Advances in Computer Vision and Pattern Recognition

For further volumes:
www.springer.com/series/4205

Gernot A. Fink

Markov Models
for Pattern Recognition

From Theory to Applications

Second Edition

Gernot A. Fink
Department of Computer Science
TU Dortmund University
Dortmund, Germany

Series Editors
Prof. Sameer Singh
Rail Vision Europe Ltd.
Castle Donington
Leicestershire, UK

Dr. Sing Bing Kang
Interactive Visual Media Group
Microsoft Research
Redmond, WA, USA

ISSN 2191-6586   ISSN 2191-6594 (electronic)
Advances in Computer Vision and Pattern Recognition
ISBN 978-1-4471-7133-1   ISBN 978-1-4471-6308-4 (eBook)
DOI 10.1007/978-1-4471-6308-4
Springer London Heidelberg New York Dordrecht

Printed on acid-free paper

Springer is part of Springer Science+Business Media (www.springer.com)

To Britta and Conradin

Preface

The development of pattern recognition methods on the basis of so-called *Markov models* is tightly coupled to the technological progress in the field of automatic speech recognition. Today, however, Markov chain and hidden Markov models are also applied in many other fields where the task is the modeling and analysis of chronologically organized data as, for example, genetic sequences or handwritten texts. Nevertheless, in monographs, Markov models are almost exclusively treated in the context of automatic speech recognition and not as a general, widely applicable tool of statistical pattern recognition.

In contrast, this book puts the formalism of Markov chain and hidden Markov models at the center of its considerations. With the example of the three main application areas of this technology—namely automatic speech recognition, handwriting recognition, and the analysis of genetic sequences—this book demonstrates which adjustments to the respective application area are necessary and how these are realized in current pattern recognition systems. Besides the treatment of the theoretical foundations of the modeling, this book puts special emphasis on the presentation of algorithmic solutions, which are indispensable for the successful practical application of Markov model technology. Therefore, it addresses researchers and practitioners from the field of pattern recognition as well as graduate students with an appropriate major field of study, who want to devote themselves to speech or handwriting recognition, bioinformatics, or related problems and want to gain a deeper understanding of the application of statistical methods in these areas.

The origins of this book lie in the author's extensive research and development in the field of statistical pattern recognition, which initially led to a German book published by Teubner, Wiesbaden, in 2003. The first edition published by Springer in 2008 was basically a translation of the German version with several updates and modifications addressing an international audience. The current second edition is the result of a thorough revision of the complete text including a number of extensions and additions of material as, for example, a more thorough treatment of the EM algorithm, a description of an efficient approximate Viterbi-training procedure, a theoretical derivation of the perplexity measure, and the treatment of multi-pass decoding based on n-best search. Furthermore, this edition contains a presentation of

Bag-of-Features hidden Markov models—a recent extension of the hidden Markov model formalism developed in the author's research group.

This second edition would not have been possible without the support of a number of people. First of all, I would like to thank Simon Rees, Springer London, for encouraging me to prepare this thorough revision of the manuscript. I am also grateful to him and Hermann Engesser, Springer-Verlag, Heidelberg, for their help in resolving legal issues related to the transition of the book from its initial German version to the current second English edition. Finally, I would like to thank Leonard Rothacker for many fruitful discussions and valuable suggestions that greatly helped to improve the manuscript.

Dortmund, Germany
October 2013
Gernot A. Fink

Contents

Introduction

The invention of the first calculating machines and the development of the first universal computers were driven by the idea to liberate people from certain every-day tasks. At that time one really thought of help in computations only and by no means of helping hands in private homes. The computing machines developed thus should take over tasks which, of course, could be carried out by humans, too. However, these tasks could be performed with substantially more perseverance by an automatic system and thus more reliably and consequently also more cheaply.

The rapid progress in the development of computer technology soon allowed researchers to dream of far more ambitious goals. In the endeavor of creating so-called "artificial intelligence" (AI) one tried to outperform the capabilities of humans in certain areas. In the early days of AI, primarily the solving of mathematical or formally described problems by symbolic methods was regarded as intelligence. Therefore, for a long time the prototypical area of research was the play of chess. The victory of the chess computer Deep Blue over the world champion Kasparov in 1997 arguably meant an important public relations activity for IBM. However, in the end it proved only that playing chess is probably not such a typical achievement of intelligence as in this discipline even the best human expert can be defeated by rather brute computing power. In contrast, in the field of understanding spoken language, which is central for human capabilities, all symbolic and rule-based methods that originated from the roots of AI research could achieve moderate success only.

Meanwhile, a radical change in paradigms has been completed. Typical human intelligence now is no longer considered to be manifest on the symbolic level but rather in the capabilities for processing various sensory input data. Among these are the communication by spoken language, the interpretation of visual input, and the interaction with the physical environment by motion, touch, and grasping. Both in the area of automatic image and speech processing and in the field of robotics for many years first solutions were developed from an engineering background. Since it has been proven by the successful use of statistical methods that automatically trained systems by far outperform their "hard-wired" rule-based counterparts with respect to flexibility and capabilities realized, the concept of learning receives special attention in these areas of research. In this respect the human example is still

G.A. Fink, *Markov Models for Pattern Recognition*,
Advances in Computer Vision and Pattern Recognition,
DOI 10.1007/978-1-4471-6308-4_1, © Springer-Verlag London 2014

unsurpassed. Therefore, currently we have to be content with reproducing the respective human capabilities in strongly constrained settings within computing machines.

Central for all methods of machine learning is the availability of example data from which the parameters of the models to be created can be derived. Therefore, no complex symbolic sets of rules are necessary to describe the typical properties of the data considered. Rather, these are automatically extracted by learning algorithms during the repeated presentation of training samples.

Probably the most well known class of learning methods are the so-called artificial neuronal networks. Their elementary building blocks correspond to largely simplified models of human nerve cells—the neurons. This formalism, which can be regarded as a universal function approximator, is very powerful but also too general for some applications. Therefore, other statistical formalisms could establish themselves that are especially well adapted to certain application areas. Especially for the statistical modeling of chronologically organized data, *Markov models* are applied to a major extent.

The most common application area of this technology is the automatic recognition of speech. In the early days of speech recognition research Markov model-based approaches competed with symbolic approaches for quite a long time. However, the availability of large sample sets of speech data heralded the triumph of statistical methods. Therefore, meanwhile the standard technology for building successful automatic speech recognition systems is represented by a combination of *hidden Markov models* for describing acoustic events and *Markov chain models* for the statistical modeling of word sequences on the symbolic level.

Only in the beginning of the 1990s these methods entered a both thematically and sensorily related application area. The automatic recognition of handwritten texts—in the same way as automatic speech recognition—can be considered as a segmentation problem of chronologically organized sensor data. There the time-line either runs along the text line to be processed or along the line of writing itself. With the help of this trick statistical modeling techniques known from the field of automatic speech recognition usually can be transferred to the problem of processing handwritten documents with minor changes only.

A third important application area of Markov models takes us beyond the field of man-machine interaction. Bioinformatics research is primarily concerned with cell-biological processes and their simulation and analysis by means of computer science techniques. Currently, special attention lies on the analysis of the human genome. From the view of statistical pattern recognition this genetic information—and cell products like, e.g., RNA or proteins derived from it—essentially consists of linearly organized symbol sequences. Though for quite some years statistical techniques have been used for the analysis of such biological sequences, the attention of bioinformatics research was only drawn to Markov models towards the end of the last century. The success of the respective methods in this application area was so convincing that meanwhile several software packages for the application of Markov models as well as libraries of ready-made models for different analysis tasks are available.

1.1   Thematic Context

The thematic context for the treatment of Markov models is defined by the research area of *pattern recognition* (cf. [65, 214]). In this field of research primarily measurements of certain sensors, as, for example, images or speech signals, are regarded as *patterns*. However, pattern recognition methods can also be applied to different input data, e.g., the symbolically represented genetic information in DNA strands.

In order to separate relevant properties of the data from interfering or irrelevant ones, the patterns considered are transformed into a *feature representation*. In general, this includes several preprocessing steps which serve the purpose of "improving" the signals for future processing, e.g., by normalizing the illumination within an image or the loudness of a spoken utterance.

After feature extraction follows the *segmentation* of the data. When trying to interpret image data, for example, regions of similar color or texture are determined. For machine-printed script a segmentation into text blocks, lines, words and usually even single character shapes is performed. The segments determined thus are subsequently mapped onto a certain pattern class by *classification* methods. Thus after successful classification a symbolic representation of the data is obtained. However, not for all pattern recognition problems the tasks of segmentation and classification can be separated so clearly. In the processing of speech, for example, it is not possible to generate a segmentation without knowing what was actually spoken as word boundaries are not marked acoustically. Rather, inferences on the boundaries between the units involved cannot be drawn before the actual utterance is known.[1] For the solution of such pattern recognition tasks, therefore, integrated segmentation and classification methods are required. However, with respect to complexity such methods generally by far exceed techniques that can be applied in isolation.

The flat symbolic representation of patterns that is available after the classification step is not sufficient for many pattern recognition applications as no structural properties are represented yet. Generating these is the goal of *pattern analysis* which tries to compute structured interpretations of patterns on the basis of the classification results. For images this could be, for example, a description of the observed scene which in addition to a classification of individual objects also specifies their relative positions with respect to each other and their composition to more complex structures. In the field of spoken language processing, the analysis of an utterance usually consists in generating an internal representation of its meaning which can serve as the basis for a man-machine dialog or the automatic translation into a different language.

---

[1]In the first commercial dictation systems by the companies IBM and Dragon Systems this dilemma was solved by a methodological trick. Users had to make small pauses between words while talking. Thus by detecting the pauses, utterances could be segmented into words first and these could be classified subsequently.

1.2   Functional Principles of Markov Models

The simplest form of Markov models are the so-called *Markov chain models*, which can be used for the statistical description of symbol and state sequences. They were developed by the Russian mathematician Andrej Andrejewitsch Markov (1856–1922), after whom they are also named. At the beginning of the past century he first applied them for the statistical analysis of the character sequences in the text of "Eugene Onegin", a novel in verse by Alexander Sergeyevich Pushkin [190].

The functional principle of this model variant can be explained well with the example of texts. The states of the model then can be identified with the words of a certain lexicon from which the word sequences investigated are formed. Markov chain models then indicate how probable the occurrence of a word in a certain textual context is. A total probability for the text section considered can be obtained by evaluating this probability for a sequence of words. Thus plausible, i.e., highly probable sentences of a certain language can be discriminated from implausible ones, i.e., less probable word sequences by choosing a suitable model. In contrast to a formal language definition, this membership decision is not deterministic but probabilistic. If, for example, multiple models for different text categories are available, the generation probability can be used as the basis for a classification decision. In the simplest case, one decides for that text category for which the associated model achieves the highest probability on a certain text section.

In so-called *hidden Markov models* the concept of a state sequence that is modeled statistically is augmented with state-specific outputs of the model. It is assumed that only these outputs can be observed. The underlying state sequence, however, is hidden—a fact from which the name of this model variant is derived. In order to make the evaluation of such models tractable, strong limitations apply for the statistical regularities which underlie the generation of the state sequence and the outputs of the model. In general, a hidden Markov model can be regarded as a finite-state automaton with outputs which is augmented statistically. Both the transitions between states and the generation of outputs occur depending on certain probability distributions.

In order to be able to apply such a generative model for the analysis of data that is already available, a mental trick is necessary. First, one assumes that the data to be analyzed was generated by a natural process which obeys similar statistical regularities. Then one tries to reproduce this process with the capabilities of hidden Markov models as closely as possible. If this attempt is successful, inferences about the real process can be drawn on the basis of the artificial model. On the one hand, this may concern the probability for generating the available data. On the other hand, inferences about the internal processes within the model are possible in a probabilistic sense. In particular, one can determine the state sequence that generates a certain sequence of outputs with highest probability.

When associating pattern classes with complete models, the formalism can be used for classification purposes. However, the by far more widely used procedure is to identify parts of a larger overall model—i.e. states or state groups—with meaningful segments of the data to be analyzed. Then a segmentation of the data with simultaneous classification into the chosen units is possible by uncovering the optimal state sequence.

In automatic speech recognition, the outputs of the models correspond to a parametric feature representation extracted from the acoustic signal. In contrast, the model states define elementary acoustic events, e.g., speech sounds of a certain language. Sequences of states then correspond to words and complete spoken utterances. If one is able to reconstruct the expected internal state sequence for a given speech signal, the—hopefully correct—sequence of words spoken can be associated with it and the segmentation and classification problem can thus be solved in an integrated manner.

The possibility to treat segmentation *and* classification within an integrated formalism constitutes the predominant strength of hidden Markov models. The dilemma pointed out in the beginning, namely that classification requires prior segmentation but segmentation often is possible only with knowledge about the classification result, thus can be circumvented elegantly. Because of this important property, methods on the basis of hidden Markov models are also referred to as being *segmentation-free*.

In contrast to symbolic or rule-based approaches, both Markov chain and hidden Markov models have the important advantage that the model parameters required can be trained automatically from sample data. However, this possibility alone does not yet guarantee the success of this modeling technique. Statistical parameter estimation methods provide reliable results only if sufficiently many training samples are available. Powerful Markov models can thus be created only if sample sets of considerable size are available for the parameter training. Moreover, only the parameters of the models and not their configuration—i.e. the structure and the number of free parameters—can be determined automatically by the training algorithms. Even in the framework of statistical methods the experience of experts and extensive experimental evaluations are required for this purpose. Furthermore, almost all known estimation methods require the availability of an initial model, which is then optimized step by step. The choice of the stating point, therefore, can critically influence the performance of the final Markov model. Finally, the Markov chain and hidden Markov models offer different modeling capabilities and are, consequently, often used in combination. In the technical implementation, however, this requires algorithmic solutions that are substantially more complex than the simple combination of probabilities.

The successful application of Markov model-based techniques for pattern recognition tasks, therefore, requires the solution of a number of methodological problems which go far beyond a mere technical implementation of the underlying mathematical theory.

1.3   Goal and Structure of the Book

The extensive application and simultaneously the substantial further development of pattern recognition methods on the basis of Markov models took place in the field of automatic speech recognition. There the combination of hidden Markov models for the acoustic analysis and Markov chain models for the restriction of potential word sequences is the predominant paradigm today. This also explains the fact that the treatment of these methods in monographs is almost always coupled to the subject of automatic speech recognition (cf. [103, 123, 125, 136, 229]).

In contrast, their use in different application areas such as, for example, character or handwriting recognition or the analysis of biological sequences, becomes accessible from the respective specialized technical literature only. This is surprisingly true also for the presentation of Markov chain models which are usually referred to as statistical language models. With the exception of the monograph by Huang and colleagues [123] the necessary foundations and algorithms are almost exclusively treated in tightly focused articles that appear in conference proceedings or scientific journals. The situation is the same for questions which arise in combination with the practical application of Markov model technology. Among these are especially the successful configuration of the models, the treatment of efficient algorithms, methods for the adaptation of the model parameters to changed task conditions, and the combination of Markov chain and hidden Markov models in integrated search processes.

Therefore, this book pursues two goals. First, Markov models will be presented with respect to their nowadays extremely wide application context. Secondly, the treatment will not be concentrating on the theoretical core of the modeling only but will include all technological aspects that are relevant from today's view.

At the beginning of the book, an overview over potential application areas of Markov model technology will be given in Chap. 2. First the automatic recognition of speech will be considered as the prototypical application before the two further main application areas will be presented, namely character and handwriting recognition as well as the analysis of biological sequences. The chapter closes with an outlook on some of the many further fields of application for Markov models.

Part I of this book provides the formal framework for the treatment of Markov models. It starts with a short introduction of relevant fundamental concepts of probability theory and mathematical statistics. Furthermore, basic methods for vector quantization and the estimation of mixture density models will be presented which are applied for the modeling of high dimensional data. Afterwards the two representatives of Markov model technology are formally described, namely hidden Markov models and Markov chain models which are frequently also referred to as n-gram models. The focus of the treatment is rather on presenting a sound general concept of the theoretical foundations than on covering all possible variants of the respective formalisms.

The second part of this book deals with important aspects of the practical application of methods on the basis of Markov models. At the beginning the robust handling of probability quantities will be covered which are omnipresent when dealing with these statistical methods. Chapter 8 presents methods for the configuration of hidden Markov models for certain application areas. Subsequently, the robust estimation of the necessary model parameters will be explained. Chapter 10 introduces the most important methods for the efficient processing of Markov models. The adaptation of the models to different tasks is the topic of Chap. 11. Part II of the book concludes with the treatment of algorithms for the search in highly complex solution spaces that result from the joint application of Markov chain and hidden Markov models.

In Part III we will come back to the applications of Markov models. Here selected systems from the main application areas automatic speech recognition, handwriting recognition, and the analysis of biological sequences are presented with the focus on successfully realized combinations of different methods.

Application Areas

2

2.1 Speech

The interaction by spoken language is the dominant modality of communication between humans. By means of speech emotions can be conveyed, irony can be expressed, simply "small talk" can be made, or information can be transmitted. The last of these aspects is by far the most important for the automatic processing of speech even though approaches for recognizing emotions in spoken utterances are pursued, too. Spoken language makes it possible to transmit information without hardly any effort—at least for healthy humans—and with a rather high "data rate" of up to 250 words per minute. Thus with respect to ease of use and efficiency this modality principally outperforms all other means of communication used by humans as, for example, gesture, handwriting, or typing on a keyboard. In the literature it is, therefore, often concluded that speech would also be the best solution for the communication with technical systems. This may well be doubted, however, as an open-plan office where all employees talk to their computers or a coffee machine that can be controlled by spoken language only and not by simply pushing a button might not seem to be the best ideas.

There are, however, a number of scenarios in which man–machine communication by spoken language makes sense—if necessary including additional modalities—and can be applied successfully. In such scenarios the goal is either to control a certain device or to acquire information from an automatic system. Examples for the latter are information systems from which time-table or event information can be queried over the telephone and also the respective train, cinema, or theater tickets can be ordered, if necessary. Among the control applications are the operation of mobile phones, which make the respective connection when the appropriate name or phone number is called, the operation of machinery in an industrial context, where the use of other modalities besides speech is not possible, and also the control of so-called non-safety relevant functions in vehicles as, e.g., the car stereo or the air condition. As a very special case of device control the automatic transcription of texts by a dictation system can be viewed. Though automatic

G.A. Fink, *Markov Models for Pattern Recognition,*
Advances in Computer Vision and Pattern Recognition,
DOI 10.1007/978-1-4471-6308-4_2, © Springer-Verlag London 2014

Fig. 2.1 Example of a digitized speech signal of the phrase "`speech recognition`" with manually marked phone segments

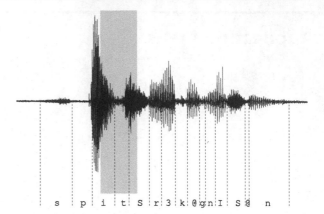

dictation did not make it to become the "killer application" of speech technology, it has had a crucial influence on the developments in the field.

In order to make spoken language man–machine communication possible, spoken utterances need to be mapped onto a suitable computer-internal symbolic representation. This internal representation later serves as the basis for determining the actions of the system. For this purpose first the physical correlate of speech—i.e. the minute changes in air pressure caused by the radiation of sound—needs to be represented digitally. Microphones convert the sound pressure level into a measurable electrical quantity. The temporal progression of these measurements corresponds to the acoustic signal. In order to represent this signal with sufficient accuracy in digital form, it is sampled, i.e., the analog values are measured at certain regular time intervals, and subsequently quantized, i.e., the analog quantities are mapped onto a finite discrete domain of values. The combination of sampling and quantization is referred to as digitization. For speech one usually works with sampling rates of 11 to 16 kHz and stores the quantized measurements with a precision of 8 to 16 bits.[1]

Figure 2.1 exemplarily shows a digitized speech signal of the utterance "`speech recognition`". For extremely simple applications of speech processing this information sometimes is already sufficient. Thus voice dialing in a mobile phone can be achieved by the direct comparison of the current speech signal with a small set of stored reference signals. In complex applications of spoken language processing, however, it is indispensable to first create a suitable intermediate symbolic representation before an interpretation of the data in the context of the application is attempted.

Besides the realization of language as an acoustic signal, there also exists the dual representation in written form. Though a number of characteristics of speech as, for example, loudness, speed, or timbre, cannot be represented in writing, still the central information content can be specified orthographically. This "encoding"

---

[1]Representing speech sampled at 16 kHz with 16 bits per sample surely is not the best possible digital representation of speech signals. However, by and large it is sufficiently accurate for the automatic processing methods applied and has become standard in the field.

of the acoustic signal can also easily be represented in and manipulated by digital computers. Therefore, it is standard to first map speech signals onto a textual representation in more complex systems for spoken language processing. This processing step is referred to as *speech recognition*. The process of *speech understanding* starts from the results of speech recognition which usually consist of a sequence of word hypotheses. On this basis methods for speech understanding try to derive a representation of the meaning for the utterance considered. In information systems the intention of the user is determined in this step and the relevant parameters of his query are extracted. An automatic dialog system of an airline, for example, needs to distinguish between a request for flight schedules and the actual order of a ticket. In both cases the airport of departure, the destination, and the desired travel time must be determined. For the syntactic-semantic analysis of so-called *natural language*, i.e., language input encoded in textual form, a multitude of different approaches were proposed in the literature (cf. e.g. [318]). The interpretation of utterances is almost exclusively achieved by applying rule-based methods which either build directly on linguistic theories or are motivated by these.

However, the mapping of a speech signal onto its textual representation, as it is the goal of automatic speech recognition, cannot be achieved with purely symbolic methods. The main reason for this is the large variability in the realization of principally identical spoken utterances by different speakers or in different environments. Furthermore, boundaries between acoustic units are generally *not* marked at all within the speech signal which makes the segmentation of spoken language extremely problematic.

The elementary unit for describing speech events is the so-called *phone* which denotes a single speech sound. In contrast to a *phoneme*, i.e., the smallest unit of speech used to distinguish meaning, phones define "building blocks" of spoken utterances that can be discriminated perceptually by listeners. The categories used for describing phones were developed on the basis of the articulation of the respective speech units (cf. e.g. [9, 47]). The articulation of speech events can be explained by a model of the speech production process, the principles of which will be described briefly in the following.

First a stream of air from the lungs is created—usually by exhalation—which passes the phonation mechanism in the larynx formed by the vocal folds. If this so-called *glottis* is closed, a series of periodic impulses of air pressure is generated. In contrast, with the glottis opened the air passing by only produces something similar to white noise. This voiced or un-voiced *excitation signal* is then modified in its spectral content in the so-called *vocal tract*, and a certain speech sound is formed. The vocal tract consists of the oral and nasal cavities and the pharynx. It can be modified in shape depending on the opening of the jaw and the position of the tongue and the soft palate. When putting it in simple terms, the two coarse classes of speech sounds *vowels* and *consonants* can be distinguished by the gross type of sound modification effected by the vocal tract. For vowels the excitation is always voiced and the vocal tract merely forms a resonant space. For example, with the largest possible opening of the vocal tract one obtains a vowel as in the word "start" (in phonetic transcription[2] ([stArt]). In contrast, consonants result from a sort of constriction formed in the vocal tract being combined with either a voiced or un-voiced excitation signal. For example, if the tip of the tongue touches the back of the lower teeth, either a voiced or un-voiced S sound as in "*raise*" or "*race*" is generated, respectively ([reIz] vs. [reIs]).

Spoken language utterances always develop as a sequence of such elementary sounds. However, the units are not represented in isolation within these and, therefore, are by no means easy to segment. As the articulatory organs cannot change their positions instantaneously from one sound to the next, this is achieved by continuous movements. Therefore, speech signals reflect the smooth transition between the characteristic features of subsequent sounds. In strong idealization of the real situation one may assume that in deliberately articulated, slow speech the typical properties of a speech sound are expressed at the center of its total duration. The border regions of the respective signal segment, however, are influenced by the neighboring sounds. This mutual influencing among sounds in the speech current is referred to as coarticulation. In reality its effects can also extend across multiple neighboring sounds. In Fig. 2.1 the segmentation of an example signal is shown. However, the discrimination between the individual phones is not uniquely defined, in general, as even by experts the segment boundaries cannot be specified beyond any doubt.

The inherent continuity of speech makes a purely data-driven segmentation without any model knowledge virtually impossible. Therefore, today exclusively socalled "segmentation-free" methods on the basis of hidden Markov models are applied for the purpose of automatic speech recognition. Though the digitized speech signal itself is already a linear sequence of samples, the statistical models of speech always start from a suitable feature representation. This aims at numerically describing the characteristic properties of speech units which are mainly defined by the local spectral composition of the signal. This feature extraction needs to be performed on sections of speech where the properties in question vary as little as possible over time as no segmentation information is available in this early stage of processing. Therefore, on the one hand the respective sections should be quite short. On the other hand, they also need to be sufficiently long in order to make the computation of useful spectral characteristics possible. Therefore, the speech signal is subdivided into sections of constant length of approximately 16 to 25 ms, which are called *frames*. In order to avoid losing important information at the boundaries created by this elementary segmentation of the signal, the frames usually overlap. A *frame rate* of 10 ms has virtually become a standard in the field. With a frame length of 20 ms the signal sections would overlap by 50 percent. Figure 2.2 shows the subdivision of a speech signal into frames of 16 ms length for a part of the example signal known from Fig. 2.1.

---

[2]The phonetic transcriptions of spoken utterances given in this book use the symbol inventory defined by SAMPA which was developed as a machine-readable version of the International Phonetic Alphabet (IPA) especially for the automated processing in digital computers [303].

Fig. 2.2 Frame segmentation for the short example section marked in the speech signal known from Fig. 2.1, which represents the transition from the vowel [i] through the plosive [t] to the fricative [S]. The model spectrum which was created by cepstral smoothing is shown as the hypothetical feature representation

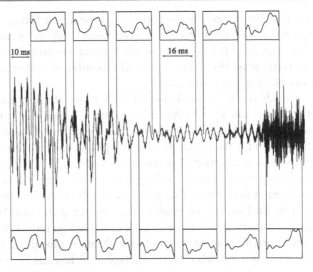

For every frame features are calculated. Thus one obtains a sequence of high-dimensional, continuous feature vectors which are identified with the outputs of a hidden Markov model. All feature extraction methods have in common that they use a measure for the signal energy and generate an abstract representation of the spectral composition of the respective section of the signal. Originally developed for the analysis of seismic data, the so-called *cepstral*[3] analysis has become the standard feature extraction method in the field of automatic speech recognition ([26], cf. also [123, pp. 306–318]). The so-called model spectrum implicitly characterizes the shape of the vocal tract during the formation of speech and thus allows to draw inferences on the speech sound articulated.[4] The combination of subdividing a speech signal into frames and carrying out a local feature extraction is referred to as *short-time analysis*. In Fig. 2.2 results of such a procedure are exemplarily shown. There the computation of a model spectrum created by cepstral smoothing was used as the hypothetical feature extraction method.

The training of hidden Markov models for acoustic units attempts to reproduce the statistical properties of the feature vector sequences that were generated by the short-term analysis. Usually, for this purpose a modular approach is applied for the description of complex structures of speech. Models for words are constructed by concatenation on the basis of models for elementary units as, e.g., phones. An arbitrary sequence of word models from a given lexicon then defines a model for spoken utterances from a certain application domain. The overall model is again a hidden Markov model. On the basis of a sequence of feature vectors that represents a spoken language utterance, its segmentation into the respective word sequence can be

---

[3]Terms as *cepstrum*, *saphe*, and also *alanysis* were artificially derived by the authors from their "equivalent" terms in the frequency domain, i.e., *spectrum*, *phase*, and *analysis*.

[4]A detailed explanation of different methods for feature extraction is, e.g., given in [123, Chap. 6 pp. 275–336].

obtained by computing the optimal state sequence through the model. This state sequence passes through certain word models which by construction are part of the utterance model. Therefore, the corresponding optimal textual representation can be derived easily. However, in general this solution will only represent an approximation of what was really said.

In addition to the modeling on the acoustic level, statistical restrictions on a symbolic level can be introduced by means of Markov chain models. This extension of the model helps to avoid the consideration of arbitrary word sequences during the search for the solution, which might be quite implausible in the context of the respective application. Therefore, an additional Markov chain model statistically describes regularities of the language fragment considered and, therefore, is usually referred to as a so-called *language model*. Principally, also purely symbolic methods can be used for this purpose as, e.g., formal grammars. However, the combination of two statistical techniques, in general, leads to more powerful integrated systems. Therefore, the combination of hidden Markov models for the acoustic modeling and Markov chain models for the language modeling has become the standard procedure within the field of automatic speech recognition.

The difficulty of an actual speech recognition task can be estimated from the restrictions which apply for the spoken utterances to be expected. The more constrained, the simpler and the more diverse, the more difficult the necessary modeling will be. The problem of speech recognition is considerably simplified if the actual speech data originates from only a single speaker. This is then said to be a *speaker-dependent* recognition task. In contrast, systems are referred to as *speaker independent* which are approximately capable of processing utterances from a wide range of different persons. The recognition problem can also be simplified by limiting the vocabulary considered. If only a simple set of command words is to be recognized, this can be achieved comparably easily and robustly. The decoding of a large vocabulary of several 10 000 words, however, requires a dramatically increased effort. Therefore, off-the-shelf dictation systems work in speaker-dependent mode in order to achieve an acceptable recognition accuracy even for very large vocabularies. Information systems accessible over the telephone, in contrast, need to be speaker independent and generally use vocabularies which are constrained to the actual task.

But not only the size of the lexicon influences the recognition performance achievable. Usually, in large vocabulary speech recognition systems one uses statistical models for the restriction of the potential or probable word sequences. Depending on how well these constraints can be brought to bear during model decoding, the recognition problem is simplified. This can be achieved especially well for utterances from clearly defined application areas in which possibly even formalized language structures might be used. Therefore, the first dictation systems that were commercially available were aimed at offices of attorneys and medical doctors.

In addition to the size of the space of potential solutions, also the speaking style critically influences the quality of the recognition results. In experiments in the laboratory one often works with speech signals that were read from given text prompts and which, therefore, exhibit considerably less variability in their acoustic realization than can be observed in spontaneous speech. In general, when speaking spontaneously, the care taken in the articulation decreases, and coarticulation effects between neighboring speech sounds increase. In certain contexts individual phones or complete phone groups are potentially not realized at all. Furthermore, spontaneous speech effects as, e.g., hesitations or false starts may occur which, of course, need to be taken into account when building the models required.

A further severe difficulty for speech recognition systems are changes in the environmental conditions in which the signal data is captured. On the one hand, these might affect the recording channel itself which is defined by the technical solutions used for signal recording and the acoustic properties of the recording environment. Therefore, in early off-the-shelf dictation systems often the special microphone required was sold together with the software package. Even today dictation systems work in a quiet office environment only and not in a large exhibition hall. In such public spaces two additional effects make the task of automatic speech recognition extremely challenging. First, interfering noises appear which adversely affect the system performance in two respects. On the one hand, they overlay the actual speech signal and thus influence the feature representations extracted. On the other hand, also the speaker himself perceives the interfering noises and, in general, modifies his articulation in consequence. This phenomenon according to its discoverer is referred to as the *Lombard effect* [181]. Therefore, the robust recognition of utterances spoken in uncontrolled acoustic environments as, for example, in a driving vehicle or in crowded public spaces where severe and unpredictable noises occur is a considerable challenge for current speech recognition systems. Secondly, speech signals recorded in public spaces are distorted by a considerable amount of reverberation not present in quiet in-door environments. Even though human listeners show a remarkable capability to understand speech in reverberant environments, automatic techniques are still not able to achieve a comparable performance.

Over decades of speech recognition research, respectable achievements were made in counteracting the manifold difficulties of automatically recognizing speech input by further and further refinements in the statistical methods as well as by special application specific techniques. Nevertheless, even today no system exists that is able to recognize arbitrary utterances of an arbitrary person on an arbitrary subject in an arbitrary environment—but these requirements are not even met by the human example. But also for less ambitious goals as, for example, the building of speaker-dependent dictation systems the actual system performances often fall short of the promises made by the manufacturers [97]. The problem of automatic speech recognition, therefore, is not solved at all, and also in the future considerable research efforts and potentially radically new methods will be required for creating systems that, at least approximately, achieve the capabilities of a human listener.

2.2 Writing

When considering writing, in the Western world first character alphabets come to mind and especially the widely used Roman alphabet, which was also used for printing this book. Alphabetic writing systems, in general, follow the phonographic principle. According to this principle the phonetic structure of the respective language is

represented by the comparably few symbols of the alphabet.[5] Even though a Western reader might consider this procedure to be the only one making sense due to his
cultural background still completely different approaches for writing down spoken
language exist today.[6] The most prominent example is the Chinese writing system
which mostly works according to the logograhic principle. In Chinese script each of
the complex symbols represents a certain word of the language. Therefore, at least
a few thousand symbols are required in order to write texts in everyday Mandarin,
e.g., in newspapers. Such a form of writing might appear overly complex in the eyes
of Western people. Nevertheless, even in the computer age such writing systems are
not replaced by alphabetic ones. However, the typing of Chinese or Japanese texts
on today's computer keyboards is usually facilitated by the use of romanized versions of the respective scripts, i.e., systems for writing Chinese or Japanese that use
Roman characters.

Japanese texts are written in a mixture of Chinese symbols (so-called *kanji*) for
representing word stems and two syllabic writing systems that were derived from
it by simplification and which again follow the phonographic principle. *Hiragana*
symbols are used for writing grammatical elements. Names and foreign words are
written with the symbols of the *katagana* writing system.

Independently from the actual writing system written texts can either be produced by machine, i.e., printed, or by handwriting on paper by using a pen or brush.
In machine print the form of the individual symbols or characters is not constrained
in principle. In contrast, in handwriting one aims at bringing the symbols of a certain
script to paper as easily and as fluently as possible. Therefore, for most writing systems also a cursive version adapted for handwriting exists in addition to the symbol
set used for producing machine-printed texts.

In contrast to the recognition of spoken language, the automatic processing of
writing is only partly carried out in the context of man–machine interaction. Rather,
the origins of this technology lie to a major extent in industrially relevant applications in the field of automation technology.

This book does not aim at treating the automatic processing of writing thoroughly
for all existing writing systems. Therefore, we will limit the considerations to the
widely used alphabetic writing systems in the following and there to the Roman
alphabet as a typical representative. The interested reader is referred to the respective
specialized technical literature for a presentation of techniques, which are used for
processing, e.g., Japanese, Chinese, or Arabic texts (cf. e.g. [36, Chap. 10 to 15]).
With the exception of highly logographic writing systems, as, e.g., Chinese, the
same principal approaches are applied. The main differences result from taking into
account the respective special appearance of the image of the writing in the selection
of methods and the combination of processing steps.

---

[5]The relationship between characters of a certain alphabet and the respective pronunciation is more
or less obviously preserved in their current writing due to the historical development of languages.

[6]In [51] a thorough overview is given over ancient writing systems and those still in use today
together with their historical development and relationships amongst each other. A brief overview
of the major scripts with examples of their appearance can be found in [112].

The classical application of automatic processing of writing is the so-called *optical character recognition* (OCR, cf. e.g. [200]). There the goal is to automatically "read" machine-printed texts which were captured optically and digitized afterwards. In other words, one aims at transforming the image of the writing into a computer-internal symbolic representation of the text. Thus the underlying data is images of document pages, as, for example, the one at hand, which are converted into a digital image by means of a scanner with a typical resolution of 300 to 2400 dots per inch. Therefore, methods for automatic image processing are predominant in the field of OCR due to the very nature of the input data itself.

Before the actual text recognition can be started, an analysis of the document layout is necessary in almost any document image analysis task. This layout analysis attempts to identify text areas and other elements of the document structure as, e.g., headlines or graphics, within the available page image. Afterwards, the text areas can be segmented into paragraphs, individual lines, and, in general, also single characters due to the usually high precision in the production of machine-printed texts. As soon as the images of the written symbols are isolated, they can be mapped onto a symbolic representation by arbitrary techniques from the field of pattern classification (cf. e.g. [36, 275]). The results of the classification are generally subject to one or more post-processing steps. These post-processing operations attempt to correct errors on the character level as far as possible by incorporating context restrictions, e.g., in the form of a lexicon (cf. e.g. [55]).

As in the field of automatic speech recognition, the complexity of the processing task is defined by the variability of the input data to be expected. The size of the lexicon used is of subordinate importance as the processing mainly is performed on the character level and the word and document context is only taken into account during post-processing. On the one hand, the variability of the data results from differences in the respective image of the writing as it is created by the printing process. On the other hand, distortions in the optical capturing of the documents may severely affect the appearance of individual characters and text sections. In the printing process itself the type face (e.g. Times, Helvetica or Courier), the font family (e.g. regular, **bold**, or *italic*), and the character size (e.g. tiny, normal, large) may vary. The difficulty of the automatic processing is increased considerably if the image of the writing could only be captured with poor quality. This can be due to aging or a comparable degradation of the original document that might be caused, for example, by contamination. A similar effect is caused by the repeated reproduction or transmission of a document, e.g., by fax or by means of copying machines, which severely reduces the quality of the source data for automatic character recognition. In such cases a segmentation on character level is generally no longer possible with sufficient reliability. Therefore, segmentation-free methods on the basis of Markov models offer substantial advantages in the processing of such "degraded" documents as opposed to classical OCR methods (cf. e.g. [75]).

The problem of automatic character recognition also becomes considerably more challenging if the texts considered were not printed by machine but written by hand. Especially the use of cursive writing which, in general, links individual characters with connecting strokes in alphabetic writing systems makes a reliable segmentation

Fig. 2.3 Example of a digitized handwritten document from *The George Washington Papers at the Library of Congress, 1741–1799*, Series 2, Letterbook 1, page 270, reprinted with permission of Library of Congress, Manuscript Division

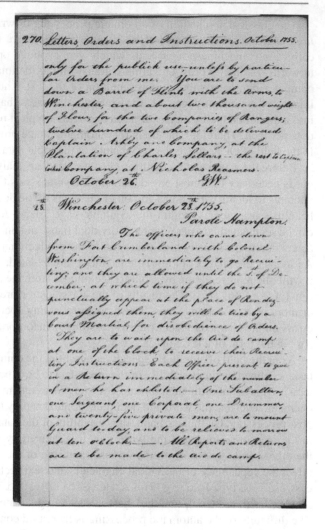

on character level virtually impossible. Therefore, segmentation-free methods on the basis of Markov models are predominant in the field of handwriting recognition today. However, the automatic reading of larger handwritten documents is currently not a relevant application possibly due to the enormous difficulty of the task. Even in the scientific area today only a few related research efforts exist. An example of a historic document in quite neatly written cursive script is shown in Fig. 2.3. In contrast, Fig. 2.4 shows a contemporary document as it was used for building a large corpus of handwritten texts within a research initiative of the University of Bern, Switzerland (cf. [192]). The challenges of automatically reading every-day texts are exemplified by the example of a historical postcard shown in Fig. 2.5.

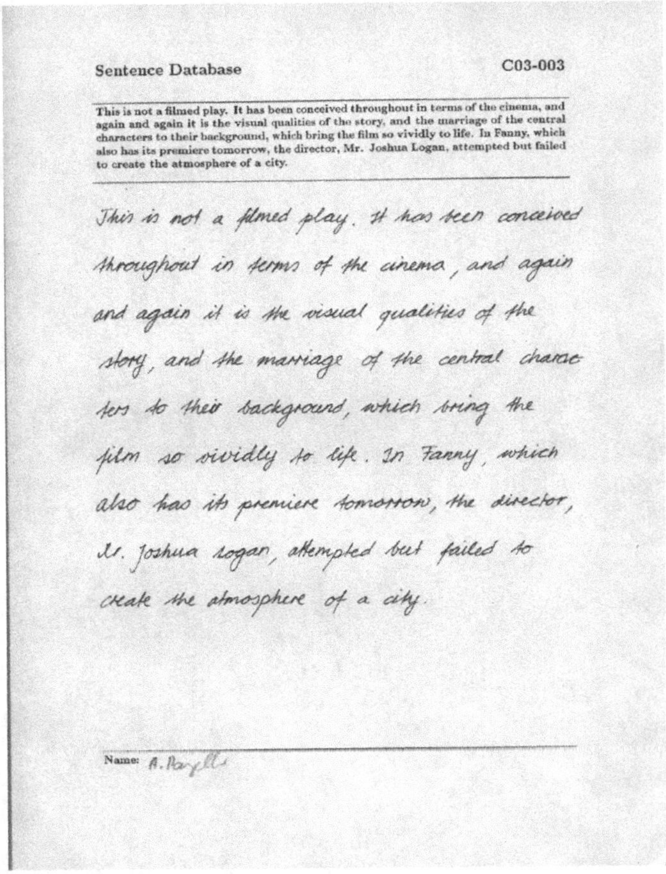

Sentence Database C03-003

This is not a filmed play. It has been conceived throughout in terms of the cinema, and again and again it is the visual qualities of the story, and the marriage of the central characters to their background, which bring the film so vividly to life. In Fanny, which also has its premiere tomorrow, the director, Mr. Joshua Logan, attempted but failed to create the atmosphere of a city.

This is not a filmed play. It has been conceived
throughout in terms of the cinema, and again
and again it is the visual qualities of the
story, and the marriage of the central characters to their background, which bring the
film so vividly to life. In Fanny, which
also has its premiere tomorrow, the director,
Mr. Joshua Logan, attempted but failed to
create the atmosphere of a city.

Name:

Fig. 2.4 Example page from the corpus of handwritten documents created by the Institute for Informatics and Applied Mathematics, University of Bern, Switzerland [192]. In the *upper part* the text section to be written together with an identification code is printed. *Below* the respective handwritten version was filled in by one of the subjects (reprinted with permission)

The complexity in the processing of handwritten documents results from the considerable larger variability in the image of the writing as opposed to machine-printed texts. Similarly to sounds in spoken language, the individual characters differ even when repeatedly realized by the same person, depending on their context, and the most severely between different writers. Without suitable restrictions on the potential character sequences, no satisfactory results are achieved in the automatic recognition of handwritten texts. Therefore, the vocabulary used and comparable contextual knowledge is of great importance for this task.

An especially important application of the automatic recognition of writing is the automated reading of postal addresses in mail sorting machines. Here the essential difficulty results from the part of handwritten addresses which is large even today. Therefore, in practice an automatic sorting of the mail pieces can be achieved only

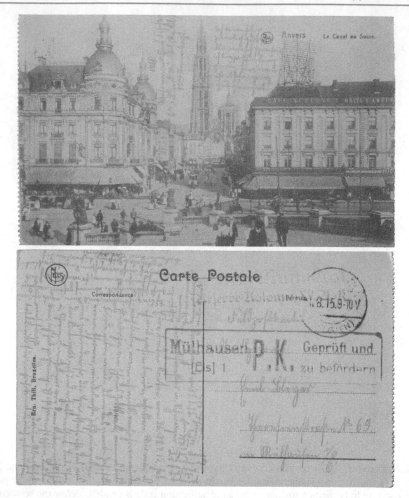

Fig. 2.5 Example of a historical postcard written in German Kurrent script during the First World War and delivered by the German Military Postal Service (Private Collection Dr. Britta Bley, Dortmund, Germany, reprinted with permission). Please note how the writer used every possible writing space by adding paragraphs with different script orientations and with ever decreasing character size—even on the image side of the postcard

partially as recognition errors by wrongly dispatched mail cause enormous costs. In order to be able to keep the error rate of such systems as low as possible, a quite large rejection rate has to be accepted. The addresses on rejected mail pieces then need to be transcribed manually.

Powerful methods for the automatic analysis of addresses—especially for machine-printed postal addresses—have been applied in practice for many years. In postal address recognition the quality of the results not only depends on the classification accuracy on character level which should be as high as possible. Additionally, it is extremely important to intelligently exploit relations in structure and content

Fig. 2.6 Example of a form for bank transfers in the European Union filled out manually. Handwritten capital characters need to be written into the appropriate fields given

between the individual elements of a postal address, e.g., city name, zip-code, street name, and house number. After the introduction of a new automatic address reading system at the end of the last century in the U.S. more than half of the handwritten addresses were analyzed automatically while the estimated error rate was below 3 percent [50].[7]

Almost exclusively devoted to the processing of handwritten input are methods for the automatic processing of forms. When automatically reading forms, the complexity of the recognition task can be considerably reduced by suitable technical measures for limiting the variability of the character images. Special fields for writing individual words or even short phrases are used in order to facilitate text segmentation. Additionally, the writing style is often restricted to the exclusive use of hand-printed characters which frequently also means that only capital letters may be used. The most restricted writing style is obtained if every character has to be written within an individual field of the form. Figure 2.6 shows this principle with the example of a form for bank transfers used in many countries sharing the Euro as currency in the European Union.

In the U.S., in contrast to Europe, checks play an especially important role in financial transactions. A multitude of approaches exist for automatically analyzing the handwritten legal amount, its numeric equivalent, the so-called courtesy amount, and the date of issue (cf. e.g. [165]). In this recognition task the lexicon

---

[7]Today, the processing of handwritten addresses will be even more reliable. Unfortunately, manufacturers of postal automation equipment or postal service providers hardly ever publish up-to-date performance figures.

Fig. 2.7 Example of a pen trajectory of the handwritten word "*handwriting*" captured online. The size of the dots representing the pen positions encodes the pen pressure in pen-down strokes (black) and the shading represents the distance to the writing surface during pen-up movements

is restricted to only a few entries consisting of numerals and digits. However, from these basic units longer sequences may be constructed without appreciable sequencing restrictions. The writing style used also satisfies no constraints. Thus the use of hand-printed characters, cursive writing, and an arbitrary mixture of those styles is possible. This mixed writing style is usually referred to as so-called unconstrained handwriting.

All methods for processing writing presented so far have in common that documents are captured digitally *after* they were completed and are then processed further independently from their generation process. This type of analysis is referred to as *offline* handwriting or character recognition. In contrast to that, also so-called *online* methods exist for the processing of handwritten documents where the motion of the pen is already captured during the process of writing. For this purpose special sensors as, e.g., pressure sensitive tablets or LC displays, are required and, in general, also the use of specialized tools for writing. In essence a sequence of two-dimensional measurements of the pen position is obtained as the digital representation of the written texts. This sequence encodes the trajectory of the pen as observed during the writing process. In simple devices as they are, e.g., used in so-called personal digital assistants (PDAs), position measurements are only obtained if the pen touches the writing surface resulting in so-called *pen-down* strokes. However, if the pen is lifted, only more sophisticated graphics tablets can still track the pen in so-called *pen-up* movements in the close vicinity of the writing surface by using inductive techniques and specialized pens. Such devices usually also provide the pen pressure and the inclination of the pen with respect to the writing surface in addition to the position measurements. Figure 2.7 shows a potential pen trajectory by the example of the word "handwriting". There the pen pressure and the distance of the pen tip to the writing surface are encoded in the size and shading, respectively, of the dots used to represent the pen positions.

Compared to the offline processing of handwriting, online methods have the advantage that they can take into account the additional information about the temporal organization of the writing process during recognition. Thus it is, for example, not possible that neighboring characters overlap in the image of the writing and, therefore, can hardly be separated in the automatic segmentation. The dynamic information is also essential for the verification of signatures. It represents a highly writer specific peculiarity of the signature which even by experts cannot be forged on the basis of an available image of the signature.

However, the main application area for online handwriting recognition is man–machine interaction. Especially for operating extremely small, portable computing devices, which would not be reasonably possible with a keyboard, this form of text entry has become very attractive for device control.[8] Usually the problem is simplified as much as possible in order to achieve satisfactory results with the limited resources of a PDA, organizer, or smart phone while at the same time reaching sufficiently high reaction times. In the well known PalmPilot and its descendants only isolated characters were captured in special input fields. Additionally, a special writing style optimized for the purposes of automatic recognition needed to be used. On today's more powerful devices usually also the input of complete handwritten words or phrases is possible.

Inspired by the success of Markov model-based methods in the field of automatic speech recognition, the principal approach of this technique was also transferred to problems of automatic character and handwriting recognition in recent years. These segmentation-free methods are mostly applied where the "classical" OCR approaches, which first segment on the level of characters and later classify, are either not reliably enough or fail completely. Therefore, Markov models are mainly used for the recognition of handwritten documents in both online and offline mode and only rarely for the processing of machine-printed texts. Similarly to automatic speech recognition, hidden Markov models are applied for modeling the appearance in writing of individual characters or whole words, and Markov chain models are used for restricting potential sequences of elementary units on character or word level.

The fundamental prerequisite for the applicability of these methods is that the signal data considered can be represented as a linear sequence. This is rather easily possible in the field of online handwriting recognition. The temporal progress of the writing process itself defines a chronological order of the position measurements which are provided by the respective sensors. The time-line of the signal thus virtually runs along the trajectory of the pen. Similarly to the short-time analysis of speech signals, local characteristic properties of the pen trajectory can be described by feature vectors. For this purpose mainly shape properties are evaluated as, for example, the writing direction or the curvature. In contrast, the writing speed is usually normalized in pure recognition systems in order to avoid variations of the signal characteristics due to different writers.

It is considerably more difficult to define a comparable procedure for the serialization of offline documents as these are principally two-dimensional images. However, in general a segmentation of the document considered into individual text lines

---

[8] With the introduction of capacitive touch-sensitive displays, pen-based input methods have often been replaced by so-called soft keyboards. Apple's former CEO Steve Jobs severely influenced the turning away from pen-based interaction. Technically, it is also more challenging to use pen input on a capacitive display. Just recently pens with conductive tips were introduced that make writing on these interactive surfaces possible. Interestingly, Apple itself may be reviving pen-based interaction in the future with its ideas of an "active stylus".

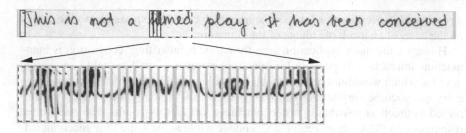

Fig. 2.8 Example for the serialization of offline handwriting: *Above*, the text line to be analyzed is shown with some of the overlapping analysis windows superimposed. *Below*, the extracted image stripes are shown for part of the text line (inspired by [241]; example based on the document image known from Fig. 2.4, used with permission; pre-processed by the author)

can be generated with sufficient reliability. When analyzing forms, which usually comprise only isolated words or phrases, the segmentation of the field contents is possible even more easily. Then a hypothetical time-line can be defined in parallel to the direction of the text. Following this direction the changing local properties of the image of the writing can be described by a sequence of feature vectors. For this purpose the text line is usually subdivided into a sequence of narrow overlapping image windows which then in principle correspond to the frames known from automatic speech recognition. Figure 2.8 shows an example of this so-called *sliding-window approach* applied to a text-line image. For each of the analysis windows extracted such a feature vector is computed. Unfortunately, in the field of offline handwriting or character recognition no generally accepted method exists for extraction of feature representations from images of writing. In some cases local structural properties are computed as, e.g., the number of line ends or arcs, which lie within a certain frame of writing. Most recent feature extraction approaches rely on the computation of statistical image descriptors as, e.g., moments or histograms. The sequence of the feature vectors generated thus is then—similarly to automatic speech recognition—identified with the outputs of hidden Markov models for characters or words.

2.3   Biological Sequences

The genetic information of all living organisms, which influences their growth, their metabolism, and to a major extent also their behavior, is encoded in a symbolic sequence. In the majority of cases this is the macro molecule *deoxyribonucleic acid* (DNA) which consists of two strands intertwined in the form of a double helix. The strands are built as sequences of so-called *bases*. There exist four different types of bases (adenine, cytosine, guanine, and thymine) which are pairwise complementary and, therefore, in addition to the chemical bonds within a DNA strand also establish pair bonds to bases from the other strand. Thus one obtains the "ladder-type" structure of the double-stranded DNA. As the pairwise bonds are unique, already a single DNA strand contains the complete genetic information. Therefore, in the double strand it is encoded redundantly.

In higher developed organisms as, for example, mammals, the DNA is not available as a single complete sequence but distributed across so-called *chromosomes*. Human cells contain 23 pairs of those, which represent the genetic information from maternal and paternal side, respectively. The entirety of the DNA strands in all chromosomes is referred to as the *genome*. Every cell of a living being contains an identical copy of this total genetic information. The size of the genome is coarsely connected to the complexity of the respective organism. While the genetic information of bacteria contains only a few million bases, the human genome comprises approximately 3 billion base pairs.

However, the majority of the DNA sequence has no cell-biological function or none that has been understood so far. In this additional "junk" material the elementary units of genetic information—the so-called *genes*—are embedded. Their relevant information that encodes the function of a gene—the so-called coding region—is generally split up into multiple *exons* which are interrupted by *introns*. A few years ago it was still assumed that the human genome contains approximately 30 000 to 40 000 genes [131, 295] while more recent estimates propose a total number of only approximately 25 000 coding regions [132].

For controlling most cell-biological functions, genes are "transformed" into *proteins* in a process called *expression*. The proteins created then influence the metabolism and the growth of the cell and control its reproduction during cell division.

In order to express a certain gene, first the genetic information available on the double-stranded DNA is read and transformed into the equivalent representation of the single-stranded *ribonucleic acid* (RNA) which also represents a sequence of bases. This process, which is referred to as *transcription*, begins in a so-called *promotor* region before the actual DNA sequence which contains the information of a specific gene. In the resulting raw version of the RNA, the coding region of a gene, in general, is still interrupted by introns without known function. Therefore, the RNA is "cleaned" in a subsequent modification process where the introns are discarded. The cleaned RNA is called *messenger* RNA or for short mRNA.

Finally, a certain protein is generated from mRNA in an additional transformation process which is referred to as *translation*. This protein realizes the functionality of the underlying gene. In contrast to DNA and RNA, proteins consist of a sequence of 20 different *amino acids*. Within the mRNA sequence a triple of bases—a so-called *codon*—encodes a certain amino acid.[9] Special start and stop codons control which area of the mRNA is covered by the translation process. After the generation of the amino acid sequence, proteins form a characteristic three-dimensional structure by folding which makes up a substantial part of their functionality. Figure 2.9 shows a part of the amino acid sequence of a protein for the example of hemoglobin as well as its representation as a sequence of codons on the level of DNA.

In contrast to sensor data, which are always affected by measurement noise, the symbolic representations of DNA sequences or proteins can in principle be given exactly. Therefore, one might assume that symbolic and rule-based methods are

---

[9]The relationship between codons and amino acids is not unique as with 4 bases there exist $4^3 = 64$ potential triples.

Amino Acid Sequence

```
MALSAEDRALVRALWKKLGSNVGVYTTEALERTFLAFPATKTYFSHLDLS
PGSSQVRAHGQKVADALSLAVERLDDLPHALSALSHLHACQLRVDPASFQ
LLGHCLLVTLARHYPGDFSPALQASLDKFLSHVISALVSEYR
```

DNA Sequence

```
atggcgctgt  ccgcggagga  ccgggcgctg  gtgcgcgccc
tgtggaagaa  gctgggcagc  aacgtcggcg  tctacacgac
agaggccctg  gaaaggacct  tcctggcttt  ccccgccacg
aagacctact  tctcccacct  ggacctgagc  cccggctcct
cacaagtcag  agcccacggc  cagaaggtgg  cggacgcgct
gagcctcgcc  gtggagcgcc  tggacgacct  accccacgcg
ctgtccgcgc  tgagccacct  gcacgcgtgc  cagctgcgag
tggacccggc  cagcttccag  ctcctgggcc  actgcctgct
ggtaaccctc  gcccggcact  accccggaga  cttcagcccc
gcgctgcagg  cgtcgctgga  caagttcctg  agccacgtta
tctcggcgct  ggtttccgag  taccgctga
```

Fig. 2.9 Part of the amino acid sequence and the underlying DNA sequence of the protein hemoglobin according the SWISS-PROT database [12]. Individual amino acids are encoded by capital letters and bases by lower case letters

completely sufficient for genome analysis. However, the sequencing of a genome poses considerable difficulties in practice (cf. [76, Chap. 5]). Therefore, even after the completion of the *"Human Genome Project"* [129], the genetic information of the human cells investigated can still not be given completely and with absolute certainty. Furthermore, genetic information is not encoded uniquely in the sequence of base pairs and is subject to a wide range of random variations within a family of organisms and also within the same species. Therefore, for complex genomes the actual number and position of the individual genes can still be estimated only even for the extensively studied human genome. In order to understand the function of the proteins expressed, it is additionally essential to consider the so-called expression pattern, i.e., under what conditions they are created from the respective genes, and to investigate the three-dimensional structure that is formed. The latter can result in functional equivalent form from different amino acid sequences.

The variations within biological sequences pointed out above, which—according to current scientific knowledge—are largely random, have helped statistical methods to become predominant for their investigation and modeling.

Depending on which data basis the analysis of genetic material starts from, different processing steps are relevant. When starting from so-called genomic DNA, i.e., virtually raw genetic information, first the coding regions of genes need to be found and the DNA sequences present there subsequently need to be cleaned from introns in the same way as in the creation of mRNA.

When applying Markov model-based methods for the analysis of genomic DNA, individual HMMs for promotor regions as well as for exons and introns need to be created. A segmentation of the DNA sequence considered then allows to localize genes and to extract their coding region in a cleaned-up representation (cf. [118, 160]). However, genes can also be identified within DNA sequences on the basis of Markov chain models which define restrictions for the occurrence of individual bases within different genetic contexts (cf. [222, 266]).

When starting directly from mRNA, this first processing step is not necessary as only a single gene is transcribed at a time and the final mRNA was already cleaned. However, depending on the life cycle of a cell, only a limited set of genes is expressed so that the investigation of a complete genome is virtually impossible on the basis of mRNA only.

Often only the final product of the transcription and translation process itself is considered, namely the proteins. When analyzing proteins, the goal is not a segmentation but the finding of similar sequences. The comparison of proteins is the most simple if they are only considered pairwise. Long before the application of hidden Markov models, probabilities for the mapping between amino acids at certain positions of the sequence as well as for their insertion and deletion were defined in order to be able to capture statistical variations of proteins. Such a statistical model can be used to associate an amino acid sequence with another one position by position. From such a position-wise pairing one obtains a so-called *alignment*. The logical positions within this mapping between two proteins are mostly directly connected to the three-dimensional structure formed.

It is considerably more demanding to apply the sequence alignment to multiple proteins of a certain family. The results of such efforts are represented in the form of so-called *multiple alignments*. From pre-existing multiple alignments the statistical properties of the respective groups of similar sequences can be derived and then be described by hidden Markov models (cf. [67, 69, 70, 161]). These so-called *profiles* can then be used to search the respective databases automatically for further similar proteins. Figure 2.10 shows a multiple alignment created by an expert for the example of different goblins.

Of course, the detection of new genes by the segmentation of a genome or the extension of a family of proteins with new members by means of statistical comparisons cannot show the cell-biological functions of the newly found structures. In the end this needs to be proven in biological experiments. However, from the structural comparison of biological sequences and the similarities found, hypotheses about the function of genes and proteins can be derived which can then be verified experimentally in a considerably more goal directed manner.

Such efforts are embedded in the endeavor of biologist and bioinformatics researchers to be able to explain the function of biological organisms. Especially an exact understanding of the human metabolism is of fundamental interest to the pharmaceutical industry. Substances constructed on the genetic level and especially adapted to a certain individual—such is the hope of the researchers—might make a substantially improved treatment of diseases possible without at the same time causing the often dramatic side effects of classical drugs. Therefore, the sequencing of more and more genetic material and its detailed analysis with respect to structure and cell-biological function is especially pushed by pharmaceutical companies.

```
Helix                   AAAAAAAAAAAAAAAA  BBBBBBBBBBBBBBBBBCCCCCCCCCCC      DDDDDDDEE
HBA_HUMAN   ---------VLSPADKTNVKAAWGKVGA--HAGEYGAEALERMFLSFPTTKTYFPHF-DLS-----HGSA
HBB_HUMAN   --------VHLTPEEKSAVTALWGKV----NVDEVGGEALGRLLVVYPWTQRFFESFGDLSTPDAVMGNP
MYG_PHYCA   ---------VLSEGEWQLVLHVWAKVEA--DVAGHGQDILIRLFKSHPETLEKFDRFKHLKTEAEMKASE
GLB3_CHITP  ----------LSADQISTVqASFDKVKG------DPVGILYAVFKADPSIMAKFTQFAG-KDLESIKGTA
GLB5_PETMA  PIVDTGSVAPLSAAEKTKIRSAWAPVYS--TYETSGVDILVKFFTSTPAAQEFFPKFKGLTTADQLKKSA
LGB2_LUPLU  --------GALTESQAALVKSSWEEFNA--NIPKHTHRFFILVLEIAPAAKDLFS-FLK-GTSEVPQNNP
GLB1_GLYDI  ---------GLSAAQRQVIAATWKDIAGADNGAGVGKDCLIKFLSAHPQMAAVFG-FSG----AS---DP

Helix                   EEEEEEEEEEEEEEEEEEE           FFFFFFFFFFFFF  FFGGGGGGGGGGGGGGGGGGGG
HBA_HUMAN   QVKGHGKKVADALTNAVAHV---D--DMPNALSALSDLHAHKL--RVDPVNFKLLSHCLLVTLAAHLPAE
HBB_HUMAN   KVKAHGKKVLGAFSDGLAHL---D--NLKGTFATLSELHCDKL--HVDPENFRLLGNVLVCVLAHHFGKE
MYG_PHYCA   DLKKHGVTVLTÄLGAILKK----K-GHHEAELKPLAQSHATKK--KIPIKYLEFISEAIIHVLHSRHPGD
GLB3_CHITP  PFETHANRIVGFFSKIIGEL--P---NIEADVNTFVASHKPRG---VTHDQLNNFRAGFVSYMKAHT--D
GLB5_PETMA  DVRWHAERIINAVNDAVASM--DDTEKMSMKLRDLSGKHAKSF--QVDPQYFKVLAAVIADTVAAG----
LGB2_LUPLU  ELQAHAGKVFKLVYEAAIQLQVTGVVVTDATLKNLGSVHVSKG---VADAHFPVVKEAILKTIKEVVGAK
GLB1_GLYDI  GVAALGAKVLAQIGVAVSHL--GDEGKMVAQMKAVGVRHKGYGNKRIKAQYFEPLGASLLSAMEHRIGGK

Helix                   HHHHHHHHHHHHHHHHHHHHHHHHHHHHH
HBA_HUMAN   FTPAVHASLDKFLASVSTVLTSKYR------
HBB_HUMAN   FTPPVQAAYQKVVAGVANALAHKYH------
MYG_PHYCA   FGADAQGAMNKALELFRKDIAAKYKELGYQG
GLB3_CHITP  FA-GAEAAWGATLDTFFGMIFSKM-------
GLB5_PETMA  -----DAGFEKLMSMICILLRSAY-------
LGB2_LUPLU  WSEELNSAWTIAYDELAIVIKKEMNDAA---
GLB1_GLYDI  MNAAAKDAWAAAYADISGALISGLQS-----
```

Fig. 2.10 Multiple alignment of the amino acid sequence of seven goblins of different organisms after [161] with the respective identifiers used in the SWISS-PROT database [12]. The line designated by `Helix` defines the mapping onto the three-dimensional structure of the proteins. Deletions of amino acids at certain positions are designated by –

2.4   Outlook

Markov models represent a formalism which has received substantial attention in the field of pattern recognition and beyond due to the success of the technique in the area of automatic speech recognition. Therefore, it would be a pointless endeavor trying to list all problems that were ever tackled by applying these methods. However, in the following we will give an overview of the most important topics for which Markov models were used to a larger extent and which do not fall into their main application areas of automatic speech recognition, character and handwriting recognition, and the analysis of biological sequences.

Alternative recognition tasks on the basis of speech signals that have been tackled by Markov model-based systems are, for example, the recognition of prosodic structures (cf. [33]) or the recognition of emotions conveyed (cf. e.g. [219]). As HMMs are generative models, they can even be successfully applied to the approximately inverse problem of speech recognition, namely speech synthesis (see [293] for a recent survey).

Similarly to the processing of speech signals, which merely represent a sequence of measurements of the sound pressure level, hidden Markov models can be applied for the analysis of other series of measurements as they are, e.g., obtained in material testing (cf. e.g. [270, 300]) in biomedical applications (cf. e.g. [4, 127, 220]), or in remote sensing (cf. e.g. [104, 173]).

Comparable to online handwriting recognition is the automatic recognition of human gestures (cf. e.g. [29, 39, 72, 74, 149, 202, 213, 253]) which includes the recognition of sign-language as a special case (cf. e.g. [62, 288]). However, the trajectories of the hands and arms of a person and, if necessary, also the respective hand postures need to be extracted from the respective image sequences with costly image processing methods before the statistical analysis of the motion sequences. In this respect these methods are comparable in their structure to a video-based online handwriting recognition system [92, 313] developed on the basis of a method for tracking pen movements during writing in image sequences [201].

The recognition of human actions or behavior can be regarded as a generalization of gesture recognition. Thus in, e.g., [323] motion sequences of tennis players and in [31] of people walking are analyzed. As human gait is quite characteristic for individuals, can easily be observed from a distance, and is hard to conceal, hidden Markov models are increasingly applied to gait recognition in the context of surveillance applications (cf. e.g. [41, 144, 179, 291]). In [121] human motion patterns learned are used for mimicking them by a robot and thus having the demonstrated action carried out by the machine. Extremely special human actions are changes in facial expressions as they are, e.g., analyzed in [120, 177]. Related to action recognition and surveillance applications is the problem of detecting unusual—and, therefore, interesting—events (cf. e.g. [249, 329]).

In all these methods, first chronologically organized sequences of feature vectors are created from the input image sequences. The Markov model-based techniques then start from the serialized feature representations. However, in the literature also methods were proposed which extend the formalism of hidden Markov models such that a modeling of two- or even three-dimensional input data is directly possible (cf. e.g. [73, 141, 175, 176, 267]).

In virtually all approaches mentioned so far, hidden Markov models are used in isolation and not in combination with Markov chain models. This is mainly due to the fact that for applications as, e.g., gesture or action recognition only a rather small inventory of segmentation units is used. Therefore, probabilistic restrictions on the respective symbol sequences are not of immediate importance.

On the purely symbolic level, Markov chain models, in contrast, are applied for describing state sequences without being complemented by a hidden Markov model. An important application area is the field of information retrieval where statistical models of texts are described by Markov chain models (cf. e.g. [244]). As a compact representation of documents in principle corresponds to a compression of their content, the same principles also form the foundation of different methods for text compression (cf. [17]). Markov chain models are also applied in slightly modified form as so-called Markov decision processes for, e.g., the solution of planning tasks (cf. e.g. [310]).

Part I
Theory

Introductory Remarks

The first part of this book presents the theoretical foundations of Markov models in Chaps. 3, 4, 5 and 6. First, a short overview will be given over the most important concepts of probability theory and mathematical statistics which are necessary for the understanding of the subsequent explanations. Afterwards, methods for the description of data distributions in high-dimensional vector spaces will be presented. This treatment will cover approaches for vector quantization as well as methods for the estimation of Gaussian mixture models which can be considered as a probabilistic extension of classical vector quantization techniques. Chapter 5 is devoted to the presentation of the theoretical foundations of hidden Markov models and the necessary fundamental algorithms. The treatment will focus on typical members of this modeling technique. The most important variants of hidden Markov models will be presented shortly in Sect. 5.8 where the interested reader will also find further bibliographical references. Chapter 6 deals with Markov chain models which are frequently referred to as n-gram models in their specialized realization for pattern recognition tasks. Their description requires less theoretical background as opposed to the treatment of hidden Markov models. Therefore, the emphasis of the presentation lies on algorithmic solutions which allow a reliable estimation of the model parameters required. We will concentrate on methods which from today's point of view can be regarded as standard techniques and, therefore, clearly stand out among the host of widely differing methods that have been proposed in this field. In the same way as in the presentation of hidden Markov models, important alternative modeling techniques will be described briefly at the end of the chapter.

A thorough understanding of the application of Markov models for pattern recognition tasks is only possible when simultaneously considering aspects relevant in practice. Nevertheless, within the scope of the following formal treatment we will present the theoretical core of these methods in a linear, consecutive way without distracting cross-references. The subsequent second part of this book is then entirely devoted to problems appearing in the practical application of hidden Markov and n-gram models and the associated technical solutions.

Foundations of Mathematical Statistics

3

Many events that can be observed in natural processes do not occur according to some well-defined law but rather exhibit a random behavior. It is, therefore, not possible to predict the outcome for any single event. However, even for random processes certain regularities can be derived if their behavior is observed in frequent repetitions and events are no longer considered in isolation.

Probability theory offers the necessary mathematical models for the treatment of regularities underlying such random processes. Mathematical statistics additionally considers the problem of how the parameters of probabilistic models can be derived from observations.

In the following some important fundamental concepts of probability theory and mathematical statistics will be introduced that are relevant for the further presentation of Markov models. The goal of this presentation is to illustrate the relevant terms. For a more detailed mathematical treatment and a derivation of these concepts the interested reader is referred to the extensive volume of specialized literature.

3.1   Random Experiment, Event, and Probability

A random *experiment*[1] is formally described as carrying out a procedure which can be repeated arbitrarily often and will produce a random result from a well-defined set of possible outcomes. This can be, for example, the rolling of a dice or the observation of the development of the stock marked. In all those cases the result of every single experiment is uncertain within the bounds of the given possibilities—the faces one to six when rolling dice or the rising and falling of the stock marked indices. Regularities can be identified only when abstracting from isolated events and considering long-term observations instead.

---

[1] The additional word "random" is usually omitted if the topic of mathematical statistics is clear from the context.

G.A. Fink, *Markov Models for Pattern Recognition*,
Advances in Computer Vision and Pattern Recognition,
DOI 10.1007/978-1-4471-6308-4_3, © Springer-Verlag London 2014

A random *event*[2] A corresponds to a single result or a set of potential results of a random experiment, e.g., the showing of the face six, any even-numbered face, or the rising of the stock market. Such an event A occurs if the result of the random experiment lies in the set A for a particular trial. The complete set of all possible results of a random experiment is the so-called sample space Ω. Events that correspond to exactly one result of the random experiment are called elementary events. The usual set operations can be applied to events, namely conjunction, disjunction, and complement (with respect to the sample space Ω).

The *relative frequency* $f(A)$ of an event A that occurred m times during an N-fold repetition of a random experiment is obtained as the quotient of its absolute frequency (or count) $c(A) = m$ and the total number of trials N:

$$f(A) = \frac{c(A)}{N} = \frac{m}{N}$$

A pragmatic derivation of the notion of probability is directly based on the relative frequency of an event. If this concept is generalized by abstracting from the actual duration of the observation, the underlying regularity for the occurrence of the event A is defined as its *probability* $P(A)$. It can be shown that the variation in the relative frequency $f(A)$ will constantly decrease with an increasing number of observations and approach a uniform, constant value—the probability $P(A)$. This relationship is supported by the so-called "law of large numbers".[3]

The *conditional probability* $P(A|B)$ of an event A is obtained if the information that event B occurred is already available before the observation of A. This probability for the occurrence of A under the condition of B having occurred before can be derived from the probability of A and B occurring jointly and the unconditional probability of B as follows:[4]

$$P(A|B) = \frac{P(A, B)}{P(B)}$$

This quantity is also referred to as the *posterior probability* of A as $P(A|B)$ is determined *after* the observation of the event B. In contrast, the unconditional probability of an event which is valid *before* the incorporation of additional restrictions is called *prior probability*.

---

[2] As with random experiments, events are also not labeled "random" if their nature is clear from the context.

[3] The "law of large numbers" was originally derived by Bernoulli (1655–1705). It says: The probability that the relative frequency of an event A will deviate more than an arbitrary but fixed threshold ε from its probability $P(A)$ will become arbitrarily small if the number of observations becomes arbitrarily large, i.e., approaches infinity.

[4] In the literature the simplified notation $P(A, B)$ is frequently used for the union or conjunctive combination of events instead of the set notation $P(A \cap B)$ for the joint probability.

If the observation of B provides no information about the occurrence of A, the events A and B are said to be *statistically independent*. Consequently, in this case the conditional probability is equal to the unconditional one and the following equality holds:

$$P(A|B) = P(A) \quad \text{and} \quad P(B) = P(B|A) \quad \text{if } A, B \text{ are statistically independent}$$

The joint probability of statistically independent events can simply be determined by the product of the individual probabilities:

$$P(A, B) = P(A)P(B) \quad \text{if } A, B \text{ are statistically independent}$$

An important relationship for computations involving conditional probabilities is stated by *Bayes' rule*:

$$P(B|A) = \frac{P(A|B)P(B)}{P(A)} \tag{3.1}$$

It allows to compute the posterior probability $P(B|A)$ of event B from the conditional probability $P(A|B)$ by taking into account model knowledge about the events A and B in the form of the associated prior probabilities. The conditional dependence in the probability expressions is thus virtually reversed.

When assuming that the sample space Ω is completely partitioned into pairwise disjoint events $B_1, B_2, \ldots, B_n$, then Bayes' rule in its general from is given by

$$P(B_j|A) = \frac{P(A|B_j)P(B_j)}{\sum_{i=1}^{n} P(A, B_i)} = \frac{P(A|B_j)P(B_j)}{\sum_{i=1}^{n} P(A|B_i)P(B_i)} \tag{3.2}$$

3.2 Random Variables and Probability Distributions

A simplification of the mathematical treatment of random events can be achieved by mapping random events appropriately onto the set of real numbers $\mathbb{R}$. Random experiments are then represented by so-called *random variables* that randomly take on certain values from $\mathbb{R}$. A random variable X is called *discrete* if it takes on a finite or countably infinite number of values $x_1, x_2, \ldots, x_N$. In contrast, so-called *continuous* random variables can take on arbitrary values $x \in \mathbb{R}$.

Random variables are characterized by means of their *distribution function*.[5] The distribution function $F_X(x)$ of a random variable X specifies how high the probability is that values taken on by X are less than or equal to x for every possible value of x:

$$F_X(x) = P(X \leq x)$$

---

[5]The distribution function is frequently also referred to as the *cumulative distribution function*.

In the discrete case $F_X(x)$ can easily be computed from the individual probabilities of the elementary events A_i which are associated with the values x_i of the random variable. The distribution function is obtained by summing over all p_i corresponding to values less than or equal to x:

$$F_X(x) = \sum_{i:x_i \leq x} P(A_i) = \sum_{i:x_i \leq x} p_i$$

In the continuous case the sum in the above equation is turned into an integral and the integrated continuous function $p_X(x)$ loses its interpretation as a probability of elementary events:

$$F_X(x) = \int_{-\infty}^{x} p_X(t)\, dt$$

The quantity $p_X(x)$ is called the *probability density* function or simply the *density* of the random variable X. Density values are always non-negative in the same way as probabilities are. However, they may also take on values larger than 1. Only the total area or probability mass under the density function must be equal to 1. The probability of some event is obtained as the integral of the density function over an appropriate interval of real numbers. The probability that an arbitrary continuous random variable takes on a certain value is, therefore, always equal to zero.

The concept of random variables can be generalized to vector-valued quantities. In order to simplify the treatment of the subject we will limit the following presentation to the most important continuous case. The relationships to the discrete versions are obtained in complete analogy to one-dimensional or scalar random variables.

A vector-valued n-dimensional random variable X formally constitutes a *random vector*[6] which is composed of n individual random variables X_i. The distribution function of the random vector X is given by

$$F_X(x) = P(X_1 \leq x_1, X_2 \leq x_2, \ldots, X_n \leq x_n)$$

It is obtained on the basis of a *joint* probability density function $p_X(x)$ of the individual random variables X_i:

$$F_X(x) = \int_{-\infty}^{x_1} \int_{-\infty}^{x_2} \cdots \int_{-\infty}^{x_n} p_X(t_1, t_2, \ldots, t_n)\, dt_1, dt_2, \ldots, dt_n$$

---

[6]Random vectors are also frequently referred to as *multivariate random variables* as opposed to the scalar or *univariate* case.

Their probability density functions p_{X_i} can be computed by integration over all remaining vector components as the *marginal distribution* of the joint density function p_X according to

$$p_{X_i}(x) = \int_{(x_1,\ldots,x_{i-1},x_{i+1},\ldots,x_n)\in\mathbb{R}^{n-1}} p_X(x_1,\ldots,x_n)\,dx_1,\ldots,dx_{i-1},dx_{i+1},\ldots,dx_n$$

If the individual random variables X_i are statistically independent, the joint density function of the random vector can simply be obtained as the product of all component densities:

$$p_X(x) = p_X(x_1, x_2, \ldots, x_n) = \prod_{i=1}^{n} p_{X_i}(x_i)$$

In any case, however, the joint density p_X can be represented as the product of conditional density functions in generalization of the notion of conditional probabilities. In order to illustrate this procedure we will consider here the simple two-dimensional case only. For the joint density of a random vector then the following relationships hold:

$$p_X(x) = p_X(x_1, x_2)$$
$$= p_{X_1}(x_1)\, p_{X_2|X_1}(x_2|x_1)$$
$$= p_{X_2}(x_2)\, p_{X_1|X_2}(x_1|x_2)$$

In the general n-dimensional case, however, there exist $n!$ different possibilities for splitting up p_X into one-dimensional conditional density functions.

3.3   Parameters of Probability Distributions

The parameters expected value and variance are used for the coarse characterization of probability distributions or the associated random variables, respectively. Both parameters are derived from the actual probability density function. The *expected value* $\mathscr{E}\{X\}$ of a random variable or the corresponding probability distribution denotes the value of X that is taken on in the statistical average. The expected value can be computed as the first moment of the probability density function if the distribution is completely known:

$$\mathscr{E}\{X\} = \int_{-\infty}^{\infty} x p_X(x)\,dx$$

For discrete distributions the following relationship is obtained:

$$\mathscr{E}\{X\} = \sum_{i=1}^{\infty} x_i p_i$$

If the expected value of a distribution is known, the *variance* characterizes the expected scatter of values taken on by X around $\mathscr{E}\{X\}$. It can be computed as the expected value of the squared difference between values of the random variable and its expected value which corresponds to the second central moment of the distribution function:

$$\text{Var}\{X\} = \mathscr{E}\left\{\left(X - \mathscr{E}\{X\}\right)^2\right\} = \int_{-\infty}^{\infty} \left(x - \mathscr{E}\{X\}\right)^2 p_X(x)\, dx$$

In the discrete case the following rule is obtained in analogy to the computation of the expected value:

$$\text{Var}\{X\} = \sum_{i=1}^{\infty} \left(x_i - \mathscr{E}\{X\}\right)^2 p_i$$

It can be shown by means of simple algebraic transformations that the variance of a distribution can alternatively be determined using the following relationship which offers advantages especially in practical applications:

$$\text{Var}\{X\} = \mathscr{E}\left\{X^2\right\} - \left(\mathscr{E}\{X\}\right)^2 \tag{3.3}$$

For random vectors, which for simplicity will be treated as vector-valued random variables in the following, moments of the distribution can be defined in the same way as for scalar quantities. The expected value of a random vector is obtained as direct generalization of the one-dimensional case from the following relationship:

$$\mathscr{E}\{X\} = \int_{x \in \mathbb{R}^n} x\, p_X(x)\, dx$$

The variance of a multivariate distribution is described by the so-called *covariance matrix* which is defined as follows:

$$\text{Var}\{X\} = \mathscr{E}\left\{\left(X - \mathscr{E}\{X\}\right)\left(X - \mathscr{E}\{X\}\right)^T\right\}$$
$$= \int_{x \in \mathbb{R}^n} \left(x - \mathscr{E}\{X\}\right)\left(x - \mathscr{E}\{X\}\right)^T p_X(x)\, dx$$

Instead of the squared difference between a scalar quantity and the expected value, here the outer product of the respective vector difference is computed. If the components X_i of a random vector X are statistically independent the main diagonal elements of the covariance matrix $\text{Var}\{X\}$ correspond directly to the variances $\text{Var}\{X_i\}$ of the individual distributions and the remaining matrix elements vanish.

Similar to the case of univariate distributions, the rule for computing the covariance matrix can be rewritten as follows:

$$\text{Var}\{X\} = \mathscr{E}\left\{X X^T\right\} - \mathscr{E}\{X\}\mathscr{E}\{X\}^T \tag{3.4}$$

3.4   Normal Distributions and Mixture Models

In the discrete case the distribution of a uni- or multivariate random variable can—in principle—be defined by storing the probabilities $P(x)$ for every outcome x of the random variable in a table. For continuous distributions, however, such an approach is not feasible as the associated densities can be very general continuous functions. Consequently, in this case it is only possible to work with parametrically defined models which also for discrete probability distributions yield considerably more compact representations.

The most important parametric distribution in the context of Markov models — and maybe even beyond—is the *normal distribution*[7] which is defined for continuous random variables only. For a univariate random variable satisfying a normal distribution one obtains the following probability density function:[8]

$$\mathscr{N}\left(x|\mu,\sigma^2\right) = \frac{1}{\sqrt{2\pi\sigma^2}}e^{-\frac{(x-\mu)^2}{2\sigma^2}} \tag{3.5}$$

The two parameters μ and σ^2 of the probability density function correspond directly to the expected value and the variance of the normal distribution. For n-dimensional random vectors one obtains the multivariate Gaussian probability density function by using a mean vector $\boldsymbol{\mu}$ and a covariance matrix $\boldsymbol{C}$ according to

$$\mathscr{N}(x|\boldsymbol{\mu},\boldsymbol{C}) = \frac{1}{\sqrt{|2\pi\boldsymbol{C}|}}e^{-\frac{1}{2}(x-\boldsymbol{\mu})^T\boldsymbol{C}^{-1}(x-\boldsymbol{\mu})} \tag{3.6}$$

In this formula $\boldsymbol{C}^{-1}$ denotes the inverse and $|2\pi\boldsymbol{C}|$ the determinant of the covariance matrix scaled by a factor of 2π.

Many natural processes can be described by means of the normal distribution. This is because it can frequently be assumed that they will satisfy a Gaussian distribution after a sufficiently long time of observation.[9] However, the normal distribution has only a single mode—i.e. a global maximum—at the position of its mean and decays exponentially from there on. Therefore, it is said to be a *uni-modal* probability density function. This simple model is no longer sufficient when aiming at the parametric representation of distributions with multiple local maxima or modes.

---

[7]Frequently, the normal distribution is also referred to as the *Gaussian distribution* after the German mathematician Carl Friedrich Gauss (1777–1855) who worked extensively on the subject. The invention of the normal distribution, however, is attributed to the French mathematician Abraham de Moivre (1667–1754).

[8]Prior to the introduction of the Euro as the standard currency in many European countries, this formula was depicted on the 10-Deutschmark bank note together with a graph showing the typical bell-shape of the probability density function.

[9]This assumption is backed up by the *central limit theorem*. In its most general form it states that the sum of N random variables with finite variances will approach a normal distribution as N tends towards infinity (cf. [155, Chap. 3.5]).

Fortunately, it can be shown that even general continuous probability density functions $p(x)$ can be approximated with arbitrary precision by a linear combination of an infinite number of normal densities [322]:

$$p(x) \stackrel{\wedge}{=} \sum_{i=1}^{\infty} c_i \mathcal{N}(x|\mu_i, C_i) \quad \text{with} \quad \sum_{i=1}^{\infty} c_i = 1$$

Generally, however, only a finite number of K component densities is considered for such *mixture density* models:

$$p(x) \approx p(x|\theta) = \sum_{i=1}^{K} c_i \mathcal{N}(x|\mu_i, C_i) \tag{3.7}$$

The parameters of this model—namely the mixture weights c_i as well as the mean vectors μ_i and covariance matrices C_i of the individual normal densities—are collected within a parameter set $\theta = \{(c_i, \mu_i, C_i)|i = 1, \ldots, K\}$. Here, the fact that such a simplified model is easily manageable in practice by far outweighs the inevitable loss in precision caused by the coarser density representation.

3.5 Stochastic Processes and Markov Chains

Obviously, the results that are generated by random variables over some period of time vary randomly. What remains unchanged, however, are the properties of the process generating these results—the probability distribution associated with the random variable. In order to be able to treat a variation of these characteristics mathematically and to describe the behavior of statistical procedures with time-varying properties, stochastic processes are used.

A *stochastic process* is defined as a sequence of random variables $S_1, S_2, \ldots$, which take on values s_t from a discrete or continuous domain according to individual probability distributions. Depending on the type of domain one distinguishes between either continuous or discrete stochastic processes. All further treatment will be limited to the simpler case of discrete stochastic processes as only these are relevant for the topic of this book. Additionally, the discrete values generated by such processes can be interpreted as discrete states being taken on. In the context of discrete stochastic processes one, therefore, frequently talks about states and state sequences generated by the processes.

In general, the distribution function corresponding to the random variable S_t at time t can be dependent on the actual time t itself and the values $s_1, \ldots, s_{t-1}$, $s_{t+1}, \ldots$, which were taken on by the other random variables defining the properties of the stochastic process. This very powerful general concept of a stochastic process is, however, usually restricted with respect to a number of aspects.

A stochastic process is said to be *stationary* if the absolute time t does not make any difference for its behavior, i.e., if the probability distribution is the same for all random variables S_t. The process is further said to be *causal* if the distribution of the random variable S_t is only dependent on past states $s_1, s_2, \ldots, s_{t-1}$. The probability distribution for a discrete, stationary, and causal stochastic process can, therefore, be written as follows:

$$P(S_t = s_t | S_1 = s_1, S_2 = s_2, \ldots, S_{t-1} = s_{t-1})$$

If the correspondence between actual values s_t and the associated random variables S_t is uniquely defined by the context, this property can be specified in simplified form:

$$P(s_t | s_1, s_2, \ldots, s_{t-1})$$

It is immediately obvious that the causality constraint is appropriate for processes evolving in time. Though causality imposes a considerable restriction on the potential characteristics of a stochastic process, the modeling is still problematic. With time t advancing and, consequently, increasing length of the state sequence an arbitrarily long set of dependencies for the necessary probability distributions will be generated. Therefore, an additional constraint is required which will make it feasible to describe stochastic processes with a finite model.

The so-called *Markov property* achieves this goal by constraining conditional dependencies within the model appropriately. It represents the additional restriction that the dependence of the properties of the process is limited to a *finite* history—in the case of a *simple* stochastic process even to the immediate predecessor state only. The probability distribution of a discrete, stationary, causal, and simple stochastic process, which is also called a *Markov chain* of first order, can be written in the following way:

$$P(s_t | s_1, s_2, \ldots, s_{t-1}) = P(s_t | s_{t-1})$$

If the total set of events—i.e. the state space considered—is finite, the necessary conditional probabilities can be compactly combined into a matrix of *state transition probabilities* which completely describes the property of the process:

$$A = [a_{ij}] = \left[P(S_t = j | S_{t-1} = i) \right]$$

Higher-order Markov chains—i.e. Markov chains with longer temporal dependencies—offer no principal advantages over first-order models. The longer influence of the context can always be encoded into a single state by an appropriate extension of the state space. However, such a structural reorganization is not always desirable or possible. Therefore, Markov chains of higher order play an important role in the statistical modeling of symbol sequences as we will see in Chap. 6.

3.6   Principles of Parameter Estimation

All statistical models are characterized by the model's type and a certain number of free parameters. Both need to be determined in an appropriate manner in order to be able to use such a model for the description of certain natural processes. The first important prerequisite for doing so are expectations set up by experts which essentially determine the type of model to be used. The second important foundation are concrete observations of the process to be described. These can either be real measurements or quantities derived from them.

Estimates of the model parameters can be computed on this set of sample data by taking into account the specified model type. The actual characteristics of these parameter estimates are, however, also dependent on the kind of optimization criterion that is applied by the selected estimation procedure.

3.6.1   Maximum Likelihood Estimation

The so-called *maximum likelihood* (ML) method is the most widely used method for estimating parameters of statistical models. On the basis of a given set of samples $\omega = \{x_1, x_2, \ldots, x_T\}$ and depending on the actual type of the model sought, estimates $\hat{\theta}$ of the model parameters are determined such that the probability—or in the continuous case the probability density, respectively—for the observation of the data will be maximized.

In order to simplify the following considerations, we will assume that the sample set corresponds to a sequence of values generated by random variables $X_1, X_2, \ldots, X_T$ satisfying an identical probability distribution. The estimation problem is then defined as determining the unknown parameters of this probability distribution function.

The individual random variables X_i are, furthermore, assumed to be statistically independent. Therefore, the joint probability of the data can be obtained as the product of all contributions from the individual distributions sharing an identical set of parameters:

$$p(\omega|\theta) = p(x_1, x_2, \ldots, x_T|\theta) = \prod_{t=1}^{T} p(x_t|\theta)$$

When maximizing this quantity by a variation of the parameter θ, not of the random variables but the model parameters themselves represent the variables. This is made explicit by introducing the so-called *likelihood function*:

$$L(\theta|\omega) = L(\theta|x_1, x_2, \ldots, x_T) = p(\omega|\theta)$$

The goal of the maximum likelihood method is now to maximize the likelihood function for a given type of stochastic model and a given sample set ω with respect to the parameters θ:

$$\hat{\theta}_{\text{ML}} = \underset{\theta}{\text{argmax}} \, L(\theta|\omega)$$

In order to solve this problem, the standard approach for finding extreme values of analytical functions can be applied. Here the derivative of $L(\theta|\omega)$ with respect to the model parameters θ is computed and equated to zero. In most practical cases one obtains exactly one extremum which then corresponds to the ML estimate for the model parameters. In general, however, the result is not uniquely defined.

Often a mathematically simpler treatment of this extreme value problem can be achieved by not considering the likelihood function itself but its logarithm instead:

$$\hat{\theta}_{\text{ML}} = \underset{\theta}{\text{argmax}} \, \log L(\theta|\omega) \tag{3.8}$$

The application of a monotonic function does not change the extremum. However, by using the log-likelihood function considerable simplifications can be obtained especially for statistical models on the basis of exponential probability densities as, e.g., normal distributions.

Let us consider a simple example in order to illustrate the principle of ML estimation. On a sample set $\omega = \{x_1, x_2, \ldots, x_T\}$ the parameters of a one-dimensional normal distribution shall be estimated. The logarithmic likelihood function is then given by

$$\log L(\theta|\omega) = \log \prod_{t=1}^{T} \mathcal{N}\left(x_t|\mu, \sigma^2\right) = \sum_{t=1}^{T} \log \frac{1}{\sqrt{2\pi\sigma^2}} e^{-\frac{(x_t-\mu)^2}{2\sigma^2}}$$

$$= -\frac{T}{2} \log\left(2\pi\sigma^2\right) - \frac{1}{2\sigma^2} \sum_{t=1}^{T} (x_t - \mu)^2$$

As derivatives of this function with respect to the two variables μ and σ^2 one obtains

$$\frac{\partial}{\partial \mu} \log L(\theta|\omega) = \frac{1}{\sigma^2} \sum_{t=1}^{T} (x_t - \mu)$$

$$\frac{\partial}{\partial \sigma^2} \log L(\theta|\omega) = -\frac{T}{2\sigma^2} + \sum_{t=1}^{T} \frac{(x_t - \mu)^2}{2\sigma^4}$$

By equating those formulas to zero one obtains the following estimates $\hat{\mu}$ for the mean and $\hat{\sigma}^2$ for the variance of the normal distribution as a result of the ML method:

$$\hat{\mu}_{\text{ML}} = \frac{1}{T} \sum_{t=1}^{T} x_t$$

$$\hat{\sigma}_{\text{ML}}^2 = \frac{1}{T} \sum_{t=1}^{T} (x_t - \hat{\mu}_{\text{ML}})^2 = \frac{1}{T} \sum_{t=1}^{T} x_t^2 - \hat{\mu}_{\text{ML}}^2$$

In the multivariate case one obtains the following relationships for computing estimates of the mean vector $\hat{\boldsymbol{\mu}}$ and the covariance matrix $\hat{\boldsymbol{C}}$ of an n-dimensional Gaussian density:

$$\hat{\boldsymbol{\mu}} = \frac{1}{T} \sum_{t=1}^{T} \boldsymbol{x}_t \tag{3.9}$$

$$\hat{\boldsymbol{C}} = \frac{1}{T} \sum_{t=1}^{T} (\boldsymbol{x}_t - \hat{\boldsymbol{\mu}})(\boldsymbol{x}_t - \hat{\boldsymbol{\mu}})^T \tag{3.10}$$

$$= \frac{1}{T} \sum_{t=1}^{T} \boldsymbol{x}_t \boldsymbol{x}_t^T - \hat{\boldsymbol{\mu}} \hat{\boldsymbol{\mu}}^T \tag{3.11}$$

Those two quantities are also referred to as the *sample mean* and the *sample covariance matrix* of a probability distribution defined by a set of samples only.

Here Eq. (3.11) is analogously derived to the alternative definition of the covariance matrix of a random vector given by Eq. (3.4). In practice it offers the advantage that an estimate for both the mean and the covariance matrix can be obtained by a single pass through the sample set $\omega = \{\boldsymbol{x}_1, \boldsymbol{x}_2, \ldots, \boldsymbol{x}_T\}$. When using Eq. (3.10) instead, the terms inside the summation can only be evaluated after an estimate of $\hat{\boldsymbol{\mu}}$ has been computed.

ML estimation has several advantageous properties[10] if it can be safely assumed that the real distribution of the data corresponds to the pre-specified model type and the available sample set is large enough. The parameter estimates $\hat{\boldsymbol{\theta}}_{\text{ML}}$ computed for the unknown distribution parameters converge to the real parameters $\boldsymbol{\theta}^*$ if the size of the sample set approaches infinity:

$$\lim_{T \to \infty} \hat{\boldsymbol{\theta}}_{\text{ML}} = \boldsymbol{\theta}^*$$

Additionally, the ML estimates exhibit the lowest variance of all possible estimates. Consequently, no other method can deliver an estimate that lies closer to the real parameters.

---

[10]The interested reader will find in-depth treatments of the asymptotic properties of ML estimators in [155] Chaps. 5.4 and 6.5, respectively.

3.6.2   Maximum a Posteriori Estimation

In contrast to maximum likelihood estimation, the so-called *maximum a posteriori estimation* (MAP) uses the posterior probability of the model parameters as the optimization criterion for a pre-specified type of model and a given sample set:

$$\hat{\theta}_{\text{MAP}} = \underset{\theta}{\text{argmax}}\, p(\theta | \omega)$$

When rewriting this formula using Bayes' rule the following relationship is obtained:

$$\hat{\theta}_{\text{MAP}} = \underset{\theta}{\text{argmax}}\, p(\theta | \omega) = \underset{\theta}{\text{argmax}}\, \frac{p(\omega|\theta)\, p(\theta)}{p(\omega)} = \underset{\theta}{\text{argmax}}\, p(\omega|\theta)\, p(\theta) \qquad (3.12)$$

The maximization of the posterior probability $p(\theta|\omega)$ of the parameters θ can thus be rewritten in terms of the conditional probability density $p(\omega|\theta)$ of the data and the prior probability $p(\theta)$ of the model parameters. The unconditional probability density $p(\omega)$ of the samples can be ignored in the maximization process as this quantity is independent of the model parameters θ. Therefore, the principle difference between MAP estimation and the ML procedure is the incorporation of a suitable prior distribution $p(\theta)$ into the optimization process which represents expectations about the characteristics of the model parameters.

This is the reason why MAP estimation offers advantages over the ML method if only a rather limited set of sample data is available. As we saw in the previous section, the ML estimation is the optimal method for deriving parameter estimates from the data alone. However, in general the size of the sample set will be limited and, as a consequence, the results obtained will be rather unreliable as no prior expectations are taken into account. When applying the MAP principle, those expectations are considered by making the prior distribution $p(\theta)$ of the parameters part of the optimization criterion. Putting it in simple terms, with this procedure an optimal combination of two principle strategies for parameter estimation is realized. Model parameters for which only few training samples are available are mainly determined according to the expectations. Those parameters, however, which can be estimated on large amounts of data are mainly derived from the sample data while largely ignoring the expectations.

In order to illustrate the principle of MAP estimation let us consider a simple example. For a given sample set $\omega = \{x_1, x_2, \ldots, x_T\}$ we want to estimate the mean μ of an univariate Gaussian distribution assuming that the variance σ^2 is known. The expectations that we have about the parameter to be estimated have to be specified by defining a prior distribution $p(\mu)$. A reasonable choice is to assume μ to be normally distributed with mean μ_0 and variance σ_μ^2:

$$p(\mu) = \frac{1}{\sqrt{2\pi\sigma_\mu^2}} e^{-\frac{(\mu-\mu_0)^2}{2\sigma_\mu^2}}$$

In order to maximize Eq. (3.12) we have to compute the derivative with respect to μ and equate it to zero:

$$\frac{\partial p(\theta|\omega)}{\partial \theta} = 0 \quad \Leftrightarrow \quad \frac{\partial p(\omega|\theta)p(\theta)}{\partial \theta} = 0$$

As in the case of ML estimation a monotonic function—here the logarithm—may be applied to the optimization function. For the conditional density of the data we again assume the individual samples to be independently and identically distributed:

$$\frac{\partial \log p(\omega|\mu)p(\mu)}{\partial \mu} = 0 \quad \Leftrightarrow \quad \frac{\partial}{\partial \mu} \log \prod_{i=1}^{T} p(x_i|\mu)p(\mu) = 0$$

This equation can now be rewritten by inserting the definitions of $p(x_i|\mu)$ and $p(\mu)$—both normal distributions—and subsequently applying rather simple algebraic transformations mainly exploiting properties of the logarithm:

$$\Leftrightarrow \quad \frac{\partial}{\partial \mu} \left\{ \sum_{i=1}^{T} \log p(x_i|\mu) \right\} + \log p(\mu) = 0$$

$$\Leftrightarrow \quad \frac{\partial}{\partial \mu} \sum_{i=1}^{T} \log \left\{ \frac{1}{\sqrt{2\pi\sigma^2}} e^{-\frac{(x_i-\mu)^2}{2\sigma^2}} \right\} + \log \left\{ \frac{1}{\sqrt{2\pi\sigma_\mu^2}} e^{-\frac{(\mu-\mu_0)^2}{2\sigma_\mu^2}} \right\} = 0$$

$$\Leftrightarrow \quad \frac{\partial}{\partial \mu} \left(\sum_{i=1}^{T} \left[-\frac{(x_i-\mu)^2}{2\sigma^2} - \log\sqrt{2\pi\sigma^2} \right] - \frac{(\mu-\mu_0)^2}{2\sigma_\mu^2} - \log\sqrt{2\pi\sigma_\mu^2} \right) = 0$$

$$\Leftrightarrow \quad \frac{\partial}{\partial \mu} \left(\sum_{i=1}^{T} -\frac{(x_i-\mu)^2}{2\sigma^2} - \frac{1}{2}\log(2\pi\sigma^2) - \frac{(\mu-\mu_0)^2}{2\sigma_\mu^2} - \frac{1}{2}\log(2\pi\sigma_\mu^2) \right) = 0$$

$$\Leftrightarrow \quad \sum_{i=1}^{T} \frac{x_i-\mu}{\sigma^2} - \frac{\mu-\mu_0}{\sigma_\mu^2} = 0$$

Multiplying this intermediate result by $\sigma^2\sigma_\mu^2$ we obtain

$$\Leftrightarrow \quad \sigma_\mu^2 \sum_i x_i - \sigma_\mu^2 T\mu - \sigma^2\mu + \sigma^2\mu_0 = 0$$

$$\Leftrightarrow \quad (\sigma^2 + T\sigma_\mu^2)\mu = \sigma^2\mu_0 + \sigma_\mu^2 \sum_i x_i$$

Solving the above equation for μ we obtain its MAP estimate:

$$\hat{\mu}_{\text{MAP}} = \frac{\mu_0 + \frac{\sigma_\mu^2}{\sigma^2} \sum_i x_i}{1 + \frac{\sigma_\mu^2}{\sigma^2} T} \tag{3.13}$$

From this equation it is immediately obvious that the MAP estimate of the mean can be interpreted as a weighted average of the expected mean μ_0 and the ML estimate obtained directly from the sample set. The MAP estimate will converge to the ML estimate if the size of the sample set goes to infinity. It will also be equivalent to the ML estimate if $\frac{\sigma_\mu^2}{\sigma^2} \gg 1$, i.e., if the uncertainty σ_μ^2 of the prior knowledge about μ is large with respect to the variance σ^2. Such a prior on a parameter estimate is called *non-informative* as it does not influence the estimate in a noticeable way.

In practice often a further simplification of Eq. (3.13) is used for computing an approximation of the MAP estimate:

$$\hat{\mu}'_{\text{MAP}} = \frac{\tau \mu_0 + \sum_i x_i}{\tau + T} \qquad (3.14)$$

Thus the necessity to explicitly specify the prior expectations in form of a probability density can be avoided by introducing a heuristically chosen parameter τ.

3.7 Bibliographical Remarks

A huge number of monographs exists on the topic of mathematical and computational statistics, many of which are of introductory nature or even explicitly intended as textbooks (cf. e.g. [46, 147, 233, 247, 292]).

Among the many monographs the book by Larsen & Marx [166] stands out because of its clear presentation and the many illustrative examples. The book by Knight [155] covers the formal aspects of mathematical statistics more thoroughly and gives many useful references. Good introductions to the fundamental concepts of statistics especially relevant for pattern recognition tasks, furthermore, can be found in the classic books by Fukunaga [102] and Duda, Hart, & Stork [65] as well as in [123, Chap. 3].

Vector Quantization and Mixture Estimation

4

When processing signal data with a digital computer, one is always faced with two basic problems: on the one hand this data needs to be stored as compactly as possible and on the other hand it must be represented with sufficient accuracy. An appropriate compromise between these two criteria has to be found by the data quantization procedure, keeping in mind that digital representations of any type of data are necessarily always finite. Therefore, the goal of a so-called *vector quantizer* is to map vectors from the input data space onto a finite set of typical reproduction vectors. Ideally, during this transformation no information should be lost that is relevant for the further processing of the data. Consequently, one tries to reduce the effort for storage and transmission of vector-valued data by eliminating redundant information contained therein.

Such a coding is, for example, applied to speech signals before transmitting them over low-bandwidth digital telephone networks. Similarly, appropriately encoded images are, for example, stored as compactly as possible in the memory of a digital camera or transmitted as feature-length movies to private homes.

Though the meaning of the data is principally not of interest during coding, the most suitable representations are achieved if "similar" vectors are grouped together when encoding the data and "dissimilar" ones are represented separately. From this point of view the goal of vector quantization corresponds to the one of so-called *cluster analysis* which aims at finding areas of high density within an unknown data distribution and representing these adequately.

The goal of finding a compact representation for the distribution of some data can also be considered from the viewpoint of statistics. Then the task can be described as trying to find a suitable probability distribution that adequately represents the input data. As we have seen in the previous chapter, a general parametric representation of such probability distributions does not exist. Therefore, an approximate parametric representation of general probability distributions is usually defined by means of mixture densities on the basis of normal densities (cf. Sect. 3.4). In this approach the individual Gaussians model the different regions of high density in the data distribution considered—the so-called *clusters*. The corresponding mean vectors can then be viewed as the reproduction vectors of a statistical quantization process.

G.A. Fink, *Markov Models for Pattern Recognition*,
Advances in Computer Vision and Pattern Recognition,
DOI 10.1007/978-1-4471-6308-4_4, © Springer-Verlag London 2014

In the following sections we will first formally define the concept of a vector quantizer and derive conditions for its optimality. Subsequently, the most important algorithms for building vector quantizers will be presented. Finally, the unsupervised estimation of mixture densities will be treated as a generalization of the vector quantization problem.

4.1 Definition

A vector quantizer—or for short a quantizer—Q is defined as a mapping of a k-dimensional vector space $\mathbb{R}^k$ onto a finite subset $Y \subset \mathbb{R}^k$:

$$Q : \mathbb{R}^k \mapsto Y$$

The set $Y = y_1, y_2, \ldots, y_N$ of reproduction or prototype vectors y_i is usually referred to as the *codebook*. The size N of the codebook is the essential parameter for characterizing a set of vector quantizers.[1]

Every vector quantizer Q of size N is always associated with a partition of the considered vector space $\mathbb{R}^k$ into regions or cells $R_1, R_2, \ldots, R_N$. The cell R_i contains all vectors $x \in \mathbb{R}^k$ which were mapped to the prototype or code word y_i by the quantizer. The respective cell can be obtained as the inverse image of the prototype vector under the mapping Q defined by the vector quantizer:

$$R_i = Q^{-1}(y_i) = \left\{ x \in \mathbb{R}^k \mid Q(x) = y_i \right\}$$

Thus a quantizer Q implicitly defines a complete and disjoint partition of $\mathbb{R}^k$ into cells R_i as it maps every vector x from the input space to exactly one prototype y_i, i.e.:

$$\bigcup_{i=1}^{N} R_i = \mathbb{R}^k \quad \text{and} \quad R_i \cap R_j = \emptyset \quad \forall i, j \text{ with } i \neq j$$

Then the behavior of a quantizer Q is uniquely defined by specifying the codebook Y used and the associated partition $\{R_i\}$ of the vector space considered.

In practice a vector quantizer can be described as the combination of a coder C and a decoder D. When introducing an index set $I = \{1, 2, \ldots, N\}$ one obtains:

$$C : \mathbb{R}^k \mapsto I \quad \text{and} \quad D : I \mapsto Y$$

---

[1] A vector quantizer with a codebook containing N prototypes is sometimes also referred to as an *N-level quantizer*. This term should, however, not be confused with the notion of a multi-stage vector quantizer which generates the quantization result in multiple subsequent processing steps for increased efficiency.

The quantization rule Q is thus obtained as a concatenation of the coding and the subsequent decoding step:

$$Q = D \circ C$$

This representation is especially useful if the transmission of compactly coded data is considered. In principle it is sufficient then to use a matched pair of coder and decoder and to transmit only the code word indices of the quantized data over the communication channel.[2] In practical applications the codebook itself also needs to be communicated during the transmission of the data as it must be ensured that the decoder uses the correct codebook for the reconstruction of the data from the quantization indices. Therefore, the size of the codebook has to be taken into account when considering the necessary capacity of the transmission channel and the total compression ratio to be achieved.

The main limitation of the quantization process is that a vector $x \in \mathbb{R}^k$ will be mapped onto a prototype vector y which will in general be different from the source vector. Therefore, an individual *quantization error* $\varepsilon(x|Q)$ results from every single quantization operation depending on the quantization rule Q used. This error can formally be described by using a suitable distance measure $d(\cdot, \cdot)$ for vector-valued data:[3]

$$\varepsilon(x|Q) = d(x, Q(x))$$

General statements about the reproduction quality of a certain quantizer Q can, however, only be derived from a global consideration of the quantization error. Therefore, the overall quantization error is computed which is to be expected in the statistical average:

$$\bar{\varepsilon}(Q) = \mathcal{E}\{\varepsilon(X|Q)\} = \mathcal{E}\{d(X, Q(X))\} = \int_{\mathbb{R}^k} d(x, Q(x))\, p(x)\, dx \qquad (4.1)$$

It is assumed here that the statistical properties of the vectors x considered can be described by a random variable X which has the probability density function $p(x)$.

4.2   Optimality

Though the size of the codebook constitutes the essential configuration parameter of vector quantizers in practice, conditions for the existence of optimal quantization

---

[2]Vector quantizers that use a variable data rate also transmit the quantized indices themselves in compressed form, e.g., by applying a Huffman coding to them (cf. e.g. [110, Chap. 17, pp. 631–633]).

[3]The quantization error $\varepsilon(x|Q) = \|x - Q(x)\|$ is obtained if the Euclidean distance is used here instead of a general distance measure.

rules are always considered for a fixed number N of prototype vectors. Then the only factor determining the quality of the quantizer is the reproduction quality achieved. Therefore, the general goal of vector quantizer design is to create a quantizer that, with a given fixed codebook size, achieves the minimal average quantization error for a certain distribution of the input data.

As we have seen before, a quantizer is defined by specifying the codebook *and* the associated partition of the data space. Starting from both components criteria can be formulated on how to choose the respective other element in an optimal way. However, a closed form definition of optimality for both codebook and partition— i.e. for the vector quantizer as a whole—is not possible.

4.2.1 Nearest-Neighbor Condition

The so-called *nearest-neighbor condition* describes the optimal selection of the partition $\{R_i\}$ for a given codebook Y. This condition specifies that every single cell R_i needs to be determined in such a way that it contains all those vectors $x \in \mathbb{R}^k$ which have minimal distance from the associated prototype vector y_i:

$$R_i \subseteq \left\{ x \mid d(x, y_i) \leq d(x, y_j) \ \forall j \neq i \right\} \tag{4.2}$$

This means that the corresponding quantizer Q maps a vector x onto its nearest neighbor in the codebook:

$$Q(x) = y_i \quad \text{if} \quad d(x, y_i) \leq d(x, y_j) \quad \forall j \neq i \tag{4.3}$$

In the case that a vector x has equal distance from two (or more) codebook vectors, it can be mapped arbitrarily to any one of the candidate cells. The resulting quantization error

$$d(x, Q(x)) = \min_{y \in Y} d(x, y) \tag{4.4}$$

is not affected by the actual choice of the tie-braking rule.[4]

It can easily be shown that the quantization of vectors by means of the nearest-neighbor rule (4.3) minimizes the average expected quantization error for a given codebook Y. A lower bound on the average quantization error $\bar{\varepsilon}(Q)$ defined in equation (4.1) can be derived by replacing every single individual error—i.e. the distance

---

[4]In [110, p. 350] it is suggested to perform the mapping in such cases onto the codebook vector with smallest index i.

to the codebook entry chosen—by the minimum achievable one:[5]

$$\bar{\varepsilon}(Q) = \int_{\mathbb{R}^k} d\big(x, Q(x)\big)\, p(x)\, dx \geq \int_{\mathbb{R}^k} \Big\{ \min_{y \in Y} d(x, y) \Big\} p(x)\, dx$$

The comparison of this result with Eq. (4.4) shows that exactly this lower bound of the average quantization error will be reached when applying the nearest-neighbor condition. Therefore, the partition defined on the basis of Eq. (4.2) is optimal for the given codebook.

4.2.2 Centroid Condition

The optimal choice of a codebook Y for a given partition $\{R_i\}$ is defined by the so-called *centroid condition*. For a cell R_i of the partition the optimal reproduction vector is given by that prototype vector y_i that corresponds to the *centroid* of the cell:

$$y_i = \text{cent}(R_i)$$

The centroid of a set of data points—here of a cell R—is defined as that vector $y^* \in R$ which in the statistical average has minimal distance to all other vectors $x \in R$, i.e.:

$$y^* = \text{cent}(R) \quad \text{if} \quad \mathcal{E}\big\{d(X, y^*) | X \in R\big\} \leq \mathcal{E}\big\{d(X, y) | X \in R\big\} \quad \forall y \in R$$

The random variable X again serves to characterize the distribution of the data vectors x in the input space.

If the centroid of R is uniquely defined,[6] it can be specified as follows:

$$\text{cent}(R) = \operatorname*{argmin}_{y \in R} \mathcal{E}\big\{d(X, y) | X \in R\big\} \tag{4.5}$$

The distance measure $d(X, y)$ can be any type of metric and has to be chosen suitably in practice. Quite commonly used are elliptic symmetric distance measures of the form $(x - y)^T C^{-1}(x - y)$. This family of distance measures includes the Euclidean distance $\|x - y\|$ as a special case if no scaling of the vector space with an

---

[5]This derivation of a lower bound on the average quantization error is possible because both factors $d(\cdot, \cdot)$ and $p(x)$ in the integral take on non-negative values. It is, therefore, sufficient to chose $d(\cdot, \cdot)$ to be locally minimal for every vector x of the input space in order to minimize the integral as a whole.

[6]Depending on the distribution of the vectors within the cell considered, it may happen that in certain cases the centroid is not uniquely defined. The minimum of the mean distance is then achieved in the same way for different prototype vectors. As with the choice of the nearest neighbor, the centroid can then be selected arbitrarily among the candidates without affecting optimality.

inverse scatter matrix C^{-1} is performed. When using an elliptic symmetric distance measure the centroid of a cell is identical to the conditional expected value of the data vectors limited to the region R considered:

$$\text{cent}(R) = \mathcal{E}\{X|X \in R\} = \int_R x\, p(x|x \in R)\, dx$$

The use of the centroid as prototype vector also minimizes the average quantization error for the cell R as all vectors within the cell have minimal average distance to the centroid. If all codebook vectors are determined in this way, the quantization by means of this codebook minimizes the error caused by the quantization process for the given partition in the statistical average. The codebook is, therefore, chosen optimally for the partition at hand.

This can easily be shown by computing the average quantization error that results from applying the centroid condition:

$$\bar{\varepsilon}(Q) = \sum_{i=1}^{N} \int_{R_i} d(x, y_i) p(x)\, dx = \sum_{i=1}^{N} P(X \in R_i) \int_{R_i} d(x, y_i) p(x|x \in R_i)\, dx$$

The total error is obtained by integration over all components corresponding to the respective cells and subsequent summation over all cells in the partition. This formula can be rewritten by introducing the prior probabilities $P(X \in R_i)$ of the cells and the conditional probability densities $p(x|x \in R_i)$ of vectors within a specific cell.

All N partial error terms can be minimized independently as all cells are disjoint and the sum runs over non-negative terms only:

$$\int_{R_i} d(x, y_i) p(x|x \in R_i) dx = \mathcal{E}\{d(X, y_i)|X \in R\} \longrightarrow \min!$$

The comparison with the definition of the centroid in Eq. (4.5) shows that this minimization can be achieved by choosing the centroid of every cell R_i as its associated prototype vector y_i. This is because exactly this choice minimizes the average distance to the other vectors in the cell.

Consequently, for an optimal quantizer, codebook and partition are immediately dependent on each other. Therefore, the specification of the codebook is sufficient for the parametrization of the procedure. The associated partition of the input space results implicitly from the optimal choice of the quantization operation by applying the nearest-neighbor rule. Therefore, it is quite common in practice to conceptually identify the codebook with the associated vector quantizer.

4.3 Algorithms for Vector Quantizer Design

In the previous sections conditions were specified for the optimality of a partition for a given codebook or vice versa. However, a closed form analytical solution does not exists for deriving an optimal vector quantizer of given size for some distribution of data vectors. Nevertheless, iterative methods can be defined that try to determine an approximately optimal vector quantizer. Starting from an initial parametrization these algorithms optimize the vector quantizer step by step. However, all these methods can not guarantee to actually find the optimal solution of the problem. They are, therefore, inherently sub-optimal.

An additional problem in the design of vector quantizers lies in the fact that the quality of the quantizer depends on the probability density $p(x)$ of the data vectors considered. In practice this distribution is usually not known and can, therefore, not be described exactly in parametric form. However, in the field of pattern recognition it can safely be assumed that a suitable sample set $\omega = \{x_1, x_2, \dots, x_T\}$ of example vectors is available. Based on this data the parameters of the actual distribution function can be approximated. In the following treatment of algorithms for vector quantizer design, this sample set will always be considered instead of the total input space $\mathbb{R}^k$ or the usually unknown true distribution of the data.

4.3.1 Lloyd's Algorithm

The idea behind the method known as *Lloyd's algorithm* lies in the exploitation of the dual view on vector quantizers. By means of the procedures defined in the previous section, the method alternates between phases that determine, in an optimal way, the partition or the codebook, respectively. In general, an optimal quantizer will not be created by applying a pair of these optimization steps, i.e., a single iteration of the algorithm. It can be shown, however, that an iterative application of the method results in a sequence of vector quantizers which achieve ever decreasing average quantization errors.

The algorithm, which is summarized in Fig. 4.1, generates a vector quantizer of size N for a given sample set, i.e., a codebook containing N prototype vectors. At the beginning of the procedure a suitable initial codebook Y^0 has to be chosen. Unfortunately, only heuristic methods can be applied for determining this initial codebook as no optimality conditions can be exploited in this early stage of the algorithm. However, the choice of this starting point obviously influences the optimization process. Nevertheless, useful results can be obtained in practice by randomly selecting N initial prototype vectors from the sample set. This disadvantage of Lloyd's algorithm is largely avoided by the algorithm proposed by Linde, Buzo & Gray that will be presented in the following section.

In the next processing step the optimal partition of the sample set is computed for the current codebook Y^m. The mapping of every element $x_t \in \omega$ onto a cell of the partition corresponds to its classification into that class R_i^m for which the data element considered has minimal distance from the associated prototype vector y_i^m.

Given a sample set $\omega = \{x_1, x_2, \ldots, x_T\}$ of example vectors, the desired
codebook size N, and a lower bound $\Delta\varepsilon_{min}$ on the relative improvement of
the quantization error.

1. **Initialization**
   choose a suitable initial codebook Y^0 of size N
   (e.g. by randomly selecting N vectors y_i^0 from ω)
   initialize iteration count $m \leftarrow 0$

2. **Optimization of the Partition**
   for the current codebook Y^m determine the optimal partition by classifying all vectors x_t with $t = 1, \ldots, T$ into cells
   $$R_i^m = \{x \,|\, y_i^m = \operatorname*{argmin}_{y \in Y^m} d(x, y)\}$$
   also determine the average quantization error
   $$\bar{\varepsilon}(Y^m) = \tfrac{1}{T} \sum_{t=1}^{T} \min_{y \in Y^m} d(x_t, y)$$

3. **Codebook Update**
   for all cells R_i^m with $i = 1, \ldots, N$ compute new reproduction vectors
   $$y_i^{m+1} = \operatorname{cent}(R_i^m)$$
   these constitute the new codebook $Y^{m+1} = \{y_i^{m+1} \,|\, 1 \le i \le N\}$

4. **Termination**
   compute the relative decrease of the quantization error with respect to the
   last iteration
   $$\Delta\varepsilon_m = \frac{\bar{\varepsilon}(Y^{m-1}) - \bar{\varepsilon}(Y^m)}{\bar{\varepsilon}(Y^m)}$$
   if the relative decrease was large enough, i.e. $\Delta\varepsilon_m > \Delta\varepsilon_{min}$
   $\qquad\qquad$ set $m \leftarrow m + 1$ and continue with step 2
   otherwise Stop!

Fig. 4.1 Lloyd's Algorithm for the design of vector quantizers

During the classification step also the quantization error is computed as the termination of the procedure is decided based on the evolution of this quantity. The
subsequent codebook update can be performed based on the newly computed partition. The new codebook simply consists of all the centroids of the cells defining
the current partition of the input space. The algorithm terminates if no sufficiently
large relative improvement of the quantization error is achieved any more by the
optimization. The lower bound $\Delta\varepsilon_{min}$ on this relative improvement is a parameter
of the method that needs to be specified by the user.[7]

---

[7]Experiments of the author have shown that a relative improvement of the quantization error of
less than a tenth of a percent usually does not result in an improvement of the codebook which is
relevant for practical applications.

A serious drawback of Lloyd's method for vector quantization is the considerable computational effort required. This effort is mainly caused by the classification of the sample vectors in step 2 of the algorithm where the nearest neighbor among the codebook entries has to be computed for every input vector. In contrast, the effort necessary for the computation of the updated codebook is negligible.[8] Therefore, it makes sense to carry out this step in any case even though the average quantization error computed corresponds to the previous codebook.

4.3.2 LBG Algorithm

The most problematic aspect of Lloyd's algorithm is its initialization. Therefore, it is a quite obvious goal to modify this part of the algorithm such that the results can no longer be adversely affected by a bad choice of the initial codebook. The *LBG algorithm*, which was named after the initials of its inventors Linde, Buzo & Gray [178], offers an elegant solution of the initialization problem. It does not construct the desired vector quantizer of size N directly but generates a sequence of quantizers with an increasing number of codebook vectors.

The algorithm, which is summarized in Fig. 4.2, also starts from an initial codebook estimate. However, this initial codebook can be considerably smaller than the desired final one. Therefore, its choice is less crucial for the successful construction of the resulting vector quantizer. If the speed of the overall algorithm is not of primary concern, even an optimum choice is possible here. An optimum codebook can be specified directly if a trivial quantizer is considered, i.e., a vector quantizer that associates the complete data set in question with a single cell of a trivial partition. The optimum codebook for this single-cell partition consists of the centroid of the data set[9] which can be computed easily.

Thus the initialization step produces a codebook of size $N_0 \ll N$. In order to reach the desired codebook size N, the number of prototype vectors is increased in the further course of the procedure. The algorithm applies a method for splitting up existing codebook vectors into two new prototypes. Therefore, a suitable distortion vector ε of small Euclidean norm is added to or subtracted from all existing prototype vectors resulting in two new codebook entries $y_i + \varepsilon$ and $y_i - \varepsilon$ that replace the original prototype. In total, this operation yields a codebook that contains twice as many reproduction vectors as the original one.[10]

---

[8]When using the Euclidean distance measure, the centroid of a cell R is given by the expected value of its data distribution. This boils down to the sample mean for empirically defined distributions: $\mathrm{cent}(R) \hat{=} \frac{1}{|R|} \sum_{x \in R} x$. The sample mean can easily be computed incrementally by performing the summation over all data vectors first and then normalizing the result.

[9]In order to speed up the procedure in the starting phase one can also choose a small codebook containing $N^0 \ll N$ randomly selected vectors without adversely affecting the final result of the algorithm.

[10]In contrast to splitting up all existing prototypes, the splitting procedure can be applied to a suitable subset only, e.g., those codebook entries that account for the highest local quantization error on the data set considered.

Given a sample set $\omega = \{x_1, x_2, \ldots, x_T\}$ of example vectors, the desired codebook size N, and a lower bound $\Delta\varepsilon_{min}$ on the relative improvement of the quantization error.

1. **Initialization**

   choose a suitable initial codebook Y^0 of size N^0

   (e.g. a trivial codebook $Y^0 = \{\text{cent}(\omega)\}$ with $N^0 = 1$)

   initialize iteration count $m \leftarrow 0$

2. **Splitting**

   from the current codebook Y^m generate a new codebook

   with $N^{m+1} = 2 N^m$ reproduction vectors

   $Y^{m+1} = \{y_1 + \varepsilon, y_1 - \varepsilon, y_2 + \varepsilon, y_2 - \varepsilon, \ldots, y_{N^m} + \varepsilon, y_{N^m} - \varepsilon\}$

   using a suitable small distortion vector ε

3. **Optimization**

   optimize the newly created codebook Y^{m+1} by applying Lloyd's algorithm (using $\Delta\varepsilon_{min}$ as a parameter)

4. **Termination**

   if the desired number of codebook vectors is not yet reached

            set $m \leftarrow m + 1$ and continue with step 2

   otherwise Stop!

Fig. 4.2 LBG Algorithm for the design of vector quantizers

Of course, it can not be expected that the codebook generated in this way is optimal with respect to the quantization error achieved. Therefore, in the third step of the procedure the current codebook is optimized by applying Lloyd's algorithm (steps 2 to 4) known from the previous section. If the desired codebook size is not yet reached, the splitting of codebook vectors is again applied to the optimized quantizer.

Compared to the method proposed by Lloyd, the LBG algorithm offers the important advantage that the initialization process is clearly defined. Thus it is avoided that a random but unfortunate choice of the initial codebook causes the iterative optimization of the quantizer to reach an unsatisfactory local optimum only. Just the distortion vector necessary for splitting codebook vectors needs to be specified in a suitable way. The method also reduces the computational costs of the necessary classification as increasingly large codebooks are created step by step. In the beginning of the optimization process where only rough estimates of the parameters of the vector quantizer are available, the method works on very small codebooks. These can be decoded much more efficiently than the final complete quantizer. During the continuous growth of the codebook, refined and more elaborate models, which require more decoding effort, are not used before a better approximation of the desired quantization rule is available.

Given a sample set $\omega = \{x_1, x_2, \ldots, x_T\}$ of example vectors and the desired codebook size N.

1. **Initialization**

   choose the first N vectors of the sample set as initial codebook Y^0

   $Y^0 = \{x_1, x_2, \ldots, x_N\}$

   the initial partition is given by $\{R_i^0 | R_i^0 = \{x_i\}\}$

   initialize iteration count $m \leftarrow 0$

2. **Iteration**

   for all vectors x_t, $N < t \leq T$ not yet processed

   a. **Classification**

      for x_t determine the optimal reproduction vector y_i^m in the current codebook Y^m

      $$y_i^m = \operatorname*{argmin}_{y \in Y^m} d(x_t, y)$$

   b. **Partition Update**

      determine the new partition by updating the cell of the codebook vector selected

      $$R_j^{m+1} = \begin{cases} R_j^m \cup \{x_t\} & \text{if } j = i \\ R_j^m & \text{otherwise} \end{cases}$$

   c. **Codebook Update**

      determine a new codebook by updating the prototype of the cell modified in the previous step

      $$y_j^{m+1} = \begin{cases} \operatorname{cent}(R_j^{m+1}) & \text{if } j = i \\ y_j^m & \text{otherwise} \end{cases}$$

   set $m \leftarrow m + 1$ and continue with next sample

Fig. 4.3 k-means algorithm for the design of vector quantizers

4.3.3 k-Means Algorithm

Both Lloyd's algorithm and the LBG algorithm are well suited for the design of vector quantizers. However, both require the repeated expensive classification of all data vectors in the sample set during the necessary optimization steps. In contrast, the so-called k-*means algorithm* defines a method that is able to generate an approximately optimal codebook with only a single pass through the data to be processed. The procedure was developed by MacQueen [187] and is based on the idea to use not a single sample mean for the characterization of some distribution of data vectors but multiple means. These k mean vectors correspond directly to the reproduction vectors of a vector quantizer of size k.

Figure 4.3 shows the associated algorithm. In order to be consistent in notation with the other methods presented, we will denote the size of the codebook by N and not by k as in the original work.

In contrast to the algorithms presented before, a surprisingly simple initialization rule can be obtained as it is the goal of the method to process every data vector x_t only once. The initial codebook just consists of the first N vectors of the sample set.

The following processing steps remind us of the two optimization phases of Lloyd's algorithm. However, in the k-means method they are applied to every vector individually. Thus a vector x_t is first mapped onto the optimal reproduction vector y_i^m in the current codebook Y^m according to the nearest-neighbor rule. Immediately afterwards the parameters of the vector quantizer are updated. Therein it is assumed that by mapping the vector x_t onto R_i^{m+1} only this very cell is changed. Therefore, it is sufficient to compute a new reproduction vector y_i^{m+1} for the modified cell only. Finally, the newly created codebook is available after a single pass through the sample set.

It might be suspected that such a codebook estimation procedure does not lead to satisfactory results. In practice, however, the method is surprisingly powerful and largely more efficient than Lloyd's algorithm or the LBG method. When quality is concerned, the vector quantizers generated by the k-means algorithm are generally not inferior to those created by the other methods. If the sample set consists of a sequence of vectors generated randomly and independently of each other, it can be shown that the method converges asymptotically to the optimal solution provided that the size of the sample set approaches infinity [187]. In practice this means that the algorithm works especially well for large sample sets which exhibit no or only very limited correlation between subsequent vectors.

Though the k-means algorithm is fundamentally different from the method attributed to Lloyd, the latter is frequently incorrectly referred to as the k-means algorithm.[11] When efficiency is concerned, the method largely outperforms all iterative optimization methods, as Lloyd's algorithm or the LBG algorithm, with its linear complexity in the size of the sample set. Still the quality of the resulting vector quantizers is comparable.

4.4   Estimation of Mixture Density Models

The result of a vector quantization method describes a given data distribution only by means of the N reproduction vectors within the codebook created. A substantially more precise representation is obtained if a mixture density model is used. Then also the characteristics of the local scatter of the data can be described. Usually, normal distributions are used as components of such a model because of their rather simple mathematical treatment (cf. Sect. 3.4).

In principle, the estimation of a mixture model for a given sample set can directly build upon the results of a vector quantization process though this naive approach

---

[11] See also the bibliographical remarks in Sect. 4.5.

yields the qualitatively worst results. After the codebook generation is finished just the parameters of a normal distribution are estimated for all cells R_i of the final partition. The necessary mean vector $\boldsymbol{\mu}_i$ is identical to the centroid $\boldsymbol{y}_i$, which is already known. Merely the sample covariance matrix needs to be computed for the respective cell (cf. Eq. (3.10)):

$$C_i = \sum_{x \in R_i} (x - \boldsymbol{\mu}_i)(x - \boldsymbol{\mu}_i)^T$$

Considerably better results are achieved if the distortion of the vector space modeled by the covariance matrix is already considered during the quantization process. The so-called *Mahalanobis distance* represents the associated extension of the Euclidean distance measure.

$$d_{\text{Mahalanobis}}(\boldsymbol{x}, \boldsymbol{\mu}) = (\boldsymbol{x} - \boldsymbol{\mu})^T C^{-1} (\boldsymbol{x} - \boldsymbol{\mu})$$

As the comparison with Eq. (3.6) shows, this formula is almost identical with the exponential term of a normal density function. It is, therefore, only a small step further to consider such a distribution directly in the quantization process.

In contrast to a distance measure, however, a density function represents a measure of membership, i.e., the higher the density the "closer" samples are to the modes of the distribution. Therefore, the rule for mapping vectors to codebook entries needs to be modified. A vector $\boldsymbol{x}_t$ is now mapped to that cell R_i for which the corresponding normal distribution $\mathcal{N}(\boldsymbol{x}|\boldsymbol{\mu}_i, C_i)$ yields the maximal density value:

$$R_i = \left\{ \boldsymbol{x} | i = \underset{j}{\text{argmax}} \, \mathcal{N}(\boldsymbol{x}|\boldsymbol{\mu}_j, C_j) \right\}$$

This modification of the quantization rule makes it possible that mixture density models can be created with traditional methods for vector quantizer design. However, the algorithms still assume that the average quantization error should be minimized which is not an appropriate optimization criterion for a probability distribution.

This becomes clearer when considering the fact that for the computation of the parameters of the normal distributions only vectors from a limited region—i.e., the respective cell—are used. The density function itself, however, is defined for the complete vector space and yields non-negative density values for all possible vectors, which may become arbitrarily small though.

4.4.1   EM Algorithm

For the correct estimation of Gaussian mixture models the so-called *EM algorithm* is used. It defines a very general method for the iterative optimization of statistical models with hidden states or variables. In the following we will first describe the general methodology and then present the EM algorithm in its concrete version for the estimation of mixture density models.

Principally, the EM algorithm defines a generalization of ML estimation to statistical models with hidden random variables. In the literature this situation is usually described as an estimation problem working on so-called incomplete data. The complete data consists of the observed samples $X = \{x_1, x_2, \ldots, x_T\}$ paired with hidden data $Y = \{y_1, y_2, \ldots, y_T\}$ that is not observable but required for evaluating the model properly. In the case of a Gaussian mixture model the observed data is the set of samples to be described by the model and the hidden data is the unknown association of the samples with components of the mixture model that are used to generate them. In such a situation the log-likelihood[12] of the observed data X

$$L(\theta|X) = \log p(X|\theta) \tag{4.6}$$

can not be maximized directly any more as it depends on the hidden data Y.

The solution to this problem proposed by the EM algorithm relies on two important ideas. First, instead of the log-likelihood of the observed but incomplete data X the log-likelihood of the so-called complete data (X, Y) is considered

$$L(\theta|X, Y) = \log p(X, Y|\theta) \tag{4.7}$$

where $p(X, Y|\theta)$ is the probability for generating the complete data given the model. It can be shown that maximizing this quantity is equivalent to maximizing the original incomplete-data log-likelihood (see sidebar *Convergence of the EM Algorithm*).

Convergence of the EM Algorithm

In order to verify that the iterative re-estimation procedure defined by the EM algorithm really converges, let us first look at the maximization of the complete-data log-likelihood (4.7) from a more formal point of view. As it depends on the hidden data Y it can not be evaluated or maximized directly. However, the unknown hidden data can be considered as a random variable which is governed by a certain probability distribution. Consequently, the complete-data log-likelihood also corresponds to a random variable and we can maximize its expected value with respect to Y

$$\mathcal{E}_Y \{ \log p(X, Y|\theta) | X, \bar{\theta} \} \longrightarrow \max$$

conditioned on the observed data X and some estimate of the parameters $\bar{\theta}$.

---

[12] As we have seen from the description of ML estimation (see Sect. 3.6.1) using the log-likelihood instead of the likelihood function is admissible and can lead to considerable simplifications in the further mathematical derivations.

Rewriting this equation using Bayes' rule we obtain:

$$\mathcal{E}_Y\{\log p(X, Y|\theta)|X, \bar{\theta}\} = \mathcal{E}_Y\{\log p(Y|X, \theta)|X, \bar{\theta}\} + \mathcal{E}_Y\{\log p(X|\theta)|X, \bar{\theta}\}$$

As $\log p(X|\theta)$ is constant with respect to the conditional expectation $\mathcal{E}_Y\{.|X, \bar{\theta}\}$, it is easy to derive the following equation for the incomplete-data log-likelihood:

$$\begin{aligned}\log p(X|\theta) &= \mathcal{E}_Y\{\log p(X, Y|\theta)|X, \bar{\theta}\} - \mathcal{E}_Y\{\log p(Y|X, \theta)|X, \bar{\theta}\}\\ &= Q(\theta|\bar{\theta}) - H(\theta|\bar{\theta})\end{aligned}$$

Here $Q(\theta|\bar{\theta})$ is the auxiliary function of the EM procedure—frequently simply referred to as the Q-function—which corresponds to the expected value of the complete-data log-likelihood that is maximized in the M-step. This maximization also achieves a maximization of the original log-likelihood $\log p(X|\theta)$ as it can be shown that $H(\theta|\bar{\theta}) \leq H(\theta|\theta)$. Consequently, iterating E- and M-step the parameter estimate $\hat{\theta}$ will eventually converge to a local maximum.

Second, the unknown values of the hidden variables Y are approximated by suitable estimates $\hat{Y}$. In order to do so, an initial guess $\bar{\theta}$ about the parameters is required. Furthermore, the fact can be exploited that the model to be estimated will always define relations between the parameters θ and the hidden data Y. Therefore, it is possible to derive expectations $\hat{Y}$ about Y from θ and the observed data X. This estimate $\hat{Y}$ can now be plugged into the log-likelihood function (4.7) which is then based on given data only, i.e., X being observed and $\hat{Y}$ being estimated. Consequently, the likelihood can now be maximized in the usual way.

The result of this optimization is an improved parameter set $\hat{\theta}$ for the model in question which replaces the current guess or estimate $\bar{\theta}$. Repeating this procedure, which is summarized in Fig. 4.4, will eventually produce an optimized parameter set of the model in question. Though the convergence of the method can be shown, it will in general compute only a local optimum of the parameters θ, more specifically, it will find that local optimum that lies closest to the initial guess on θ which the EM procedure was started with. Despite this apparent limitation, the EM algorithm is extremely useful in practice for the optimization of complex statistical models.

The name of the EM algorithm is derived from the two main processing steps that are executed within the iterative re-estimation framework. First, the values of the hidden random variables are estimated depending on the current model and the given data. This step is called expectation or simply E-step. Afterwards, new model parameters are computed which locally optimize the objective function, i.e. the complete-data log-likelihood (4.7). This second phase is referred to as the maximization or M-step.

Given a data set of observed but incomplete data $X = \{x_1, x_2, \ldots, x_T\}$.

1. **Initialization**
   choose a suitable initial estimate θ^0 of the model parameters
   initialize iteration count $m \leftarrow 0$

2. **E-Step**
   compute estimates $\hat{Y}$ of the hidden data given the current parameters θ^m
   and the observed data X

3. **M-Step**
   compute ML estimate θ^{m+1} that maximizes the expected value of the
   complete-data log-likelihood (Q-function):

$$\theta^{m+1} = \operatorname*{argmax}_{\theta} Q(\theta|\theta^m) = \operatorname*{argmax}_{\theta} \mathcal{E}_Y \{\log p(X, Y|\theta)|X, \theta^m\}$$

4. **Termination**
   if there was a sufficient improvement in the log-likelihood $\log p(X|\theta^m)$
   $\qquad$ set $m \leftarrow m + 1$ and continue with step 2
   otherwise Stop!

Fig. 4.4 General EM framework for the estimation of statistical models with hidden random variables

4.4.2 EM Algorithm for Gaussian Mixtures

With the general EM framework laid out, we can now apply it to the estimation
of Gaussian mixture models. A model with N component densities is defined as
follows (cf. Eq. (3.7))

$$p(x|\theta) = \sum_{i=1}^{N} c_i \, \mathcal{N}(x|\mu_i, C_i)$$

where the mixture weights c_i have to sum up to one, i.e., $\sum_i c_i = 1$. In contrast
to a vector quantization model, every component density statistically represents the
distribution of similar vectors or patterns in the input space rather than describing
a clearly bounded region or cell. The set of parameters consists of the prior probabilities c_i of the individual pattern classes and the associated density parameters μ_i
and C_i and will be collected into a parameter vector θ.

In order to be able to apply the EM algorithm for the estimation of mixture models, a set of example data and the desired number of component distributions must
be given. As stated before, the hidden variables here consist of the unknown correspondences between data vectors and normal distributions or pattern classes, respectively.

Given a sample set $\omega = \{x_1, x_2, \ldots, x_T\}$ of example vectors, the desired number of mixture components N, and a lower bound $\Delta L_{\min}$ on the relative improvement of the log-likelihood.

1. **Initialization**
   choose initial parameters $\theta^0 = (c_i^0, \mu_i^0, C_i^0)$ of the mixture model
   (e.g. on the basis of a pre-computed vector quantization codebook)
   initialize iteration count $m \leftarrow 0$

2. **Estimation**
   for every vector $x \in \omega$ compute estimates of the posterior probabilities of the pattern classes using the current model θ^m
   $$P(\omega_i | x, \theta^m) = \frac{c_i^m \mathcal{N}(x | \mu_i^m, C_i^m)}{\sum_j c_j^m \mathcal{N}(x | \mu_j^m, C_j^m)}$$
   compute the log-likelihood of the data for the current model θ^m
   $$L(\theta^m | \omega) = \log p(x_1, x_2, \ldots, x_T | \theta^m) = \sum_{x \in \omega} \log \sum_j c_j^m \mathcal{N}(x | \mu_j^m, C_j^m)$$

3. **Maximization**
   compute updated parameters $\theta^{m+1} = (c_i^{m+1}, \mu_i^{m+1}, C_i^{m+1})$

   $$c_i^{m+1} = \frac{\sum_{x \in \omega} P(\omega_i | x, \theta^m)}{|\omega|}$$

   $$\mu_i^{m+1} = \frac{\sum_{x \in \omega} P(\omega_i | x, \theta^m) x}{\sum_{x \in \omega} P(\omega_i | x, \theta^m)}$$

   $$C_i^{m+1} = \frac{\sum_{x \in \omega} P(\omega_i | x, \theta^m) x x^T}{\sum_{x \in \omega} P(\omega_i | x, \theta^m)} - \mu_i^{m+1} (\mu_i^{m+1})^T$$

4. **Termination**
   compute the relative change in the log-likelihood with respect to the previous iteration
   $$\Delta L_m = \frac{L(\theta^m | \omega) - L(\theta^{m-1} | \omega)}{L(\theta^m | \omega)}$$
   if the relative improvement was large enough, i.e. $\Delta L_m > \Delta L_{\min}$
           let $m \leftarrow m + 1$ and continue with step 2
   otherwise Stop!

Fig. 4.5 EM algorithm for the estimation of mixture models

For the initialization of the procedure, which is summarized in Fig. 4.5, first some suitable initial parameters of the mixture model need to be determined. Unfortunately, a random initialization is no longer possible as the complexity of the model is significantly higher compared to a vector quantizer and, therefore, the method is extremely sensitive to the choice of the initial model. However, a suitable initial model can easily be determined with one of the two simpler methods described earlier in this section. In addition to the initial parameters of the component densities $\boldsymbol{\mu}_i^0$ and $\boldsymbol{C}_i^0$ only the mixture weights $c_i^0 = \frac{|R_i|}{\sum_j |R_j|}$ need to be defined which correspond to estimates of the prior probabilities $P(\omega_i)$ of the pattern classes ω_i.

In the E-step probabilities for the mapping of every vector onto one of the code-book classes ω_i are derived given the current model $\boldsymbol{\theta}^m$. These posterior probabilities can be computed for arbitrary vectors $\boldsymbol{x} \in \omega$ in the following way:

$$P(\omega_i|\boldsymbol{x},\boldsymbol{\theta}^m) = \frac{P(\omega_i|\boldsymbol{\theta}^m)p(\boldsymbol{x}|\omega_i,\boldsymbol{\theta}^m)}{p(\boldsymbol{x}|\boldsymbol{\theta}^m)} = \frac{P(\omega_i|\boldsymbol{\theta}^m)p(\boldsymbol{x}|\omega_i,\boldsymbol{\theta}^m)}{\sum_j P(\omega_j|\boldsymbol{\theta}^m)p(\boldsymbol{x}|\omega_j,\boldsymbol{\theta}^m)}$$

$$= \frac{c_i^m \mathcal{N}(\boldsymbol{x}|\boldsymbol{\mu}_i^m, \boldsymbol{C}_i^m)}{\sum_j c_j^m \mathcal{N}(\boldsymbol{x}|\boldsymbol{\mu}_i^m, \boldsymbol{C}_i^m)}$$

Here first Bayes' rule is applied to rewrite the expression. As the overall density function $p(\boldsymbol{x}|\boldsymbol{\theta}^m)$ is described by current model it can be substituted by the mixture density itself in the second rewriting step.

Furthermore, it makes sense to compute the likelihood of the current model during the estimation of the posterior probabilities. It is defined as the sum over the logarithmic density values of the mixture evaluated for every sample.

In the next step, the M-step, new parameters of the mixture density are derived based on the probability estimates for associating data vectors and pattern classes $P(\omega_i|\boldsymbol{x},\boldsymbol{\theta}^m)$. The new parameter estimates maximize the complete-data log-likelihood given the sample data and the previous parameter estimates. Technically, this maximization requires to solve a Lagrangian optimization problem for the complete-data log-likelihood taking into account the constraint that the mixture weights c_i need to define a discrete probability distribution. One obtains the following relationships for computing estimates of the prior probabilities c_i, the mean vectors $\boldsymbol{\mu}_i$, and the associated covariance matrices $\boldsymbol{C}_i$:

$$c_i = \frac{\sum_{\boldsymbol{x} \in \omega} P(\omega_i|\boldsymbol{x})}{|\omega|}$$

$$\boldsymbol{\mu}_i = \frac{\sum_{\boldsymbol{x} \in \omega} P(\omega_i|\boldsymbol{x})\boldsymbol{x}}{\sum_{\boldsymbol{x} \in \omega} P(\omega_i|\boldsymbol{x})}$$

$$\boldsymbol{C}_i = \frac{\sum_{\boldsymbol{x} \in \omega} P(\omega_i|\boldsymbol{x})(\boldsymbol{x} - \boldsymbol{\mu}_i)(\boldsymbol{x} - \boldsymbol{\mu}_i)^T}{\sum_{\boldsymbol{x} \in \omega} P(\omega_i|\boldsymbol{x})}$$

In the same way as in the design of vector quantizers, also in the EM algorithm it is necessary to decide about the termination of the procedure in a suitable way. In analogy to the termination criterion used for Lloyd's algorithm, this decision can be based on the relative improvement of the likelihood $L(\boldsymbol{\theta}|\omega)$ which is obtained for the current model parameters given the sample set.

In contrast to classical vector quantization techniques, for Gaussian mixture models the mapping of data vectors to pattern classes—i.e. the individual component densities—is not performed via the binary decision of a classifier but probabilistically instead. The estimation of mixture densities with this method is, therefore, sometimes also referred to as "soft vector quantization".

4.5   Bibliographical Remarks

An in-depth treatment of the field of vector quantization can be found in the fundamental monograph by Gersho & Gray [110]. The presentation of the topic in this
chapter was partially based on [110, Chap. 10, pp. 309–340 and Chap. 11, pp. 345–
400]. A good summary of the most important aspects can also be found in [123,
Chap. 4.4, pp. 163–175].

The *k-means algorithm* for the design of vector quantizers was developed by
MacQueen [187]. A description of this original *k*-means algorithm and related clustering methods can be found in [25].

The *LBG algorithm* was named after the initials of its inventors Linde, Buzo &
Gray [178]. Descriptions of this method can also be found in [110, pp. 361–362],
[103, pp. 395–396] or [123, pp. 169–170].

The origin of *Lloyd's algorithm* dates back to 1957 where a manuscript by
its inventor was internally circulated at Bell Labs. According to the author this
manuscript was almost literally published as [180] later. The generalization of the
method to vector-valued input data is presented in [178]. An analysis of the convergence properties of the generalized Lloyd algorithm is given in [263]. A good
overview of the algorithm can also be found in [110, pp. 362–370]. Frequently,
the method is incorrectly referred to as *k*-means algorithm in the literature (cf. e.g.
[252, p. 125], [136, p. 11], [103, pp. 394–395], and [123, pp. 166–169]) though it is
fundamentally different from this method (see also Sect. 4.3).

The *EM algorithm* for the parameter estimation of statistical models with hidden
variables goes back to work of Dempster, Laird & Rubin [53]. Summarizing descriptions of this very general method and proofs of its convergence can, e.g., be found in
[125, pp. 29–35], [22], [123, pp. 170–175], and [23, Sect. 9.4, pp. 450–455]. Extensions of the EM procedure to the MAP estimation principle are presented in [109].

Hidden Markov Models

In the field of pattern recognition, signals are frequently thought of as the product of sources that act statistically. Therefore, the primary goal of the analysis of such signals is to model the statistical properties of the assumed signal sources as exactly as possible. As a basis of the model building, merely the observed example data and assumptions about limitations in the model's degrees of freedom are available. However, the model to be determined should not only replicate the generation of certain data as exactly as possible but also deliver useful information for segmenting the signals into some meaningful units.

Hidden Markov models are able to account for *both* these modeling aspects. First, they define a generative statistical model that is able to generate data sequences according to rather complex probability distributions and that can be used for classifying sequential patterns. Second, information about the segmentation of the data considered can be derived from the two-stage stochastic process that is described by a hidden Markov model. Consequently, hidden Markov models possess the quite remarkable ability to treat segmentation and classification of patterns in an integrated framework.

The great popularity of this modeling technique results from its successful application and consequent further development in the field of automatic speech recognition. In this area of research, hidden Markov models have effectively replaced all competing approaches and constitute the dominant processing paradigm. This success is due to their superior ability to describe processes or signals evolving over time. As a consequence, artificial neural networks are used for speech recognition and comparable segmentation problems only in very few cases despite their success in other areas of pattern recognition. However, there exist a number of hybrid systems that combine hidden Markov models and artificial neuronal networks within an integrated modeling framework and try to make use of the advantages of both techniques (see Sect. 5.8.2).

G.A. Fink, *Markov Models for Pattern Recognition*,
Advances in Computer Vision and Pattern Recognition,
DOI 10.1007/978-1-4471-6308-4_5, © Springer-Verlag London 2014

5.1   Definition

Hidden Markov models (HMMs) describe a two-stage stochastic process. The first stage consists of a discrete stochastic process which is stationary, causal, and simple. The state space considered is finite. The process, which is also known as a Markov chain model, probabilistically describes the state transitions within a discrete and finite state space. It can be visualized as a finite state automaton with edges between any pair of states which are labeled with transition probabilities. The behavior of the process at a given time t is only dependent on the immediate predecessor state and can be characterized as follows:

$$P(S_t \mid S_1, S_2, \ldots, S_{t-1}) = P(S_t \mid S_{t-1})$$

This limitation of the temporal extension of the statistical dependencies within the model corresponds to the so-called *Markov property*. As we will se later, it is essential for being able to define efficient algorithms for HMMs.

In the second stage of the stochastic process defining an HMM, for every point in time t an output or observation O_t is generated. The associated probability distribution is only dependent on the current state S_t and not on any previous states or observations:[1]

$$P(O_t \mid O_1, \ldots, O_{t-1}, S_1, \ldots, S_t) = P(O_t \mid S_t)$$

This property of HMMs is referred to as the *output independence assumption* in the literature.

The sequence of outputs generated is the only thing that can be observed of the behavior of the model. In contrast, the state sequence taken on during the generation of the data cannot be observed. It is said to be "hidden"—a phrasing from which the term *hidden* Markov model is derived. From the outside view on the model—i.e. the observation of its behavior—also the more common reference to the sequence $O_1, O_2, \ldots, O_T$ of outputs as *observation sequence* is motivated. We will be referring to individual elements of this sequence as observation elements or simply *observations* in the following.

In the pattern recognition literature the behavior of HMMs is always considered over a finite time interval of length T. For the initialization of the model at the beginning of this period, additional start probabilities are used that describe the probability distribution of the states at time $t = 1$. An equivalent termination criterion is usually missing, however. The actions of the model are, therefore, terminated as

---

[1]In the tradition of research at IBM, HMMs are described in a slightly different way. There outputs are generated during state transitions, i.e., on the edges of the model ([11], cf. e.g. [136, p. 17]). With respect to its expressive power this formulation is, however, completely equivalent to the one which is used in this book and also throughout the majority of the literature as is also shown in [136, pp. 35–36].

soon as an arbitrary state at time T is reached. Neither a statistically nor a declarative criterion is used to specifically mark end states.[2]

A hidden Markov model which is usually denoted as λ is, therefore, completely described by

- a finite set of states $\{s \mid 1 \leq s \leq N\}$ that are usually only referred to by their indices in the literature,
- a matrix A of state-transition probabilities

$$A = \left\{ a_{ij} \mid a_{ij} = P(S_t = j \mid S_{t-1} = i) \right\}$$

- a vector π of start probabilities

$$\pi = \left\{ \pi_i \mid \pi_i = P(S_1 = i) \right\}$$

- and state specific probability distributions

$$\left\{ b_j(o_k) \mid b_j(o_k) = P(O_t = o_k \mid S_t = j) \right\} \quad \text{or} \quad \left\{ b_j(x) \mid b_j(x) = p(x \mid S_t = j) \right\}$$

for the outputs of the model.

However, the output distributions need to be distinguished depending on the type of observations the model is generating. In the simplest case, the outputs are generated from a discrete inventory $\{o_1, o_2, \ldots, o_M\}$ and, therefore, have a symbolic nature. Then the quantities $b_j(o_k)$ represent discrete probability distributions which can be grouped together in a matrix of output probabilities:

$$B = \left\{ b_{jk} \mid b_{jk} = P(O_t = o_k \mid S_t = j) \right\}$$

For this choice of output modeling one obtains so-called *discrete HMMs*.

If the observations are vector valued quantities $x \in \mathbb{R}^n$ instead, the output distributions are described on the basis of continuous probability density functions:

$$b_j(x) = p(x \mid S_t = j)$$

Current applications of HMMs to problems of signal analysis exclusively use these so-called *continuous HMMs*, even though the necessity to model continuous distributions significantly increases the complexity of the formalism.

5.2 Modeling Outputs

The description of the model's outputs by discrete probability distributions is normally used for the introduction of HMMs in the literature. This variant is also applied to the analysis of biological sequences, as there one can work with discrete

---

[2]In [125, p. 150] analogously to the start probabilities also termination probabilities are defined. The HMM architectures used for analyzing biological sequences usually contain special non-emitting start and end states (see also Sect. 8.4).

symbolic inventories of either the four bases used to build DNA strands or the 20 possible amino acids (cf. e.g. [67]). For applications in the field of signal processing, however, discrete models are hardly considered any more as they require the use of a vector quantizer which converts continuous feature representations of speech signals or handwritten script into discrete observation sequences prior to the analysis.

The expressive power of the HMM formalism is considerably increased if this quantization step is avoided or included into the model building process, respectively. In order to achieve this, it is necessary, however, to represent continuous probability distributions over $\mathbb{R}^n$ in a suitable way.

In the discrete case probability distributions can be directly represented by the empirical distribution. In the continuous case the use of empirical distributions or approximations thereof is hardly possible in practice.[3] However, parametric representations of continuous density functions are only known for a small number of families of distributions as, for example, the normal or Gaussian distribution. For the desired application area such "simple" models cannot be used as they all represent uni-modal distributions. With only a single region of high density in the area of the expected value of the probability density function only extremely "well-behaved" data can be described.

In order to be able to nevertheless deal with arbitrary continuous distributions with multiple modes or regions of high density in general, approximate techniques are applied. The most well known and most widely used method consists in the use of *mixture densities* on the basis of Gaussian densities. It can be shown that every general continuous probability distribution $p(x)$ can be approximated to arbitrary precision with a linear combination of, in general, infinitely many component normal distributions (cf. [80]):

$$p(x) \hat{=} \sum_{k=1}^{\infty} c_k \mathcal{N}(x \mid \boldsymbol{\mu}_k, \boldsymbol{C}_k) \approx \sum_{k=1}^{M} c_k \mathcal{N}(x \mid \boldsymbol{\mu}_k, \boldsymbol{C}_k)$$

If a finite number M of mixtures is used for the approximation an error results which, however, can be kept small by using a suitable number of component densities. The mixture weights which may vary between zero and one need to sum up to unity:

$$\sum_{k} c_k = 1 \quad \text{with} \quad 0 \leq c_k \leq 1 \quad \forall k$$

This gives a convex combination of the component densities and guarantees that the resulting mixture again is a probability distribution.

---

[3]The empirical distribution of a continuous random variable would assign non-zero density values only to known data points and, therefore, would be useless in practice. An approximation of the true density function by a Parzen estimate (cf. e.g. [65, Sect. 4.3]) would be possible in principle but require the storage of the complete data set.

The general form of continuous HMMs uses one mixture density per state j for the description of the output probability density function:

$$b_j(x) = \sum_{k=1}^{M_j} c_{jk} \mathcal{N}(x \mid \mu_{jk}, C_{jk}) = \sum_{k=1}^{M_j} c_{jk} g_{jk}(x) \qquad (5.1)$$

The number M_j of mixture components used may vary from state to state. Every such output probability density $b_j(x)$ is parametrized by a set of state-specific mixture weights c_{jk} and a set of normal densities $\mathcal{N}(x \mid \mu_{jk}, C_{jk})$ which is also state specific. Furthermore, each component density, which will be denoted by $g_{jk}(x)$ in the following, possesses an individual set of parameters consisting of a mean vector μ_{jk} and a covariance matrix C_{jk}.

A continuous HMM can thus also be considered as a discrete model with a state specific "soft" quantization stage. The discrete output distributions can be found in the mixture weights and the component densities used define the quantization rule. In contrast to a discrete HMM, no "hard" decisions are made here, but the density values of all normal distributions used are incorporated into the computation.

For continuous HMMs the number of parameters is drastically increased with respect to the discrete case. Therefore, a number of techniques has been developed in order to reduce the number of parameters by jointly using parts of the model. Such methods are usually referred to as the *tying* of parameters. They will be treated in greater detail in Sect. 9.2.

The most well known of these approaches are the so-called *semi-continuous HMMs* which are frequently referred to as *tied-mixture models* in the literature. In such models only a single set of component densities is used to construct all state-specific output probability density functions:

$$b_j(x) = \sum_{k=1}^{M} c_{jk} \mathcal{N}(x \mid \mu_k, C_k) = \sum_{k=1}^{M} c_{jk} g_k(x) \qquad (5.2)$$

This global set of mixture components $g_k(x)$ is frequently also referred to as the codebook as in this variant of the model the relationship to a discrete model with initial quantization stage becomes the most obvious. The definition of the output probability densities is completely analogous to the general continuous case. However, there is no longer a state dependency of the parameters of the underlying normal distributions. Additionally, in semi-continuous HMMs every mixture density consists of the same number M of component distributions.

5.3   Use Cases

The application of HMMs for pattern recognition tasks is always based on the fundamental assumption that the patterns considered—at least in principle—are outputs of a comparable stochastic model and that the properties of this model can be described reasonably well by HMMs.

A relevant question for a given model is, therefore, how well this model describes some pattern, i.e., a certain observation sequence. For this purpose the total output probability $P(O \mid \lambda)$ of the data for a known model—or a reasonable approximation thereof—needs to be computed. On the one hand, this quantity indicates how well some model λ is capable of representing the statistical properties of certain example data $O = O_1, O_2, \ldots, O_T$ that it was built for. On the other hand, the total output probability can be used as the basis for a classification decision.

If two or more HMMs λ_i are available, which resemble the statistical properties of patterns from different pattern classes Ω_i, some given sequence of test data O can be classified into that class Ω_j for which the posterior probability $P(\lambda_j \mid O)$ becomes maximum:

$$P(\lambda_j \mid O) = \max_i \frac{P(O \mid \lambda_i)P(\lambda_i)}{P(O)} \tag{5.3}$$

When evaluating this expression, the probability $P(O)$ of the data itself represents a quantity irrelevant for the classification—or the maximization of $P(\lambda_i \mid O)$—because it is independent of λ_i and, therefore, constant. Thus for determining the optimal class it is sufficient to consider the denominator of Eq. (5.3) only:

$$\lambda_j = \operatorname*{argmax}_{\lambda_i} P(\lambda_i \mid O) = \operatorname*{argmax}_{\lambda_i} \frac{P(O \mid \lambda_i)P(\lambda_i)}{P(O)} = \operatorname*{argmax}_{\lambda_i} P(O \mid \lambda_i)P(\lambda_i)$$

For this procedure to be applicable, the prior probabilities $P(\lambda_i)$ of the individual models need to be specified. As this might be non-trivial, these priors are frequently neglected for the sake of simplicity so that the classification decision is solely based on the total output probability $P(O \mid \lambda_i)$.

Such an approach can be applied to the classification of isolated sample patterns that do not need to be further segmented into smaller units. The models for describing the different pattern classes are defined completely independently of each other. For example, isolated word recognition tasks can be solved this way or local similarities of biological sequences can be analyzed (cf. [67, pp. 87–91]).

However, the mere evaluation of the total output probability makes only classification decisions possible on completely segmented data. Therefore, in the context of HMM technology a different model of usage is of greater importance which allows for the integrated segmentation and classification of sequences of sample data. Therein one assumes that the possibility exists to associate individual meaningful units of a longer observation sequence with partial structures within a larger model. Usually this is achieved by a constructive approach. First, small models for certain elementary segmental units are created as, e.g., for speech sounds, handwritten characters, or short amino-acid sequences. These can then be combined to form larger compound models taking into account certain restrictions about the sequencing possibilities. In automatic speech recognition thus from single speech sounds models for words and finally whole spoken utterances are constructed. In the field of bioinformatics models for families of proteins can be built in a similar way.

For such a complex HMM the total output probability $P(O \mid \lambda)$ provides hardly any relevant information about the data considered. Instead the internal processes involved in the generation of the observation sequence $O = O_1, O_2, \ldots, O_T$ using the model λ need to be uncovered, i.e., the associated state sequence $s = s_1, s_2, \ldots, s_T$. On this basis inferences about the partial models involved and, consequently, a segmentation of the observation sequence into these units can be achieved. In a stochastic formalism inferences can, however, always be drawn in a probabilistic way only. Therefore one determines that state sequence s^* that maximizes the joint probability $P(O, s \mid \lambda)$ of the data and some state sequence for a given model λ. This procedure is usually referred to as the *decoding* of the model as the generation of observations by the model can be viewed as the encoding of the internal state sequence into observable entities.

Finally, the important question needs to be clarified how a model can be built that resembles the statistical properties of certain data with sufficient accuracy in order to be used for purposes of classification or recognition. Though it can be evaluated how well a certain model describes given data by considering the total output probability, no algorithm is known which could create the optimal model for a certain task on the basis of example data. It is merely possible to improve an existing model λ such that the optimized model $\hat{\lambda}$ better resembles—in the statistical sense—the example data used. As with most iterative optimization methods, the choice of a suitable initial model is of essential importance here.

The use cases outlined above are frequently described as three fundamental problems for HMMs in the literature.[4] The so-called *evaluation problem* is concerned with the question how the probability can be computed to generate a given observation sequence with a given model. The so-called *decoding problem* considers the drawing of inferences about the internal processes within HMMs. Finally, the challenging search for the model which will be optimal to represent the properties of certain example data is called the *training problem*.

When following classical presentations of HMMs, there exists an algorithm for the solution of each of these problems. In this view it is totally ignored, however, that in many cases alternative methods exist and that some algorithms can also be used for the solution of different tasks. Therefore, we will break up the quite restrictive structuring of HMM theory into pairs of problems and associated algorithms in the following. Instead, the presentation will be oriented at the respective use case, i.e., we will present methods for evaluation and decoding of HMMs as well as for the estimation of the models' parameters.

---

[4]According to Rabiner ([251], [252, p. 322]) the idea of characterizing the possible use cases of HMMs in the form of three fundamental problems paired with three corresponding algorithms for their solution goes back to Jack Ferguson, Institute for Defense Analyses [79].

5.4   Notation

In formal descriptions of HMMs, a rather homogeneous notation can be found in the literature. Start probabilities and transition probabilities, the model itself, as well as many of the derived quantities which will be presented in the following sections are always denoted with the same mathematical symbols. This "standardization" can probably be explained to the major part by the influence of the classical article by Rabiner [251].

However, the consistence in notation ends as soon as the transition from discrete to continuous models is performed. Due to the very nature of the model, outputs can no longer be described with discrete probability distributions now but need to be represented by continuous density functions. As a further consequence, many derived probability quantities are transformed into densities.

In order to achieve an HMM notation with a maximum of uniformity we will keep the "discrete" view on the models in the following as long as a differentiation or specialized treatment of continuous models is not necessary. This means that we will always be talking about probabilities even if those would need to be densities in the continuous case. The outputs of the models will also be uniformly denoted as a sequence O of observation elements $O_1, O_2, \ldots, O_T$.

The discrimination between discrete and continuous models will exclusively be achieved on the basis of the values that can be taken on by these random variables O_t. In the discrete case we will be denoting the observation symbols as o_k, in the continuous case, however, as vectors $x \in \mathbb{R}^n$. In analogy to the notation of discrete output probabilities $P(O_t = o_k)$ we will use the notation $p(O_t = x)$ or $p(O_t = x_t)$ for continuous output densities, respectively. The latter can be transformed into the notation $p(x_t)$ for continuous model outputs of an HMM that is commonly used in the literature by leaving away the explicit specification of the random variable O_t.

These conventions will, however, not lead to an absolute consistency in the notation, but as Duda & Hart [64, p. 173] state quite pointedly...[5]

> ... we shall recall Emerson's remark that a foolish consistency is the hobgoblin of little minds and proceed.

5.5   Evaluation

The total production probability is the most widely used measure for assessing the quality with which an HMM describes the statistical properties of certain data. It yields the probability that the observation sequence considered was in some arbitrary way—i.e. along an arbitrary state sequence—generated by a certain model. A similar but slightly modified evaluation criterion is obtained if only that state sequence is considered which for the given data yields the maximum generation probability.

---

[5]Original quote from Ralph Waldo Emerson (American Philosopher, 1803–1882) from the essay *"Self Reliance"* (1841).

5.5.1 The Total Output Probability

In order to compute the *total output probability* $P(O \mid \lambda)$ of a certain observation sequence O for a given model λ we will first consider an intuitively simple but quite inefficient method.

Obviously, an observation sequence $O_1, O_2, \ldots, O_T$ needs to be generated along a corresponding state sequence $s = s_1, s_2, \ldots, s_T$ of the same length as the output of observation elements O_t can only result from corresponding states of the model. The probability for this happening is obtained as the product of the output probabilities along the state sequence, as the model is given and also the concrete state sequence can be assumed to be fixed:

$$P(O \mid s, \lambda) = \prod_{t=1}^{T} b_{s_t}(O_t) \tag{5.4}$$

The probability that a given model λ runs through an arbitrary state sequence is in turn simply obtained as the product of the respective state-transition probabilities. At the beginning of the sequence in principle the start probability π_{s_1} needs to be used. However, the notation can be greatly simplified by the definition of $a_{0i} := \pi_i$ and $s_0 := 0$:

$$P(s \mid \lambda) = \pi_{s_1} \prod_{t=2}^{T} a_{s_{t-1},s_t} = \prod_{t=1}^{T} a_{s_{t-1},s_t} \tag{5.5}$$

The probability that a given model λ generates a certain observation sequence O in a specific way—i.e. along a certain state sequence s—can be obtained immediately by combining Eqs. (5.4) and (5.5):

$$P(O, s \mid \lambda) = P(O \mid s, \lambda) P(s \mid \lambda) = \prod_{t=1}^{T} a_{s_{t-1},s_t} b_{s_t}(O_t) \tag{5.6}$$

It corresponds to the joint probability of the observation sequence O and the state sequence s given the model. By interleaving the computations involved, an expression results that immediately reflects the internal processes of the model: In turn state transitions are carried out according to a_{s_{t-1},s_t} and state-specific outputs are generated according to $b_{s_t}(O_t)$.

Due to their statistical nature, HMMs are principally capable of generating a desired observation sequence O along every arbitrarily chosen sequence of states s of the same length, though possibly with arbitrarily low probability. Therefore, all state sequences of length T through the model need to be taken into account as possible "causes" for the computation of the total output probability $P(O \mid \lambda)$ of a certain observation sequence O. The overall probability is obtained as the sum over all individual probabilities for jointly generating the observation sequence O and a specific state sequence s:

$$P(O \mid \lambda) = \sum_{s} P(O, s \mid \lambda) = \sum_{s} P(O \mid s, \lambda) P(s \mid \lambda)$$

This "brute force" method thus consists in the enumeration of all possible state sequences of length T through the model, the computation of the path-specific output probability $P(O \mid s, \lambda)$ along every state sequence, and the summation of the results obtained. However, with a complexity of $O(TN^T)$ the computational effort for this conceptually simple method is exponential in the length of the observation sequence. Therefore, the method is out of question for practical applications.

5.5.2   Forward Algorithm

The widespread use of HMM technology can essentially be attributed to the fact that for this formalism efficient algorithms are known for the solution of the central problems. All these methods exploit the Markov property valid for all HMMs which is their limited "memory" that only allows for the storing of *a single* internal state. If a model λ has taken on a certain state j at time t it is totally irrelevant for the future behavior of the model on which path this state was arrived at and which outputs were generated in this course. At the respective next point in time $t + 1$ it is, therefore, sufficient to consider all possible states at time t only—this is the N states of the model. Thus the elementary computations for HMMs can *always* be carried out in a strictly time-synchronous way and in parallel for all model states.

For the computation of the total output probability $P(O \mid \lambda)$ this principle leads to the so-called *forward algorithm*[6] the actions of which are summarized in Fig. 5.1. First, the so-called *forward variables* $\alpha_t(i)$ are defined as auxiliary quantities. They yield the probability that for a given model λ the first part of the observation sequence up to O_t is generated and that the state i is reached at time t:

$$\alpha_t(i) = P(O_1, O_2, \ldots, O_t, s_t = i \mid \lambda) \tag{5.7}$$

Based on these quantities a recursive procedure for the computation of the total output probability for the entire observation sequence can be formulated. As already outlined above, the method works in parallel for all model states in a strictly time-synchronous manner. The resulting computation scheme is graphically visualized in Fig. 5.2.

---

[6] As the name indicates already, there exists a matching counterpart of the forward algorithm which is referred to as the backward algorithm. Taken together they constitute the so-called forward–backward algorithm which will be presented in its entirety during the description of the HMM parameter training in Sect. 5.7.

Let $\alpha_t(i) = P(O_1, O_2, \ldots, O_t, s_t = i \mid \lambda)$
1. **Initialization**
   $$\alpha_1(i) := \pi_i b_i(O_1)$$
2. **Recursion**
   for all times $t, t = 1, \ldots, T - 1$:
   $$\alpha_{t+1}(j) := \sum_i \{\alpha_t(i) a_{ij}\} b_j(O_{t+1})$$
3. **Termination**
   $$P(O \mid \lambda) = \sum_{i=1}^{N} \alpha_T(i)$$

Fig. 5.1 Forward algorithm for the computation of the total output probability $P(O \mid \lambda)$ of an observation sequence O for a given model λ

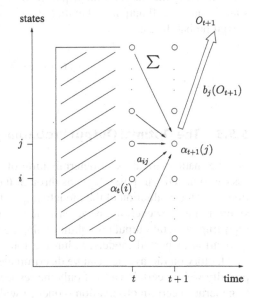

Fig. 5.2 Computation scheme for determining the forward variables $\alpha_t(i)$ by means of the forward algorithm

For the initialization of the computations or the anchoring of the recursion, respectively, the forward probabilities $\alpha_1(i)$ at the beginning of the time-line, i.e., at time $t = 1$ need to be determined. The probability for generating the first observation element O_1 at the initial point in time and for reaching state i is obtained as the product of the start probability π_i for state i and the output probability $b_i(O_1)$ of the first observation element in this state:

$$\alpha_1(i) = \pi_i b_i(O_1)$$

For the further course of the computations one can now assume that according to the induction principle the computation of the $\alpha_t(i)$ is possible for all past times t. It is, therefore, sufficient to specify a rule how the forward variables $\alpha_{t+1}(j)$ can be computed from these quantities at the next point in time.

In order to generate the prefix of the observation sequence $O_1, O_2, \ldots, O_t, O_{t+1}$, which is extended by the observation element O_{t+1}, and to reach state j all possibilities need to be considered for generating $O_1, O_2, \ldots, O_t$—which is equivalent to $\alpha_t(i)$—and then proceeding by one further step in time. The forward variable $\alpha_{t+1}(j)$ is, therefore, obtained as the sum of the $\alpha_t(i)$ over all possible predecessor states i including the respective transition probabilities a_{ij} to the current state. Additionally, the observation element O_{t+1} needs to be generated according to $b_j(O_{t+1})$:

$$\alpha_{t+1}(j) := \left\{ \sum_i \alpha_t(i) a_{ij} \right\} b_j(O_{t+1}) \tag{5.8}$$

At the end of the computations N different probabilities $\alpha_T(i)$ are obtained at time T for generating the observation sequence O in an arbitrary way and finally reaching state i. The overall output probability $P(O \mid \lambda)$ is obtained by summation over these partial probabilities:

$$P(O \mid \lambda) = \sum_{i=1}^{N} \alpha_T(i)$$

5.5.3   The Optimal Output Probability

For the mathematical exact determination of the total output probability it is necessary to include all possible paths through the respective model into the computations. For the evaluation of the modeling quality of an HMM this summarizing consideration is, however, not necessarily the only procedure that makes sense. When reporting the total output probability only, the possibility is lost to evaluate the specialization of partial models within the total model. However, a model which is satisfactory on the average can be discriminated from another one which works especially well in certain cases if only the respective optimal possibility is considered to generate a certain observation sequence with a given model.

When disregarding efficiency considerations, the optimal output probability $P^*(O \mid \lambda)$—i.e. the optimal probability $P(O, s^* \mid \lambda)$ for generating the observation sequence along a specific path—can be determined by maximization over all individual output probabilities given by Eq. (5.6):

$$P^*(O \mid \lambda) = P(O, s^* \mid \lambda) = \max_s P(O, s \mid \lambda)$$

A much more efficient method for the computation of this quantity is obtained as a slight variation of the forward algorithm by again applying the considerations about the finite memory of HMMs which were already pointed out there. The resulting

Let $\delta_t(i) = \max_{s_1,s_2,\dots,s_{t-1}} P(O_1, O_2, \dots, O_t, s_1, s_2, \dots, s_{t-1}, s_t = i \mid \lambda)$

1. **Initialization**

$\delta_1(i) = \pi_i b_i(O_1)$

2. **Recursion**

for all times $t, t = 1, \dots, T - 1$:

$\delta_{t+1}(j) = \max_i\{\delta_t(i)a_{ij}\}b_j(O_{t+1})$

3. **Termination**

$P^*(O \mid \lambda) = P(O, s^* \mid \lambda) = \max_i \delta_T(i)$

Fig. 5.3 Algorithm for the computation of the maximum production probability $P^*(O \mid \lambda)$ of an observation sequence O along the respective optimal path for a given model λ

method, for which the computation procedure is summarized in Fig. 5.3, is part of the *Viterbi algorithm*, which, however, aims at determining the optimal path itself. Therefore, only part of the complete procedure will be described here. The overall algorithm will be presented when treating the model decoding in Sect. 5.6.

As an auxiliary quantity for this procedure one defines the maximum probability $\delta_t(i)$ to produce the initial segment of the observation sequence up to time t along an arbitrary path ending in state i:

$$\delta_t(i) = \max_{s_1,s_2,\dots,s_{t-1}} P(O_1, O_2, \dots, O_t, s_1, s_2, \dots, s_{t-1}, s_t = i \mid \lambda) \qquad (5.9)$$

The recursive scheme for the computation of these partial path probabilities $\delta_t(i)$ then works completely analogously to the computation of the forward probabilities $\alpha_t(i)$ in the forward algorithm. The resulting procedure is graphically visualized in Fig. 5.4. At time $t = 1$ one obtains the initial $\delta_1(i)$ trivially as the product of the start probability π_i of the respective state and the output probability $b_i(O_1)$ of the first element of the observation sequence. An optimization over variable parts of the state sequence is not necessary yet.

$$\delta_1(i) = \pi_i b_i(O_1)$$

As the probabilities of the respective optimal partial paths $\delta_t(i)$ can be assumed to be known for all past times according to the induction principle, merely the optimal probabilities $\delta_{t+1}(i)$ of the paths extended by one element need to be computed. Therefore, all possible predecessors i of the current state j are considered. The maximum probability is determined for continuing the paths ending in one of the predecessor states up to the current state according to the transition probability a_{ij}. Finally, the current observation element O_{t+1} needs to be generated according to $b_j(O_{t+1})$:

$$\delta_{t+1}(j) = \max_i\{\delta_t(i)a_{ij}\}b_j(O_{t+1})$$

Fig. 5.4 Calculation scheme for the computation of the partial path probabilities $\delta_t(i)$

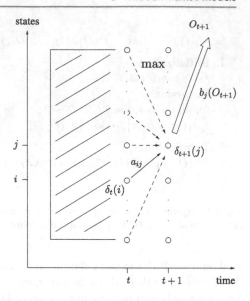

After finishing the computations, the optimal production probability $P^*(O \mid \lambda)$ is obtained as the maximum over all optimal possibilities $\delta_T(i)$ to reach a certain state i at the final time step T. Here we assume, as usually done for HMMs, that all possible states can be considered as the final state of a valid path:[7]

$$P^*(O \mid \lambda) = P\big(O, s^* \mid \lambda\big) = \max_i \delta_T(i)$$

Analogously to the forward algorithm, one thus obtains a computation scheme for determining the quality of a model λ depending on example data O. In contrast to the total output probability, therein only the optimal possibility for generating the observation sequence is taken into account. The optimal state sequence s^* can, however, not be determined based on the computation steps alone which were presented so far.

Especially in the field of speech recognition, the probability $P^*(O \mid \lambda)$ of the optimal path is frequently used instead of the total output probability $P(O \mid \lambda)$. This approach can be justified by the observation that the probability for generating the data O along the optimal path s^* will dominate the summation over all possible paths which is necessary for the computation of $P(O \mid \lambda)$ and, therefore, will be highly correlated with that quantity [197]. Additionally, the computation of the partial path probabilities $\delta_t(i)$ in practice is considerably more efficient compared to the forward probabilities. As will be explained in more detail in Chap. 7, when

---

[7]If specially marked end states are used (cf. e.g. [67, p. 51]), the maximization needs to be restricted to the appropriate set. Alternatively, also additional termination probabilities can be considered when computing the final path probabilities (cf. e.g. [125, p. 150]).

carrying out computations for HMMs the probabilities are usually transformed into the logarithmic domain. The multiplications necessary for determining the $\delta_t(i)$ are then transformed into summations. The maximizations are not affected by such a monotonic mapping. The summation necessary for the computation of the forward probabilities, however, can only be realized with considerable computational effort in the logarithmic domain.

5.6 Decoding

If the individual states of a larger model can be associated with certain meaningful segments of the modeled data, the consideration of a global quality measure as, e.g., the total output probability, is no longer sufficient for the analysis. Rather, it is necessary to uncover the internal processes during the generation of the observation sequence.

However, due to the probabilistic nature of HMMs, a given observation sequence can, in principle, be generated from any state sequence through the model with the same length. Therefore, an inference of the corresponding state sequence is only possible in the probabilistic sense. Consequently, for a given model one determines that state sequence s^* that produces the observations with maximum posterior probability:

$$s^* = \operatorname*{argmax}_{s} P(s \mid O, \lambda) \qquad (5.10)$$

The posterior probability of a certain state sequence s on the right hand side of Eq. (5.10) can be rewritten as follows by applying Bayes' rule:

$$P(s \mid O, \lambda) = \frac{P(O, s \mid \lambda)}{P(O \mid \lambda)} \qquad (5.11)$$

For a maximization of this quantity the contribution of the total output probability $P(O \mid \lambda)$ is, however, irrelevant as it is constant for a fixed model and a given observation sequence. By exploiting this fact, Eq. (5.10) can be simplified and the optimal state sequence can be determined as follows:

$$s^* = \operatorname*{argmax}_{s} P(s \mid O, \lambda) = \operatorname*{argmax}_{s} P(O, s \mid \lambda)$$

This optimal path s^* exactly corresponds to that state sequence for which the maximum probability $P^*(O \mid \lambda)$ of generating the observation sequence is obtained. Thus for determining s^* one could in principle use the "brute force" approach for computing the optimal production probability which was outlined in the previous Sect. 5.5.3. After enumerating all possible state sequences of length T and computing the respective individual production probabilities using Eq. (5.6), one selects the state sequence s^* with maximum probability. As this method exhibits an exponential complexity $O(TN^T)$ in the length of the state sequence, however, it is not suitable for practical applications. Rather the method for efficiently computing $P(O, s^* \mid \lambda)$,

Let $\delta_t(i) = \max\limits_{s_1,s_2,\dots,s_{t-1}} P(O_1, O_2, \dots, O_t, s_1, s_2, \dots, s_{t-1}, s_t = i \mid \lambda)$

1. **Initialization**

   $\delta_1(i) := \pi_i b_i(O_1)$ $\psi_1(i) := 0$

2. **Recursion**

   for all times t, $t = 1, \dots, T-1$:

   $\delta_{t+1}(j) := \max\limits_{i}\big\{\delta_t(i)a_{ij}\big\} b_j(O_{t+1})$ $\psi_{t+1}(j) := \mathrm{argmax}\limits_{i}\{\delta_t(i)a_{ij}\}$

3. **Termination**

   $P^*(O \mid \lambda) = P(O, s^* \mid \lambda) = \max\limits_{i} \delta_T(i)$

   $s_T^* := \mathrm{argmax}\limits_{j} \delta_T(j)$

4. **Back-Tracking of the Optimal Path**

   for all times t, $t = T-1, \dots, 1$:

   $s_t^* = \psi_{t+1}(s_{t+1}^*)$

Fig. 5.5 Viterbi algorithm for computing the optimal state sequence s^*, which maximizes the production probability $P(O, s^* \mid \lambda)$ of an observation sequence O for a given model λ

which was described in Sect. 5.5.3, is extended such that not only the optimal score but also the associated state sequence s^* can be determined.

5.6.1 Viterbi Algorithm

The efficient computation of the optimal state sequence s^* by means of the so-called *Viterbi algorithm* uses a recursive procedure which is quite similar to the forward algorithm and which also exploits the Markov property. As already explained in Sect. 5.5.3, one defines probabilities $\delta_t(i)$ for partially optimal paths which generate the initial segment of the observation sequence up to O_t with maximum probability and end in state i:

$$\delta_t(i) = \max\limits_{s_1,s_2,\dots,s_{t-1}} P(O_1, O_2, \dots, O_t, s_1, s_2, \dots, s_{t-1}, s_t = i \mid \lambda)$$

The computation scheme for the $\delta_t(i)$ largely corresponds to the one for determining the forward variables $\alpha_t(i)$. The only difference is that instead of a summation over the probabilities associated with the predecessor states a maximization is performed. The resulting algorithm for the computation of the optimal path is presented in Fig. 5.5.

In a similar way as in dynamic time warping, which computes an optimal path for mapping two patterns onto each other by a comparable scheme (cf. e.g. [125, pp. 71–78]), every decision in the computation of the $\delta_t(i)$ is only locally optimal. The globally optimal probability of the optimal state sequence s^* is only known after the evaluation of the final $\delta_T(i)$, i.e., after the observation sequence has been considered in its entire length. That state that maximizes $\delta_T(i)$ corresponds to the final state of the optimal state sequence. The remaining members of the sequence now need to be determined based on the decisions made during the computations of the $\delta_t(i)$. Therefore, one defines "backward pointers" $\psi_t(j)$ along the partial paths which store the associated optimal predecessor state for every corresponding $\delta_t(j)$:

$$\psi_t(j) = \underset{i}{\operatorname{argmax}}\ \delta_{t-1}(i)a_{ij}$$

Starting from its final state

$$s_T^* = \underset{i}{\operatorname{argmax}}\ \delta_T(i),$$

the optimal path can then be reconstructed recursively according to

$$s_t^* = \psi_{t+1}(s_{t+1}^*)$$

in reversed chronological order.[8]

For practical applications this reversing of the direction of the order of computations means a significant limitation. The optimal state sequence can, therefore, only be determined *after* the end of the observation sequence is reached, i.e., only after all the data to be analyzed is known in its entirety. Especially for interactive systems it is, however, frequently desirable to be able to generate feedback to the user in the form of partial results—i.e. after a prefix of the optimal state sequence has been decided for—already while the computations are still ongoing. But such incremental decoding methods can in general find sub-optimal solutions only.

5.7 Parameter Estimation

Ideally, for all application areas of HMMs models should be used that resemble the statistical properties of certain data as closely as possible. Unfortunately, no method is known that is able to create for a given sample set a model which is optimal in some respect, as already pointed out in Sect. 5.3. However, an iterative optimization of the model with respect to the data considered can be performed if one succeeds in defining a suitable model structure—i.e. the number of states and the type of output distributions—and useful initial estimates of the model's free parameters by applying know-how of experts. This step-by-step improvement of the model parameters up to some quality which is sufficient for the respective task is usually called *training* of the model.

---

[8]In general, the decision for the optimal predecessor state is not unique. Multiple sequences s_k^* with identical scores maximizing Eq. (5.6) might exist. In practical applications, therefore, a rule for breaking up such ambiguities is necessary which might, e.g., be a preference for states with lower indices.

5.7.1 Foundations

The methods presented in the following mainly differ with respect to the measure used for evaluating the modeling quality of a certain model. In the so-called Baum–Welch algorithm this is achieved by using the total output probability $P(O \mid \lambda)$. In Viterbi training and the closely related segmental k-means method only the probability $P(O, s^* \mid \lambda)$ of the respective optimal state sequence is considered instead.

All these methods are based on the principle that the parameters of a given model λ are subject to a growth transformation, i.e., the model parameters are modified such that the score $P(\ldots \mid \hat{\lambda})$ of the changed model $\hat{\lambda}$ exceeds the one achieved for the original model. It is, however, possible that a certain model represents a fixed point of the optimization method applied so that an improvement of the quality measure is no longer possible and the respective score remains unchanged.[9] In general the parameter estimation methods, therefore, guarantee a monotonic increase of the modeling quality only:

$$P(\ldots \mid \hat{\lambda}) \geq P(\ldots \mid \lambda)$$

Considered intuitively, the parameter estimation methods for HMMs are based on the idea to "observe" the actions of the model during the generation of an observation sequence. The original state-transition and output probabilities are then simply replaced by the relative frequencies of the respective events. As pointed out previously, the inference of the internal processes of HMMs is only possible in the probabilistic sense due to the statistical nature of the models. It is, however, possible to determine the *expected* number of relevant events—i.e. the transition between states and the generation of observations—depending on the given model and the observation sequence considered. If we consider only discrete models[10] for the sake of simplicity and ignore the estimation of start probabilities for the moment,[11] the updated model parameters can in principle be determined as follows:

$$\hat{a}_{ij} = \frac{\text{expected number of transitions from } i \text{ to } j}{\text{expected number of transitions out of state } i}$$

$$\hat{b}_i(o_k) = \frac{\text{expected number of outputs of } o_k \text{ in state } i}{\text{total number of outputs in state } i}$$

In order to be able to infer the expected state transitions or outputs of the model, respectively, it is necessary to determine the probability that at a given time t the model was in a certain state i. We will refer to this probability as the *state probability* in the following.

---

[9] In practice this means that the chosen quality measure does not change any more within the scope of the available computational accuracy.

[10] Of course the optimization of general continuous mixture densities is possible with all training methods. However, it always represents the most challenging part of the procedure.

[11] The updated start probabilities $\hat{\pi}_i$ can be considered as a special case of the transition probabilities $\hat{a}_{ij}$ and can, therefore, be computed analogously.

For its computation two fundamentally different possibilities exist. If the probability $P(O, s^* \mid \lambda)$ to create the observation sequence along the optimal path only is considered, it can be verified directly whether or not a certain state i was present at time t. The state probability $P^*(S_t = i \mid O, \lambda)$, therefore, takes on the values zero and one only. It can be described by a characteristic function that operates on the optimal state sequence s^*:

$$P^*(S_t = i \mid O, \lambda) = \chi_t(i) = \begin{cases} 1 & \text{if } s_t^* = i \text{ and } s^* = \operatorname{argmax}_s P(s, O \mid \lambda) \\ 0 & \text{otherwise} \end{cases} \tag{5.12}$$

However, the computation of the posterior probability of a certain state at a given time becomes somewhat more demanding if the quality measure is the total output probability $P(O \mid \lambda)$ for which all paths through the model are considered.

5.7.2 Forward–Backward Algorithm

Of course, a "brute force" approach could be used in order to compute the posterior probability $P(S_t = i \mid O, \lambda)$ of a state i at time t for a given observation sequence O and a known model λ. However, with the forward variables $\alpha_t(i)$ we already came to know quantities in Sect. 5.5 which, to a limited extent, make predictions about the presence of a state at a given time. What is missing is the probability for completing the rest of the partial observation sequence from the current state onward.

This quantity is known as the *backward variable*. It represents the probability for generating the partial observation sequence $O_{t+1}, O_{t+2}, \ldots, O_T$ from time $t + 1$ onward starting at state j and given the model λ.

$$\beta_t(j) = P(O_{t+1}, O_{t+2}, \ldots, O_T \mid s_t = j, \lambda) \tag{5.13}$$

It can be efficiently computed with the counterpart of the forward algorithm—the so-called *backward algorithm*—and represents the companion piece to the forward variable $\alpha_t(i)$. Both algorithms taken together are frequently considered as a coherent unit in the literature and are referred to as the *forward–backward algorithm*.

In order to compute the desired state probability $P(S_t = i \mid O, \lambda)$ on the basis of the forward and backward variables let us first rewrite this expression using Bayes' rule as follows:

$$P(S_t = i \mid O, \lambda) = \frac{P(S_t = i, O \mid \lambda)}{P(O \mid \lambda)} \tag{5.14}$$

The total output probability $P(O \mid \lambda)$ can be computed by means of the forward algorithm. The numerator of the right hand side of Eq. (5.14) directly corresponds to the product of the respective forward and backward variables (cf. Eqs. (5.7) and (5.13)):

$$P(S_t = i, O \mid \lambda) = P(O_1, O_2, \ldots, O_t, S_t = i \mid \lambda) P(O_{t+1}, O_{t+2}, \ldots, O_T \mid S_t = i, \lambda)$$

$$= \alpha_t(i)\beta_t(i)$$

Therefore, the posterior probability of the state i at time t, which is usually denoted as $\gamma_t(i)$, can be computed as follows:

$$\gamma_t(i) = P(S_t = i \mid \boldsymbol{O}, \lambda) = \frac{\alpha_t(i)\beta_t(i)}{P(\boldsymbol{O} \mid \lambda)} \tag{5.15}$$

The evaluation of the backward variable $\beta_t(i)$—as already indicated by its name—almost corresponds to a mirrored version of the forward algorithm. The anchoring of the inductive computation procedure takes place at time T, which is the end of the time interval defined by the observation sequence. Trivially, the probability for not generating any further observations from time T onward is equal to 1:

$$\beta_T(i) := 1$$

If the $\beta_{t+1}(j)$ are assumed to be known for all future times $t + 1$ according to the induction principle, a recursive computation rule for the backward variables $\beta_t(i)$ can be derived by considering all possible continuations of a state sequence starting from the current state i:

$$\beta_t(i) := \sum_j a_{ij} b_j(O_{t+1})\beta_{t+1}(j) \tag{5.16}$$

Similarly to the forward algorithm, the total output probability $P(\boldsymbol{O} \mid \lambda)$ is obtained at the termination of the procedure by summation over all backward variables $\beta_1(i)$ at time $t = 1$ taking into account the start probabilities and the generation of the first observation element O_1 in the respective state:[12]

$$P(\boldsymbol{O} \mid \lambda) = \sum_{i=1}^{N} \pi_i b_i(O_1)\beta_1(i)$$

In Fig. 5.6 both algorithms are presented together in order to illustrate the extraordinary symmetry of the computational procedures. The computation scheme resulting for the backward variables is graphically visualized in Fig. 5.7.

5.7.3   Training Methods

The probabilistic possibility for defining the state probability via $\gamma_t(i)$ or its deterministic variant $\chi_t(i)$, respectively, form the basis for the training methods treated in the following. By means of the chronological mapping between model states and elements of the observation sequence, not only state-transition probabilities can be estimated but also the parameters of the state specific output distributions. Thus

---

[12]The fact that the total output probability $P(\boldsymbol{O} \mid \lambda)$ may be computed both via the forward and the backward algorithm can be exploited in practice to check the computations for consistency and accuracy.

Let
$$\alpha_t(i) = P(O_1, O_2, \ldots, O_t, s_t = i \mid \lambda)$$
$$\beta_t(i) = P(O_{t+1}, O_{t+2}, \ldots, O_T \mid s_t = i, \lambda)$$

1. **Initialization**
$$\alpha_1(i) := \pi_i b_i(O_1) \qquad\qquad\qquad\qquad\qquad \beta_T(i) := 1$$

2. **Recursion**
   for all times $t, t = 1, \ldots, T-1$:   respectively $t = T-1, \ldots, 1$:
$$\alpha_{t+1}(j) := \sum_i \{\alpha_t(i) a_{ij}\} b_j(O_{t+1}) \qquad \beta_t(i) := \sum_j a_{ij} b_j(O_{t+1}) \beta_{t+1}(j)$$

3. **Termination**
$$P(O \mid \lambda) = \sum_{i=1}^{N} \alpha_T(i) \qquad\qquad\qquad P(O \mid \lambda) = \sum_{i=1}^{N} \pi_i b_i(O_1) \beta_1(i)$$

Fig. 5.6 Forward–backward algorithm for the joint computation of the forward and backward variables, respectively

Fig. 5.7 Computation scheme for determining the backward variables $\beta_t(i)$ via the backward algorithm

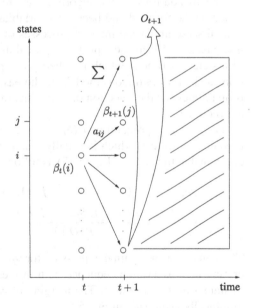

quite simple estimation formulas can be derived in discrete models. The increased complexity of parameter estimation when using mixture densities for describing the output distributions is due to the fact that even when considered in isolation no closed form solutions exist for estimating the parameters of such models. In fact *iterative* optimization strategies have to be applied which, however, can be combined with the training methods applied for HMMs as a whole.

5.7.4 Baum–Welch Algorithm

The most widely used method for the optimization of HMMs is given by the so-called *Baum–Welch algorithm*. It uses the total production probability $P(O \mid \lambda)$ as the optimization criterion. Thus the algorithm improves a given model λ depending on certain example data O in such a way that the optimized model generates the training set with equal or greater probability:

$$P(O \mid \hat{\lambda}) \ge P(O \mid \lambda)$$

The equality of those two expressions is valid only if a local maximum with respect to the optimization in the space of all possible models was already reached with the parameters of the original model.

In this method all model parameters are replaced by their conditional expected values with respect to the given original model λ and the training data O. The Baum–Welch algorithm, therefore, represents a variant of the EM algorithm which in general optimizes parameters of multi-stage stochastic processes with hidden variables following the maximum likelihood criterion (see Sect. 4.4).

The foundations of the algorithm are represented by some quantities which, based on the forward and backward variables, allow to draw inferences in the statistical sense about the internal processes of the model λ when generating certain given data O. Besides the posterior probability $P(S_t = i \mid O, \lambda)$ for the occurrence of a state i at time t, which is called $\gamma_t(i)$, posterior probabilities for state transitions and—for continuous models on the basis of mixture densities—also posterior probabilities for the selection of individual mixture components M_t at a given time are required.

The posterior probability $P(S_t = i, S_{t+1} = j \mid O, \lambda)$ of a transition from state i to state j at time t, which is usually denoted as $\gamma_t(i, j)$ in the literature,[13] can be computed in the style of Eq. (5.15) as follows:

$$\begin{aligned}
\gamma_t(i, j) &= P(S_t = i, S_{t+1} = j \mid O, \lambda) \\
&= \frac{P(S_t = i, S_{t+1} = j, O \mid \lambda)}{P(O \mid \lambda)} = \frac{\alpha_t(i) a_{ij} b_j(O_{t+1}) \beta_{t+1}(j)}{P(O \mid \lambda)}
\end{aligned}$$

The numerator of the final expression for $\gamma_t(i, j)$ represents the probability for generating the observation sequence with the restriction that a transition from state i to state j occurs at time t. The merging of computation paths within the model is graphically visualized in Fig. 5.8.

In the literature the state probability is frequently defined on the basis of the posterior probabilities for state transitions. The probability $\gamma_t(i)$ of some state i occurring at time t irrespective of any successor state can be obtained as the marginal

---

[13]Due to the close connection in their meaning and in order not to unnecessarily make the notation any more complex, the state probability is denoted with a single argument as $\gamma_t(i)$ and the state-transition probability with two arguments as $\gamma_t(i, j)$.

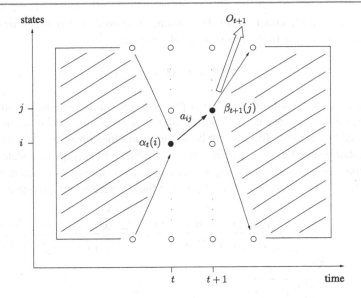

Fig. 5.8 Computation scheme for determining the $\gamma_t(i, j)$

distribution of $\gamma_t(i, j)$ by summation over all possible state successors:

$$\gamma_t(i) = P(S_t = i \mid \mathbf{O}, \lambda) = \sum_{j=1}^{N} P(S_t = i, S_{t+1} = j \mid \mathbf{O}, \lambda) = \sum_{j=1}^{N} \gamma_t(i, j)$$

However, this relationship can only be exploited for times $t < T$ as $\gamma_t(i, j)$ is only defined for those points in time. In practice $\gamma_t(i)$ will, therefore, be computed directly via Eq. (5.15). Otherwise a suitable extension of the definition of $\gamma_t(i, j)$ will be required.

On the basis of the γ_t all updated parameters $\hat{\lambda}$ for HMMs with discrete output distributions can be computed. The number of state transitions from i to j that can be expected in the statistical average is obtained as the sum of the individual transition probabilities $\gamma_t(i, j)$ over all points in time $t = 1, 2, \ldots, T - 1$ to be considered.[14] One obtains the improved estimates $\hat{a}_{ij}$ for the transition probabilities of the model when normalizing this quantity by the expected total number of transitions out of state i:

$$\hat{a}_{ij} = \frac{\sum_{t=1}^{T-1} P(S_t = i, S_{t+1} = j \mid \mathbf{O}, \lambda)}{\sum_{t=1}^{T-1} P(S_t = i \mid \mathbf{O}, \lambda)} = \frac{\sum_{t=1}^{T-1} \gamma_t(i, j)}{\sum_{t=1}^{T-1} \gamma_t(i)} \tag{5.17}$$

---

[14] According to common opinion, HMMs do not perform a state transition into a specially marked end state when reaching the end of the observation sequence at time T. Therefore, the restriction to all prior points in time is necessary here.

The following simple equation for determining improved start probabilities is obtained as a special case of the transition probabilities:

$$\hat{\pi}_i = P(S_1 = i \mid \boldsymbol{O}, \lambda) = \gamma_1(i) \tag{5.18}$$

In general, the improved discrete output probabilities can be obtained in an analogous way. First, the expected number of outputs of a specific symbol o_k in state j is computed by checking for a match between o_k and the corresponding element of the observation sequence in addition to the occurrence of the respective state. When normalizing this quantity by the expected total number of outputs which are generated by state j one obtains estimates $\hat{b}_j(o_k)$ of the discrete output probabilities:

$$\hat{b}_j(o_k) = \frac{\sum_{t=1}^{T} P(S_t = j, O_t = o_k \mid \boldsymbol{O}, \lambda)}{\sum_{t=1}^{T} P(S_t = j \mid \boldsymbol{O}, \lambda)} = \frac{\sum_{t:O_t = o_k} P(S_t = j \mid \boldsymbol{O}, \lambda)}{\sum_{t=1}^{T} P(S_t = j \mid \boldsymbol{O}, \lambda)}$$

$$= \frac{\sum_{t:O_t = o_k} \gamma_t(j)}{\sum_{t=1}^{T} \gamma_t(j)} \tag{5.19}$$

Whether or not a certain observation symbol o_k was present at a given time t can be determined unambiguously. Therefore, the probabilities $P(S_t = j, O_t = o_k \mid \boldsymbol{O}, \lambda)$ contribute positive portions to the sum in the numerator of Eq. (5.19) only for those points in time. All other terms vanish and the summation can be restricted accordingly and thus be simplified.[15]

In contrast, when modeling output distributions by mixture densities it is necessary to optimize the parameters of the component densities themselves—i.e. of the individual normal distributions—and the associated mixture weights. If the evaluation of the mixture densities is viewed as some sort of quantization, which realizes a probabilistic mapping of the observations onto abstract but not yet meaningful symbolic units, it becomes immediately evident that the computation of updated mixture weights can be performed in analogy to the procedure for discrete output probabilities.

Therefore, similarly to the state probability an auxiliary quantity $\xi_t(j, k)$ is defined which represents the probability of selecting the kth mixture component in state j at time[16] t for generating the continuous observation O_t:

$$\xi_t(j, k) = P(S_t = j, M_t = k \mid \boldsymbol{O}, \lambda) = \frac{\sum_{i=1}^{N} \alpha_{t-1}(i) a_{ij} c_{jk} g_{jk}(O_t) \beta_t(j)}{P(\boldsymbol{O} \mid \lambda)} \tag{5.20}$$

---

[15]For any given time t the symbol o_k was either present in the observation sequence or not. Therefore, the probability $P(S_t = j, O_t = o_k \mid \boldsymbol{O}, \lambda)$ either takes on the value zero or is equal to $P(S_t = j \mid \boldsymbol{O}, \lambda)$ which is simply $\gamma_t(j)$.

[16]For time $t = 1$ in Eq. (5.20) the term $\sum_{i=1}^{N} \alpha_{t-1}(i) a_{ij}$ needs to be replaced by the respective start probability π_j of the associated state.

Based on Eq. (5.20) a formula for the estimation of the mixture weights can be derived as follows:

$$\hat{c}_{jk} = \frac{\sum_{t=1}^{T} P(S_t = j, M_t = k \mid \mathbf{O}, \lambda)}{\sum_{t=1}^{T} P(S_t = j \mid \mathbf{O}, \lambda)} = \frac{\sum_{t=1}^{T} \xi_t(j,k)}{\sum_{t=1}^{T} \gamma_t(j)} \qquad (5.21)$$

The updating of the parameters of the kth mixture component $g_{jk}(\mathbf{x})$ of state j— i.e. of the mean vector $\boldsymbol{\mu}_{jk}$ and the covariance matrix $\mathbf{C}_{jk}$—is performed in analogy to the estimation formulas for mixture density models presented in Sect. 4.4. The posterior probability $P(\omega_i \mid \mathbf{x}, \theta)$ of the individual pattern class merely needs to be replaced by the term $\xi_t(j,k)$. In contrast to the estimation Eqs. (3.9) and (3.10) for individual normal distributions presented in Sect. 3.6, observations are not incorporated deterministically but probabilistically into the computation process. The probability that a certain observation vector $\mathbf{x}_t$ is used for the estimation of the parameters of $g_{jk}(\mathbf{x})$ exactly corresponds to the probability $P(S_t = j, M_t = k \mid \mathbf{O}, \lambda)$ of selecting the respective mixture component for its generation at the time in question.

Therefore, one obtains the following formulas for the computation of updated mean vectors $\hat{\boldsymbol{\mu}}_{jk}$ and covariance matrices $\hat{\mathbf{C}}_{jk}$ of the individual component densities:

$$\hat{\boldsymbol{\mu}}_{jk} = \frac{\sum_{t=1}^{T} P(S_t = j, M_t = k \mid \mathbf{O}, \lambda)\mathbf{x}_t}{\sum_{t=1}^{T} P(S_t = j, M_t = k \mid \mathbf{O}, \lambda)} = \frac{\sum_{t=1}^{T} \xi_t(j,k)\mathbf{x}_t}{\sum_{t=1}^{T} \xi_t(j,k)} \qquad (5.22)$$

$$\hat{\mathbf{C}}_{jk} = \frac{\sum_{t=1}^{T} P(S_t = j, M_t = k \mid \mathbf{O}, \lambda)(\mathbf{x}_t - \hat{\boldsymbol{\mu}}_{jk})(\mathbf{x}_t - \hat{\boldsymbol{\mu}}_{jk})^T}{\sum_{t=1}^{T} P(S_t = j, M_t = k \mid \mathbf{O}, \lambda)}$$

$$= \frac{\sum_{t=1}^{T} \xi_t(j,k)(\mathbf{x}_t - \hat{\boldsymbol{\mu}}_{jk})(\mathbf{x}_t - \hat{\boldsymbol{\mu}}_{jk})^T}{\sum_{t=1}^{T} \xi_t(j,k)} \qquad (5.23)$$

The estimation formula for the covariance matrix $\mathbf{C}_{jk}$ of the mixture component can be rewritten by exploiting the relationship given by Eq. (3.4) in order to obtain the following computation scheme:

$$\hat{\mathbf{C}}_{jk} = \frac{\sum_{t=1}^{T} P(S_t = j, M_t = k \mid \mathbf{O}, \lambda)\mathbf{x}_t\mathbf{x}_t^T}{\sum_{t=1}^{T} P(S_t = j, M_t = k \mid \mathbf{O}, \lambda)} - \hat{\boldsymbol{\mu}}_{jk}\hat{\boldsymbol{\mu}}_{jk}^T$$

$$= \frac{\sum_{t=1}^{T} \xi_t(j,k)\mathbf{x}_t\mathbf{x}_t^T}{\sum_{t=1}^{T} \xi_t(j,k)} - \hat{\boldsymbol{\mu}}_{jk}\hat{\boldsymbol{\mu}}_{jk}^T \qquad (5.24)$$

In practice, it offers the advantage that only a single pass through the data is required for computing both $\hat{\boldsymbol{\mu}}_{jk}$ and $\hat{\mathbf{C}}_{jk}$.

In semi-continuous models all states share a set of component densities $g_k(\mathbf{x})$ for building the mixture models as introduced in Sect. 5.2. As the mixture weights are still state specific, the respective estimation formula remains unchanged. In order to estimate the parameters μ_k and C_k used jointly via the shared component densities, it has to be taken into account that the probability for the selection of a certain density at a given time is independent of some concrete state in semi-continuous models. It is obtained from Eq. (5.20) as the marginal distribution of $\xi_t(j,k)$ by summation over all possible states:

$$P(M_t = k \mid O, \lambda) = \xi_t(k) = \sum_j \xi_t(j,k)$$

When replacing $\xi_t(j,k)$ by $\xi_t(k)$ in Eqs. (5.22) and (5.24) one obtains the following estimation formulas for μ_k and C_k in semi-continuous models:

$$\hat{\mu}_k = \frac{\sum_{t=1}^{T} P(M_t = k \mid O, \lambda) x_t}{\sum_{t=1}^{T} P(M_t = k \mid O, \lambda)} = \frac{\sum_{t=1}^{T} \xi_t(k) x_t}{\sum_{t=1}^{T} \xi_t(k)} \tag{5.25}$$

$$\hat{C}_k = \frac{\sum_{t=1}^{T} P(M_t = k \mid O, \lambda) x_t x_t^T}{\sum_{t=1}^{T} P(M_t = k \mid O, \lambda)} - \hat{\mu}_k \hat{\mu}_k^T = \frac{\sum_{t=1}^{T} \xi_t(k) x_t x_t^T}{\sum_{t=1}^{T} \xi_t(k)} - \hat{\mu}_k \hat{\mu}_k^T \tag{5.26}$$

The updating of the model parameters according to the estimation equations (5.17), (5.18), and (5.19) for discrete models, by applying Eqs. (5.17), (5.18), (5.21), (5.22), and (5.24) for models with continuous output distributions, and by means of Eqs. (5.17), (5.18), (5.21), (5.25), and (5.26) for semi-continuous models corresponds to one step in an iteratively optimizing training process. Starting from an initially given model λ^0 the updating of the parameters needs to be repeated until the resulting model reaches a sufficient descriptive quality or no further improvements are to be expected any more. For "fully" continuous models the complete algorithm is put together in Fig. 5.9.

5.7.5 Viterbi Training

In contrast to the Baum–Welch algorithm, in the so-called *Viterbi training* only the probability $P^*(O \mid \lambda) = P(O, s^* \mid \lambda)$ that the observation sequence is generated along the best-scoring path s^* is optimized during the training process. It can be shown that the method realizes a growth transformation starting from an existing model λ so that the modified model $\hat{\lambda}$ achieves a higher or at least equal probability for the optimal path:

$$P^*(O \mid \hat{\lambda}) \geq P^*(O \mid \lambda)$$

The method follows the intuitive understanding of the principle of HMM training outlined at the beginning of the chapter by proceeding in two working phases. First, by means of the Viterbi algorithm the optimal state sequence s^* for the training data is computed depending on the given model parameters. In the second step the estimates for updating the model parameters are determined on the basis of the

Let

$$\gamma_t(i) \quad = P(S_t = i \mid O, \lambda) \qquad = \frac{\alpha_t(i)\beta_t(i)}{P(O \mid \lambda)}$$

$$\gamma_t(i,j) = P(S_t = i, S_{t+1} = j \mid O, \lambda) = \frac{\alpha_{t-1}(i)a_{ij}b_j(O_{t+1})\beta_{t+1}(j)}{P(O \mid \lambda)}$$

$$\xi_t(j,k) = P(S_t = j, M_t = k \mid O, \lambda) \quad = \frac{\sum_{i=1}^{N} \alpha_t(i)a_{ij}c_{jk}g_{jk}(O_t)\beta_t(j)}{P(O \mid \lambda)}$$

1. **Initialization**
   Choose a suitable initial model $\lambda = (\pi, A, B)$ with initial estimates
   - π_i for start and
   - a_{ij} for transition probabilities as well as for
   - mixture weights c_{jk} and
   - component densities $g_{jk}(x) = \mathcal{N}(x \mid \mu_{jk}, C_{jk})$ for the definition of output probability density functions $b_{jk}(x) = \sum_k c_{jk}g_{jk}(x)$.

2. **Optimization**
   Compute updated estimates $\hat{\lambda} = (\hat{\pi}, \hat{A}, \hat{B})$ for all model parameters:

$$\hat{a}_{ij} = \frac{\sum_{t=1}^{T-1} \gamma_t(i,j)}{\sum_{t=1}^{T-1} \gamma_t(i)} \qquad \hat{\pi}_i = \gamma_1(i)$$

$$\hat{c}_{jk} = \frac{\sum_{t=1}^{T} \xi_t(j,k)}{\sum_{t=1}^{T} \gamma_t(j)}$$

$$\hat{\mu}_{jk} = \frac{\sum_{t=1}^{T} \xi_t(j,k)x_t}{\sum_{t=1}^{T} \xi_t(j,k)} \qquad \hat{C}_{jk} = \frac{\sum_{t=1}^{T} \xi_t(j,k)x_t x_t^T}{\sum_{t=1}^{T} \xi_t(j,k)} - \hat{\mu}_{jk}\hat{\mu}_{jk}^T$$

3. **Termination**
   if the quality measure $P(O \mid \hat{\lambda})$ was considerably improved by the updated model $\hat{\lambda}$ with respect to λ

   let $\lambda \leftarrow \hat{\lambda}$ and continue with step 2

   otherwise Stop!

Fig. 5.9 Baum–Welch algorithm for estimating the parameters of general continuous HMMs. For modifications necessary for discrete or semi-continuous models see the text

empirical distributions which result from the explicit mapping of observations to individual model states along the optimal state sequence.

Formally this mapping can be described via the state probability $\chi_t(i)$ known from Eq. (5.12) which merely corresponds to the evaluation of a characteristic function on the optimal state sequence s^*. When replacing the probabilistic version $\gamma_t(i)$

by the deterministic mapping using $\chi_t(i)$ in the Baum–Welch algorithm, one obtains the formulas necessary for computing updated parameters of discrete models by means of the Viterbi training. Estimates for the state-transition probabilities, which can principally be obtained by counting state pairs in the optimal state sequences, are obtained as

$$\hat{a}_{ij} = \frac{\sum_{t=1}^{T-1} P(S_t = i, S_{t+1} = j \mid s^*, O, \lambda)}{\sum_{t=1}^{T-1} P(S_t = i \mid s^*, O, \lambda)} = \frac{\sum_{t=1}^{T-1} \chi_t(i)\chi_{t+1}(j)}{\sum_{t=1}^{T-1} \chi_t(i)} \tag{5.27}$$

However, useful estimates for start probabilities cannot be obtained by means of the Viterbi training. As a special case of Eq. (5.27) one would obtain a value of one for the start probability $\pi_{s_1^*}$ of the first state s_1^* of the optimal state sequence and zero for all other states. Nevertheless, this is not a significant limitation of the method as start probabilities are of hardly any importance in practical applications.

The estimates for discrete output probabilities are directly determined by the empirical distributions. The latter are obtained by simply counting all observation symbols o_k which are mapped to a certain model state via the optimal state sequence:

$$\hat{b}_j(o_k) = \frac{\sum_{t:O_t=o_k} P(S_t = j \mid s^*, O, \lambda)}{\sum_{t=1}^{T} P(S_t = j \mid s^*, O, \lambda)} = \frac{\sum_{t:O_t=o_k} \chi_t(j)}{\sum_{t=1}^{T} \chi_t(j)} \tag{5.28}$$

The overall algorithm for the Viterbi training of discrete HMMs is summarized in Fig. 5.10.

The estimation of continuous mixture models by means of the Viterbi training is, however, considerably more demanding as no analytical methods are known for deriving optimal parameters of such models from training examples. It is usually assumed, however, that the number M_j of the baseline distributions remains constant. Nevertheless, an estimation of the mixture weights c_{jk} as well as of the parameters of the component densities $g_{jk}(x)$ cannot be performed directly.

For this purpose the maximum likelihood criterion is applied in [301] for the improvement of the optimal output probability $P(O, s^* \mid \lambda)$ depending on the model parameters λ. This optimization can be carried out separately for the transition probabilities a_{ij} (see Eq. (5.27)) and for the output probability densities $b_j(x)$. Though one obtains a system of constraint equations, no explicit relationship for computing updated model parameters can be derived. Rather, this must be achieved in a complex embedded optimization process.

In [209, pp. 42–44] an approximate version of Viterbi training for output probability densities of continuous mixture HMMs was proposed. The method applies the Viterbi criterion not only in the usual way for determining the optimal state s_t^* at time t. In addition to this, a similar maximization is carried out during the computation of output probability densities:

$$b'_j(x_t) = \max_k c_{jk} g_{jk}(x_t)$$

Let

$$\chi_t(i) = \begin{cases} 1 & \text{if } s_t^* = i \text{ and } s^* = \text{argmax}_s \, P(s, O \mid \lambda) \\ 0 & \text{otherwise} \end{cases}$$

1. **Initialization**
   Choose a suitable initial model $\lambda = (\pi, A, B)$ with initial estimates of π_i for start and a_{ij} for transition probabilities as well as discrete output probabilities $b_j(o_k)$.
2. **Segmentation**
   Compute the optimal state sequence s^* for generating the data O given the model λ by means of the Viterbi algorithm (see Fig. 5.5).
3. **Optimization**
   Compute updated estimates $\hat{\lambda} = (\hat{\pi}, \hat{A}, \hat{B})$ for all model parameters (except π, explanations see text):

$$\hat{a}_{ij} = \frac{\sum_{t=1}^{T-1} \chi_t(i) \chi_{t+1}(j)}{\sum_{t=1}^{T-1} \chi_t(i)} \qquad \hat{b}_j(o_k) = \frac{\sum_{t:O_t=o_k} \chi_t(j)}{\sum_{t=1}^{T} \chi_t(j)}$$

4. **Termination**
   if the quality measure $P^*(O \mid \hat{\lambda})$ was considerably improved by the updated model $\hat{\lambda}$ with respect to λ

   $$\text{let } \lambda \leftarrow \hat{\lambda} \text{ and continue with step 2}$$

   otherwise Stop!

Fig. 5.10 Viterbi training for parameter estimation of discrete HMMs

In contrast to the usual computation of $b_j(x_t)$ in Eq. (5.1), this can be considered as an approximation of the true output probability density that is obtained by a weighted summation over all mixture components. The approximation of $b_j(x_t)$ by the maximum of the (weighted) component densities can be justified by the observation that in mixture models usually a single density will dominate the contribution of the other components.

The consistent application of the Viterbi criterion on state and mixture level can now be exploited for obtaining a Viterbi-style training procedure. In addition to the characteristic function $\chi_t(j)$ (see Eq. (5.12)) that specifies whether a certain state j was part of the optimal state sequence s^* at time t, a similar characteristic function $\zeta_t(j, k)$ can be defined on the level of mixture components:

$$\zeta_t(j, k) = \begin{cases} 1 & \text{if } s_t^* = j \text{ and } k = \text{argmax}_m \, c_{jm} g_{jm}(x_t) \\ 0 & \text{otherwise} \end{cases} \qquad (5.29)$$

It takes on the value of one if state j was part of the optimal state sequence at time t and mixture k was the optimal mixture for generating the respective output x_t of the model.

This information can now be used for updating the model's mixture parameters. Figure 5.11 shows the resulting training algorithm.[17] Even though no formal proof of convergence can be found in the literature for this approximate Viterbi-training procedure, the continued success of HMM-based recognizers developed in the tradition of the Philips research system impressively demonstrates its suitability for the training of continuous mixture HMMs (see also Sects. 13.1 and 14.2). However, as pointed out in [209], the method is not suitable for semi-continuous HMMs due to the sharing of mixture components among all output probability densities.

5.7.6 Segmental k-Means Algorithm

With respect to its theoretical derivation the so-called *segmental k-means algorithm* is identical with the Viterbi training presented in the preceding section. The output probability $P(O, s^* \mid \lambda)$ of the training data along the optimal path through the model is also used as optimization criterion. In the practical application, however, the procedure offers a solution for the problem of estimating parameters of mixture models on example data only with the embedding of a method for vector quantization—namely the k-means algorithm.

Similar to Viterbi training the method proceeds in two phases. In a first step a segmentation of the training data is generated with the existing model. Subsequently new output probability density functions can be estimated from the resulting mapping between feature vectors and model states without any further reference to the original parameters. The resulting algorithm is summarized in Fig. 5.12.

As in all training procedures for HMMs, suitable initial model parameters need to be chosen before the optimization begins. However, the method can be extended such that also an initialization of HMMs is possible for models with a certain limited structure. This aspect of the segmental k-means algorithm will be presented in greater detail in Sect. 9.3.

By means of the Viterbi algorithm the optimal state sequence for the observations considered is computed in the next step. As in Viterbi training this already serves as a basis for computing estimates for the transition probabilities of the updated model (see Eq. (5.27)). Furthermore, one obtains a mapping between feature vectors x_t and corresponding model states which can formally be derived from the discrete state probability $\chi_t(i)$ (see Eq. (5.12)). Let us now collect all vectors which

---

[17]Please note that in [209] and in subsequent works using this method, covariance modeling and state-transition probabilities hardly play any role. The update equation for covariances is, therefore, given in analogy to Eq. (5.24). Parameter updates for transition probabilities can be obtained in the same way as for discrete models (see Eq. (5.27)).

Use

$$\delta'_t(j) = \max_i \left\{ \delta'_t(i) a_{ij} \right\} \max_k c_{jk} g_{jk}(x_t)$$

for computing partial path probabilities.
Let

$$\chi_t(i) = \begin{cases} 1 & \text{if } s_t^* = i \text{ and } s^* = \text{argmax}_s P(s, O \mid \lambda) \\ 0 & \text{otherwise} \end{cases}$$

$$\zeta_t(j, k) = \begin{cases} 1 & \text{if } s_t^* = j \text{ and } k = \text{argmax}_m c_{jm} g_{jm}(x_t) \\ 0 & \text{otherwise} \end{cases}$$

1. **Initialization**
   Choose a suitable initial model $\lambda = (\pi, A, B)$.
2. **Segmentation**
   Compute the optimal state sequence s^* by means of the Viterbi algorithm
   (see Fig. 5.5) using $\delta'_t(j)$.
3. **Optimization**
   Compute updated estimates $\hat{\lambda} = (\hat{\pi}, \hat{A}, \hat{B})$ for all model parameters (except π, explanations see text):

$$\hat{a}_{ij} = \frac{\sum_{t=1}^{T-1} \chi_t(i) \chi_{t+1}(j)}{\sum_{t=1}^{T-1} \chi_t(i)} \qquad \hat{c}_{jk} = \frac{\sum_{t=1}^{T-1} \zeta_t(i, k)}{\sum_{t=1}^{T-1} \chi_t(i)}$$

$$\hat{\mu}_{jk} = \frac{\sum_{t=1}^{T} \zeta_t(j, k) x_t}{\sum_{t=1}^{T-1} \chi_t(i)} \qquad \hat{C}_{jk} = \frac{\sum_{t=1}^{T} \zeta_t(j, k) x_t x_t^T}{\sum_{t=1}^{T} \chi_t(k)} - \hat{\mu}_k \hat{\mu}_k^T$$

4. **Termination**
   if the quality measure $P^*(O \mid \hat{\lambda})$ was considerably improved by the updated model $\hat{\lambda}$ with respect to λ

   let $\lambda \leftarrow \hat{\lambda}$ and continue with step 2

   otherwise Stop!

Fig. 5.11 Approximate Viterbi training for parameter estimation of continuous mixture HMMs

are mapped to a particular state i into a partial set $X(i)$ of the sample data considered:

$$X(i) = \left\{ x_t \mid \chi_t(i) = 1 \right\} = \left\{ x_t \mid s_t^* = i \right\}$$

These state specific partial sample sets form the basis for the estimation of new output probability density functions. First a cluster analysis of the respective partial set $X(i)$ is performed using a principally arbitrary method for vector quantiza-

Given the number M_j of mixture components to be estimated per model state (frequently $M_j = M$ is chosen identically for all states j)

1. **Initialization**
   Choose a suitable initial model $\lambda = (\boldsymbol{\pi}, \boldsymbol{A}, \boldsymbol{B})$
2. **Segmentation**
   Compute the optimal state sequence $\boldsymbol{s}^*$ for the generation of the data $\boldsymbol{O}$ given the model λ by means of the Viterbi algorithm (see Fig. 5.5). Compute updated transition probabilities $\hat{a}_{ij}$:

$$\hat{a}_{ij} = \frac{\sum_{t=1}^{T-1} \chi_t(i)\chi_{t+1}(j)}{\sum_{t=1}^{T-1} \chi_t(i)}$$

3. **Estimation**
   For all states $j, 0 \le j \le N$:
   a. **Cluster Analysis**
      For the partial sample set $X(j)$ compute a vector quantization codebook $Y = \{y_1, \ldots, y_{M_j}\}$ and the associated partition $\{R_1, \ldots, R_{M_j}\}$, e.g., using the k-means algorithm (see Fig. 4.3)
   b. **Updating the Model**
      Compute updated parameters of the output distributions:

$$\hat{c}_{jk} = \frac{|R_k|}{|X(j)|}$$

$$\hat{\boldsymbol{\mu}}_{jk} = \boldsymbol{y}_k$$

$$\hat{\boldsymbol{C}}_{jk} = \frac{1}{|R_k|} \sum_{\boldsymbol{x} \in R_k} \boldsymbol{x}\boldsymbol{x}^T - \hat{\boldsymbol{\mu}}_{jk}\hat{\boldsymbol{\mu}}_{jk}^T$$

4. **Termination**
   if the quality measure $P^*(\boldsymbol{O} \mid \hat{\lambda})$ was considerably improved by the updated model $\hat{\lambda}$ with respect to λ

$$\text{let } \lambda \leftarrow \hat{\lambda} \text{ and continue with step 2}$$

   otherwise Stop!

Fig. 5.12 Segmental k-means algorithm for estimating parameters of continuous HMMs

tion.[18] The parameters of the output distribution of the corresponding model state are then obtained in the same way as in the simple estimation of mixture models

---

[18]For reasons of efficiency it is rather obvious to use the k-means algorithm as vector quantization method as it achieves competitive results with only a single pass through the data. However, principally any algorithm for vector quantizer design or the unsupervised estimation of mixture densities could be applied.

(see Sect. 4.4). Analogously to vector quantizer design, however, it is necessary to specify the number of desired codebook classes or mixture components, respectively.

When assuming that exactly one mixture density with M_j individual component densities is used per model state j for modeling the output distribution, the mean vectors μ_{jk} correspond directly to the centroids of the M_j codebook classes which were determined by the vector quantization procedure for the partial sample set $X(j)$. The covariance matrices are computed as the sample covariances of the feature vectors that were mapped to a specific reproduction vector. The necessary mixture weights correspond to the prior probabilities of the individual codebook classes.

The segmental k-means method converges significantly faster than a comparable iterative estimation using the Baum–Welch algorithm because the parameters of an HMM including the complex mixture density models are completely newly computed in every step of the optimization on the basis of the example vectors only.

5.7.7 Multiple Observation Sequences

In general, sample sets that are used for parameter training are subdivided into individual segments—in automatic speech recognition in utterances or turns and in the analysis of biological sequences into protein domains or motifs, respectively. From the view of the HMM formalism these are considered individual observation sequences. In order to be able to estimate model parameters on such a set of isolated sequences, too, the training procedures do not need to be modified fundamentally. Only the statistics gathered for the updating of the parameters need to be accumulated across all the observation sequences considered. One then obtains modified estimation formulas with an additional outer summation over the observation sequences. For the sake of clarity however, these were omitted in the presentation of the individual methods in the preceding sections.

The fundamental principle will now be explained for the estimation of the mean vectors of continuous output probability densities.[19] Let us assume that a sample set $\omega = \{O^1, O^2, \ldots, O^L\}$ of L individual observation sequences O^l is available for the training of the models. In this case one obtains the updated mean vectors according to

$$\hat{\mu}_{jk} = \frac{\sum_{l=1}^{L} \sum_{t=1}^{T} \xi_t^l(j,k) x_t}{\sum_{l=1}^{L} \sum_{t=1}^{T} \xi_t^l(j,k)}$$

In this expression the inner sums in the numerator and denominator, respectively, correspond to the original estimation formula (5.22) that considered a single observation sequence only. The mapping probability $\xi_t^l(j,k)$ between feature vectors and

---

[19]The estimation of transition probabilities and discrete output probabilities is, for example, explained in [125, pp. 157–158].

mixture components, however, needs to be computed depending on the lth observation sequence O^l. The accumulated statistics are finally summed over all partial
sequences of the sample set.

5.8 Model Variants

For hidden Markov models a number of variants in the algorithmic treatment and in
the models themselves were proposed due to their widespread use and their long-
lasting development history. The most important of those aspects shall be outlined
shortly in the following. For a detailed treatment of the respective methods the interested reader is referred to the referenced specialized literature.

5.8.1 Alternative Algorithms

The majority of recognition systems with implicit segmentation that are based on
HMMs use the Viterbi algorithm for decoding. Differences merely result from necessary improvements in efficiency (see Sect. 10.2) or the incorporation of additional
modeling parts as, e.g., statistical language models (cf. Chap. 12). It is, however, also
possible to apply the principle of the A* graph-search algorithm (cf. [217, Sect. 9.2,
pp. 141–154]) to the decoding of HMMs. The resulting algorithm is known as *stack
decoding*. The basic method was first proposed in [134]. In [232] the method was
extended to use the A* criterion for the selection of theories that should be taken off
the stack and expanded.

For the estimation of model parameters a number of alternative approaches exist besides the established methods that were presented in the preceding section.
The best known group of methods applies techniques for discriminative training.
Similarly to Viterbi training the goal is therein to improve the probability of the
optimal path through the model for given data. However, this is not achieved in
isolation. Rather, it is attempted to reduce the probability of all competing paths
at the same time. In this way a higher discriminative power of the models shall
be achieved which, however, results in a substantially higher computational effort.
Mathematically a maximization of the mutual information is performed. Therefore,
these methods are frequently found under the topic of maximum mutual information (MMI) in the literature (cf. e.g. [44], [125, pp. 213–214], [123, pp. 150–152]).
Closely related to these methods is a technique known as corrective training [10].

5.8.2 Alternative Model Architectures

Besides the "classical" HMM architecture there exists a multitude of variants that
attempt to either avoid or at least compensate for the inherent limitations of the
models by using special modifications. Especially the improvement of the modeling
of duration by HMMs, which is possible rather inadequately with simple transition probabilities only, has been the aim of several approaches (cf. e.g. [37, 174],

[123, pp. 406–408]). In the main application area of HMMs, however, transition probabilities constitute a rather unimportant modeling aspect compared to output probability densities. For that reason and because of the increased computational effort of alternative duration modeling approaches none of the proposed techniques could establish itself as a standard method.

The best known modification of the classical HMM architecture undoubtedly is constituted by hybrid systems with a combination of HMMs and artificial neuronal networks (NN) (cf. e.g. [199], [123, pp. 458–459]). The neuronal networks which are incorporated into the model are used either as a vector quantizer in combination with discrete HMMs [254], as a replacement of the modeling of output distributions on the basis of mixture densities [260], or directly for the estimation of posterior probabilities of individual model states [199]. The combination of the scores obtained such with probabilities derived from the HMM formalism is, however, quite problematic and requires special mapping rules.

Due to the increase in the models' degrees of freedom, which results from the omission of the restrictions to mixture density models, an improved potential can be expected from such hybrid systems. This is also frequently demonstrated exemplarily in the literature. However, for this advantage the poor convergence properties of the training of neuronal networks have to be accepted. Also the optimization of those parameters is usually performed separately from the actual HMM and not in an integrated training process as with classical model architectures based on mixture densities. Furthermore, no standardized design strategies exist for hybrid HMM/NN-systems. As a consequence, until now these methods could not establish themselves as real or even better alternatives alongside the standard architectures.

5.9 Bibliographical Remarks

Hidden Markov Models were named after the Russian mathematician Andrej Andrejewitsch Markov (1856–1922) [190]. Books and articles from the mathematical literature mainly treat the theoretical aspects of these models. The primary application area of HMMs, in which they were successfully applied and consequently further developed, is the field of automatic speech recognition. Therefore, the treatment of HMMs within monographs related to the field of pattern recognition is almost always coupled with that special topic.

The treatment of HMMs in the monograph by Huang, Acero, & Hon [123] is especially convincing. The core of the model building process is also treated in the partially outdated book by Rabiner & Juang [252] as well as in the monograph by Jelinek [136]. A nice introduction to the use of HMMs in the domain of bioinformatics is given by Durbin et al. [67].

Descriptions of the algorithms relevant for HMMs can be found in all the above-mentioned works. A summary of these is also presented in the classical article by Rabiner [251] which had a significant influence on the HMM literature and the notation used therein.

The *Viterbi algorithm* was named after its inventor and goes back to his works in the field of coding theory [296]. An in-depth early presentation and analysis of the method is given by [98]. Later descriptions can, for example, be found in [125, pp. 151–152] or [123, pp. 387–389].

The most widely used method for estimating parameters of HMMs is the *Baum–Welch algorithm*, which was developed by Baum and colleagues [15]. Though the algorithm surely was named after its inventors, there exists no accessible publication with Welch as co-author. The method represents a variant of the *EM algorithm* [53]. The relationship between the two algorithms is, e.g., presented in [123, pp. 389–393]. A proof of the convergence of the Baum–Welch algorithm can besides [15] also be found in, e.g., [125, pp. 158–164]. The principle method is furthermore described in [251, pp. 342–348], [125, pp. 152–158], and [136, pp. 149–161].

Viterbi training constitutes an alternative method for estimating parameters of HMMs and is described, e.g., in [168]. Especially for continuous models the method was elaborated in [301]. An approximate version of Viterbi training that is attractive due to its computational efficiency was proposed by Ney and colleagues [209, pp. 42–44]. Principally comparable to this method is the segmental k-means algorithm, which was developed by Juang & Rabiner [142]. The actual embedding of a vector quantization procedure into a method for HMM training is mentioned in [142] but not elaborated as, e.g., in [168]. A short description of the method can also be found in [252, p. 427].

The most well-known variant of HMMs, the so-called semi-continuous or tied mixture models, were first proposed by Huang and Jack [126] and subsequently further developed by Huang and colleagues (cf. [125]). A recent comparison of continuous and semi-continuous HMMs can be found in [123, Sect. 8.3, pp. 394–398].

n-Gram Models

6

A *statistical language model* in its most general form defines a probability distribution over a set of symbol sequences from some finite inventory. These methods are referred to as "language models" because their origin, their development, and their spreading in use is closely related to the statistical modeling of texts as well as to the restriction of possible sequences of word hypotheses in automatic speech recognition.

An especially simple yet very powerful concept for the formal description of statistical language models is formed by their representation using Markov chains. Today, the most widely used version of these models is based on this formalism, the so-called *n-gram models*. The description of the statistical properties of symbol sequences by stochastic grammars is also well understood but considerably more complicated as the parameter training of such models is technically extremely demanding. Additionally, the definition of the grammar rules needs to be done by experts as no general inference methods are known for learning these automatically from data. Therefore, stochastic grammars have been used for pattern analysis tasks to a rather limited extent only which is why the term language model is mostly used synonymously for n-gram models in the literature. These models shall, therefore, be considered as the only class of statistical language modeling techniques in the following. For different methods the interested reader is referred to the respective specialized literature.

6.1 Definition

A statistical n-gram model corresponds to a Markov chain of order $n - 1$. The probability $P(w)$ of a certain symbol sequence $w = w_1, w_2, \ldots, w_T$ of length T is first decomposed into a product of conditional probabilities according to Bayes' rule:

G.A. Fink, *Markov Models for Pattern Recognition*,
Advances in Computer Vision and Pattern Recognition,
DOI 10.1007/978-1-4471-6308-4_6, © Springer-Verlag London 2014

$$P(\boldsymbol{w}) = P(w_1)P(w_2 \mid w_1) \cdots P(w_T \mid w_1, \ldots, w_{T-1}) = \prod_{t=1}^{T} P(w_t \mid w_1, \ldots, w_{t-1})$$

However, with increasing length T of the symbol sequence this factorization will require conditional probabilities with arbitrarily long dependencies as already pointed out when introducing stochastic processes. Therefore, for practical applications the maximal length of the context is limited to $n - 1$ predecessor symbols:

$$P(\boldsymbol{w}) \approx \prod_{t=1}^{T} P(\underbrace{w_t \mid w_{t-n+1}, \ldots, w_{t-1}}_{n \text{ symbols}})$$

Motivated by the chronological order of symbol or word sequences, this context is frequently also referred to as the *history*. The respective predicted symbol w_t and the associated history form a tuple of n symbols which is the reason why the models are referred to as *n*-gram models. A concrete *n*-tuple of symbols is called *n*-gram. In the language modeling literature it is usually referred to as an *event*.

Thus a given *n*-gram model defines probabilities for the prediction or evaluation of the occurrence of symbols from a finite inventory within a sequence on the basis of a context of $n - 1$ known predecessor elements. The total probability of a certain sequence can be computed directly from these individual contributions. The set of necessary conditional probability distributions forms the statistical language model. In contrast to HMMs, such a model is never denoted with an explicit mathematical symbol in the literature. Therefore, we also will not use an explicit designation in the further elaborations as long as the implicit assignment of probabilities to the respective model is clear.

Besides the principal difficulties to estimate such a model and to apply it in practice, also the required amount of memory increases substantially with increasing context length. Therefore, the most widely used variants of *n*-gram models are bi- and tri-grams while 4-gram models are hardly used any more in statistical recognition systems. In the field of automatic speech recognition bi-gram models complementing the HMM modeling can be regarded as a standard procedure today. In the field of handwriting recognition the use of statistical language models has become increasingly popular in recent years though it can still be regarded as a rather special model component. In contrast, in the more recently opened application areas of statistical modeling techniques like the analysis of gestures or biological sequences statistical language models to date are used only to a very limited extent. This is mainly due to the fact that in the latter research areas the general availability of sufficiently large database is not yet granted, whereas for the purpose of speech and handwriting recognition language models can rather easily be estimated on text corpora which are more readily available in suitable sizes.

6.2   Use Cases

In the same way as for HMMs, the usage of statistical language models for the description of texts and other symbol sequences is based on the assumption that their underlying generation principle obeys statistical rules which can be described or at least can be sufficiently approximated using Markov chains.

Therefore, it is a relevant question for n-gram models how well a given model is able to describe available data. For this purpose essentially the probability of this symbol sequence—or some information theoretic measure derived from it—needs to be computed by means of the model being used. Then inferences about the quality of the language model can be drawn or different models can be evaluated with respect to their suitability for describing the respective data. For example, paragraphs of text can be assigned to a certain category or to a specific topic on this basis if for each topic or category a suitable model was built.

The second relevant question concerns the construction of the n-gram models themselves. In contrast to the necessary iteratively optimization procedures used for HMMs, for statistical language models methods are conceivable that compute a model which is in some sense optimal directly depending on the sample data. The naive, immediately obvious solution of the problem is to count the absolute frequencies $c(w_1, w_2, \ldots, w_n)$ of all symbol tuples and all possible contexts $w_1, \ldots, w_{n-1}$ within the available sample set. The conditional probabilities $P(w_n \mid w_1, w_2, \ldots, w_{n-1})$ can then be defined via the relative frequencies $f(w_n \mid w_1, w_2, \ldots, w_{n-1})$:

$$P(w_n \mid w_1, w_2, \ldots, w_{n-1}) := f(w_n \mid w_1, w_2, \ldots, w_{n-1}) = \frac{c(w_1, w_2, \ldots, w_n)}{c(w_1, \ldots, w_{n-1})}$$
(6.1)

However, even for a moderately sized inventory of symbols and already for short context lengths it must be assumed that the majority of the theoretically possible n-grams are not contained in the sample set considered—even if this is rather large. The n-grams that have not been observed are usually referred to as so-called *unseen events*. According to Eq. (6.1) all conditional probabilities involving such tuples will be defined to be zero. Consequently, a probability of zero results for every sequence considered that contains a single of those unseen events when evaluating the resulting model on new data.

Such a behavior of the model is, however, extremely undesirable as it can be assumed that the estimation of vanishing probabilities is extremely unreliable and only due to the limited size or representativity of the sample set considered. Therefore, for n-gram models the probability distributions determined empirically are always subject to a post-processing or smoothing operation which aims at delivering robust estimates especially for very small conditional probabilities. As the application of such smoothing techniques is crucial for the success of language modeling, it is quite obvious that these methods constitute the relevant algorithmic know-how for applying statistical language models to pattern recognition tasks.

6.3   Notation

In the treatment of n-gram models mainly the terms for computing the individual conditional probabilities are considered and not their evaluation on a longer text. Therein the distinction between the predicted word and the current history is essential. In order to be able to also make this more explicit in the formal treatment, a notation will be used in the following that is inspired by the one defined by Federico and colleagues [77].

An arbitrary isolated n-gram will be denoted as yz where z stands for the predicted symbol and $y = y_1, y_2, \ldots, y_{n-1}$ for its history. In the notationally simple case of tri- or bi-gram models, all symbols of a tri-gram can be denoted individually—if this is required—as xyz and those of a bi-gram as yz. The conditional n-gram probabilities will be denoted as $P(z \mid y)$ in general and as $P(z \mid xy)$ for tri- and $P(z \mid y)$ for bi-gram models, respectively. That symbol within the n-gram which is the last with respect to the chronological order will always be referred to as z.

Besides the frequency of occurrence $c(yz)$ of an n-gram yz in the training set considered, also several derived quantities are important which either characterize properties of n-gram contexts or provide meta-information about the empirical frequency distribution. The absolute frequency—or count—of all n-grams with history y will be denoted as $c(y \cdot)$ by using the joker symbol '$\cdot$'. It is in principle equal to the frequency $c(y)$ of the context y of an n-gram yz. Differences merely result from border phenomena in the sample set considered. If the training text or a specially marked section therein ends with y then no further event yz exists at this position having this very context and $c(y) > c(y \cdot)$ holds. For this reason we will use $c(y \cdot)$ throughout the whole presentation as this quantity always yields the correct normalization in practical applications. By $d_k(y \cdot)$ we will denote how many events with context y occur exactly k times in the training data. Especially important is the frequency $d_1(y \cdot)$ of so-called *singletons*, i.e., events that occur exactly once in a given context. In generalization of this notation, the number of different events occurring at all is referred to as $d_{1+}(y \cdot)$. When also replacing the context restrictions in this quantity by the joker symbol one obtains the total number of all n-grams $c(\cdot \cdot)$ or the number of events occurring k times in total $d_k(\cdot \cdot)$. In order to simplify the representation the arguments $(\cdot \cdot)$ can be omitted completely in the last two cases mentioned.

6.4   Evaluation

In order to evaluate a statistical language model,—as in many fields of statistical pattern analysis—its descriptive power on unknown data has to be determined, i.e., on test data that was not used for creating the model. The so-called *perplexity* has become the relevant quality measure [139]. For a given test text or test symbol sequence $w = w_1, w_2, \ldots, w_T$ of length $|w| = T$, one obtains the perplexity $\mathcal{P}$ of the language model considered as the reciprocal value of the geometric mean of the individual symbol probabilities:

$$\mathscr{P}(\boldsymbol{w}) = \frac{1}{\sqrt[|\boldsymbol{w}|]{P(\boldsymbol{w})}} = \frac{1}{\sqrt[T]{P(w_1, w_2, \ldots, w_T)}} = P(w_1, w_2, \ldots, w_T)^{-\frac{1}{T}} \quad (6.2)$$

Formally, perplexity is defined via the entropy of a language or of an information source (see sidebar *Foundations of Perplexity*). However, the wide-spread use of this measure in the literature is to a substantial extent due to the possibility of interpreting it in an intuitively illustrative way. In order to do so, one assumes that the text considered was created by an information source which generates symbols from a finite vocabulary V with some probability. For purposes of the analysis it is now desired to be able to predict this process as exactly as possible, i.e., only as few as possible symbols should be considered for continuing a sequence. However, such a deterministic statement is strictly speaking not possible due to the statistical behavior of the source. In principle all symbols might occur at any time, even though with an arbitrarily low probability. In the statistical average, however, a relationship to the deterministic behavior can be established.

Foundations of Perplexity

Perplexity is an evaluation measure for the modeling quality of statistical language models. The formal derivation of perplexity is based on an information theoretic view on the problem (cf. e.g. [125, pp. 97–100], [252, pp. 449–450], [136, pp. 141–142]. In this view it is assumed that a text is generated by an information source that emits symbols or words from some lexicon according to a discrete probability distribution. This probability distribution that corresponds to the statistical language model defines—in a statistical sense—a formal language. The complexity of that formal language can be measured by computing the entropy of the underlying symbol probability distribution $P(s_i) = p_i$:

$$H(p) = -\sum_i p_i \log_2 p_i$$

Entropy measures the uncertainty that is encountered when trying to predict the behavior of the information source given full knowledge about the actual statistical model being used. It corresponds to the average number of bits per element that are necessary to optimally encode symbol sequences that are generated according to the distribution p.

In practice the true language model defined by p is not known but is approximated by estimating a model q on some training data. The question how well this estimated model approximates the true one could be answered by computing the cross-entropy between the two probability distributions:

$$H(p|q) = -\sum_i p_i \log_2 q_i$$

It represents the uncertainty about texts generated according to p when using q as a prediction model.

As, however, the true model p is unknown, the respective probability distribution can only be approximated based on some observed data. Therefore, instead of computing the cross-entropy between the estimated language model q and the true model p, the cross-entropy between q and an empirically defined approximation of p is computed. This approximation $\hat{p}$ is derived from test data that has not been used to estimate q.

When approximating the true language model by an empirical estimate, it is a priori not clear how specific the respective probabilistic model really would be. Therefore, every element of the test data $\boldsymbol{w} = w_1, w_2, \ldots, w_T$ is considered as a unique event occurring with probability $\frac{1}{T}$. The cross-entropy can then be computed by summing over all elements of the test set:

$$H(\hat{p}|q) = H(\boldsymbol{w}|P(\cdot\,|\ldots)) = -\sum_{t=1}^{T} \underbrace{\frac{1}{T}}_{\hat{=}\hat{p}} \underbrace{\log_2 P(w_t\,|\ldots)}_{\hat{=}q}$$

$$= -\frac{1}{T} \log_2 \prod_t P(w_t\,|\ldots)$$

Based on this cross-entropy measure, perplexity—or more specifically *test set perplexity*—is defined as the size of the virtual lexicon of an information source that generates equally complex texts according to a uniform distribution:

$$\mathscr{P}(\boldsymbol{w}) = 2^{H(\boldsymbol{w}|P(\cdot\,|\ldots))}$$

This equation can now be rewritten to obtain the definition of perplexity found in Eq. (6.2):

$$\mathscr{P}(\boldsymbol{w}) = 2^{H(\boldsymbol{w}|P(\cdot\,|\ldots))} = 2^{-\frac{1}{T} \log_2 \prod_t P(w_t|\ldots)} = 2^{\log_2 P(w_1, w_2, \ldots, w_T)^{-\frac{1}{T}}}$$

$$= P(w_1, w_2, \ldots, w_T)^{-\frac{1}{T}}$$

In the "worst" case the generation is performed according to a uniform distribution over the lexicon V, which means that every additional symbol w_t will be generated with probability $P(w_t) = \frac{1}{|V|}$ independently of the context. Then a prediction of successor symbols is not possible as all words of the lexicon can occur equally likely. The probability of a text of length T is obtained as $\{\frac{1}{|V|}\}^T$ and its perplexity is equal to the size $|V|$ of the lexicon used.

If the generation principle relies on any other probability distribution, which generates certain words with higher and others with lower frequency, always a lower perplexity $\rho < |V|$ is obtained compared to the case of the uniform distribution. The precision of the prediction based on this model can now be related to the one of an "uninformed" source with equal perplexity that acts according to a uniform distribution. The vocabulary of that source, which is identical with respect to the evaluation criterion, would consist of exactly $|V'| = \rho < |V|$ words—i.e. less than contained in the original lexicon. It can, therefore, be said that the perplexity of a statistical language model specifies how many words are in the statistical average likely for the continuation of a symbol sequence even if at every time—from the statistical point of view—an arbitrary continuation with possibly lower probability is possible.

Therefore, it is the central goal of language model design to construct precise statistical models for predicting the text data to be expected, i.e., models that achieve perplexities as low as possible on unseen text material. Thereby the generalization capability of the model is essential as a model too specifically tuned to a certain training situation is useless for practical applications.[1]

A generalization of n-gram models can always be achieved quite well if sufficiently precise restrictions for possible successor words can be derived based on the considered context of $n - 1$ predecessor words. However, it must be possible to estimate the parameters of the conditional probabilities, which are necessary for describing these restrictions, sufficiently robustly on the available training material.

An important task for automatic speech recognition is the recognition of sequences of digits for telephony applications. Here the "worst case" perplexity of 10 can hardly be reduced any more by techniques of statistical language modeling due to the almost complete absence of restrictions for such symbol sequences. For "normal" texts in natural languages, however, a significant reduction in perplexity to values well below the unrestricted case—i.e. the size of the lexicon—is always possible. Consequently, the compression of texts is another important application area for statistical language models (cf. e.g. [17]).

n-gram models are applicable especially well for the English language—not only because this language is probably among the most well studied in this respect. The relatively linear sentence structure with reduced degrees of freedom in word order and the almost complete absence of inflected forms provide ideal conditions for statistical language modeling. Inflecting languages with rather free word order as French or German are considered to be much more challenging. In German, the extremely productive creation of compound words makes language modeling even more complicated and either requires the analysis of complex word constructs or a substantial increase of the possible lexicon (cf. e.g. [2, 111, 299, 311]). A similar problem can be found in agglutinative languages as, e.g., Turkish or Finnish where many syntactic phenomena are described by concatenating morphemes (cf. e.g. [5, 40, 283]).

However, it is not necessarily required that language models are built on the basis of the orthographic word definition of a certain language. In order to simplify the

---

[1]On the training material of a language model always a perplexity of one can be achieved by completely storing this data. But even with standard techniques arbitrarily low perplexities on the training set are possible which, however, allow no predictions whatsoever about the modeling quality on unknown texts.

modeling, for example, a normalization of the lexicon can be applied (cf. e.g. [1]) or a direct modeling of morpheme sequences by the statistical model can be considered (cf. e.g. [5, 40, 111, 312]).

6.5   Parameter Estimation

In contrast to HMMs, n-gram models usually contain no hidden state variables. Therefore, their parameters can in principle be computed directly based on example data, i.e., without the need of some iterative optimization procedure. Provided that one is satisfied with defining the conditional probabilities via the relative frequencies, the model can directly be specified after counting the events observed in the sample set.

However, for a robust application of n-gram models it is essential that the problem of events not observed in the data is dealt with. Therefore, in all approaches to statistical language modeling known from the literature the empirical distributions are never used directly. Rather a suitable smoothing is applied to them. The most important task of this smoothing is to replace vanishing probabilities of unseen events by plausible and robust estimates. Due to the normalization conditions necessary for probability distributions, however, this cannot be performed in isolation, but the estimates of the remaining events have to be included in the process.

The most widely used class of methods for solving this problem proceeds in two steps. First the empirical distributions are modified such that a redistribution of probability mass from seen to unseen events takes place. As those manipulations usually result in very small changes only, the probabilities of seen events are hardly modified. The relevant effect of that approach is, therefore, the gathering of "probability mass" in order to be able to define new, very small probabilities for n-grams not observed in the sample set.

In a second step robust estimates are calculated on the basis of the modified empirical distributions by incorporating one or even several more general distributions. For frequently observed events the influence of this modification can be kept small or can be omitted completely. For unseen n-grams it is, however, important not to distribute the gathered probability mass uniformly but on the basis of a more general distribution—usually the one of the associated $(n - 1)$-gram model. Otherwise *all* unseen events would be assigned the same probability which would not be very plausible.

In practice also robust estimates for $(n - 1)$-grams are not necessarily available directly. Therefore, the two steps of the method outlined above are recursively applied to the resulting model hierarchy starting from the n-gram and proceeding down to the uni-gram or zero-gram, respectively. The term *uni-gram model* refers to the prior probability of the words in the lexicon and the term *zero-gram model* is used to denote the uniform probability distribution over a lexicon of given size.

6.5.1 Redistribution of Probability Mass

A quite intuitive possibility to get rid of the problem of unobserved events consists in raising their frequencies of occurrence, which were empirically determined to be zero, to some positive value. In order not to discard the differences between seen and unseen events, a positive constant—usually 1—is added to all n-gram counts. The normalization condition for probability distributions is not violated by this manipulation if the sum over all newly determined counts of individual events $\sum_z c^*(yz)$ is used instead of the frequency of the respective n-gram context $c(y\cdot)$ for the computation of the relative frequencies.

This relatively old method is referred to as *adding one* or *Laplace's rule* in the literature. Though it is maximally simple on the algorithmic side, it, unfortunately, achieves *substantially* worse results than the more advanced methods which will be presented in the following. This is due to the fact that the probability of rare events is systematically over-estimated (cf. [205]).

All other methods for smoothing n-gram probabilities are based on the principle of redistributing probability mass. This means that the frequency counts which are necessary for removing unseen events are first gathered at some other position in the original probability distribution. Hereby not only the normalization condition of the relative frequencies remains unaltered but it is also possible that a different amount of probability mass is obtained for unseen events depending on the properties of the initial distribution considered and the redistribution strategy applied. Thus it can be controlled to some extent whether the observation of such an event, which is assumed to be extremely rare, is more or less probable in a certain context.

6.5.2 Discounting

In order to be able to gather probability mass for unseen events without a modification of the occurrence frequencies in total, the empirical counts $c(yz)$ of observed n-grams need to be reduced by a certain amount $\beta(yz)$. Therefore, this class of methods is referred to as so-called *discounting*. The modified relative frequencies $f^*(z \mid y)$ are obtained directly from the modified n-gram counts $c^*(yz)$ according to

$$f^*(z \mid y) = \frac{c^*(yz)}{c(y\cdot)} = \frac{c(yz) - \beta(yz)}{c(y\cdot)} \quad \forall yz, c(yz) > \beta(yz)$$

The discounting function $\beta(yz)$ may be chosen such that for certain events yz it will become equal to their count $c(yz)$. Then the effect can be observed that these events first contribute all their probability mass to the redistribution process but themselves belong to the effectively unseen events after the discounting.

The total probability mass that is obtained for improving the empirical distribution and especially for removing unseen events is referred to as the so-called *zero probability* $\lambda(y)$. It depends on the respective n-gram context and is calculated as a sum over the accumulated probability mass:[2]

$$\lambda(y) = \frac{\sum_{yz:c(yz)>0} \min\{\beta(yz), c(yz)\}}{c(y \cdot)}$$

In case that the modified relative frequency $f^*(\cdot)$ is directly used as an estimate for the conditional probability of seen events, this quantity specifies the probability that any unseen event can be expected to occur in a given context. As will be elaborated in more detail in the following Sect. 6.5.3, there also exist methods that perform a redistribution of the zero probability to *all* events in the respective context. For both strategies, however, additional knowledge is required as otherwise the redistribution would only be possible according to a uniform distribution.

The methods for the definition of special discounting strategies known from the literature—i.e. for the choice of $\beta(yz)$—can be divided into two groups. All methods which perform the reduction of a certain n-gram count proportional to its value $c(yz)$ are referred to as *linear discounting*. In contrast, so-called *absolute discounting* is applied if the discounting constant β is specified independently from the actual frequency of events.

In the simplest form of linear discounting $\beta(yz)$ is defined by means of a proportionality factor α depending on $c(yz)$:

$$\beta(yz) = \alpha c(yz)$$

The modified relative frequencies $f^*(yz)$ for all observed events are consequently obtained as

$$f^*(z \mid y) = \frac{(1-\alpha)c(yz)}{c(y \cdot)} = (1-\alpha)f(z \mid y) \quad \forall yz, c(yz) > 0 \quad \text{and} \quad 0 < \alpha < 1$$

A good choice for α is given by the relative frequency of singletons, i.e., events observed exactly once in the data [206]:

$$\alpha = \frac{d_1(\cdot\cdot)}{c(\cdot\cdot)} = \frac{d_1}{c}$$

If the proportionality constant is not defined globally but individually for every n-gram context, one obtains a more general definition of linear discounting. In this case it is easy to verify that the context dependent proportionality factor becomes equivalent to the respective zero probability $\lambda(y)$ and one obtains the following modified distribution of relative frequencies [77, 206]:

$$f^*(z \mid y) = \frac{(1-\lambda(y))c(yz)}{c(y \cdot)} = (1-\lambda(y))f(z \mid y) \quad \forall yz, c(yz) > 0 \qquad (6.3)$$

---

[2]In general, the discounting function $\beta(yz)$ can take on values larger than the absolute frequencies $c(yz)$. Therefore, during the modification only the minimum of the respective values might be gathered as probability mass.

The most serious drawback of linear discounting lies in the fact that the counts of frequently observed events are modified the most. This does, however, not comply with the basic statistical assumption backed up by the "law of large numbers" that more robust estimates are obtained the more example data is available for a certain event. Furthermore, in the general formulation of Eq. (6.3) the choice or optimization, respectively, of the zero probability $\lambda(y)$ is required for all n-gram contexts. Though this can be performed on additional data (cf. e.g. [206]) the effort for computing the n-gram model is significantly increased.

In contrast, methods for absolute discounting are substantially easier in the application. They are also among the best methods known with respect to their effectiveness. Here large frequencies remain almost unchanged and mainly events observed rarely contribute to the gathering of probability mass. Therefore, these techniques in general tend to assign smaller probabilities to unseen events than methods for linear discounting do.

In absolute discounting every count $c(yz)$ determined empirically is decreased by a constant amount β. On the basis of the counts $c^*(yz)$ modified such one obtains the following new distribution of relative frequencies:

$$f^*(z \mid y) = \frac{c^*(yz)}{c(y\cdot)} = \frac{c(yz) - \beta}{c(y\cdot)} = \quad \forall yz, c(yz) > \beta \tag{6.4}$$

In this case the zero probability $\lambda(y)$ can simply be given as

$$\lambda(y) = \frac{\sum_{yz:c(yz)>0} \beta}{c(y\cdot)} = \beta \frac{d_{1+}(y\cdot)}{c(y\cdot)}$$

In all variants of absolute discounting the discounting constants β are usually chosen such that they do not lie above the original frequencies. This is especially true for the widely used choice of $\beta \leq 1$, which already achieves very good results in practice.

Under certain conditions the discounting constants can be chosen better though not necessarily optimal. If exactly one constant is used for every context length, one obtains the following upper bound for its choice according to [205]:

$$\beta \leq \frac{d_1(\cdot\cdot)}{d_1(\cdot\cdot) + 2d_2(\cdot\cdot)} = \frac{d_1}{d_1 + 2d_2} < 1$$

In [43] even three different constants are proposed for events seen once, twice, or more frequently. However, the improvements achieved with this refinement of the model are quite marginal in the majority of cases.

6.5.3 Incorporation of More General Distributions

The gathering of probability mass alone is not sufficient for determining suitable estimates for conditional n-gram probabilities. It has to be complemented by a strategy for redistributing the zero probability in order to remove unseen events and to obtain improved estimates for low probability events. Such a redistribution strategy always requires the incorporation of additional, more reliable knowledge. However, this knowledge cannot be contributed by experts but also needs to be determined from the example data. Therefore, only probability distributions can be considered for that purpose which are less complex and, consequently, can be estimated more easily than the *n*-gram model to be improved.

For tasks of language modeling the strategy most frequently applied for choosing such more general distributions is the shortening of the context restriction of the *n*-gram models by one word. The resulting $(n - 1)$-gram distribution is less specific than the initial model and, therefore, chances are also higher that its parameters can be estimated robustly on the available data.

For the combination of the more general distributions with the smoothed empirical distributions two fundamental classes of methods exist. When applying *interpolation* a weighted averaging of the two parts of the model is performed. In the case of the so-called *backing off* the more general distribution is only taken into account for redistributing the gathered zero probability in a clever way onto unseen events.

6.5.4 Interpolation

Interpolation methods (cf. [138]) are widely used in the field of language modeling for improving empirically determined estimates $f(z \mid y)$ of a special distribution $P(z \mid y)$. Robust estimates are obtained for the special probability distribution considered by a linear combination with a suitably chosen more general distribution $q(z \mid y)$:

$$P(z \mid y) = (1 - \alpha) f(z \mid y) + \alpha q(z \mid y) \quad 0 \le \alpha \le 1 \tag{6.5}$$

This approach is based on the assumption that principally *all* empirically determined frequencies $f(z \mid y)$ can be estimated better—i.e. more robustly—by also taking into account additional knowledge in the form of the more general distribution $q(z \mid y)$. Thus, vanishing frequencies and those that are based on a sufficient number of samples are treated in the same way.

In this method the interpolation weight α needs to be chosen such that on the one hand the coarser information of the more general distribution does not dominate the special estimates too much but on the other hand suitably supports less robustly estimated or vanishing relative frequencies. The interpolation weight α can either be determined experimentally or can be optimized in a mathematically exact way on the basis of additional training material which was not used for determining the empirical distributions.[3]

---

[3]The training material of the *n*-gram model cannot be used for the optimal choice of the interpolation weight α as on this data the most special model—i.e. the empirical distribution $f(z \mid y)$ itself—would always be optimal. Consequently, one would obtain $\alpha = 0.0$ [136, p. 63]. Rather, additional material needs to be available that is exclusively used for the optimization of the interpolation weight.

In the context of language modeling almost always the $(n-1)$-gram distribution $P(z \mid \hat{y})$ associated with the n-gram model $P(z \mid y)$ considered is chosen as more general distribution:

$$q(z \mid y) = q(z \mid y_1, y_2, \ldots, y_{n-1}) \leftarrow P(z \mid y_2, \ldots, y_{n-1}) = P(z \mid \hat{y})$$

Thus the generalization lies in the shortening of the context restriction $y = y_1, y_2, \ldots, y_{n-1}$ by one word to yield $\hat{y} = y_2, \ldots, y_{n-1}$ which achieves a lower specificity of the model and at the same time a better trainability of its parameters. When applying this strategy to tri- and bi-gram models, $q(\cdot)$ can easily be given as follows:

$$q(z \mid xy) \leftarrow P(z \mid y)$$

$$q(z \mid y) \leftarrow P(z)$$

In general, the interpolation principle is applied recursively here as the more general distribution $q(\cdot)$ is again described by an n-gram model:

$$\begin{aligned}
P(z \mid y) &= (1 - \alpha_n) f(z \mid y) + \alpha_n q(z \mid y) \\
&= (1 - \alpha_n) f(z \mid y_1 \ldots, y_{n-1}) \\
&\quad + \alpha_n \big[(1 - \alpha_{n-1}) f(z \mid y_2 \ldots, y_{n-1}) \\
&\quad + \alpha_{n-1} q(z \mid y_2 \ldots, y_{n-1}) \big] \\
&= \cdots \quad \forall i: \ 0 \le \alpha_i \le 1
\end{aligned}$$

Thus as the final model one obtains a linear combination[4] of all empirically determined relative frequencies by repeated shortening[5] of the n-gram context for choosing the respective more general distribution $q(\cdot)$:

$$\begin{aligned}
P(z \mid y) &= \lambda_n f(z \mid y) \\
&\quad + \lambda_{n-1} f(z \mid y_2 \ldots, y_{n-1}) \\
&\quad + \cdots \\
&\quad + \lambda_1 f(z) \\
&= \sum_{i=1}^{n} \lambda_i f(z \mid y_{n-i+1} \ldots, y_{n-1}) \quad \forall i: \ 0 \le \lambda_i \le 1 \quad \text{and} \quad \sum_i \lambda_i = 1
\end{aligned}$$

---

[4] For the sake of clarity here the resulting products of the pairwise interpolation weights α_i were replaced by new constants λ_i.

[5] The incorporation of a zero-gram model usually is not necessary if one assumes that every word of the lexicon V considered was observed at least once. However, if this is not the case, as, e.g., the sample set and the lexicon were defined completely independently of each other, the interpolation scheme can be extended by the additional term $\lambda_0 \frac{1}{|V|}$.

The interpolation formula for robust tri-gram models developed by Jelinek & Mercer used in the tradition of research at IBM can be obtained as a special case from this general interpolation equation (cf. e.g. [136, pp. 60–61]):

$$P(z \mid xy) = \lambda_3 f(z \mid xy) + \lambda_2 f(z \mid y) + \lambda_1 f(z)$$

In the derivation so far the interpolation method directly started from the empirically determined relative frequencies $f(\cdot)$ and made no use of the reduced frequency distribution $f^*(\cdot)$ generated in the preparatory step described previously. The principal possibility for its incorporation into the interpolation becomes evident most easily if *linear discounting* is used for obtaining $f^*(z \mid y)$:

$$f^*(z \mid y) = (1 - \alpha)f(z \mid y) \quad \forall yz$$

This expression directly corresponds to the first term in the weighted sum of the classical interpolation Eq. (6.5). When distinguishing between sufficiently frequently observed events, for which estimates $f^*(z \mid y)$ exist, and effectively unseen n-grams, one obtains a generalized recursive interpolation rule. Therein the reduced frequency distribution $f^*(z \mid y)$ is combined with the general distribution $q(z \mid y)$ with the interpolation weight being equal to the gathered zero probability $\lambda(y)$:

$$P(z \mid y) = \begin{cases} f^*(z \mid y) + \lambda(y)q(z \mid y) & c^*(yz) > 0 \\ \lambda(y)q(z \mid y) & c^*(yz) = 0 \end{cases} \tag{6.6}$$

As in this case the interpolation weights are not defined for a distribution in general but are chosen depending on the context y, the method is also called *non-linear interpolation*.

The crucial conceptual drawback of interpolation models is directly caused by their very design principle. When assuming that counts which were determined on a large basis of sample data represent robust estimates already, it does not seem to be useful to modify these by an interpolation with a coarser model. In the end this leads to a smoothing of the resulting distributions which at the same time also causes a partial loss of their specificity.

6.5.5 Backing off

In contrast to interpolation methods the principle of *backing off* incorporates the more general distribution into the computation of the n-gram model only if the reduced frequencies $f^*(\cdot)$ vanish. In all other cases these values are directly used as estimates for the conditional probabilities of the respective event. The redistribution of the gathered zero probability $\lambda(y)$ onto the unseen events is, however, performed proportional to the more general distribution $q(\cdot)$:

$$P(z \mid y) = \begin{cases} f^*(z \mid y) & c^*(yz) > 0 \\ \lambda(y)K_y q(z \mid y) & c^*(yz) = 0 \end{cases} \tag{6.7}$$

An additional scaling factor K_y needs to be introduced in order to guarantee the normalization constraint for the distribution $P(z \mid y)$ constructed such. It makes sure that the zero probability is completely—i.e. with weight 1.0—incorporated into the resulting model according to a probability distribution $K_y q(z \mid y)$ defined for unseen events only. Therefore, the scaling factor can be computed as the reciprocal value of the probability sum that is obtained for unseen events according to the more general distribution:

$$K_y = \frac{1}{\sum_{yz:c^*(yz)=0} q(yz)} \qquad (6.8)$$

In the same way as with interpolation methods the more general distribution $q(\cdot)$ is usually chosen by simply shortening the n-gram context. Likewise the principle of backing off is recursively applied to the whole hierarchy of n-gram models. For a back-off tri-gram model one thus obtains the following computation scheme:

$$P(z \mid xy) = \begin{cases} f^*(z \mid xy) & c^*(xyz) > 0 \\ \lambda(xy)K_{xy} \begin{cases} f^*(z \mid y) & c^*(xyz) = 0 \wedge c^*(yz) > 0 \\ \lambda(y)K_y \begin{cases} f^*(z) & c^*(yz) = 0 \wedge c^*(z) > 0 \\ \lambda(\cdot)K.\frac{1}{|V|} & c^*(z) = 0 \end{cases} \end{cases} \end{cases}$$

Extremely powerful n-gram models for a wide range of applications can be obtained rather easily by combining backing off and absolute discounting. In general, only marginally lower perplexities can be achieved even with considerably more expensive methods.

6.5.6 Optimization of Generalized Distributions

In the previous section it was assumed that the more general distributions necessary for interpolation methods or backing off can be obtained by shortening the context of the respective n-gram model. This heuristic definition is, however, not necessarily the best possible strategy.

Illustratively, this can be made plausible with the example of a word z which in fact occurs very frequently in a given sample set but only in a certain context y. Depending on the text category this could be for example "York" in the context "New" or "machine" after the preceding phrase "support vector". In all other contexts y', however, z was never observed. The problem with the standard choice of generalized distributions arises from the fact that both in interpolation and in backing off the more general distribution $q(z \mid y')$ is crucial for determining the conditional probability $P(z \mid y')$. If $q(z \mid y') \leftarrow P(z)$ is chosen, the predicted probability $P(z \mid y')$ is proportional to the frequency of occurrence $c(z)$ of the considered word z. Therefore, one obtains a relatively high probability for its observation in a context y' in which z never occurred in the sample data. A relatively low probability would be more plausible as in this situation the considered word is seen frequently in exactly one context but was not observed in any other. A more general distribution which comes close to that intuitive idea defines $q(z \mid y')$ proportional to the number of different contexts in which a certain word was observed. The more unique the context specificity of an event is the lower the respective predicted probability would be compared to other events.

In the method for determining the more general distribution proposed by Kneser & Ney, which is usually referred to as *Kneser–Ney smoothing* in the literature, $q(\cdot)$ is not defined heuristically but derived in an analytical way [153]. Using two different optimization criteria principally comparable distributions $q(\cdot)$ are obtained which are not based on the absolute frequencies of events but on the number of contexts in which a word was observed.

In the first approach proposed it is required that the conditional $(n-1)$-gram distribution $P(z \mid \hat{y})$, which results from shortening the context, can also be obtained as the marginal distribution of the joint distribution $P(y, z \mid \hat{y})$. The more general distribution $q(z \mid y)$ is then given by

$$q(z \mid y) = \frac{d_{1+}(\cdot\hat{y}z)}{d_{1+}(\cdot\hat{y}\cdot)} = \frac{d_{1+}(\cdot\hat{y}z)}{\sum_{z'} d_{1+}(\cdot\hat{y}z')} \tag{6.9}$$

In the second derivation, which applies the principle of *leaving-one-out*—a special technique of parameter estimation by means of cross validation (cf. [206] or [71])—a similar formula for the computation of $q(\cdot)$ is obtained:

$$q(z \mid y) = \frac{d_1(\cdot\hat{y}z)}{d_1(\cdot\hat{y}\cdot)} = \frac{d_1(\cdot\hat{y}z)}{\sum_{z'} d_1(\cdot\hat{y}z')} \tag{6.10}$$

Thus in the first case $q(z \mid y)$ is proportional to the number of different contexts $\hat{y}$ in which the word z to be predicted is occurring. From these contexts only those are considered in the expression (6.10) determined by leaving-one-out in which z was observed *exactly once*. In general, the quantity $d_1(\cdot\hat{y}z)$ also accounts for a significant portion of the total number of different contexts $d_{1+}(\cdot\hat{y}z)$ so that the two possibilities for the choice of $q(\cdot)$ do not differ substantially. In practical applications, however, often situations occur in which $d_1(\cdot\hat{y}z)$ vanishes for certain words. This is the case if these words that usually occur quite frequently in the training data were always observed more than once in their respective contexts. Therefore, Eq. (6.9) is better suited for the robust estimation of optimized generalized distributions as the probability estimates obtained never vanish.

Though the principle of determining more general distributions for n-gram models in an optimal way is immediately convincing, the advantages of the method are rather small in practice.

For the derivation of Eqs. (6.9) and (6.10) the authors in fact rely on backing off. However, significant improvements in the modeling quality are only obtained in practice with the proposed smoothing technique if it is combined with non-linear interpolation.[6] This behavior is quite plausible as in backing off the more general distribution is used for the evaluation of unseen events only. Therefore, its optimization has a noticeable effect only if a large number of unseen events occurs in the test set. This means, however, that the n-gram model being used is rather unsuitable for the task which will rarely happen in practice. In contrast, with non-linear interpolation the more general distribution is *always* incorporated into the probability computations and, therefore, has a significantly greater effect on the modeling quality.

The possible improvements are, however, obtained with an extremely high computational effort. Already for tri-gram models this effort by far dominates the other computations necessary for building the model. The reason for this behavior is the repeated evaluation of expressions of the form $d_k(\cdot yz)$. These counts cannot be determined locally due to the leading joker symbol. Rather, always all contexts xy have to be taken into account which makes searching a large portion of the stored count data necessary.

6.6   Model Variants

Besides the "classical" definition of n-gram models also several variants of the basic concept were proposed in the literature. In general, these try to overcome limitations or deficiencies of the standard formalism.

6.6.1   Category-Based Models

The most well known variant of the n-gram technique tries to exploit the fact that natural languages alongside a syntagmatic structure exhibit a paradigmatic structure, too. This means that in different linguistic contexts not only a certain word but a whole group of words or phrases can occur likewise. In every case one obtains a syntactically well formed utterance even if its meaning will, in general, be altered by such an exchange.

Thus in the sentence *"I moved to Dortmund seven years ago"* the city name could be replaced by an arbitrary one as, e.g., *Los Angeles* or *Paris*. Additionally the number could, in principle, be varied arbitrarily and the respective unit of time might be exchanged, too. But also in many other positions paradigmatic replacements could be made.

When trying to capture such a situation with an n-gram model, one will notice that all possible combinations need to occur at least once in the sample set considered. Still no paradigmatic rules can be represented in an abstract way. In order to make, for example, the occurrence of city names equally probable in all relevant contexts *all* these names would need to be observed in the respective context.

---

[6]Inconsistently Kneser & Ney themselves use non-linear interpolation in order to demonstrate the potential of their smoothing technique in experimental evaluations [153].

Therefore, all words which should be exchangeable in a certain context are grouped to form a word class or *category*. Thus *Dortmund*, *Los Angeles*, and *Paris* would form the category of city names in our small example.

The language models extended in this way are referred to as *category-based n-gram models* or simply as *class n-grams* provided that the thematic context is unique. The categories used should comprise such words that—in the statistical sense—occur in similar contexts or generate comparable restrictions for the joint occurrence of other words or categories. Brown and colleagues describe this situation quite illustratively as follows [35, Sect. 3]:

> *Clearly, some words are similar to other words in their meaning and syntactic function. We would not be surprised to learn that the probability distribution of words in the vicinity of Thursday is very much like that for words in the vicinity of Friday. Of course, they will not be identical: we rarely hear someone say Thank God it's Thursday! or worry about Thursday the 13th.*

When using a categorial *n*-gram model for the computation of the probabilities of word sequences, the possible sequences of categories which might correspond to these must be taken into account. In principle, any sequence $C = C_1, C_2, \ldots, C_T$ of length T can be associated with a word sequence $w = w_1, w_2, \ldots, w_T$ with a certain probability $P(w_1, w_2, \ldots, w_T \mid C_1, C_2, \ldots, C_T)$ as the mapping of words to categories is not unique in general. The probability of the word sequence is then obtained as the marginal distribution over all possible category sequences of the same length:

$$
\begin{aligned}
P(w) &= P(w_1, w_2, \ldots, w_T) \\
&= \sum_{C_1, C_2, \ldots, C_T} P(w_1, w_2, \ldots, w_T, C_1, C_2, \ldots, C_T) \\
&= \sum_{C_1, C_2, \ldots, C_T} P(w_1, w_2, \ldots, w_T \mid C_1, C_2, \ldots, C_T) P(C_1, C_2, \ldots, C_T)
\end{aligned}
$$

As a first simplification one now defines the occurrence of a word at a specific position not to be dependent on the total sequence of categories but only on the respective corresponding element. The probability of the word sequence can then be rewritten as

$$
P(w_1, w_2, \ldots, w_T \mid C_1, C_2, \ldots, C_T) = \prod_{t=1}^{T} P(w_t \mid C_t)
$$

Furthermore one describes the joint probability of the category sequence by approximating it with an *n*-gram model:

$$
P(C_1, C_2, \ldots, C_T) \approx \prod_{t=1}^{T} P(C_t \mid C_{t-n+1}, \ldots, C_{t-1})
$$

The evaluation of a word sequence by means of a categorial language model restricted in this respect is then obtained according to

$$P(\boldsymbol{w}) \approx \sum_{C_1, C_2, \ldots, C_T} \prod_{t=1}^{T} P(w_t \mid C_t) P(C_t \mid C_{t-n+1}, \ldots, C_{t-1}) \qquad (6.11)$$

Furthermore, one obtains the following simplified computation rule if also the category n-gram model being used is restricted to consist of a bi-gram model only:

$$P(\boldsymbol{w}) \approx \sum_{C_1, C_2, \ldots, C_T} \prod_{t=1}^{T} P(w_t \mid C_t) P(C_t \mid C_{t-1}) \qquad (6.12)$$

The comparison with Eq. (5.6) immediately shows that this model is equivalent to a discrete HMM. The internal states of the model correspond to the categories and the outputs generated correspond to the words from a certain lexicon. Unfortunately, this also means that the evaluation of the model is substantially more expensive than in the case of an "ordinary" n-gram model. For the latter only the multiplication of a sequence of conditional probabilities is necessary. For a categorial bi-gram model, however, the probability of a word sequence can be computed only by means of the forward algorithm. Nevertheless, this means a significant improvement in efficiency when compared to the general formulation of a categorial n-gram model in Eq. (6.11) where in principle category sequences of arbitrary length are allowed as contexts.

The most dramatic reduction in the evaluation effort of categorial n-gram models is achieved by the use of strictly disjoint categories. Then a unique mapping between the word and the corresponding category sequence is possible. Equation (6.11) can then be further simplified to

$$P(\boldsymbol{w}) \approx \prod_{t=1}^{T} P(w_t \mid C_t) P(C_t \mid C_{t-n+1}, \ldots, C_{t-1}) \qquad (6.13)$$

The main advantage of categorial models lies in the fact that they require a significantly smaller number of parameters as opposed to "ordinary" word-based n-gram models. Therefore, they can be estimated robustly even on limited training material and promise improved generalization capabilities on unknown data provided that the paradigmatic conditions were captured sufficiently well.

A "conventional" n-gram model is, however, always superior to a categorial model if large amounts of training material are available. Therefore, category-based n-gram models are often used as a supplement to an existing word-based model only. They then serve the purpose to provide robust estimates for the more general distributions required for which it is the primary concern to define useful probabilities for rare or completely unobserved events (cf. e.g. [216, 268]).

However, the need to specify a suitable category system makes the application of categorial models substantially more difficult. In some domains which are also analyzed on a syntactic-semantic level the linguistic categories lend themselves to be used directly for the purpose of language modeling (cf. e.g. [215]). However, methods for automatically determining a suitable category system on the basis of a sample set only are more powerful in general but also significantly more costly (cf. e.g. [35, 154, 215]).

6.6.2   Longer Temporal Dependencies

The most important limitation in the modeling capabilities of n-gram language models results from the fact that only rather short contexts of usually no more than two or three predecessor words can be taken into account in practice. The training sets usually available are not sufficient to robustly estimate parameters of more complex models. Therefore, a number of methods was proposed in the literature which allow to capture longer context dependencies while at the same time achieving a reduced model complexity.

In so-called long-distance bi-grams pairs of words are considered in certain predefined distances. In this way language models are created which are similar to bi-gram models from a computational point of view. The total model results from a linear combination of the component models [124]. A similar principle is also applied by the so-called distance tri-grams where word triplets are generated by skipping one context word at a time [193].

The methods presented above represent techniques for explicitly capturing longer contextual restrictions within a statistical language model. A quite different approach is pursued by methods that try to adapt an existing model in a suitable way to a concrete textual or thematic context, respectively. Some methods of this group of techniques will be described in the view of model adaptation in Sect. 11.3.

6.7   Bibliographical Remarks

Markov chain models originated from the work of the Russian mathematician Andrej Andrejewitsch Markov (1856–1922), after whom they were also named. He used such a modeling the first time for the statistical analysis of the character sequences in the text of "Eugene Onegin", a novel in verse by Alexander Sergeyevich Pushkin [190]. In the mathematical technical literature mainly theoretical aspects of Markov chain models are covered. Their practical application occurs primarily in the field of automatic speech recognition or the statistical modeling of texts, respectively, where the models are referred to as *n-gram* or *language models*.

A very thorough treatment of the topic can be found in the monograph by Huang, Acero & Hon [123, pp. 558–590]. In contrast, the treatment of language models in [136] is strongly limited to the author's view on the topic. Bell *et al.* describe *n*-gram models in the context of text compression [17]. A compact introduction to the subject is given in the article by Federico *et al.* [77]. Especially the historical perspective on the development of techniques for language modeling is covered by Rosenfeld [256].

Stochastic grammars, which in the same way as n-gram models can be used for the statistical description of sequencing constraints in symbol chains or texts, respectively, are, e.g., described in [123, pp. 554–558]. An overview of language modeling techniques in general can be found in [123, Chap. 11, pp. 545–553] or [229, p. 417].

The probably oldest method for removing vanishing probability estimates of unobserved events is *adding one* (cf. e.g. [77], "Method A" in [319], "Jeffrey's estimate" in [205]). The method which is also referred to as *Laplace's rule* is, however, applied in the analysis of biological sequences [67, p. 108,115]. Considerably better model parameters are obtained by *interpolation methods* which date back to works by Jelinek & Mercer ([138], cf. also [135] or [136, S. 62ff]). Ney, Essen & Kneser proposed the use of *non-linear interpolation* [205]. The principle of *backing off* was developed by Katz [148].

The gathering of the probability mass required can be performed by means of *linear discounting* ([148], cf. also [77, 206]) or *absolute discounting* ("Method B" in [319], [205, 206]). A method for the optimization of the more general distributions required for both backing off and interpolation was developed by Kneser & Ney [153]. Comparisons of different smoothing techniques can be found in Federico et al. [77] and also in Chen & Goodman [42, 43] where extensive experimental evaluations are reported.

Category-based n-gram models are, for example, described in [35] or [123, pp. 565–570].

Part II
Practice

Introductory Remarks

The theoretical foundations of Markov models were introduced in Chaps. 3, 4, 5 and 6 of the preceding part of this book. Though they are extremely important for the conceptional understanding of the properties of HMMs and n-gram models, they are not sufficient for realizing working implementations of these techniques and systems that are successful in real-world applications. For this purpose, additionally know-how related to practical aspects is necessary. In spite of its great importance, the presentation of these aspects is usually disregarded in the literature. Jelinek proceeds in a especially extreme way with respect to practical aspects in his monograph on statistical methods for speech recognition. Right at the beginning he clarifies in a remark [136, p. 11]:

> As presented here, the algorithm contains the idea's essence. In practice, [. . .], many refinements are necessary that are the results of intensive experimentation. [. . .] This is the case with the vast majority of algorithms presented in this book: We describe the basic idea that must then be worked out in practice.

Especially from a pioneer of automatic speech recognition and of statistical methods in the field of pattern analysis, one would have expected more than such a disappointing statement.

In contrast to that, we want to put an emphasis of this book on the practical applications of Markov model technology. Therefore, in the following chapters, essential aspects of HMMs and n-gram models relevant in practice will be covered. In addition to a theoretical understanding of the underlying concepts, the reader will thus be enabled to realize his own applications of the techniques presented.

At the beginning, methods will be presented for the numerically stable handling of probabilities which are ubiquitous when dealing with Markov models. Chapter 8 is dedicated to the challenging problem of configuring Markov models, i.e., the choice of a suitable model architecture. Different methods for robust parameter estimation which are especially relevant for complex models are presented in Chap. 9. In Chap. 10, efficient algorithms for model utilization are described. Additionally, techniques are presented which achieve a gain in efficiency in practical applications by a reorganization of the models' representation. The topic of Chap. 11 is the adaptation of models to the operating conditions which will, in general, be different from the ones of the training phase. Especially for hidden Markov models, such methods have gained increased importance lately. In the last chapter of the part on practical aspects of Markov models several methods for integrated search are presented which make the joint use of HMMs and n-gram models for challenging tasks possible.

In general, methods from *all* topics mentioned above are implemented in a successful recognition system based on Markov models be it for spoken language or handwritten script. In contrast, methods for model adaptation, integration of n-gram models, and the robust estimation of continuous distributions hardly play a role in the analysis of biological sequences.

Computations with Probabilities

At first sight the handling of probability values in real computing systems seems to be a trivial problem as the range of values of these quantities is limited to the interval $[0.0 \ldots 1.0]$. Nevertheless, problems arise especially in longer computational procedures as *extremely small* values lying close to zero need to be represented and manipulated.

The following simple example illustrates that such nearly vanishing probability values can appear easily in computations for Markov models. Let us consider the computation of the probability $P(s|\lambda)$ of a state sequence $s = s_1, s_2, \ldots, s_T$ for a given model λ. It is performed by multiplying all transition probabilities involved (cf. Eq. (5.5)):

$$P(s|\lambda) = \prod_{t=1}^{T} a_{s_{t-1}, s_t}$$

Let us furthermore consider a simple model structure—only two successors per state—and a trivial parametrization—uniformly initialized transition probabilities, i.e., all a_{ij} are equal to 0.5. In this situation it can easily be verified that already from a length of the observation sequence of $T > 100$ onwards numerical values smaller than $5 \cdot 10^{-100}$ are obtained for $P(s|\lambda)$ which can hardly be represented in today's digital computers.[1] And yet in these considerations strongly simplifying assumptions were made which will never be met in reality. Additionally, in usual situations the handling of considerably longer observation sequences will be required as $T = 100$ in automatic speech recognition usually corresponds to utterances of

---

[1]On virtually all modern computer architectures, floating-point numbers are represented in formats which were standardized in the framework of the ANSI/IEEE standard 854 [130]. When considering the absolute value only, single precision numbers can be represented in the range of approximately $3.4 \cdot 10^{38}$ to $1.4 \cdot 10^{-45}$ and such with double precision in the range of $1.8 \cdot 10^{308}$ to $4.9 \cdot 10^{-324}$.

G.A. Fink, *Markov Models for Pattern Recognition*,
Advances in Computer Vision and Pattern Recognition,
DOI 10.1007/978-1-4471-6308-4_7, © Springer-Verlag London 2014

one second in length[2] and in handwriting recognition of only a few consecutive characters. Furthermore, scores for partial paths also include output probabilities or probability densities which themselves tend to become quite small numerically.

Therefore, it is extremely important for the practical use of Markov models to be able to effectively counteract the phenomenon of de facto vanishing probabilities. In order to do so, the most important mechanism is an improved numerical representation of these quantities. In addition, probabilities may be limited to suitable lower bounds algorithmically, if necessary.

7.1   Logarithmic Probability Representation

The probably oldest method for improving the dynamic range of probability values in computations consists in scaling these appropriately (cf. [251], [125, pp. 241–242]). Unfortunately, this is only possible locally as especially in longer computations the occurring quantities tend more and more to extremely small probability values. As a consequence, the necessary scaling factors need to be determined for every normalization operation anew which makes the method extremely costly and error prone.

Therefore, the representation of probabilities on a negative-logarithmic scale has become the method of choice for handling even extremely small probability values (cf. [125, pp. 243–244]). Instead of using the real probability or density values p in computations, the following transformation is applied to them:

$$\tilde{p} = -\log_b p \qquad\qquad (7.1)$$

After this transformation the probability values, which were combined in a multiplicative way before, can be interpreted as additive costs.

The choice of the base b of the logarithm used has no noticeable influence on the representational possibilities. In practice the natural logarithm to base e is mostly used for this purpose as it makes an additional simplification of the evaluation of normal densities possible (cf. Sect. 3.6.1). Furthermore, also in virtually all standard computing libraries efficient implementations of the natural logarithm and its inverse are available as log() and exp(), respectively. Therefore, we will use the pair of functions $\ln x = \log_e x$ and e^x for the transformation of probability values to and from the logarithmic domain in the following.

This transformation maps the original range of values $[0.0 \ldots 1.0]$ for probabilities to the entire non-negative floating-point numbers that can be represented. As density values can also become larger than 1.0—though only in rather rare cases in practice—their logarithmic representation comprises principally even the whole dynamic range of floating-point numbers. The resolution of the negative-logarithmic

---

[2]Feature vectors are extracted from the speech signal with a spacing of 10 ms in virtually all current speech recognition systems.

representation is limited though due to the limited precision of today's floating-point formats. However, the accuracy is sufficient for the practical application of the method.

In order to be able to fully exploit the advantages of the logarithmic representation, it is necessary to carry out all computations on probabilities as consistently as possible in the logarithmic domain. This is achieved easily as long as only multiplications and maximizations are involved in the calculations. Let us consider, for example, the formula for computing the partial path probabilities $\delta_{t+1}(i)$ in the Viterbi algorithm (cf. Eq. (5.9)). It is transformed from

$$\delta_{t+1}(j) = \max_i\{\delta_t(i)a_{ij}\}b_j(O_{t+1})$$

in linear, i.e., "normal" probability representation, into

$$\tilde{\delta}_{t+1}(j) = \min_i\{\tilde{\delta}_t(i) + \tilde{a}_{ij}\} + \tilde{b}_j(O_{t+1})$$

when using the negative-logarithmic representation. The computational effort required it, therefore, not affected by the transformation.

However, if computations with probability quantities require summations, it is considerably more complex to carry them out in the logarithmic domain. In the most unfavorable of situations, it would be necessary to convert the quantities $\tilde{p}_1$ and $\tilde{p}_2$ involved to the linear domain, add their linear representations, and finally transform the result back to the logarithmic domain again:

$$\tilde{p}_1 +_{\log} \tilde{p}_2 = -\ln\left(e^{-\tilde{p}_1} + e^{-\tilde{p}_2}\right)$$

This operation is not only extremely costly but also will almost cancel out the advantages of the log-domain representation. The so-called *Kingsbury–Rayner formula* ([150], see also [169, p. 29]) addresses both the issue of computational complexity and of numerical precision:

$$\tilde{p}_1 +_{\log} \tilde{p}_2 = -\ln(p_1 + p_2) = -\ln\left(p_1\left(1 + \frac{p_2}{p_1}\right)\right)$$
$$= -\left\{\ln p_1 + \ln\left(1 + e^{\ln p_2 - \ln p_1}\right)\right\}$$
$$= \tilde{p}_1 - \ln\left(1 + e^{-(\tilde{p}_2 - \tilde{p}_1)}\right) \tag{7.2}$$

The obvious effect of Eq. (7.2) is that only one exponentiation is required as opposed to the naive computation scheme. In addition, instead of converting both log-domain probabilities back to the linear representation, this is only necessary for their ratio, i.e., their difference in the logarithmic representation. If this difference is small,

Relation Between Linear and Log-Domain Probability Representations
When transforming all probability values from their linear representation p
into a log-domain representation $\tilde{p}$ according to

$$\tilde{p} = -\ln p$$

all further computations have to be adjusted appropriately. The following table gives an overview over the most important mathematical operations and
constants used in probability computations and how they are related between
linear and log-domain representations.

Linear Representation	Log-domain Representation
p	$\tilde{p} = -\ln p$
0	∞
1	0
min	max
max	min
$p \cdot q$	$\tilde{p} + \tilde{q}$
$p + q, \quad p > q$	$\tilde{p} - \ln(1 + e^{-(\tilde{p}-\tilde{q})}), \quad \tilde{p} < \tilde{q}$

representing it in the linear domain is not harmful. If it becomes large, however, the
computation can be avoided altogether as then the term $e^{-(\tilde{p}_2-\tilde{p}_1)}$ will vanish and
the result of the summation can be approximated by the larger of the arguments p_1
and p_2, respectively.[3]

Even though the Kingsbury–Rayner formula requires considerable effort for
computing a log-domain probability sum, it offers the advantage that sequences of
computations involving summations of probability values can be carried out in the
logarithmic domain in an integrated manner and with sufficient precision.[4] The forward and backward variables $\alpha_t(i)$ and $\beta_t(j)$ (cf. Eqs. (5.7) and (5.13) and Fig. 5.6)
and also the probability sums for the normalization of n-gram scores (cf. Eq. (6.8))
can be calculated with sufficient accuracy by applying the method of Kingsbury &
Rayner. The observable loss in efficiency in the training phase of a model constitutes a negligible limitation only compared to the extension of the dynamic range
achieved.

---

[3]In log-domain representations this will correspond to picking the smaller of $\tilde{p}_1$ and $\tilde{p}_2$.

[4]The precision of the "logarithmic summation" can be improved further if a function for directly
computing $\ln(1 + x)$ also for small x is used, e.g., the function `log1p()` available in the standard
C-library.

However, the evaluation of output probability density functions described by mixture models requires the summation over all component densities even when decoding the model (cf. Eq. (5.1)):

$$b_j(\boldsymbol{x}) = \sum_{k=1}^{M} c_{jk}\, g_{jk}(\boldsymbol{x})$$

In this case the application of the "logarithmic summation" after Eq. (7.2) is not advisable as per density computation M exponentiations and M computations of the logarithm are necessary in addition to the computational effort in the linear domain.[5] In order to avoid this considerable increase in computational complexity, the output probability density $b_j(\boldsymbol{x})$ can be approximated by the respective maximum of the component densities with slightly reduced accuracy:

$$b_j(\boldsymbol{x}) \approx \max_{k}\{c_{jk}\, g_{jk}(\boldsymbol{x})\}$$

This approximation assumes that the maximum component within a mixture dominates the overall density, which is true in most practical situations. As this approximation of the mixture evaluation does not involve any summation, the computation of $\tilde{b}_j(\boldsymbol{x})$ can be performed completely in logarithmic representation:

$$\tilde{b}_j(\boldsymbol{x}) \approx \min_{k}\{\tilde{c}_{jk} + \tilde{g}_{jk}(\boldsymbol{x})\}$$

7.2 Lower Bounds for Probabilities

The logarithmic representation of probability values presented in the previous section can effectively transfer numerically vanishing quantities into a range of values that can be safely manipulated by digital computers. However, if *real* zeros appear in computations—for example probabilities of unobserved events—these would need to be mapped to the largest representable positive floating-point number.[6] Such values then dominate all computation processes in which they are used in the same way as the equivalent quantities in the linear representation. This effectively creates situations where states or state sequences can no longer be part of any solution if a single vanishing probability occurred during their evaluation.

In general, such a behavior is not desired in statistical models, however. Similarly to the creation of statistical language models (cf. Sect. 6.5), it can never be safely assumed that a probability computed to be zero and the associated final rejection of

---

[5]This problem does not arise in the usual decoding of semi-continuous HMMs. When replacing density values of individual mixtures by class posterior probabilities (cf. Sect. 7.3), the resulting quantities can safely be manipulated in the linear domain.

[6]When applying Eq. (7.1) in a naive way, even an error in the floating-point computation would result.

certain solutions are reliable enough. Rather, it always has to be ensured that probability values never fall below a certain minimal value p_{min}. In negative-logarithmic representation this means to use a respective maximal value $\tilde{p}_{max} = -\ln p_{min}$. Such a lower bound is also referred to as the *floor* and the associated procedure as *flooring*.

Flooring can—and should—be applied in all situations where a safe and moderately strict lower bound on the expected quantities can be defined which is usually the case for transition or output probabilities. Whenever this is not possible, no absolute limitation should be introduced. This is, for example, the case if scores of paths through HMMs or n-gram models are computed that grow depending on the length of the path considered. In this case, one rather relies on the fact that the use of suitably limited component scores in combination with the increased dynamic range of the logarithmic representation will ensure the computability and comparability of the overall results. In practice this assumption is de facto justified as concrete observation or word sequences are always of finite length and, therefore, only a finite number of partial scores will be accumulated.

The limitation of $b_j(x) > b_{min}$ already proposed in [251] causes two effects in the practical application. During the training phase of the model, it is avoided that certain states are not considered for parameter estimation, the current parameters of which are still totally unsuitable for the generation of certain observations. In decoding the limitation avoids that paths through states with vanishing output probabilities are immediately discarded as possible solutions. A principally similar effect can be achieved by limiting the mixture weights according to $c_{jk} > c_{min}$.

Though this so-called flooring is a mandatory measure for the robust application of Markov models, it has the crucial disadvantage that the necessary bounds need to be determined heuristically and, therefore, in general also need to be optimized in the context of the application. Furthermore, always interactions with methods for the limitation of the search space arise as those try to eliminate less promising solutions from the search space early.

7.3   Codebook Evaluation for Semi-continuous HMMs

When using semi-continuous HMMs, a special method for the evaluation of the densities within the commonly shared codebook has proven useful in practice. It can essentially be viewed as a technique for reducing the dynamic range of the quantities involved.

The output probability densities $b_j(x)$ of semi-continuous HMMs are defined as mixture densities over a common inventory of component densities (cf. Eq. (5.2)):

$$b_j(x) = \sum_{k=1}^{M} c_{jk} g_k(x) = \sum_{k=1}^{M} c_{jk} p(x|\omega_k)$$

The individual component densities $g_k(x)$ therein correspond to the class-conditional densities $p(x|\omega_k)$ of the features depending on the codebook classes ω_k. Using Bayes' rule this quantity can be related to the posterior probability $P(\omega_k|\boldsymbol{x})$ of the respective class:

$$p(\boldsymbol{x}|\omega_k)P(\omega_k) = p(\boldsymbol{x},\omega_k) = P(\omega_k|\boldsymbol{x})p(\boldsymbol{x})$$

In this expression still neither the prior probabilities $P(\omega_k)$ of the codebook classes nor the density $p(\boldsymbol{x})$ of the data itself is known. However, the fact can be exploited that in the semi-continuous modeling a global codebook is used. Ideally this should approximate reasonably well the distribution of all feature vectors—namely $p(\boldsymbol{x})$—with the baseline distributions contained therein. Therefore, $p(\boldsymbol{x})$ can be approximated by a mixture density as follows:

$$p(\boldsymbol{x}) \approx \sum_{m=1}^{M} P(\omega_m)p(\boldsymbol{x}|\omega_m)$$

When further assuming that the partitioning of the feature space into classes ω_k generates regions of high density of approximately equal size, the prior probabilities $P(\omega_k)$ can be approximated by a uniform distribution. The conditional probability $P(\omega_k|\boldsymbol{x})$ of a class ω_k can then be computed depending on the feature vectors $\boldsymbol{x}$ as follows:

$$P(\omega_k|\boldsymbol{x}) = \frac{p(\boldsymbol{x}|\omega_k)P(\omega_k)}{p(\boldsymbol{x})} \approx \frac{p(\boldsymbol{x}|\omega_k)P(\omega_k)}{\sum_{m=1}^{M} P(\omega_m)p(\boldsymbol{x}|\omega_m)} \approx \frac{p(\boldsymbol{x}|\omega_k)}{\sum_{m=1}^{M} p(\boldsymbol{x}|\omega_m)}$$

In practice this corresponds to a scaling of the density values $p(\boldsymbol{x}|\omega_k)$ such that they sum up to unity—a normalization operation which is widely used in the application of semi-continuous HMMs [125, p. 200]. The definition of the output probabilities is then achieved on the basis of the posterior probabilities of the codebook classes:

$$b'_j(\boldsymbol{x}) = \sum_{k=1}^{M} c_{jk} P(\omega_k|\boldsymbol{x}) = \sum_{k=1}^{M} c_{jk} \frac{p(\boldsymbol{x}|\omega_k)}{\sum_{m=1}^{M} p(\boldsymbol{x}|\omega_m)}$$

Therefore, the semi-continuous model can directly be considered as the combination of a "soft" vector quantization stage, which computes probabilistic class memberships $P(\omega_k|\boldsymbol{x})$, and a discrete HMM with output probabilities $b_j(\omega_k)$ that correspond to mixture weights c_{jk}.

7.4 Probability Ratios

When decoding HMMs for biological sequences, often a modification of the computation of output probabilities is performed. The output probability $b_j(o_k)$ for the symbol o_k in state j given by the model is normalized onto a suitable background distribution which is identical for all states:

$$b'_j(o_k) = \frac{b_j(o_k)}{P(o_k)}$$

In the simplest case $P(o_k)$ is assumed as a random model, i.e., as a uniform distribution over all K possible symbols of the output alphabet:

$$b'_j(o_k) \approx \frac{b_j(o_k)}{\frac{1}{K}}$$

One obtains a modified probability $P'(O, s|\lambda)$ for the generation of the sequence $O_1, O_2, \ldots, O_T$ considered and jointly running through a certain state sequence $s_1, s_2, \ldots, s_t$ for a given model λ (see also Eq. (5.6), page 79):

$$P'(O, s|\lambda) = \prod_{t=1}^{T} a_{s_{t-1}, s_t} \frac{b_{s_t}(O_t)}{P(O_t)} = \prod_{t=1}^{T} \frac{1}{P(O_t)} \prod_{t=1}^{T} a_{s_{t-1}, s_t} b_{s_t}(O_t) = \frac{P(O, s|\lambda)}{\prod_{t=1}^{T} P(O_t)}$$

The normalization of the original output probabilities $b_j(o_k)$ onto a background distribution causes a non-linear length normalization of the path score $P'(O, s|\lambda)$. If only a random model is used, one obtains a linear length normalization by a factor of $(\frac{1}{K})^T$.

In the logarithmic probability representation, which is also used in the analysis of biological sequences, the actual score for the output of a symbol o_k in state j is computed as follows:

$$\tilde{b}'_j(o_k) = \ln \frac{b_j(o_k)}{P(o_k)} = \ln b_j(o_k) - \ln P(o_k) \tag{7.3}$$

The procedure is referred to as *log-odds scoring* in the literature (cf. [160], [67, pp. 108–110]). This normalization step ensures that the scores of the optimal state sequence determined for different biological sequences can be compared directly. Otherwise these would vary largely depending on the length of the observation sequence considered and, consequently, could not constitute a useful basis for a classification decision.

Frequently, the reliability of such a classification needs to be determined on the basis of a single sequence only. Then, a rejection criterion can easily be defined using log-odds scoring. In principle, the approach corresponds to the use of a very general separate HMM—a so-called *garbage model*—for modeling all the observation sequences to be expected. If this model achieves a higher total probability than the model associated with a special class of patterns, a rejection is performed.

In the field of automatic speech recognition the use of garbage models can be found for the detection of unknown words. There a general HMM for sequences of arbitrary speech sounds of the language considered is created in addition to the models for words from the recognition lexicon. If this garbage model achieves the best score for a certain acoustic event, it can be assumed that this part-of-speech was not sufficiently well described by the models of the "known" words and, therefore, is not part of the recognition lexicon—in other words it is "unknown" (cf. [6, 119, 143, 327]).

Configuration of Hidden Markov Models

8

The vital configuration parameters for n-gram language models are given by the size of the lexicon used and the length of the context to be considered. In contrast, when creating HMMs for a certain application, it is not immediately clear what model size should be chosen, which type of output modeling should be used, and whether the number of possible paths through the model could possibly be restricted in a suitable way.

8.1 Model Topologies

In the main application areas of HMM-based modeling—automatic speech and handwriting recognition as well as the analysis of biological sequences—the input data to be processed exhibits a chronological or sequential structure. Therefore, it does not make sense for such applications to allow arbitrary state transitions within an HMM as it is the case for so-called *ergodic* models (see Fig. 8.1(d)).

Rather, one assumes that the models are run through in causal chronological sequence and, therefore, the model states can be arranged sequentially. Transition probabilities to states that describe data segments lying backwards in time are constantly set to zero. In graphical representations of HMMs, such edges which are excluded from possible state sequences are omitted for the purpose of simplification.

The most simple model topology that can be derived from this assumption is found in the so-called *linear* HMMs. As shown schematically in Fig. 8.1(a), in these models only transitions to the respective next state and to the current state itself are possible with some positive probability. With the help of the self-transitions or *loops* the model is able to capture variations in the temporal extension of the patterns described.

A larger flexibility in the modeling of duration is achieved if the skipping of individual states within a sequence is possible, too. When adding skips to the linear topology one obtains so-called *Bakis* models. This topology, which is widely used in the field of automatic speech and handwriting recognition, is exemplarily depicted

G.A. Fink, *Markov Models for Pattern Recognition*,
Advances in Computer Vision and Pattern Recognition,
DOI 10.1007/978-1-4471-6308-4_8, © Springer-Verlag London 2014

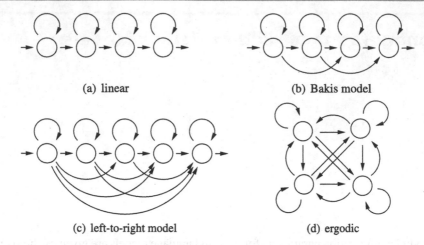

Fig. 8.1 Schematic representation of different HMM topologies: (**a**) linear model, (**b**) Bakis model, (**c**) left-to-right model, and (**d**) completely connected structure of an ergodic model

in Fig. 8.1(b). When modeling acoustic events, it is desirable that articulatory reductions caused by mutual influences between neighboring segments can be described. Bakis models offer this possibility to some limited extent as they allow the omission of short portions of a signal in its statistical description.

Larger variations in the temporal structure of the data can be described by so-called *left-to-right* models. In this model topology, which is shown in Fig. 8.1(c), longer parts of the data to be processed may be missing as an arbitrary number of states may be skipped in forward direction within a sequence. Only jumping back to "past" states within a model is not allowed.

The more flexibly the model topology is chosen the more parameters are to be trained and the more variable the possible paths through the model are, too. Therefore, the choice of a certain baseline topology always represents a compromise between flexibility and tractability. However, not only the parameter training becomes more difficult for larger numbers of successors per model state but also the effort in decoding is increased. Consequently, linear models undoubtedly represent the most efficient model topology. In contrast, the best compromise between number of parameters, decoding cost, and flexibility is offered by Bakis models which are used in many of today's recognition systems (see also Part III).

8.2   Modularization

In the theoretical view on HMMs, always exactly one model λ with N states exists which is considered as a unit. In practice it is, however, hardly possible to specify non-trivial models directly without any suitable measures of modularization. The most obvious possibility for structuring larger HMMs is based on the segmentation units that are considered in the respective application domain. In the field of speech or handwriting recognition these usually are spoken or written words from a certain language.[1] As will be shown in the next section, complex models for spoken utterances or written texts can be constructed on this basis.

In principle, an individual word model can be created directly with one of the topologies presented in the previous section. However, when following this approach, the problem arises that for every model as a whole sufficiently many training samples need to be available. For a system intended for the recognition of isolated digits or a few command words only, a suitable sample set could probably be created. However, for recognition systems with large vocabularies, such a whole-word modeling is totally infeasible.

Therefore, it is necessary to consider a further modularization of the segmentation units considered by a suitable reuse of partial models in order to assure the trainability of the parameters of the overall model. At the same time, one obtains an HMM which is considerably more compact with respect to the number of independent parameters used (see also Sect. 9.2). As this technique was developed and brought to perfection in the field of speech recognition, the resulting elementary models which describe certain segments of words are also referred to as *sub-word units*.

Many different methods for the definition of sub-word units have been developed. The solutions found are frequently based on principles that are quite specific to the application considered. Therefore, we do not attempt to give a complete overview of the proposed approaches here. Rather, in the following sections, methods shall be described that are applicable in a relatively general way. For the more detailed treatment of the topic the interested reader is referred to the associated specialized literature and the references given therein (cf. e.g. [169, Chap. 6, pp. 91–114], [136, Chap. 3, pp. 39–56], [123, pp. 428–439]).

8.2.1 Context-Independent Sub-word Units

The most simple methods for the definition of sub-word units are based on the segmentation of words into a sequence of short segments. It is most natural to use their orthographic representation for this purpose. One then obtains a segmentation into a sequence of characters which is used for defining sub-word units in many systems for automatic handwriting recognition. In the field of speech recognition, however, it makes sense to start from a phonetic transcription of the words considered. The symbolically represented sequence of speech sounds associated with a word gives a relatively good indication of its actual realization as an acoustic event.[2]

---

[1] When analyzing biological sequences a somewhat different philosophy is followed in structuring HMMs. The most important of those techniques are described in Sect. 8.4.

[2] Even in the field of automatic speech recognition satisfactory results can be achieved based on an orthographic modeling of words [269, 273] in case that no phonetic transcription is available or its generation causes too much effort.

In both cases one obtains a quite compact inventory of approximately 50 to 100 units[3] which is ideally suited for the construction of arbitrary written or spoken words and, therefore, can be used quite universally.[4] However, the accuracy of such a modeling is rather low in comparison as the realizations of the individual units are heavily influenced by their context and, consequently, may vary largely in their concrete realizations.

The correct number of states for context-independent phone or character units results from the length of the associated signal segments to be expected. Furthermore, in linear topology the number of model states corresponds to the minimal length of possible events as all states have to be passed through exactly once. Thus for speech recognition applications one obtains three to six states and up to approximately 15 for character models in handwriting recognition.

8.2.2 Context-Dependent Sub-word Units

The main drawback of simple phone or character models lies in the fact that they can not capture sufficiently the variability of the units described which results from their embedding in different contexts. In the early days of automatic speech recognition one tried to tackle this problem among others by using longer sub-word units or by defining segment boundaries between partial models in regions of the signal which were assumed to be approximately stationary (cf. e.g. [169, pp. 93–94]). A very elegant method for defining sub-word units that became a standard procedure meanwhile consists in discriminating elementary units simply depending on their respective contexts. However, the context itself is not included in the acoustic event modeled. Thus one obtains so-called *context-dependent sub-word units*.

The most prominent representatives of this kind of models are the so-called *triphones* which date back to work of Schwartz and colleagues at BBN ([277, 278], cf. also [169, pp. 95–96]). They correspond to phone units in the context of the left and right immediately neighboring speech sound. Consequently, three phone symbols are necessary to uniquely define a triphone. In the same way as a *monophone*—i.e. a context-independent phone model—a triphone thus describes the realization of only a *single* speech sound, however, of a very special one.

---

[3]For English one uses approximately 45 different phonetic units depending on the basis of definition. For German the size of the inventory ranges from 40 to 50. In character or handwriting recognition, models for all characters of the alphabet—in upper and lower case, if necessary—and for digits have to be created for most languages. Therefore, one obtains 62 elementary models for English and 69 for German including the umlauts.

[4]For character or handwriting recognition, the inventory of character and digit models needs to be complemented by HMMs for punctuation symbols and white space. In speech recognition systems, it is likewise indispensable to define a model for speech pauses. Furthermore, it may make sense to use additional models for human and non-human noises, hesitations, and other spontaneous speech effects in challenging applications (cf. e.g. [274]).

We want to illustrate the resulting triphone modeling with the example of the word `speech`. In its phonetic transcription this word corresponds to the symbol sequence `/spitS/` when using the SAMPA alphabet (cf. [303]). Without the consideration of the context, the necessary model for the speech sound `/i/` would not be distinguished from occurrences in, e.g., `achieve` (`/@tSiv/`), `cheese` (`/tSiz/`), or `reality`(`/riEl@ti/`). The corresponding triphone `p/i/t`, however, restricts the use of this model quite exactly to the respective phonetic context.

The basic idea of triphone modeling can be generalized in different ways. In the case that one wants to describe contexts in even more detail, this can be achieved by specifying a larger number of context phones. Principally arbitrarily long contexts are allowed in the so-called *polyphones* [272]. Two left and right context phones each are considered by so-called *quinphones* as they are, e.g., used in the speech recognition system BYBLOS (cf. [20], see also Sect. 13.2).

The main advantage of context-dependent models, namely their high degree of specialization achieved, also represents their main disadvantage. When starting from an inventory of approximately 50 phonetic units, one obtains a set of $125,000$ potential triphones. Even if not all of these phone combinations can actually occur in the data, it is nevertheless hardly possible in practice to supply a sufficient amount of training material for each of these highly specialized models. Therefore, comparable models or similar model parameters need to be grouped together in order to ensure the trainability. Different methods for achieving this will be presented in Sect. 9.2. In principle, these techniques always relax the context restrictions such that modeling units result that can be used more generally. When applying such a procedure to a baseline set of triphone models, one obtains *generalized triphones* ([169, pp. 103–106], [170], cf. also [123, pp. 432–436]).

Though context dependency is clearly an issue in any larger HMM architecture built on the basis of elementary units, it has to date only been applied extensively in the field of automatic speech recognition. In contrast, in automatic handwriting recognition context-dependent sub-word units have been used to a quite limited extent only. Most successfully they have been applied for the online recognition of handwriting (cf. [90, 158, 294]). The gains achieved for offline recognition of handwriting are, however, rather small still (cf. [87, 246]). This is most probably due to the fact that for this task the nature of the contextual influence that appears in the data can not be described as clearly yet [87].

8.3 Compound Models

When decomposing models for spoken or written words into a sequence of sub-word units, we implicitly assumed that more complex models can be created from existing partial HMMs by concatenation. Such construction principles are either explicitly or implicitly applied in order to define compound models for different recognition tasks. This principle is also the basis of Profile-HMMs which will be the topic of the following Sect. 8.4. However, due to their rather special nature these models will be described separately.

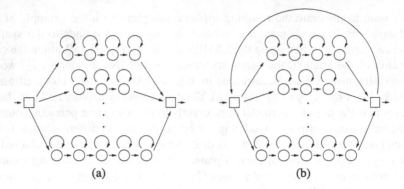

Fig. 8.2 Schematic representation of HMM structures for (**a**) isolated and (**b**) connected word recognition. Model states are represented by *circles* and non-emitting states by *squares*

In any lexicon-based recognition system, HMMs for the words contained in the recognition lexicon are usually created by concatenating the respective sub-word units. On this basis a total model for the recognition of isolated spoken or written words can be defined by a parallel connection of all individual word models. Figure 8.2(a) schematically shows the resulting model structure. All start and end states of the individual word models become start and end states of the total model. The representation of such complex HMMs can be considerably simplified by the introduction of so-called *non-emitting states*. These special states do not generate any outputs and have uniformly distributed transition probabilities to their respective successor states. In the compound model considered here, they serve the purpose of grouping together similar edges such that the simplified total HMM has only one start and end state.

In automatic speech recognition the importance of systems for isolated word recognition is constantly decreasing. In contrast, for the automatic processing of forms one can frequently assume that the writing contained in a certain field should correspond to exactly one word or phrase. Also in the recognition of machine-printed or handwritten texts, in many cases the text lines are first segmented into a sequence of words. Subsequently an HMM for the recognition of words typed or written in isolation can be applied.

However, for the recognition of continuously spoken speech, always arbitrary sequences of words have to be processed by the statistical model as no easy and reliable methods for segmenting continuously spoken utterances exist. When adding a looping edge to the isolated word recognition model that connects the end state of the model to the start state, a model structure results that is represented in Fig. 8.2(b). In order to restrict the search through such a model during decoding to plausible word sequences, usually an n-gram language model is used in addition to the HMM (see also Chap. 12).

In case that the word or segment sequences to be expected in a certain domain are heavily restricted or formalized, these can also be directly represented as a graph of partial HMMs (cf. [326]). Such a model architecture was first used successfully

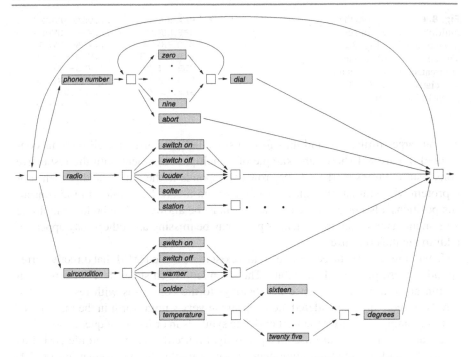

Fig. 8.3 Example of a grammar coded into the structure of an HMM that could be used by a speech recognition system for controlling non-safety-relevant functions in a car

in the speech recognition system HARPY [185]. Due to the inherent limitations of HMMs only regular languages can be captured in this way as the resulting total model also is just another HMM. Figure 8.3 shows the example of a simple grammar that is encoded within the HMM structure. A similar model might be used in luxury cars for the control of so-called non-safety-relevant vehicle functions by spoken language—e.g. mobile phone, radio, or air condition.

During the decoding of grammar HMMs only word sequences can be found that are valid in the respective domain. Therefore, such models have difficulties in rejecting invalid input. In contrast, the probabilistic restriction of potential word sequences by a language model is less vulnerable in this respect.

8.4 Profile HMMs

The most widely used HMM structure for applications in the domain of bioinformatics consists in the so-called *profile HMMs* proposed by Krogh and colleagues ([161], cf. also [67, 70]). The structuring of the models is directly derived from the data that forms the basis of the parameter training. Similarities between proteins are analyzed or represented, respectively, by a position-wise alignment of sequences of amino acids. One obtains so-called *multiple alignments* (see also Sect. 2.3 page 24). Within these the respective positions can be identified where different sequences

Fig. 8.4 Section from the
multiple alignment of seven
globins shown in Fig. 2.10.
The columns marked with *
are treated as matches in the
associated profile HMM
(after [67, p. 106])

HBA_HUMAN	...VGA--HAGEY...
HBB_HUMAN	...V----NVDEV...
MYG_PHYCA	...VEA--DVAGH...
GLB3_CHITP	...VKG------D...
GLB5_PETMA	...VYS--TYETS...
LGB2_LUPLU	...FNA--NIPKH...
GLB1_GLYDI	...IAGADNGAGV...
	*** *****

exhibit large similarities and thus form a so-called consensus for all proteins considered. Figure 8.4 shows an example of a multiple alignment with the respective consensus columns marked. Every row corresponds to the amino acid sequence of a protein with similar biological function within a cell. In addition to the consensus positions, also insertions and deletions must be allowed when building multiple alignments as in concrete sequences parts may be missing and others may appear in addition to the consensus.

Therefore, exactly three types of states exist in a profile HMM that directly correspond to these possible distinctions. The so-called match states describe a position within an amino acid sequence that belongs to the consensus with respect to the family of sequences considered, i.e., appears in very similar form in the majority of training samples. In order to insert or delete symbols in or from a sequence so-called insert and delete states are used, respectively. Figure 8.5 shows a profile HMM as it is obtained for a multiple alignment as, for example, the one shown in Fig. 8.4. In addition to the three state types derived from the data, the model also contains specially marked start and end states. In the same way as delete states, these do not generate outputs.[5] The possible state transitions within the model allow for passing through it from left to right. By means of the delete states, it is possible to skip one or more match states. Additionally, between match states as well as at the beginning and at the end of the model, arbitrarily many amino acids can be inserted into a sequence via the insert states. The required discrete output probability distributions of the match states are estimated on the consensus positions of the multiple align-

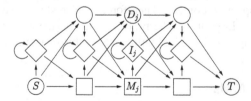

Fig. 8.5 Schematic representation of the structure of a profile HMM as it is obtained on the basis of a multiple alignment. Match states are represented by *squares*, insert states by *rhombuses*, and delete states by *circles*. Additionally, for the grouping of edges one non-emitting start and end state exist

---

[5]In principle these are ordinary non-emitting states. However, in this case transition probabilities are used, which are specially adapted to the model.

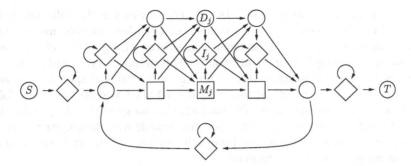

Fig. 8.6 Schematic representation of the extended structure of a profile HMM for the detection of multiple partial sequences embedded into a longer sequence

ment which defines the protein family to be modeled. In analogy, the distributions for modeling symbol insertions are obtained.

In a similar way as a model for the recognition of isolated words, a profile HMM can be used for determining the degree of similarity between an unknown sequence and the protein family that is described by the model.[6] Furthermore, an existing multiple alignment can automatically be extended with alignments of new sequences by using a profile HMM trained on it. Therefore, merely the optimal state sequence through the model needs to be determined which then yields the association of the individual sequence elements with the positions in the alignment.

The insert states at the beginning and at the end of the model can describe a prefix or suffix of a sequence to be analyzed. The corresponding output distributions are, however, specialized on the actual initial and final sequences occurring in the respective multiple alignment. Therefore, finding multiple partial sequences that match the structure of the protein family within a longer sequence of amino acids is only possible with an extension of the model. This was proposed by Eddy and colleagues and is part of the analysis tool HMMER ([70], see also Sect. 15.1 page 250). The principle structure of such a model is shown in Fig. 8.6. It uses additional insert states that serve to bridge partial sequences that have nothing in common with the amino acid sequences described by the core model. A looping edge allows to describe a sequence of the data modeled in a similar way as in connected word recognition. Thus it is possible to detect matches with members of the protein family considered at several positions within a longer sequence of amino acids.

8.5   Modeling Outputs

After the structure of the HMMs to be used is specified for a certain application, it remains to be decided how the associated modeling of the model's outputs is to be achieved.

---

[6]With PFAM there exists a library of ready-made profile HMMs which is available on the Internet [250].

In the field of bioinformatics this decision is rather easy as there the data to be processed usually consist of discrete symbols of DNA base pairs or amino acids. Unless additional properties of the data are considered (cf. e.g. [239]), discrete output distributions using four or 20 different symbols, respectively, are sufficient.

When describing continuous feature vectors in the fields of speech and handwriting recognition, however, mixture models need to be used (see also Sect. 5.2). Unfortunately, no generally applicable method exists for specifying the possible degrees of freedom of the models to be used in a suitable way. Rather, experience in dealing with the respective data and frequently also the experimental evaluation of different parametrizations are required.

In particular, it is necessary to determine the degree of specialization of the output probability densities, i.e., to specify how many model states define mixtures based on the same inventory of component densities. Additionally, the sizes of the respective codebooks must be determined. These decisions, in general, represent a compromise between the precision of the model, its generalization capabilities, and the effort needed for decoding, i.e., the computation time.

In semi-continuous models usually some 100 up to a few 1000 densities are used for the common codebook shared by all states. The more individually mixture densities are associated with model states the less training samples are available and the less component densities can be estimated. As a single normal density per model state is, however, hardly appropriate, generally 8 to 64 component densities are used in continuous HMMs that do not use mixture tying.[7]

A fundamental problem of mixture-density models in HMMs is the complexity issue. In the same way as in the case of context-dependent modeling units, it is easily possible to define highly specialized models with huge numbers of parameters. When trying to estimate these models on limited data sets, however, they will overspecialize on the training data and the necessary generalization to new data will be poor.

In order to avoid such unwanted behavior, techniques for so-called parameter tying can be applied to mixture models (see Sect. 9.2). Tying identifies parameter sets within a complex model that can be shared between model structures based on expert knowledge or automatic procedures. Even though quite sophisticated models can be designed this way, in practice preference is usually given to rather simple structures. How this is done for the modeling of HMM output distributions in typical recognition systems and in different application scenarios will be described in the course of the system presentations in Part III.

---

[7]Frequently, component densities of mixture models in continuous HMMs are significantly simplified with respect to covariance modeling in order to ensure trainability. This simplification might range from the use of diagonal covariances to that of a single shared (diagonal) covariance for all component densities of a specific mixture or a set of mixtures.

Robust Parameter Estimation

In the field of statistical pattern recognition one is always faced with the problem to robustly estimate the parameters of a desired model on the available training samples. Consequently, robust parameter estimation is a primary problem when applying HMMs in practice. However, the situation is not as critical as in the case of n-gram models for which no useful models could be created without suitable measures (cf. Sect. 6.5). Nevertheless, also with HMMs one is confronted with the so-called *sparse data problem* when working with more complex model architectures. Then chances are high that either the model parameters can no longer be computed due to numerical reasons or that an overfitting of the model to the sample data considered occurs. In extreme cases this can lead to the situation that the models estimated have learned the sample set "by heart", i.e., they describe nothing but known samples. Yet, such a behavior can be detected by an accompanying evaluation on an independent cross-validation set and the training procedure can then be stopped at a suitable position.

However, such a rather brute-force decision is not helpful in order to modify the configuration of the model purposefully for a simplified parameter estimation. Therefore, it would be extremely useful in practice to have a well-founded basis for deciding how much training material is necessary for dimensioning a given model. Unfortunately, from the mathematical side this question can only be answered by the law of large numbers. From the view of statistical pattern recognition this principle was rephrased pointedly by Robert L. Mercer [196]:

There is no data like more data!

A very rough estimate of the amount of data necessary can be derived from the assumption that there exists a linear relationship between the number of model parameters P and the minimal size T of the sample set, i.e., that P is directly proportional to T:

$$T \propto P \qquad (9.1)$$

Even though such a trivial model is hardly justified from a mathematical point of view, it can nevertheless be used quite well in practice for approximately defining

G.A. Fink, *Markov Models for Pattern Recognition*,
Advances in Computer Vision and Pattern Recognition,
DOI 10.1007/978-1-4471-6308-4_9, © Springer-Verlag London 2014

lower bounds on the number of training samples that need to be available per model parameter.[1] Furthermore, the relationship can also be exploited in reverse for approximately defining how many model parameters can be trained from a sample set of given size. As the model quality in general increases with an increased number of parameters, one is always interested in the most special model that can still be estimated robustly.

As soon as it is clear that a certain parameter set can hardly be trained in a satisfactory way with the available sample data, the factors need to be considered that cause such a situation of data sparseness. Primarily the following three reasons or a combination of them have to be taken into consideration.

Model Complexity

It has been attempted to estimate too many independent models or modeling parts on the basis of the available data. In classification problems this number usually is bounded from below by the number of pattern classes that need to be distinguished. Frequently, however, many more considerably more specialized models are used for representing variants of the patterns considered more precisely in order to improve the overall model quality.

Dimensionality

The number of features used is too large. Especially if features are determined heuristically, a large number of characteristic quantities can be computed that—considered in isolation—make a certain contribution for the solution of the problem. The adding of new components to feature vectors, however, also leads to a considerably increase in the demand for sample data. If this demand cannot be satisfied, the modeling quality decreases despite the putatively improved description of the data as the parameters can no longer be estimated robustly—a situation which is often referred to as the so-called *curse of dimensionality* (cf. e.g. [23, Sect. 1.4]).

Correlation

Mutual dependencies exist within the data to be modeled which need to be described by additional parameters. Here the following considerations will concentrate on the correlation between components of the feature vectors as they are frequently found in heuristically generated feature sets. Correlations over the temporal sequence of the features, however, are not captured parametrically in HMMs but approximately via the model structure.

Consequently, the effective size of the parameter set required is defined by the specificity of the model, the dimension of the feature space, and the need for describing correlations in the data. In general, an improvement in the trainability can

---

[1]For example, a proportionality factor of 5 achieves good results in the estimation of mixture models. For establishing individual HMM states in tied-mixture models usually 50 to 100 samples are sufficient.

be achieved by reducing the complexity with respect to one or more of these modeling aspects.

In the following section we will first consider analytical methods which allow to optimize a given feature representation such that the model built on top of it requires less parameters without a change in its descriptive quality. For this purpose either internal correlations are approximately eliminated or the dimension of the feature vectors is reduced in total. Then methods for the reduction of model complexity are presented in Sect. 9.2. They are all based on the principle of identifying "similar" parameters within the model by applying expert knowledge or by means of automatic procedures. The parameters identified as being approximately equal are then merged during the training process. Thus the number of parameters required is reduced so that the trainability can be improved and usually also the quality of the model as a whole.

Additionally, for all iteratively optimizing training procedures, as they are used for HMMs, it is of fundamental importance to start the optimization process with a suitable initial estimate. Therefore, methods for determining initial model parameters for HMMs will be presented at the end of the chapter.

9.1   Feature Optimization

The computation of features that are most suitable for certain signal analysis tasks is the topic of countless publications in the field of pattern recognition. Even though more and more approaches try to automatically derive suitable feature representations from a data set at hand, finding the optimal feature representation for a given pattern recognition task is still an unsolved problem. Therefore, we do not want to treat feature extraction methods in general here. Rather, we want to consider methods which allow to optimize the properties of an existing feature representation with respect to the model used.

In the following, we will assume that a feature extraction method exists which is principally suited for the task at hand. This procedure, which will most likely consist of a combination of heuristic methods, yields a baseline representation for the signals to be analyzed in the form of n-dimensional feature vectors $x \in \mathbb{R}^n$. In general, the probability distribution of this data is unknown. However, we also assume that the required distribution parameters can be determined sufficiently accurately on the basis of a representative set of sample vectors:

$$\omega = \{x_1, x_2, \ldots, x_N\}$$

Usually, the statistical properties of these baseline features are not optimally matched with the subsequent modeling. Therefore, we will consider a class of methods in the following which carry out an optimization of the data representation with respect to the properties and capabilities of the subsequent modeling. This is achieved by estimating a suitable transformation that maps every feature vector x from the baseline representation onto a corresponding feature vector y with equal or smaller dimension. When considering possible transformations in full generality the problem becomes intractable, however. Therefore, for reasons of simplicity we will consider only *linear* transformations in the following. They are especially well understood mathematically and offer reasonable modeling capabilities.

A linear feature space transformation is completely defined by a transformation matrix T:

$$y = Tx \quad \text{with} \quad x \in \mathbb{R}^n, \; y \in \mathbb{R}^m, \; T \in \mathbb{R}^m \times \mathbb{R}^n \quad \text{where } m \leq n$$

In the context of feature space transformations it makes sense to apply the transformation in a *centered* way, i.e., after a compensation of the sample mean $\bar{x}$:

$$y = T(x - \bar{x})$$

Centering the original data only results in a translation of the transformed feature vectors by the vector $-T\bar{x}$ that could easily be corrected again, if necessary. The fundamental statistical properties of the data, however, are not affected by this operation, and a centered feature transform is better suited as a starting point for the further considerations.

After applying a certain transformation to the original data ω one obtains a transformed sample set

$$\tilde{\omega} = \left\{ y_k \mid y_k = T(x_k - \bar{x}), 1 \leq k \leq N \right\}$$

which replaces the original one in the further modeling process. The goal of all methods presented in the following is to determine the transformation T such that unwanted variability in the feature representations that is irrelevant for the modeling will be eliminated from the data to the greatest possible extent. Simultaneously, however, relevant differences shall be preserved and thus the modeling process shall be simplified in the end.

9.1.1 Decorrelation

In general, the baseline representation of the features is the result of a heuristic procedure. Therefore, it has to be assumed that statistical dependencies exist between the individual components x_i of the feature vectors x. Figure 9.1(a) illustrates this situation with a simple two-dimensional example. In the distribution shown large values of the first feature x_1 mostly go along with the large values of the second feature x_2. The data shown can be described by a two-dimensional normal distribution with mean $\mu = \begin{bmatrix} 1 \\ 1 \end{bmatrix}$ and covariance matrix $C = \begin{bmatrix} 2 & 1 \\ 1 & 2 \end{bmatrix}$. Thus five independent parameters need to be estimated from the example data when training the respective model.

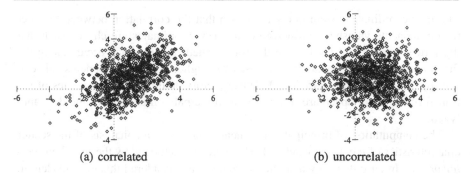

(a) correlated (b) uncorrelated

Fig. 9.1 Examples of a simple two-dimensional distribution with (**a**) correlated and (**b**) uncorrelated feature vector components

In contrast, in the distribution shown in Fig. 9.1(b) the components of the feature vectors are statistically independent[2] and, therefore, uncorrelated in particular. Consequently, this data can be described by a simplified model which only uses a diagonal covariance matrix. Thus one model parameter can be saved and a robust estimation of the remaining parameters—according to the rule-of-thumb put up at the beginning in Eq. (9.1)—can be achieved on approximately 20 % less samples.

Of course such a reduction of the number of model parameters has a more notable effect in real systems, e.g., from the domain of automatic speech recognition. With an inventory of $M = 10\,000$ Gaussian distributions and a feature dimension of $n = 39$, one obtains $10\,000 \cdot (3n + n^2)/2 = 8.19 \cdot 10^6$ independent parameters for a system with full covariance matrices, but only $10\,000 \cdot 2n = 7.8 \cdot 10^5$ degrees of freedom when using diagonal covariance matrices. Thus when using "diagonal" models either a tenth of the training material is sufficient or the ten-fold number of densities can be estimated.

However, statistical dependencies between components of a feature vector cannot principally be excluded in practice. Though the possibility exists to at least achieve a decorrelation of the features by a transformation of the feature space. In the case of normally distributed data this is equivalent to the creation of statistically independent feature vectors.

9.1.2 Principal Component Analysis I

The so-called *principal component analysis*[3] (PCA) computes a new coordinate system for a distribution of data vectors given either parametrically or empirically.

---

[2]As the covariance matrix C is symmetric, all components C_{ij} are equal to C_{ji} for $i < j$. In general, an $n \times n$ matrix C has n degrees of freedom for the diagonal elements and $(n^2 - n)/2$ for the independent off-diagonal elements, i.e., $(n + n^2)/2$ in total.

[3]The method is also known as *Karhunen–Loève transform* in the literature. However, there the transformation is not applied in a centered way so that the Karhunen–Loève transform is only completely equivalent to the principal component analysis for zero-mean data.

The new coordinate system is oriented such that the correlation between the vector components vanishes. Furthermore, the new coordinates are chosen such that the largest variance of the data in the transformed feature space occurs along the first coordinate and constantly decreases for higher vector components (cf. e.g. [56, pp. 302ff], [65, pp. 115–117]). Those vectors defining the coordinates of the transformed vector space are referred to as principal components of the data analyzed.

The computation of principal components consists in an analysis of the scatter characteristics of the data considered. These are characterized by the so-called *scatter matrix*. In case that only a single distribution is considered this is equivalent to its covariance matrix.[4] The total scatter matrix S_T of a sample set $x_1, x_2, \ldots, x_N$ of data vectors is defined as (cf. also Eq. (3.10)):

$$S_T := \frac{1}{N} \sum_{i=1}^{N} (x_i - \bar{x})(x_i - \bar{x})^T \qquad (9.2)$$

Here $\bar{x}$ denotes the sample mean (cf. also Eq. (3.9)):

$$\bar{x} := \frac{1}{N} \sum_{i=1}^{N} x_i$$

After applying a transformation T, one obtains the following total scatter matrix for the transformed sample set $\tilde{\omega}$:

$$\tilde{S}_T = \frac{1}{N} \sum_{i=1}^{N} T(x_i - \bar{x})\left[T(x_i - \bar{x})\right]^T = T S_T T^T$$

In order to decorrelate the data, therefore, a transformation T is sought which "diagonalizes" S_T, i.e., causes $\tilde{S}_T$ to become a diagonal matrix. However, the relative position of the data vectors with respect to each other should remain unchanged during this operation. Therefore, the transformation in question needs to be orthonormal as Euclidean distances in the vector spaces involved are not affected by this class of transformations (cf. sidebar *Orthonormal Transformations*).

Unfortunately, the property of the total scatter $\tilde{S}_T$ being a diagonal matrix cannot be derived by formulating a criterion and analytically computing a suitable transformation. Rather, one needs to resort to the fact known from linear algebra that every

---

[4]In presentations that assume zero-mean data or that compensate the sample mean during the transformation, the so-called *correlation matrix* is used, which is defined as follows: $C := \frac{1}{N} \sum_{i=1}^{N} x_i x_i^T$.

Orthonormal Transformations

Orthonormal transforms constitute a special class of linear transformations. Orthonormal transformations are equivalent to the expansion of the data $x \in \mathbb{R}^n$ to be transformed according to a system of orthonormal base vectors. Therefore, such a transform only causes a rotation of the original data onto a new system of orthogonal coordinates.

The rows of the transformation matrix T correspond exactly to the vectors t_i which form the new orthonormal basis of the data space $\mathbb{R}^n$:

$$T = [t_1, t_2, \ldots, t_n]^T \quad \text{with} \quad t_i^T t_j = \begin{cases} 1 & i = j \\ 0 & \text{otherwise} \end{cases} \quad \text{and} \quad \|t_i\| = 1 \; \forall i, j$$

Due to the pairwise orthogonality of the row-vectors of T one obtains

$$T^T T = I$$

from which it follows directly that for orthonormal transforms the inverse T^{-1} of the transformation matrix is identical with its transpose:

$$T^{-1} = T^T$$

By exploiting this property, it can easily be verified that the norm of the transformed vectors is preserved by an orthonormal transformation:

$$\|y\| = \sqrt{y^T y} = \sqrt{[Tx]^T Tx} = \sqrt{x^T T^T Tx} = \sqrt{x^T x} = \|x\|$$

This is equivalent to the fact that Euclidean distances between data vectors are not changed by the transformation.

non-singular matrix can be brought to diagonal form by a suitably chosen orthonormal transform (cf. sidebar *Diagonalization of Symmetric Matrices*).

Thus the diagonalization of the total scatter matrix S_T is achieved my means of the transpose Φ^T of its eigenvector matrix Φ the columns of which consist of the n normalized eigenvectors ϕ_i of S_T. For the mere diagonalization of $\tilde{S}_T$ the arrangement of these vectors to a matrix is in fact irrelevant. With respect to the following considerations, however, which also include a reduction of the dimensionality, Φ is constructed such that the eigenvectors are arranged according to the size of the associated eigenvalue. The first column of Φ thus corresponds to the eigenvector with the largest associated eigenvalue and the last column to the one with the smallest.

Diagonalization of Symmetric Matrices

Every non-singular symmetric matrix Q can be brought to diagonal form by means of a suitable orthonormal transformation $T = \Phi^T$ (cf. e.g. [102, pp. 27–28]). Here Φ corresponds to the so-called *eigenvector matrix* of Q:

$$\Phi = [\phi_1, \phi_2, \dots, \phi_n] \quad \text{with} \quad \phi_i^T \phi_j = \begin{cases} 1 & i = j \\ 0 & \text{otherwise} \end{cases} \quad \text{and} \quad \|\phi_i\| = 1 \ \forall i, j$$

The column vectors ϕ_i of Φ are formed by the normalized eigenvectors[5] of Q with the associated eigenvalue λ_i and thus satisfy the eigenvalue equation:

$$Q\phi_i = \phi_i \lambda_i \quad \forall i$$

In correspondence to the eigenvector matrix the so-called *eigenvalue matrix* is defined on the basis of the eigenvalues λ_i as follows:

$$\Lambda = \begin{bmatrix} \lambda_1 & & & \\ & \lambda_2 & & 0 \\ & & \ddots & \\ 0 & & & \lambda_n \end{bmatrix}$$

Thus a generalization of the eigenvalue equation holds

$$Q\Phi = \Phi\Lambda$$

and one obtains the following decomposition into eigenvector and eigenvalue matrix for Q:

$$Q = \Phi\Lambda\Phi^T$$

When applying the transformation Φ^T to Q

$$\Phi^T Q \Phi = \Phi^T \Phi \Lambda \Phi^T \Phi = \Lambda$$

one obtains the diagonal eigenvalue matrix of Q as the result.

---

[5]The computation of eigenvalues and eigenvectors of matrices is a challenging numerical problem. Because of its relatively general applicability the most widely used method for solving this problem is the so-called *power method* (cf. e.g. [140, p. 233]). For symmetric matrices—as scatter matrices always are—in practice good results can also be achieved by the so-called *Jacobi method* (cf. e.g. [140, p. 196], [248, p. 360]).

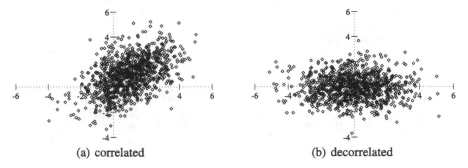

(a) correlated   (b) decorrelated

Fig. 9.2 Example for the decorrelation of a simple two-dimensional distribution: (**a**) original data (see also Fig. 9.1(a)) and (**b**) after the decorrelation by means of PCA

$$\boldsymbol{\Phi} = [\boldsymbol{\phi}_1, \boldsymbol{\phi}_2, \dots, \boldsymbol{\phi}_n] \quad \text{with} \quad \boldsymbol{S}_T \boldsymbol{\phi}_i = \boldsymbol{\phi}_i \lambda_i \quad \text{and} \quad \lambda_1 \geq \lambda_2 \geq \cdots \geq \lambda_n \quad (9.3)$$

When applying this transformation to zero-mean data vectors

$$\boldsymbol{y} = \boldsymbol{\Phi}^T (\boldsymbol{x} - \bar{\boldsymbol{x}})$$

one obtains the following transform of the scatter matrix:

$$\tilde{\boldsymbol{S}}_T = \boldsymbol{\Phi}^T \boldsymbol{S}_T \boldsymbol{\Phi} = \boldsymbol{\Phi}^T \boldsymbol{\Phi} \boldsymbol{\Lambda} \boldsymbol{\Phi}^T \boldsymbol{\Phi} = \boldsymbol{\Lambda} = \begin{bmatrix} \lambda_1 & & & \mathbf{0} \\ & \lambda_2 & & \\ & & \ddots & \\ \mathbf{0} & & & \lambda_n \end{bmatrix}$$

The total scatter matrix $\tilde{\boldsymbol{S}}_T$ of the transformed sample set thus corresponds to the eigenvalue matrix $\boldsymbol{\Lambda}$ of $\boldsymbol{S}_T$ as $\boldsymbol{\Phi}^T$ simultaneously is the inverse of $\boldsymbol{\Phi}$. In the transformed space the variance of the data along the coordinates is thus given by the eigenvalues λ_i. Additionally, all correlations between vector components vanish. Therefore, the goal of bringing the scatter matrix of the optimized feature representation to diagonal form is achieved.

For the example used in the introduction one obtains

$$\boldsymbol{\Phi} = \begin{bmatrix} \frac{1}{\sqrt{2}} & -\frac{1}{\sqrt{2}} \\ \frac{1}{\sqrt{2}} & \frac{1}{\sqrt{2}} \end{bmatrix} \quad \text{and} \quad \boldsymbol{\Lambda} = \begin{bmatrix} 3 & 0 \\ 0 & 1 \end{bmatrix}$$

as eigenvector and eigenvalue matrix. The transformation of the sample data according to

$$\boldsymbol{y}_i = \boldsymbol{\Phi}^T (\boldsymbol{x}_i - \bar{\boldsymbol{x}})$$

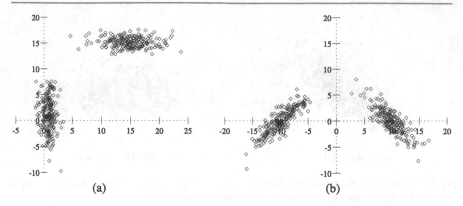

Fig. 9.3 Example of a data distribution with multiple regions of high density and local correlations (**a**) before and (**b**) after applying principal component analysis

yields the distribution shown in Fig. 9.2(b). The diagonalized total scatter matrix $\tilde{S}_T$ of the transformed data is given by the eigenvalue matrix Λ.

The decorrelation of a given feature set always causes the total scatter matrix to become a diagonal matrix and thus, considered globally, causes the correlations between the components of the transformed feature vectors to vanish. When assuming that the data are approximately normally distributed one even obtains features that are approximately statistically independent.

If such a data set is described by mixture models it is, therefore, justified—within certain limits—to use only diagonal covariance matrices and thus to save a considerable number of model parameters. However, only *global* correlations are eliminated by principal component analysis. Therefore, local statistical dependencies may occur within individual regions of high density in the data as shown exemplarily in Fig. 9.3. These are captured only inadequately or cannot be represented at all by the simplified model. Usually, however, one gives precedence to the considerable reduction of the number of parameters over the possibility to model such class regions more exactly. In the example shown, simply more baseline densities need to be estimated for the description of an "elongated" region in feature space when using diagonal models only.

9.1.3 Whitening

In practical applications it is in general undesirable that the dynamic range numerically varies largely between individual components of the feature vector. Therefore, it may make sense to also normalize the variance parts after the decorrelation of the features by means of the principal component analysis in order to simplify the further model building.

When additionally applying the transformation

$$\Lambda^{-\frac{1}{2}} = \begin{bmatrix} \lambda_1^{-\frac{1}{2}} & & & \\ & \lambda_2^{-\frac{1}{2}} & & 0 \\ & & \ddots & \\ 0 & & & \lambda_n^{-\frac{1}{2}} \end{bmatrix}$$

to the data decorrelated by PCA, this effects that the final total scatter matrix $\hat{S}_T$ will become the identity matrix I.

$$\hat{S}_T = \Lambda^{-\frac{1}{2}} \tilde{S}_T \Lambda^{-\frac{1}{2}} = \Lambda^{-\frac{1}{2}} \Phi^T S_T \Phi \Lambda^{-\frac{1}{2}} = \Lambda^{-\frac{1}{2}} \Lambda \Lambda^{-\frac{1}{2}} = I$$

The total transformation of the data which is necessary for achieving this, i.e., the combination of decorrelation and subsequent variance normalization is referred to as *whitening*:

$$z = \Lambda^{-\frac{1}{2}} y = \Lambda^{-\frac{1}{2}} \Phi^T (x - \bar{x})$$

The variances in all coordinates are normalized to 1 by this transformation. In particular this means that after a whitening the global scatter characteristics of the data are invariant to additional orthonormal transformations as the total scatter was made to become an identity matrix.

In contrast to principal component analysis, this transformation is not orthonormal so that Euclidean distances between the transformed vectors are *not* preserved. Intuitively this is also immediately clear as the feature space is scaled along the coordinates by a factor of $\frac{1}{\sqrt{\lambda_i}}$, respectively.

A whitening of the example data from Fig. 9.4(a) results in the distribution shown in Fig. 9.4(c). One obtains a radially symmetric point cloud as the variance of the distribution is equal to 1 in both coordinates.

9.1.4 Dimensionality Reduction

In addition to a decorrelation of the data frequently also a reduction of the dimensionality is performed as a second important method for optimizing feature representations. The methods applied build on top of each other so that the decorrelation step is either implicitly or explicitly performed in the preparation phase of the actual dimensionality reduction.

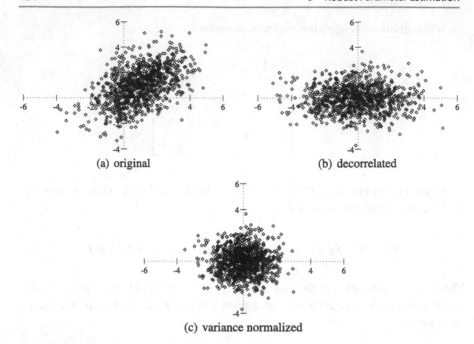

(a) original   (b) decorrelated

(c) variance normalized

Fig. 9.4 Example for the combined decorrelation and variance normalization by whitening: (**a**) original data, (**b**) after decorrelation, and (**c**) after variance normalization

9.1.5   Principal Component Analysis II

The simplest method for reducing the dimension of the features consists in using only a subset of $m < n$ eigenvectors of the scatter matrix S_T for the construction of the transformation matrix Φ^T of the principal component analysis. For this purpose only those m eigenvectors corresponding to the largest eigenvalues of S_T are selected (see Eq. (9.3)). Thus one obtains a mapping of the feature vectors $x \in \mathbb{R}^n$ onto a lower-dimensional space in which the largest variance components of the original data are preserved.

Of course, a certain error arises from this reduction of the vector dimension. This can be described quantitatively if for every original vector x its reconstruction

$$x' = \sum_{i=1}^{m} y_i \phi_i$$

on the basis of the lower-dimensional representation y is generated and the resulting average reconstruction error ε is computed. It can be shown (cf. [56, p. 304-305]) that the expected error is given by the sum of the eigenvalues of those eigenvectors of S_T that were not considered for the construction of the transformation matrix $\boldsymbol{\Phi}^T$:

$$\varepsilon = \mathcal{E}\{\|\boldsymbol{x} - \boldsymbol{x}'\|^2\} = \mathcal{E}\left\{\left\|\sum_{i=m+1}^{n} y_i \boldsymbol{\phi}_i\right\|^2\right\} = \sum_{i=m+1}^{n} \lambda_i$$

Thus selecting the eigenvectors associated with the largest eigenvalues for the transformation not only maximizes the variance preserved in the vector components but also minimizes the reconstruction error resulting from the dimensionality reduction. By considering the proportions of the eigenvalues λ_i, it can be estimated to which dimension $m < n$ the data available can be reduced with only negligible losses in the accuracy of the representation.

A reduction of dimensionality by PCA is, however, mainly used when analytically generating features directly from signal data and hardly for the optimization of existing feature representations with respect to mixture models or HMMs.[6] In fact, the global maximization of the preserved variance does not take into account the separability of the pattern classes considered.

9.1.6 Linear Discriminant Analysis

In contrast to a simple dimension reduction on the basis of global variance criteria, the so-called *linear discriminant analysis* (LDA) tries to determine a feature space transform that improves the separability of the pattern classes considered while simultaneously reducing the dimensionality (cf. e.g. [102, pp. 441–459], [65, pp. 117–124]). Therefore, criteria are applied for the computation of the transformation matrix that characterize the distribution of class regions and their separability on the basis of the features available. Consequently, for applying LDA a *labeled sample set* is mandatory. Intuitively, a transformation is sought that generates class regions that are as compact as possible while at the same time preserving the total variance of the data.

For the further considerations we will, therefore, assume that within the available sample set ω subsets ω_κ are defined which contain features of patterns originating from a class Ω_κ only:

$$\omega = \bigcup_\kappa \omega_\kappa$$

---

[6]In the field of automatic speech recognition, a further important reason for this is that the *cepstral coefficients* used as features in the majority of systems can already be assumed to be approximately decorrelated [198].

The compactness of these classes can be described by the average variance of the features *within* the respective regions. By first computing class-conditional scatter matrices

$$\frac{1}{|\omega_\kappa|} \sum_{x \in \omega_\kappa} (x - \bar{x}_\kappa)(x - \bar{x}_\kappa)^T$$

one obtains the so-called within class scatter matrix S_W

$$S_W := \sum_\kappa p_\kappa \frac{1}{|\omega_\kappa|} \sum_{x \in \omega_\kappa} (x - \bar{x}_\kappa)(x - \bar{x}_\kappa)^T \qquad (9.4)$$

as the weighted average over all class-conditional scatter matrices. Here $\bar{x}_\kappa$ denotes the mean of the respective class region, i.e., the conditional sample mean of the feature vectors from class Ω_κ. The class-conditional scatter matrices are weighted according to the prior probabilities p_κ of the respective classes which can be estimated from the proportion of feature vectors from Ω_κ contained in the sample set:

$$p_\kappa = \frac{|\omega_\kappa|}{|\omega|}$$

The relative position of the individual class regions with respect to each other can be described by means of the so-called between class scatter matrix S_B. It is, however, not completely clear how S_B should be defined. Therefore, different approaches can be found in the literature (cf. e.g. [101, p. 260]). The simplest method is to compute a scatter matrix on the basis of the individual class centers $\bar{x}_\kappa$:

$$S_B := \sum_\kappa p_\kappa (\bar{x}_\kappa - \bar{x})(\bar{x}_\kappa - \bar{x})^T \qquad (9.5)$$

This definition also allows to derive an analytical relationship between the three scatter matrices introduced so far. The total scatter matrix is then obtained as the sum of the between and the within class scatter matrix:

$$S_T = S_B + S_W$$

Different measures may be considered as optimization criteria for LDA, all of which basically try to capture the relation between within and between class scatter in the sample set (cf. e.g. [102, pp. 446–447]). On the basis of such a compactness criterion the optimization task can be defined as follows: The between class scatter should become as small as possible while the average distance between the patterns should become as large as possible at the same time—or at least remain constant.

In the literature the following criterion is used most frequently for this purpose:[7]

$$\text{tr}\{S_W^{-1} S_B\} \rightarrow \max!$$

After a quite lengthy mathematical derivation, which the interested reader can find in the respective specialized literature (cf. e.g. [102, pp. 448–459]), it can be shown that this maximization problem—similarly to the case of the principal component analysis—leads to the solution of an eigenvalue problem. The transformation matrix $\boldsymbol{\Phi}^T$ sought for LDA is created from the $m < n$ eigenvectors $\boldsymbol{\phi}_i$ of the matrix $S_W^{-1} S_B$ corresponding to the largest eigenvalues:

$$\boldsymbol{\Phi} = [\boldsymbol{\phi}_1, \boldsymbol{\phi}_2, \ldots, \boldsymbol{\phi}_m] \quad \text{with} \quad S_W^{-1} S_B \boldsymbol{\phi}_i = \boldsymbol{\phi}_i \lambda_i \quad \text{and} \quad \lambda_1 \geq \lambda_2 \geq \cdots \geq \lambda_m \tag{9.6}$$

In order to avoid problems in the eigenvalue computation for $S_W^{-1} S_B$ which may result from the necessary inversion of S_W or from the fact that $S_W^{-1} S_B$ not necessarily is a symmetric matrix, the solution can also be reduced to the simultaneous diagonalization of the matrices S_W and S_B (cf. e.g. [102, pp. 31–34]).

In this method the computation of the transformation matrix for LDA is performed in two steps. First, the between scatter matrix S_W is transformed into an identity matrix by applying a whitening. Therefore, one computes the eigenvalue and eigenvector matrix of S_W:

$$S_W \boldsymbol{\Phi} = \boldsymbol{\Phi} \boldsymbol{\Lambda}$$

Then the original data is transformed according to

$$y = \boldsymbol{\Lambda}^{-\frac{1}{2}} \boldsymbol{\Phi}^T (x - \bar{x})$$

and one obtains the identity matrix as the between class scatter matrix of the transformed data:

$$\tilde{S}_W = \boldsymbol{\Lambda}^{-\frac{1}{2}} \boldsymbol{\Phi}^T S_W \boldsymbol{\Phi} \boldsymbol{\Lambda}^{-\frac{1}{2}} = I$$

Of course, the between class scatter matrix S_B is also modified by this process, but in general it will not be brought to diagonal form:

$$\tilde{S}_B = \boldsymbol{\Lambda}^{-\frac{1}{2}} \boldsymbol{\Phi}^T S_B \boldsymbol{\Phi} \boldsymbol{\Lambda}^{-\frac{1}{2}}$$

In the second step, the fact is exploited that the within class scatter, which has become an identity matrix, is now invariant to further orthonormal transforms. Therefore, one carries out a principal component analysis of the class centers and thus

---

[7]As shown in [114], this criterion can also be applied for the evaluation of different feature sets with respect to their suitability for a certain modeling task.

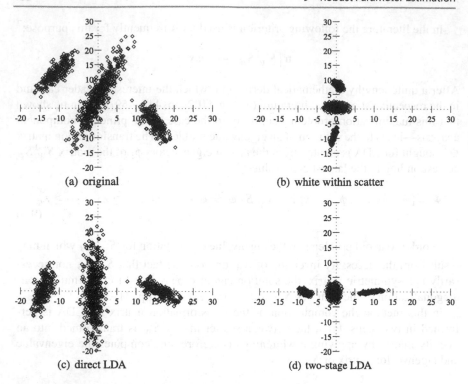

Fig. 9.5 Example of linear discriminant analysis: (**a**) original data, (**b**) after whitening the within class scatter matrix, (**c**) result of the direct solution and (**d**) of the two-stage method

diagonalizes $\tilde{S}_B$. For this purpose one computes the eigenvector matrix $\boldsymbol{\Psi}$ of $\tilde{S}_B$ and carries out a second transformation step:

$$z = \boldsymbol{\Psi}^T y = \boldsymbol{\Psi}^T \boldsymbol{\Lambda}^{-\frac{1}{2}} \boldsymbol{\Phi}^T (x - \bar{x})$$

It can be shown that the resulting total transformation matrix $\boldsymbol{\Psi}^T \boldsymbol{\Lambda}^{-\frac{1}{2}} \boldsymbol{\Phi}^T$ is identical with the one that is obtained from the direct solution of the eigenvalue problem for $S_W^{-1} S_B$ except for the normalization of the eigenvectors (cf. e.g. [102, pp. 31–33], [56, p. 330]). This means that both transformations map the feature space to the same new coordinate system with the difference that in the two-stage method additionally a scaling by $\boldsymbol{\Lambda}^{-\frac{1}{2}}$ is performed.

The advantage of the second method—besides its greater clarity—lies in the fact that it exhibits a better numerical stability. Neither a matrix inversion nor the computation of eigenvalues for a not necessarily symmetric matrix need to be performed.

The effects of the LDA transformation on a sample distribution with three pattern classes is illustrated in Fig. 9.5. In the upper left the original distribution is shown as well as its LDA transform after the application of the one-step method. For comparison, the figure shows the intermediate result that is generated by the whitening of the within class scatter matrix in the upper right. The final result of the two-stage LDA transformation, which is shown in the lower right, then results from this by the application of a PCA to the between class scatter matrix. Except for a scaling and a mirroring of the data it is identical with the result of the one-stage method.

A serious problem in the application of linear discriminant analysis that should not be overlooked when deriving mathematical solutions lies in the fact that for LDA a labeling of the sample set is mandatory. Therefore, the question arises how the underlying pattern classes should be chosen in a suitable way. In fact this choice directly influences the between and within class scatter matrices and, in the end, the result of the whole transformation.

From a more detailed analysis of the significance of the between class scatter matrix at least a lower bound for the number of pattern classes can be derived. Because of its very definition (cf. Eq. (9.5)), S_B has at most rank $K - 1$ where K is the number of pattern classes used. As only the positions of the K class centers x_κ are taken into account in the construction of S_B, at most $K - 1$ linearly independent vector components can exist. The between class scatter matrix, therefore, spans a $K - 1$-dimensional sub-space and consequently only possesses $K - 1$ positive eigenvalues. In the two-stage computation of LDA, a diagonalization of S_B forms the last step which then can only map to a sub-space with a dimension m smaller than $K - 1$.

LDA was used extensively for purposes of automatic speech recognition in the tradition of the Philips research systems (cf. [8, 115, 289] and [210]). There the underlying pattern classes are practically always defined on the basis of the model states of the context-independent sub-word unit HMMs used. Therefore, the number of classes by far exceeds the feature dimension. The use of elementary segmental units as, e.g., speech sounds—i.e. considerably fewer pattern classes—is agreed to be considerably less powerful in comparison.

These results were also confirmed in extensive experiments of our own. They suggest the assumption that what matters most when choosing the class definition is to ensure a robust estimation of the between class scatter matrix as it cannot be seriously expected that a linear transform is actually capable of perfectly separating a few 100 pattern classes. At the same time a more sophisticated class definition also ensures that the within class scatter more precisely approximates the local situations within individual regions of high density. In total, it can be concluded that the number of classes used for an LDA transformation should considerably exceed the desired dimension of the feature vectors.

9.2 Tying

The methods presented in the previous section implicitly decrease the number of model parameters by reducing the degrees of freedom present in the data, i.e., the dimension of the feature vectors themselves. In contrast, methods that try to group "similar" model parameters together work towards an explicit reduction of the number of parameters. As a consequence, their estimation on the available sample data is improved and finally the robustness of the model as a whole is increased. These methods are usually referred to as *tying* and can be applied to many different parts of the modeling. Three principal methods can be distinguished in such a procedure for the merging of model parameters.

In *constructive* tying the merging of model parameters implicitly results from the construction of more complex models from building blocks that are given by certain elementary models. All copies of the subunits reused then naturally reference the same set of parameters.

In contrast to this, the following two approaches take an already existing model as the basis and try to improve its trainability by parameter tying.

By *generalization* of modeling parts which are realized in a very special way and for which, therefore, only few training samples are available, more general units can be derived. The parameters of these can be estimated on a broader basis of data and thus also more robustly. The special models are then no longer used themselves but are replaced by suitable generalizations. The necessary generalization rules usually are set up by exploiting expert knowledge. In contrast, the creation of the generalized models themselves can be performed automatically.

A similar result can also be achieved by *agglomerative* tying. On the basis of already existing model parameters, similar parameters can be identified by a suitable distance measure. By applying an algorithm for cluster analysis to the parameter space, groups of model parameters can be constructed which serve a similar "purpose" within the overall model and for which a sufficient number of training samples is available. These methods have the big advantage of being able to compute a suitable form of tying for an arbitrary model automatically in a data-driven manner. However, it should not be forgotten that this method in fact proceeds in a quite paradoxical way: The parameter clusters which are supposed to ensure robust trainability are determined on the basis of initial parameters which could just *not* be estimated reliably. In practice one nevertheless achieves good results with data-driven tying for a wide range of applications in spite of this Münchhausen-like trick.[8]

How these principles of tying are applied to existing or yet to be constructed models, is of course left to the developer. Depending on the task at hand, different procedures may make sense. Unfortunately, no strategy can be given which would perform optimally in any case. Therefore, we want to give an overview over the most well known methods in the following in order to support this decision-making process. First we will present such methods that apply tying at the level of partial models. Afterwards, we will consider comparable methods that identify similar groups of model states or merge parameters within the mixture models used.

9.2.1 Sub-model Units

The creation of a complex HMM is generally not achieved by a direct training of all parameters. Rather, one constructs larger models on the basis of smaller partial models with well defined descriptive potential. This procedure not only leads to a

---

[8]In the fantastic stories about the supposed adventures of the German Baron Münchhausen (1720–1797) he claims to have pulled himself from a swamp by his own hair.

Fig. 9.6 Example of simple
parameter tying on the level
of elementary models as it
results from the model
construction process

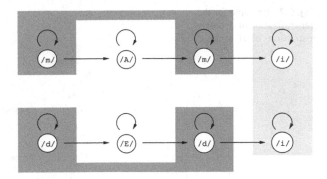

modularization of complex HMMs but also allows the economic exploitation of the
available example data for the parameter training.

This method was developed and brought to perfection in the field of automatic
speech recognition. Furthermore, the use of so-called *sub-word units* can be considered state of the art in recognition tasks structured similarly as, for example, in the
recognition of machine printed or handwritten script (see Sect. 8.2). In contrast, for
the analysis of biological sequences hardly any measures are taken in order to build
the models created in a modular way on the symbolic level.

As described in Sect. 8.2, HMMs for complex units as, e.g., whole words, spoken
utterances, or sections of a text, are created starting from a limited inventory of
baseline models. An implicit tying of model parameters results from the fact that,
though new model states originate from every replication of an elementary model,
these always share the same set of parameters with all other copies of the original
model.

Figure 9.6 shows a simple example for this situation from the domain of automatic speech recognition. For the description of a simple "baby's vocabulary" we
want to create models for the words mommy and daddy. As in the phonetic transcriptions /mAmi/ and /dEdi/ two pairs of speech sounds appear at different positions, one obtains already a word-internal tying of the respective models (/m/ and
/d/). Here it is assumed, of course, that for such a toy application speech sounds
occurring in different contexts can be modeled identically. When concatenating both
words to a primitive compound model, it furthermore becomes clear that the parameters of the partial model for the speech sound /i/ are identical in the overall model
and, therefore, can also be tied.

In simple cases of model-driven tying, thus parameters of partial models named
identically are shared within a complex overall model. This simply corresponds to
a reuse of parameter sets when constructing HMMs via the composition of existing
models. For the training phase this means that all example sequences contained in
the sample set corresponding to an arbitrary copy of a model are taken into account
for the estimation of the shared set of parameters.

Fig. 9.7 Example for the generalization of context restrictions of triphones

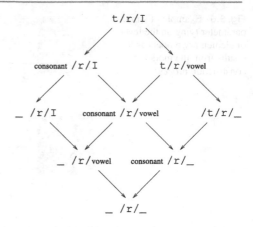

Model Generalization

Model-driven tying becomes more complex if the similarity of partial models cannot be derived directly from their names but must be determined by inference processes. Such methods are mainly applied in conjunction with the use of context-dependent sub-word units (see also Sect. 8.2.2). In these cases the number of possible models usually is so large that a direct estimation of robust parameters cannot be performed for the majority of those. Therefore, one tries to group similar models together in order to ensure their trainability.

A rule-based method for the generalization of context-dependent sub-word units, which are constructed according to the principle of triphones, was proposed in [272]. For such models the generalization of the context restriction on a symbolic level can either be achieved by a shortening of the segmental extension of the context or by an explicit introduction of contextual super-classes.

Figure 9.7 shows a possible simple generalization hierarchy starting from the triphone model $t/r/I$. As every generalization of the context restriction applies either to the left or to the right context, always two possible generalizations exist for every triphone model. The generalization of an individual context is performed in two steps in the example. First, coarse phonetic classes like vowels, nasals, and plosives are used and, finally, the context restriction is omitted completely. Thus the respective context-independent phone model is reached at the end of the generalization process.

If the context restriction applies to more than only one neighboring unit as, e.g., in so-called polyphones, the generalization of the respective models is performed by simple shortening the length of the context restriction. Again the context-independent variant of the modeled unit is reached at the end of the generalization hierarchy—for polyphones the respective monophone.

In the resulting hierarchy of generalized models, those need to be selected that are sufficiently special and at the same time can be trained robustly. These are then used for constructing more complex HMMs instead of the specialized original context-dependent units. A good indication of the trainability of HMMs is given by the frequency of occurrence of the respective units in the available sample data. In the generalization hierarchy one simply chooses the most special models that occur more frequently in the training material than a certain threshold. In practice good results are achieved with minimal frequencies in the range of 50 to a few 100 occurrences.

Model Clustering

A different view on the generalization relation between HMMs for more or less specialized sub-word units results when methods are used on the basis of *decision trees*, which are also known as *classification and regression trees* [32]. In contrast to the definition of generalization relations between context-dependent sub-word units, criteria are formulated that combine similar units into groups or clusters (cf. e.g. [163]). Therefore, these techniques constitute methods for cluster analysis which, however, work on the symbolic representation of the models and within which similarity relations are defined by rules.

We want to explain the principal approach briefly using an example for the grouping of similar triphone models. Here, every node in the decision tree corresponds to a possible group of triphones with identical central phone. A certain model is assigned to such a model group by a sequence of binary decisions starting from the root node of the tree. In every tree node, therefore, a criterion set up by experts is evaluated which tests for a certain property of the model context.[9] Depending on whether or not the property is true for the triphone considered, either the left or the right successor of the current tree node is reached. The individual leaf nodes of the decision tree correspond to one HMM each which is used for the actual modeling of all triphones that are assigned to this node by the decision rules.

By means of this technique, a grouping of context-dependent sub-word units is possible which can be parametrized in a very detailed way. The main disadvantage of the method is, however, that the necessary decision rules need to be set up by experts. Furthermore, the respective rule sets tend to become quite large in practice and are given only exemplarily or as quite limited abridgments in the literature (cf. [163]).

A severe limitation of the method outlined above lies in the fact that for the grouping of models first expert knowledge needs to be formalized in a suitable way. Agglomerative techniques try to avoid this problem by deriving similarities between different partial models in a purely data-driven manner. Still a suitable distance measure between the parameters of the HMMs considered needs to be pre-specified for these methods. Then groups of models that have similar parameters and can thus be represented by a shared HMM can be computed automatically by applying a method for cluster analysis. Kai-Fu Lee used such a purely data-driven method for determining suitable generalized triphones as one of the first researchers [169, pp. 103–106]. However, the general applicability of the method is limited as, in general, the model structure of individual HMMs may vary and multiple states of a model have to be

---

[9]In the literature it is said quite often that nodes "ask questions" which is, however, a rather inappropriate anthropomorphic description of this automatic procedure.

taken into account in the distance calculation. As a consequence, automatic techniques for tying on the level of sub-word unit models did not prevail. In contrast, the application of equivalent methods on the level of model states can be considered state of the art today. Therefore, we want to present the respective techniques within the framework of the automatic generation of state clusters in the following section.

9.2.2 State Tying

The tying of individual HMM states can be viewed as a generalization of the merging of similar model subunits. On the level of model states, parameter groups may be chosen with substantially increased granularity. At the same time the application of automatic procedures becomes easier as the structure of the units processed is considerably simpler than the one of partial models.

Simple Duration Modeling

In general, no constructive tying is applied on the state level. This is because in contrast to model subunits no symbolic meaning within more complex models is associated with individual states. The only application of constructive state-based tying lies in the modification of the duration modeling of HMMs. An individual model state describes data segments with a duration that satisfies a geometric distribution. The maximal probability is reached for a segment length of a single time step independently from the actual values of the transition probabilities. For longer segment durations the occupancy probability decays exponentially (cf. [125, p. 218]). This duration behavior can be modified such that it satisfies a binomial distribution by a linear concatenation of multiple identical copies of a certain state. Thus in linear models a minimal segment duration is specified that corresponds to the number of replicated states. By means of the transition probabilities, the state group can be parametrized such that the maximal probability of occupancy is achieved for an arbitrary longer segment duration.

It can be assumed that a binomially distributed segment duration is better suited for the modeling than an exponentially decaying distribution. However, such rather moderate changes of the duration properties (cf. also Sect. 5.8.2) hardly have a strong influence on the modeling quality in practice as it is always dominated by the substantially more important part of the output distributions.

State Clustering

In contrast to constructive state tying, the rule-based or data-driven generation of state clusters has become a state of the art procedure. In many current systems such techniques are applied in order to achieve an optimal exploitation of the training data and simultaneously a high modeling quality in a flexible and conceptual simple way.

Especially for the field of automatic speech recognition, a number of rule-based methods for state clustering have been proposed. There linguistic-phonetic knowledge about similarities between the states within context-dependent phone models is represented in the form of decision trees (cf. [32], see also page 173). These can then be used to generate a generalization hierarchy of possible groups of model states. Such state groups describe phonetic events which appear as part of a speech sound in many different contexts. Parameter sets are then trained for those clusters for which sufficiently many samples are available and which allow a modeling as specialized as possible (cf. e.g. [99, 157, 218], [123, pp. 432–436]). The main disadvantage of these methods lies in the fact that it is necessary to acquire extremely specialized expert knowledge and to represent it suitably for the application within an automatic clustering method.

This problem is avoided if the state clusters are determined in a purely data-driven manner. In order to do so, first a similarity or distance measure between states needs to be defined that can be computed only on the basis of the state parameters or the samples associated with the state. Subsequently state groups, for which parameters can be trained robustly, can be identified by a principally arbitrary method for vector quantization or cluster analysis.

Figure 9.8 shows a simple greedy algorithm for the automatic generation of state clusters in HMMs of arbitrary structure. It proceeds similarly to the methods described in [169, p. 104] or [324]. The algorithm assumes that a suitable distance measure $d(C_j, C_k)$ for the parameter sets of individual states or state groups C_j and C_k has been defined. Furthermore, a criterion must be given that specifies when the clustering algorithm is to be terminated as otherwise all states would be merged into a trivial cluster.

First, in the initialization step a simple state cluster is generated for every given model state that contains the respective state only. Taken together these trivial clusters form the initial set of state clusters. Then, in every optimization phase that pair of clusters C_j and C_k is selected that has minimal distance with respect to the chosen distance measure. The two selected clusters are subsequently merged. If the termination criterion is not yet satisfied for the current set of clusters, the selection of the nearest neighboring state clusters will be repeated. Otherwise the procedure is finished.

A simple and robust termination criterion can be defined on the basis of the frequency of occurrence of the clusters generated in the training data—similarly to the tying of partial models. In this case it merely needs to be checked whether all state clusters generated so far cover a sufficient number of feature vectors. If this condition is met for every cluster, one assumes that the modified model can be trained robustly. Unfortunately, however, the minimal number of training samples per state cluster is application dependent and, in general, needs to be determined empirically. Similarly to the tying of partial models minimal frequencies from 50 up to a few 100 training samples achieve good results in practice which could be confirmed in numerous experiments of our own.

The most important model parameters of an HMM state consists in the respective output probability density function. In contrast, transition probabilities are of inferior importance and are not taken into account when determining state clusters. However, it is quite problematic to define a distance measure for general output distributions described by mixture density models. Therefore, suitable simplifications are usually made in practice.

Given the parameters of an HMM for which the number of states shall be optimized, a distance measure $d(C_i, C_j)$ for model states or state clusters, respectively, and a suitable termination criterion.

1. **Initialization**

   Create an individual state cluster for all model states i

   $C_i = \{i\} \quad \forall i, 0 \leq i \leq N$

   and combine these to form the initial set of clusters $\mathcal{C}$:

   $$\mathcal{C} = \bigcup_{i=1}^{N} \{C_i\}$$

2. **Selection**

   Choose from the current set $\mathcal{C}$ of state clusters that pair C_j, C_k that minimizes the distance measure:

   $$(C_j, C_k) = \underset{C_p, C_q \in \mathcal{C}}{\operatorname{argmin}} \, d(C_p, C_q)$$

3. **Reorganization**

   Construct a new state cluster C by merging C_j and C_k:

   $C \leftarrow C_j \cup C_k$

   Remove the original clusters C_j and C_k from $\mathcal{C}$ and insert the newly created cluster C instead:

   $\mathcal{C} \leftarrow \mathcal{C} \setminus \{C_j, C_k\} \cup \{C\}$

4. **Termination**

   if the termination criterion is not yet satisfied for the current set $\mathcal{C}$ of state clusters

         continue with step 2

   otherwise Stop!

Fig. 9.8 Algorithm for the automatic computation of a set of state clusters for a given HMM

The model parameters used to determine the state clusters do not need to correspond to those that are finally used for the modified model. Those can be chosen arbitrarily after the optimization of the model structure. Therefore, a simpler modeling can be used as the basis of the cluster analysis that is applied to the state space. In [324] output distributions with only a single normal density are used to determine the state clusters. Then the divergence can be used as a distance measure between states or state clusters, respectively. For two multi-variate normal densities it is defined as follows (cf. e.g. [102, pp. 458–459]):

$$d_{\text{divergence}}(\mathcal{N}_j, \mathcal{N}_k) = \frac{1}{2}(\boldsymbol{\mu}_j - \boldsymbol{\mu}_k)^T (\boldsymbol{C}_j^{-1} + \boldsymbol{C}_k^{-1})(\boldsymbol{\mu}_j - \boldsymbol{\mu}_k)$$

$$+ \frac{1}{2}\text{tr}\{\boldsymbol{C}_j^{-1}\boldsymbol{C}_k + \boldsymbol{C}_k^{-1}\boldsymbol{C}_j - 2\boldsymbol{I}\} \qquad (9.7)$$

A considerable simplification of this computation rule results if only diagonal covariance matrices are taken into account as they are also used in [324]. There the
clustering is furthermore limited to model states that occur in context-dependent
models having the same base phone. The termination criterion requires a minimal
number of 100 training samples per state group created. The HMM structure optimized in such a way then serves as a basis for the creation of a more complex model
where the output distributions are described by mixture density models. A comparable approach using a single normal density per state while clustering is described
in [210].

A distance measure for mixture models that can be evaluated particularly easily
was proposed in [66]. The underlying modeling of mixture densities uses one shared
global covariance only. Therefore, the distance of two state clusters can be defined
simply on the basis of the mean vectors of the respective component densities. The
maximal distance between all possible pairs of mean vectors μ_l and v_m is defined
to represent the cluster distance and can be computed as follows:

$$d(C_j, C_k) = \max_{\mu_l \in C_j, v_m \in C_k} \| \mu_l - v_m \|$$

This distance measure is referred to as furthest neighbor criterion as only the base
densities lying the furthest apart of each other are considered for computing the
cluster distances.

State specific output distributions can be compared in an especially simple way
for discrete HMMs and also for mixture models which are based on shared codebooks as, e.g., semi-continuous HMMs. In tied-mixture models the underlying component densities are not modified by the state clustering. Furthermore, state groups
are usually formed only for states sharing the same codebook. Therefore, the distributions are completely defined by the mixture weights c_{jk} or the discrete output
probabilities for individual symbols, respectively.

For such discrete distributions, the entropy $H(C_j)$ can be computed which represents a measure for how special or how general the generation of outputs is performed in the model state or state cluster C_j considered:

$$H(C_j) = -\sum_{k=1}^{K} c_{jk} \log c_{jk}$$

The entropy of a discrete distribution is non-negative and takes on its maximal value
$\log K$ for a uniform distribution. It becomes zero, if the distribution of model outputs is uniquely defined, i.e., exactly one discrete output probability or mixture
weight takes on the value one and all others vanish (cf. e.g. [65, pp. 630–631],
[123, pp. 120–122]).

The merging of states and the modeling of the respective outputs by a *single*
shared distribution causes an increase of the entropy. This can be used as a distance
measure for the generation of state clusters. In order to avoid that large clusters
which cover a huge number of feature vectors dominate the grouping process, the

increase in entropy is weighted by the number of underlying training samples. For a pair of clusters C_i and C_j for which the output distributions are given by mixture weights c_{ik} and c_{jk} the weighted increase in entropy is then defined as follows (cf. [169, p. 105]):

$$d(C_i, C_j) = (N_i + N_j)H(C_i \cup C_j) - N_i H(C_i) - N_j H(C_j)$$

Here N_i and N_j denote the number of training samples, which are assigned to the respective cluster. The new mixture weights of a state cluster C_m, which was formed from C_i and C_j, result as the weighted averages of the individual mixture weights according to

$$c_{mk} = \frac{N_i}{N_i + N_j} c_{ik} + \frac{N_j}{N_i + N_j} c_{jk}$$

Therefore, they can be computed easily during the clustering process.

9.2.3   Tying in Mixture Models

Compared to state clusters, an even more fine-grained form of tying can be achieved by merging similar parameters within the mixture models used to describe the output distributions.

Mixture Tying

The most well known variant of tying on the level of mixture densities is represented by the so-called *semi-continuous* or *tied-mixture HMMs* (see also Sect. 5.2). In such models a shared set of baseline densities is used for all mixture densities within an HMM, i.e., the individual components of the mixtures are tied across all distributions. One then obtains the following definition for the output probability densities (cf. Eq. (5.2)):

$$b_j(x) = \sum_{k=1}^{M} c_{jk} \mathcal{N}(x|\mu_k, C_k) = \sum_{k=1}^{M} c_{jk} g_k(x)$$

Semi-continuous HMMs offer a number of practical advantages as opposed to "fully continuous" models where the state specific mixtures are described completely independently of each other.

The use of a single shared codebook is able to ensure in a simple way that all baseline densities can be reliably estimated on the sample data available. These component densities result from the application of vector quantization procedures that often tend to produce class regions of similar size. Therefore, when computing an initial codebook for a semi-continuous HMM it can be ensured easily that on average sufficiently many feature vectors per parameter of the baseline distributions are available in the sample set. A subsequent training of the model modifies the individual densities, though. Only in exceptional cases, however, this re-estimation causes the parameter estimation to fail due to sparseness of example data. Another advantage of semi-continuous models lies in the improved numerical stability of the mixture evaluation process. This is due to the fact that in semi-continuous models the dynamic range of the scores can effectively be limited during the computation process by transforming the density values to posterior probabilities (see Sect. 7.3).

The principal idea of semi-continuous HMMs, namely to use shared baseline densities for the modeling of mixture densities, can be generalized to the use of multiple codebooks. However, the developer needs to specify which model states share a common codebook. It makes sense to merge those states in this respect that are meant to describe similar data and that can, therefore, be expected to use similar output distributions.

The most well known example of such a modeling are the so-called *phonetically tied-mixture HMMs*, which were developed for purposes of automatic speech recognition.[10] In phonetically tied-mixture models, all states of basic modeling units that from a phonetic view belong to similar phones or phone classes share common codebooks. For example, in the case that triphones are used as sub-word units, all models with the same central phone share an inventory of baseline densities.

Clustering of Densities

In addition to constructive techniques of mixture tying there also exist automatic methods for the tying of baseline densities within mixture models. However, for individual component densities in general no symbolic description of the context of occurrence can be specified. Therefore, no methods on the basis of decision trees that rely on declarative rules are applicable. In contrast, agglomerative techniques can be applied in complete analogy to the automatic determination of state clusters as presented in the previous section. Thus an even finer granularity in the merging of similar model parameters is obtained.

Agglomerative state clustering techniques require a suitable distance measure between individual densities. Similarly to the generation of state groups a possible choice for this distance measure is the divergence (see Eq. (9.7)).

In contrast, in [66] a measure is applied which can be computed extremely easily. It only evaluates the weighted Euclidean distance of the respective mean vectors μ_i and μ_j of the density groups C_i and C_j:

$$d(C_i, C_j) = \frac{N_i N_j}{N_i + N_j} \| \mu_i - \mu_j \|$$

Here N_i and N_j denote the number of training samples which are associated with the respective density. A more expensive method, which also takes into account the covariance matrices of the densities involved, was proposed in [145].

---

[10]The idea of using phonetically tied mixtures for the modeling of HMM output distributions was independently proposed in [328] and [230], respectively.

In contrast to the generation of state clusters, the merging of parameters on the level of mixture densities does not aim at defining more general modeling units. Rather, all methods serve the primary purpose of reducing the model's complexity. As a consequence, the model's number of parameters is reduced, too, and it can be estimated more robustly on the training data available. In addition, a simpler model can also be evaluated more efficiently, in general.

Tying of Covariance Matrices

In mixture density models, the mean vector of a baseline density describes the center of a region of high density in the data distribution considered. The associated covariance matrices define the local distortion of the feature space. Therefore, the mean vectors are of greater importance for the representation of the data distribution. However, in contrast to the estimation of mean vectors, covariance matrices require considerably more training samples for a robust estimation. Consequently, in larger mixture models the covariance matrices are frequently tied, i.e., shared across multiple or all baseline densities.

The most radical approach of this type is applied in automatic speech recognition systems which originated from the tradition of Philips research (cf. e.g. [210, 289]). In contrast to the usual definition of continuous HMMs, there output probability densities are defined on the basis of Laplacian densities with a position vector r_{jk} and a scaling factor $v(l)$ per dimension of the feature space:

$$g_{jk}(x \mid r_{jk}, v) = \frac{1}{\prod_{l=1}^{n} 2v(l)} e^{-\sum_{l=1}^{n} \frac{|x(l) - r_{jk}(l)|}{v(l)}}$$

In essence, this corresponds to the use of Gaussian densities with mean vectors r_{jk} and a commonly shared diagonal covariance matrix, the elements of which are given by the scaling factors $v(l)$. The success of such a drastic simplification of the covariance modeling is most likely due to the fact that in the respective recognition systems always also a linear discriminant analysis is applied, too. Its first computation step consists in bringing the covariance matrices of the individual pattern classes to the form of identity matrices approximately (see Sect. 9.1.6). Thus the modeling of the local distortion of the feature space considerably loses importance and can be successfully described by a single global diagonal covariance matrix even for mixture models with some $10, 000$ or several $100, 000$ densities.

A very sophisticated method for parameter tying of covariances in mixture models was proposed in [106]. The approach uses so-called semi-tied covariance matrices. A semi-tied covariance is defined on the basis of a diagonal covariance matrix that is estimated individually per density. The effective covariance matrix used in computations is constructed from the density-specific diagonal elements by applying a non-diagonal transform matrix which is shared across a set of component densities. In simple terms, the method distinguishes between core parameters of a covariance matrix, i.e., the diagonal elements, and sharable less density-specific parameters, i.e., the off-diagonal parts, which may be shared between mixtures.

9.3 Initialization of Parameters

The training methods for HMMs presented in Sect. 5.7 always require the specification of a suitable initial model. Based on this initial estimate, the model parameters are then iteratively improved. However, it is hardly dealt with in the literature how such a starting point of the optimization procedures should be chosen, even though this decision fundamentally influences the whole subsequent parameter training. For models with some practical relevance it is by no means sufficient to choose initial parameters randomly or according to a uniform distribution.

The *segmental k-means* algorithm is the only well defined method that offers the possibility to compute initial parameters for HMM training [168]. This method for parameter estimation alternates between a segmentation of the training data and a computation of new model parameters on the basis of this segmentation alone. The structure of the model is not changed by this procedure (see Sect. 5.7.6). Therefore, it is sufficient to specify a segmentation of the training set and the desired model structure for the initialization of the method. The definition of a suitable model structure, in general, comprises a modularization into model subunits (see Sect. 8.2), the choice of a suitable topology for the baseline models (see Sect. 8.1), and the specification of the number of baseline densities that should be used for describing the output distributions.

In the segmental k-means algorithm the initial segmentation of the sample set is derived from a reference annotation of the data. The manual mapping of feature vectors to model states is, however, de facto not possible in practice and even a manual segmentation of data into elementary description units as, e.g., phones or characters requires an extraordinary effort which can only be afforded in the rarest of cases.

Therefore, in [168] a radically simplified approach was proposed for the initialization of linearly structured models. First, a modeling framework for every section of the training data can be derived from the reference annotation by concatenating the respective HMMs. For example, in the field of automatic speech recognition an overall HMM for the respective utterance can be created by concatenating word models according to the orthographic transcription. The newly constructed model also has a linear structure as it was composed of component models with linear topology. Therefore, the associated data will be generated by this model while passing through its states in a linearly ordered sequence. This linear sequence can then be mapped to the available feature vectors. As no information about the relative durations of segments is available during model initialization, the segmental k-means algorithm simply assumes equal lengths for all segments associated with HMM states. Though this extremely simple initial segmentation will, in general, be quite inadequate, it is usually sufficient for the definition of a starting point for the subsequent optimization of the model by the training process.

Considerably better results can be achieved if more accurate segmentation information is taken into account for the initialization of the model parameters. This is usually derived from an existing recognition system which is used for segmenting the training data into a sequence of words, phones, or characters.[11] The linear mapping between feature vectors and model states is then merely performed within those rather small segments so that an acceptable alignment accuracy is achieved.

In general, the choice of an initial model on the basis of an optimized segmentation has a positive effect on the parameter training. Therefore, even without changes in the model structure an improvement in the modeling quality will be achieved after such a second initialization phase. Moreover, with a sufficiently precise segmentation, it is possible in particular to initialize the training of a complex model considerably better than on the basis of an uninformed linear mapping. Therefore, large HMM systems are frequently built in a sequence of design phases. One starts with a rather simple model and refines its structure in a number of subsequent optimization steps. The parameters of the next more complex model are then newly initialized with the improved segmentation information derived from the previous model.

---

[11]In the rare case that a manual segmentation on the level of elementary units is available for a given sample set, this can obviously be used as an alternative in this phase of the method.

Efficient Model Evaluation

10

With the Viterbi algorithm a method for decoding HMMs was presented in Sect. 5.6. Also for the evaluation of n-gram models, algorithms exist as, e.g., the so-called backing-off described in Sect. 6.5.5. However, these methods only represent the basic foundations on which algorithms for the efficient integrated evaluation and decoding of Markov models are developed in practice.

All these methods are based on the idea to save "unnecessary" computations as much as possible. In some cases this can be achieved by a suitable reorganization of the representation of the search space or of the model itself. In the majority of the methods, however, "less promising" solutions are explicitly discarded early from the further search process. Thus the search space is reduced to a tightly focused "promising" part. This procedure is frequently referred to as search space *pruning*. The problem with all those techniques is to find a method for identifying "less promising" solutions. With absolute certainty this is only possible *after* the actual optimal solution is known. Every premature decision holds the risk of possibly deleting the hypothesis from the search space which was actually sought for. In practice, however, often the exact computation of the optimal solution is out of question anyway because of the tremendous computational costs. Therefore, one usually accepts that manageable efficient methods in general produce approximate solutions only. Such methods are then also called *suboptimal*.

The following sections give an overview over the most important methods for the efficient evaluation of Markov models. At the beginning methods for speeding up the computation of output probability densities on the basis of mixture models are presented. Then the standard method for the efficient application of Viterbi decoding to larger HMMs is described. The following section presents methods for efficiently generating first-best segmentation result as well as alternative solutions organized in the form of so-called n-best lists. In Sect. 10.4 methods are explained that apply techniques of search space pruning for the acceleration of the parameter training of HMMs. The chapter concludes with a section on tree-like model structures, which can be used both in HMMs and in n-gram models in order to increase the efficiency when processing these models.

G.A. Fink, *Markov Models for Pattern Recognition*,
Advances in Computer Vision and Pattern Recognition,
DOI 10.1007/978-1-4471-6308-4_10, © Springer-Verlag London 2014

10.1   Efficient Evaluation of Mixture Densities

In typical applications of continuous HMMs, where output distributions are approx-imated by mixture densities, the evaluation of these models may dominate the total resulting search effort. Especially if a large number of baseline densities is used for representing the outputs as precisely as possible, more than half of the decoding effort may result from the evaluation of probability density functions (cf. [231]). Therefore, methods for limiting the effort in the mixture evaluation are applied in most larger HMM-based systems. Unfortunately, however, the actual procedures are not always well documented in the literature.

All these methods are based on the same principle idea. First a subset of rele-vant baseline densities is identified by some method that can be evaluated extremely fast. Here densities are considered relevant that make significant contributions to the computation of the required output probability densities. Afterwards, the density is computed exactly for all mixture components in this subset. In contrast, for all re-maining distributions some constant value is used[1] as an approximation of the actual density value which is expected to be quite small. The overall effort in decoding the mixture density is reduced because these nearly vanishing densities are "inferred" rather than computed explicitly.

The best known method for predicting the actual baseline densities to be eval-uated is the so-called *Gaussian selection* which was first proposed in [24] (cf. e.g. [52, 156, 231]). First the available Gaussian densities are grouped by applying a method for vector quantization. Overlaps between the density groups are explicitly allowed in order to improve the subsequently performed accelerated density evalu-ation. Furthermore, the centroid is calculated for every group of baseline densities. During the decoding of the HMM only those Gaussian densities are computed ex-actly that lie in the density group for which the centroid has minimal distance to the current feature vector. In general, a group of densities only defines a short list of those distributions that seem promising for being evaluated exactly. Therefore, the technique is also referred to as the method of *Gaussian short lists* in the literature. Depending on the system configuration an acceleration of the density evaluation by a factor of 3 to 10 can be achieved when using this method.

A similar principle is the basis of the method proposed in [271]. It uses a se-quence of vector quantization processes that are carried out more and more exactly. First, a coarse model of the available densities is evaluated. This coarse model is built only on a subset of the available dimensions of the feature vectors in the repre-sentation used. Then, more exact and thus more costly computations are carried out for promising density candidates in one or more subsequent processing steps.[2]

---

[1]The actual choice of this lower bound for vanishing density values is actually a quite critical parameter for the overall performance of the system. An empirical investigation of its influence is, for example, presented in [156].

[2]Whether or not a density candidate is promising can be determined by a pruning strategy similar to the beam-search method presented in Sect. 10.2.

In [100] a method was proposed that is especially suited for baseline densities with diagonal covariance matrices which are frequently used in larger HMM-based systems. The regions where these densities contribute a relevant amount to a mixture density are approximated by hyper-cuboids. Then, those hyper-cuboids in which a certain feature vector lies can be determined very efficiently by representing the feature space as an n-dimensional tree. Finally, the actual values are computed exactly for the associated densities. The resulting error of the approximation defined such can be controlled by a suitable choice of the extension of the hyper-cuboids.

An extensive empirical investigation of different methods for accelerating the evaluation of mixture densities is presented in [224]. The method of Gaussian selection described above, i.e., the preselection of certain Gaussian densities by a vector quantization process, is identified as the best performing single technique. However, the densities in the three to five density groups lying closest to the current feature vector are evaluated exactly which constitutes a modification with respect to the original method [24]. The authors report a reduction by a factor of more than five in the effort for evaluating mixture densities and an overall reduction in the computational effort to approximately 30 %.

10.2   Efficient Decoding of Hidden Markov Models

With its linear time complexity, the Viterbi algorithm for decoding HMMs represents already a considerable improvement in efficiency as opposed to the naive computation scheme with exponential costs. However, the method still has quadratic complexity in the number of model states. In most applications of HMMs this quadratic complexity can be reduced to an almost linear one by choosing a suitable restricted model topology (cf. Sect. 8.1). Thus it can be ensured that only a few possible predecessor states have to be considered per computation of a partial path probability. Nevertheless, the Viterbi matrix of the $\delta_t(i)$ grows linearly with the number of model states such that, in practice, a complete evaluation is possible for quite limited problems only.

In a speech recognition system with large vocabulary the acoustic-phonetic model usually consists of several $10,000$ states. When applying the Viterbi algorithm directly for each of these states, partial path scores need to be computed at every time step. However, all these states encode quite different acoustic events. Consequently, it can be safely assumed that the majority of possible state sequences represents spoken utterances which hardly exhibit any similarities with the signal analyzed and, therefore, do not need to be considered at all.

These "less promising" solutions need to be identified both as early as possible during the decoding process and with sufficiently reliability. It is immediately clear that an absolute threshold of the path score is out of question for solving this problem as the values of $\delta_t(i)$ in total vary largely in dependence on the data considered and especially with the length of the observation sequence. Furthermore, a real vanishing of the partial path probabilities is usually avoided by the methods for flooring presented in Sect. 7.2, i.e., by limiting individual contributions to the path score to certain minimal values. Therefore, only the *differences* in the scores can give indications for promising partial results or for such paths that could be eliminated.

10.2.1 Beam Search Algorithm

In the so-called *beam-search* algorithm developed by Lowerre ([185, pp. 25–31], cf. also [184], [123, pp. 606–608])[3] an extremely robust dynamic criterion for pruning the search space is used. It is based on the relative differences in the partial path scores. Thus, the search is virtually focused within a tight "beam" around the currently best partial solution.

The basic idea of the method is to restrict the evaluation of the partial path scores in the Viterbi matrix to so-called active states, that is, to a rather limited set. States are defined as being active for which the scores $\delta_t(i)$ do not deviate too much from the locally optimal solution $\delta_t^* = \max_j \delta_t(j)$. The maximally admissible score difference is specified by a factor B proportional to the currently optimal score δ_t^*. The set of active states $\mathscr{A}_t$ at time t is, therefore, defined as follows:

$$\mathscr{A}_t = \{i \,|\, \delta_t(i) \geq B\delta_t^*\} \quad \text{with} \quad \delta_t^* = \max_j \delta_t(j) \text{ and } 0 < B \ll 1$$

Only these active states are considered as potential predecessors when computing the local path scores (cf. Eq. (5.9)) in the further evaluation of the Viterbi matrix for the respective next time step $t + 1$. Consequently, the following modified computation rule is obtained:

$$\delta_{t+1}(j) = \max_{i \in \mathscr{A}_t} \{\delta_t(i) a_{ij}\} b_j(O_{t+1}) \tag{10.1}$$

The proportionality factor B is chosen as a very small positive constant and typically lies in the range of 10^{-10} to 10^{-20}. The smaller B is the more states according to their scores fall into the interval $[B\,\delta_t^* \dots \delta_t^*]$ and thus are active, i.e., are considered in the search process.

This concept can intuitively be understood better when using the negative-logarithmic representation of probability quantities (cf. Sect. 7.1). The proportionality factor B then becomes an additive offset $\tilde{B}$, and one obtains the following rule for determining the set of active states:

$$\mathscr{A}_t = \{i \,|\, \tilde{\delta}_t(i) \leq \tilde{\delta}_t^* + \tilde{B}\} \quad \text{with} \quad \tilde{\delta}_t^* = \min_j \tilde{\delta}_t(j) \text{ and } \tilde{B} > 0 \tag{10.2}$$

---

[3]Despite the enormous practical relevance of the method hardly any descriptions of it can be found in the relevant monographs. Instead, the interested reader is referred to the original work of Lowerre [185] which, unfortunately, is rather difficult to access.

Thus around the respective locally optimal path score $\tilde{\delta}_t^*$ a "corridor" of constant width is created. The optimal solution is only sought for within this tightly focused search space. Therefore, the only free parameter $\tilde{B}$ of this search method is usually referred to as the *beam width*.

For an implementation of the method it is, however, inconvenient to select a small subset of active states as potential *predecessors* from the usually quite large total number of states as given in Eq. (10.1). Despite the focusing of the computations on active states only, all possible states j would need to be considered at time $t + 1$ in order to check whether their predecessors lie in the set of active states $\mathscr{A}_t$ for the previous time step. With respect to the effort necessary, such a verification operation would be almost comparable to an actual computation of the respective score.

Therefore, in the beam-search algorithm the "viewing direction" during the recursive computation of the partial path probabilities is changed. Instead of considering all potential predecessors, the calculations are directly propagated from the respective active states to the potential *successors*.[4] In order to be able to formulate this procedure exactly, we define a successor relation between states of an HMM as follows:

$$ j = \mathrm{succ}(i) \quad \Leftrightarrow \quad a_{ij} > 0 $$

For "entering" into the model we, furthermore, introduce a non-emitting state 0 which has all possible start states as successors:

$$ j = \mathrm{succ}(0) \quad \Leftrightarrow \quad \pi_j > 0 $$

The resulting algorithm, which is summarized in Fig. 10.1, now proceeds as follows: First the set of active states is initialized by the single non-emitting state 0. Afterwards follows the propagation of the path probabilities which is carried out for all times $t = 1, \ldots, T$.

At the beginning of every propagation step, the locally optimal score $\tilde{\delta}_t^*$ is not yet known and is set to a suitable large value. Then for all active states i the respective possible successors j are considered. Given a certain fixed predecessor state i one obtains the score $\tilde{\delta}_t(i, j)$ for a path to state j. The optimal partial path score of state j is now computed anew if no solution was known so far, or is updated if an improved score results from successor i. Simultaneously, the pointers $\psi_t(j)$ necessary for tracking back the optimal path are updated. For the completion of a propagation step, then the set $\mathscr{A}_t$ of states is determined that will be further active.

As soon as this computation scheme reaches the end of the observation sequence, i.e. time T, the approximately optimal path $\hat{s}^*$ can be determined starting from its last sequence element $\hat{s}_T^*$ in the same way as in the Viterbi algorithm (cf. also Fig. 5.5). The sub-optimal solution found by the beam-search procedure will, in general, be different from the theoretically optimal state sequence s^*. However, in

---

[4]This computation scheme is conceptually similar to the propagation of tokens representing partial path hypotheses in the so-called token-passing framework [326].

1. **Initialization**
   initialize the set of active states with the non-emitting state 0
   $$\mathscr{A}_0 \leftarrow \{0\}$$
2. **Propagation**
   for all times $t, t = 1, \ldots, T$:
   - initialize the locally optimal path score $\tilde{\delta}_t^* \leftarrow \infty$
   - for all $i \in \mathscr{A}_{t-1}$ and all $j \in \{j \mid j = \text{succ}(i)\}$
     - compute the local path score from state i to its successor j
       $$\tilde{\delta}_t(i, j) = \tilde{\delta}_{t-1}(i) + \tilde{a}_{ij} + \tilde{b}_j(O_t)$$
     - update the partial path score for state j, if necessary
       if $\tilde{\delta}_t(j)$ has not yet been computed or $\tilde{\delta}_t(i, j) < \tilde{\delta}_t(j)$
       $$\tilde{\delta}_t(j) \leftarrow \tilde{\delta}_t(i, j)$$
       $$\psi_t(j) \leftarrow i$$
     - update the locally optimal path score
       if $\tilde{\delta}_t(i, j) < \tilde{\delta}_t^*$
       $$\tilde{\delta}_t^* \leftarrow \tilde{\delta}_t(i, j)$$
   - determine the set $\mathscr{A}_t$ of active states
     - initialize the new set of active states $\mathscr{A}_t \leftarrow \emptyset$
     - add all successors j of active states i which lie within the beam
       for all $i \in \mathscr{A}_{t-1}$ and all $j \in \{j \mid j = \text{succ}(i)\}$
       if $\tilde{\delta}_t(j) <= \tilde{\delta}_t^* + \tilde{B}$
       $$\mathscr{A}_t \leftarrow \mathscr{A}_t \cup \{j\}$$
3. **Termination**
   determine the optimal end state
   $$\hat{s}_T^* := \underset{j \in \mathscr{A}_T}{\arg\min} \tilde{\delta}_T(j)$$
4. **Backtracking of the approximately optimal path**
   for all times $t, t = T - 1, \ldots, 1$:
   $$\hat{s}_t^* = \psi_{t+1}(\hat{s}_{t+1}^*)$$

Fig. 10.1 Beam-search algorithm for the efficient computation of the approximately optimal state sequence $\hat{s}^*$ in HMMs with large numbers of states. Probability quantities are represented in the negative-logarithmic domain (cf. Sect. 7.1)

practice the exhaustive search of the whole Viterbi matrixi, which is necessary for determining s^* exactly, is possible in the rarest of cases only due the computational effort required.

The beam-search algorithm constitutes the core of every method for decoding HMMs and can also be applied to the search with n-gram models in slightly modified form (cf. Chap. 12). In the realization of the algorithm presented here and shown in Fig. 10.1 further improvements in efficiency are possible that may result from the chosen internal representation of the HMMs. Thus, for example, the explicit computation of $\mathscr{A}_t$ can be avoided if the decision about active states is made only at the beginning of the respective next propagation step. Also the evaluation of the output probabilities $b_j(O_t)$ is in fact not required until after the recombination of the potential paths.

10.3   Efficient Generation of Recognition Results

The basis of all decoding results generated for HMMs is defined by traceback information accumulated during the application of the Viterbi algorithm (see Sect. 5.6.1) or the considerably more efficient beam-search procedure described in the previous section. Usually, this traceback information consists of the—potentially sparse—matrix of backpointers $\psi_t(j)$ that specify the locally optimal predecessor of the respective model state j at time t. First, from this traceback information the optimal state sequence can be derived by backtracking from the optimal endpoint. With reference to the predefined semantics of the model structure it can be translated into an optimal sequence of segmentation units afterwards.

Though the matrix of backpointers stores considerably more information than immediately required for representing the optimal state sequence, these additional back-links are still not sufficient for extracting alternative segmentation results. However, if the traceback information is extended appropriately, the generation of alternative solutions becomes possible.

In the following, we will first describe how the first-best segmentation result can be generated efficiently from a suitably reorganized traceback data structure. Afterwards, we will present algorithms for extracting not only the first-best solution but also alternative segmentation results with lower scores in order to form so-called n-best lists, i.e., sets of the top n best-scoring recognition results.

10.3.1   First-Best Decoding of Segmentation Units

In principle, the optimal segmentation hypothesis can be generated from the optimal state sequence which was obtained by applying Viterbi decoding. However, segmentation units will, in general, span longer time intervals. The actual state sequence within these intervals is irrelevant for the segmentation result. Therefore, a considerable amount of memory can be saved if the traceback information stored is limited to the relevant one.

This can be achieved by directly generating hypotheses about segmentation units during decoding and linking these to each other appropriately. These hypothesis data structures, which are frequently referred to as *word-link records* [326], can be created whenever a transition from a final state of a segmentation unit is made into an initial state of another one. The only additional information that has to be available is the backpointer to the previous word-link record representing the previous

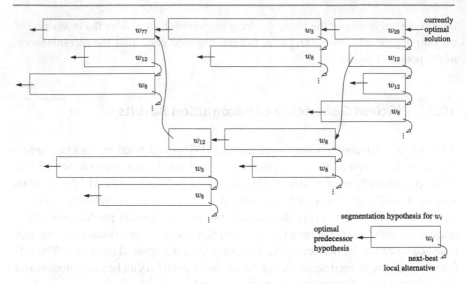

Fig. 10.2 Example of hypothesis data structures generated during HMM decoding of a recognition task with a hypothetical lexicon of segmentation units $\{w_1, w_2, \ldots\}$. Individual segmentation hypotheses are back-linked to their optimal predecessor. Additionally, references to the respective next-best scoring hypotheses ending at the same time establish a linked list of local alternative solutions

segmentation hypothesis lying on the currently optimal state sequence.[5] Figure 10.2 shows an example of such a set of back-linked hypothesis data structures representing high-level segmentation information.

10.3.2 Algorithms for N-Best Search

The goal of methods for *n-best search*, which were first proposed by researchers at BBN [45, 279], is to compute $n - 1$ additional alternative segmentation results with decreasing scores. Ideally, the n solutions produced would correspond to the top n best-scoring state sequences. Unfortunately, generating these alternative solutions only comes at considerable costs.

Let us recall the basic principle of Viterbi decoding. In a dynamic programming style algorithm the optimal scores $\delta_t(j)$ for producing a prefix $O_1, \ldots, O_t$ of the data and reaching a specific model state j are computed. Each local computation is a maximization over all possible predecessor states and only stores the back-link to the optimal predecessor $\psi_t(j) := \mathrm{argmax}_i \{\delta_{t-1}(i)a_{ij}\}$. When this process reaches the final time step T, the optimal end state of the best-scoring state sequence

---

[5]This additional back-linking can, for example, be represented as individual path identifiers (cf. [326]) or as a pair of state-identifier and end-time that augments the information associated with active states during model decoding.

can be determined. Following the back-links from there produces the optimal state sequence.

The problem is now that no alternative decisions have been stored locally. Therefore, no possibility exists for extracting the second-best scoring solution. In order to do so in an exact way, not a single back-link $\psi_t(j)$ but also the back-link to the locally second-best predecessor would need to be stored. As n-best search does not make too much sense for small n, this exact n-best algorithm that requires n backpointers per entry of the Viterbi matrix is not feasible in practice.

Consequently, approximate solutions have been proposed for n-best search. The basic idea behind these methods is to store alternative predecessor states only if this information is relevant for an alternative segmentation, i.e., on the level of word or character hypotheses.

In *sentence-dependent n-best* [45, 279] any back-link to a predecessor state is retained if the paths associated with these alternatives represent different segmentations. Therefore, this algorithm is optimal in producing the n best-scoring segmentation hypotheses that are different on the segmentation level. However, the necessity to store and compare partial segmentation results during the search process requires considerable computational effort.

The so-called *word-dependent n-best* algorithm [276] preserves back-links to alternative predecessors only if these are associated with different segmentation units, i.e., not taking into account the associated partial segmentations. Alternative paths within the same segmentation unit are recombined as in the usual Viterbi decoding.

An even more radical simplification is used by *lattice n-best* [276]. This algorithm stores alternative predecessor states only at the boundaries between segmentation units. Though this seems sufficient for retaining relevant alternatives at first sight, competing solutions representing different segmentation hypotheses might be recombined within segmentation units.

An important problem that all n-best methods have to solve is how the bookkeeping of the alternative solutions found is arranged. The first methods proposed generated all alternatives found during decoding and recombined sets of such solutions dynamically during the search process (cf. [45]). A much more efficient and widely successful solution to this problem is to produce n-best results in a two-phase algorithm [286]. In a forward Viterbi-style search only the necessary backpointers for alternatives are stored. Afterwards, a backward search process based on the A* graph-search algorithm (cf. [217, Sect. 9.2, pp. 141–154]) is used to generate the n-best solutions. This process is extremely efficient as the Viterbi scores computed during the forward pass not only define the necessary admissible heuristics for completing paths in the A* algorithm but represent the actual optimal scores. Consequently, the search for the n-best solutions is focused as much as possible.

The idea of n-best search can easily be combined with the representation of traceback information in the form of word-link records as described in the previous section. Backpointers to alternative word-level predecessors of hypotheses can be represented quite compactly if the data structure is extended appropriately. Instead of storing references to a certain number of alternative predecessors in the successor node, every note stores only the link to the optimal predecessor and to the next-best alternative hypothesis ending at the same time t [326]. Figure 10.2 shows an example of such a set of doubly linked hypothesis data structures that can serve as the basis for generating n-best results by an A*-based backward search.

10.4   Efficient Parameter Estimation

The computational effort necessary for parameter estimation usually is not of primary concern in efficiency considerations as the design and parametrization process of HMMs can be performed in advance. However, in all methods applied for this purpose an iterative optimization is required which causes the running time of an individual optimization step to contribute multiple times to the total effort. Furthermore, frequently different parametrizations or configurations need to be created in order to select the best performing version after completed parameter training. It is, therefore, quite obvious to also try to avoid "unnecessary" computations in training, unless these measures have some negative effects on the quality of the parameter estimation.

10.4.1 Forward–Backward Pruning

In the Baum–Welch algorithm the complete matrix of forward and backward probabilities needs to be evaluated for every segment of the training data. In fact, the idea of the beam-search algorithm can also be applied to this method in order to carry out necessary computations for relevant parts of the search space only (cf. [125, p. 244]).

During the computation of the forward and backward variables, for every time t active states are defined depending on the optimal values $\alpha_t^* = \max_j \alpha_t(j)$ or $\beta_t^* = \max_j \beta_t(j)$ of the respective probability quantity. The set of active states, which are considered during the computation process, is then defined as

$$\mathcal{A}_t = \left\{ i \,|\, \alpha_t(i) \geq B\,\alpha_t^* \right\} \quad \text{with} \quad \alpha_t^* = \max_j \alpha_t(j) \text{ and } 0 < B \ll 1$$

for the forward variable and as

$$\mathcal{B}_t = \left\{ i \,|\, \beta_t(i) \geq B\,\beta_t^* \right\} \quad \text{with} \quad \beta_t^* = \max_j \beta_t(j) \text{ and } 0 < B \ll 1$$

for its counterpart in the backward algorithm (cf. also Eq. (10.2)). The constant B specifies the beam width in the same way as in the *beam-search* algorithm and thus implicitly determines the size of the part of the total search space which is searched for solutions.

Thus one obtains modified recursive computation rules for the forward and backward variables. In these modified equations only those states are considered that have been active at the respective previous time step (cf. Eqs. (5.8) and (5.16)):

$$\alpha_{t+1}(j) := \sum_{i \in \mathscr{A}_t} \{\alpha_t(i)a_{ij}\} b_j(O_{t+1}) \tag{10.3}$$

$$\beta_t(i) := \sum_{j \in \mathscr{B}_{t+1}} a_{ij} b_j(O_{t+1})\beta_{t+1}(j) \tag{10.4}$$

The state probability $\gamma_t(i)$ is central for the parameter training and is essentially obtained as a product of the forward and backward probability (see Eq. (5.15)). As a consequence of the search space pruning, it vanishes for all those times t and states i for which no calculation of $\alpha_t(i)$ or $\beta_t(i)$ is performed. Especially at the beginning of the parameter training, the proportionality factor B should, therefore, be chosen very small and, consequently, the beam width large (cf. Sect. 10.2.1) such that only a moderate limitation of the search is achieved. Otherwise, possible solutions might be excluded due to still unsatisfactory estimates of the model parameters.

A simplification of the method is obtained, if the principle of the beam-search algorithm is only applied within a modified forward algorithm. The calculation of the backward variables then can be limited to those states for which a non-vanishing value of $\alpha_t(i)$ was determined without the need to compute $\mathscr{B}_t$ explicitly.

10.4.2 Segmental Baum–Welch Algorithm

A further possibility for limiting the search effort during Baum–Welch training results if the chronological structure of the data is exploited for reorganizing the model training. The basic assumption underlying this procedure is that the observation sequences to be processed represent signals which evolve linearly in time. Consequently, unnecessary computations can be avoided by using appropriately constrained model topologies. For a given sample set the reference annotation defines the sequence of meaningful units for every section O of the data, e.g., the orthographic transcription of spoken utterances. From this annotation a linearly organized HMM can be constructed by concatenation of the corresponding partial models for, e.g., words. Here interactions between the partial models can only occur to a limited extent at model boundaries. In contrast, the association of a state of a partial model with a far away segment of the data is extremely unlikely. Therefore, one may assume that the forward and backward probabilities will take on positive values only within the segments which are defined by the mapping between a partial model and the corresponding data. Consequently, the associated forward and backward matrices will approximately have a block-diagonal structure.

When neglecting the interactions across segment boundaries, the block structure can be fixed *before* the beginning of the training and the evaluation of the probability quantities can be limited accordingly. The segmentation of the data by means of the current model serves as the basis for this decision. However, only an approximate solution of the segmentation problem can be determined such as the current model is not yet optimally adapted to the sample data.

The Baum–Welch algorithm is then applied on a per-segment basis and the statistics necessary for parameter estimation are computed locally for every segmentation hypothesis. The cumulative statistics for determining updated model parameters result in complete analogy to the method for handling multiple observation sequences (cf. Sect. 5.7.7). The individual statistics gathered for all segments simply need to be summed up and normalized appropriately.[6]

The combination of a segmentation of the training data by means of the Viterbi algorithm and a subsequent parameter training on the individual segments only corresponds to the evaluation of a block-diagonal matrix of forward and backward probabilities. In [54] this method is called segmented training. However, a certain loss in the accuracy or flexibility, respectively, of the method may result from the strict specification of the segment boundaries *before* the start of the parameter training. In the so-called semi-relaxed training this disadvantage is avoided by working with overlaps between the respective neighboring blocks or segments [54].

By means of a "pre-segmentation" of the data before the application of the training procedure, considerable improvements in efficiency can be achieved especially on long observation sequences. Consider, for example, an HMM with 100 states that shall be trained on a sequence of length $T = 1000$. In this case matrices of size 100×1000 need to be computed for forward and backward probabilities, i.e., $1 \cdot 10^5$ values each. In contrast, when partitioning the data into 10 segments of an average length $T' = 100$, which are associated with partial models of on average 10 states each, only matrices of size 10×100 need to be processed ten times and thus only $2 \cdot 10^4$ probabilities must be evaluated. Therefore, already in this simple case one obtains a considerable improvement in the efficiency by a factor of 10. In general, this efficiency gain will be roughly proportional to the number of segments used.

10.4.3 Training of Model Hierarchies

In HMM-based recognition systems one is principally interested in the use of models that are as specific as possible. However, general HMMs are usually also required for the description of rare events. These models need to be trained in addition to the special ones. In the field of speech recognition it is, for example, common practice to also include general context independent phone models into an overall recognition system in addition to the widely used triphone models.

In order to be able to correctly estimate the parameters of different modeling components, typically a separate training of the respective models would be required. However, in most complex recognition models, a generalization hierarchy exists between the HMMs. Therefore, under certain conditions the parameters of more general models can approximately be derived from the statistics gathered during the estimation of more special HMMs.

---

[6]In fact, the segmentation of a larger sample set into partial observation sequences already applies this principle procedure.

Let us assume that not only a unique relation exists between special and general models, but that also the states of specialized models can be uniquely associated with the ones of the more general HMMs. Furthermore, in continuous HMMs the output probability density functions of the corresponding model states need to be "compatible", i.e., they must use the same set of baseline densities. This is trivially the case for semi-continuous HMMs but can also be achieved in all other variants of tied mixture models.

Under these conditions the statistics for the estimation of the parameters of the respective general states are obtained by simple summation over the values which were computed for the associated special model states. As an example we want to consider a triphone modeling which uses the same number of states for all baseline models. The respective n-th state of the triphone model x/a/y then corresponds to the n-th state of the monophone model /a/. For updating the model parameters of the context independent model, all training samples have to be considered which are assigned to one of the associated special model states. Therefore, one obtains the state probability $\gamma_t(/a/_n)$ for the n-th monophone state approximately as a sum over all the state probabilities of the respective triphone states:

$$\gamma_t(/a/_n) = \sum_x \sum_y \gamma_t(x/a/y_n)$$

In analogy to this, the mapping probability $\xi_t(j, k)$ for the mixture components can be approximated. Then estimates for the model parameters of the general HMM can be computed in the usual way on the basis of those two quantities (cf. Sect. 5.7 page 87).

Nevertheless, the parameter estimates obtained such constitute only approximate solutions. In fact, the existing model parameters of the general model would need to be used for correctly determining the state probability and all other statistics. However, in practice the general models are only used to complement the modeling with robust baseline models. Therefore, it is mostly irrelevant whether their parameter estimates were only determined approximately.

10.5   Tree-Like Model Organization

In order to increase the processing efficiency of Markov models, modifications of the model structure can be applied in addition to the use of special algorithms. Both for HMMs and for n-gram models, tree-like structures offer good possibilities here.

10.5.1 HMM Prefix Trees

In all larger HMM model structures the number of model states by far exceeds the number of different state parameter sets used. Methods for tying of model parameters either group similar parameter sets in a data-driven manner in order to ensure their robust trainability. Alternatively, they exploit structural properties of the models created in order to reuse partial models at different positions (cf. Sect. 9.2). However, tying alone cannot reduce the size of the total model as then unwanted paths through the model would become possible in general.

In HMM systems with large inventories of segmentation units, as they are common in the fields of speech or handwriting recognition, a rather simple possibility exists for deriving a compression of the model structure from the tying of partial models. In such systems the necessary word models of the recognition lexicon are usually built from a sequence of elementary sub-word units, e.g., phone or character models. The total model then principally results from a parallel connection of the respective individual models (cf. Sect. 8.3). For the correct evaluation of the path score, however, it is irrelevant whether identical state sequences at the beginning of a word model were passed through separately or whether these were combined into a single sequence. The structure of the overall model, therefore, can be simplified considerably by merging identical model prefixes of the individual partial models contained within the total recognition lexicon. The resulting tree-like model structure is referred to as *prefix tree* or phonetic prefix tree if identical sequences of phone models are represented only once (cf. [207, 208, 225]).

In systems for speech or handwriting recognition that use large lexica, this technique can be considered to be standard today. Depending on the application, a compression of the search space by a factor of 2 to 5 can be achieved. The gain in efficiency is even larger as the reduction of the model complexity mostly affects the beginning of word models. In this area the largest search effort arises. This is because the scores computed for partial paths that have been extended into a new segmentation unit by a few time steps only are extremely unreliable still [207].

However, organizing HMMs as a prefix tree has also a quite obvious disadvantage. When using such a "tree lexicon", it is not known which word from the recognition lexicon was hypothesized before a leaf node has been reached. This fact needs to be taken into account appropriately if an n-gram model shall be integrated into the search procedure (cf. Sect. 12.3).

Figure 10.3 shows an example for the organization of the recognition lexicon of a hypothetical speech recognition system in the form of a phonetic prefix tree. The root node of the tree serves the purpose of merging paths and corresponds to a non-emitting HMM state. When using a linear organization of the lexicon, this root node would be connected to all start nodes of all word models. With the prefix tree this is no longer the case. Rather, the successor nodes of the root of the prefix tree collect the paths trough those word models that start with the same phone model, respectively. As soon as a phone sequence corresponds to a complete word from the recognition lexicon, the path loops back to the root node. In addition, such a word model can also be the prefix of additional paths in the lexicon tree. Consequently, connections to the model states representing the respective suffixes may be present.

Fig. 10.3 Example of the tree-like organization of the recognition lexicon for a hypothetical speech recognition system

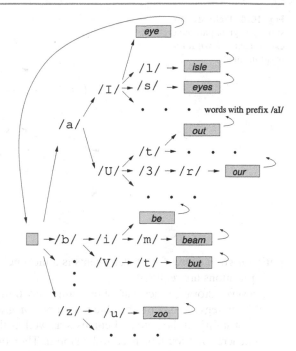

10.5.2 Tree-Like Representation for n-Gram Models

At first sight, n-gram models seem to have no appreciable structure at all. The conditional probabilities $P(z|y)$ for all combinations of predicted word z and history y could principally be stored in a table. However, such a trivial representation is manageable only for very small lexica and very limited context lengths in practice. For a tri-gram model with a lexicon of 20,000 words already $8 \cdot 10^{12}$ probabilities would need to be stored. When representing every individual probability in 4-byte floating-point format this would take up approximately 29 terra-bytes of memory. Therefore, an efficient representation is mandatory in order to be able to apply such models to realistic tasks.

The possibilities for structuring the storage of n-gram models immediately result from the scheme used to compute the model parameters. A dramatic reduction in the amount of memory required already results if only scores of *observed* events are represented explicitly. The conditional probabilities of unseen n-grams can be computed by backing-off or interpolation when needed (cf. Sect. 6.5.3). Thus a reduction in the storage requirements to manageable sizes is achieved as the majority of events is not observed in practice.[7] The computational effort necessary for com-

---

[7]A further considerable compression of n-gram models can be achieved if rare events are neglected. For singletons—i.e. n-grams observed only once—this results from the application of absolute discounting with a discounting constant $\beta = 1$. Additionally, also parameters of other rarely observed n-grams can be eliminated from the model if the modeling quality is not of primary concern, but a representation as compact as possible should be generated.

Fig. 10.4 Prefix tree for
storing n-gram parameters
exemplarily shown for a
tri-gram model

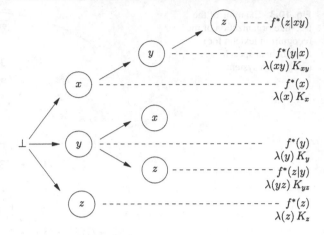

puting n-gram scores for unseen events is almost negligible, however, as only a few
multiplications are required.

However, storage space cannot be completely traded for computational effort using this strategy. In order to be able to compute n-gram scores of unseen events the
zero probability of the potential contexts as well as the parameters of the necessary
more general distributions need to be stored. Thus one obtains a hierarchical organization of the model parameters. This principle can be applied recursively as the
more general distributions are usually also represented by n-gram models.

The parameters of such an n-gram model hierarchy could principally be stored in
individual tables [308]. However, a much more flexible storage method results from
a tree-like representation of the overall model. Individual tree nodes then represent
different observed events. In every node the n-gram score and the normalized[8] zero
probability is stored which results for $n + 1$-grams with this history. The successor
relation in the tree corresponds to an extension of the event y by a word z to the
right. Thus the successors of node y are all $n + 1$-grams $y\cdot$. When only considering
how a certain n-gram is found in that representation, one deals with a *prefix tree*.

Figure 10.4 illustrates this representation of n-gram models with the example of
a tri-gram model. In order to be able to specify the score $P(z|y)$ of an observed
event in a simple way, in the example the principle of backing-off is applied. Then
the score is directly given by the respective value of the reduced frequency distribu-
tion $f^*(z|y)$. Furthermore, for reasons of simplification the respective $n - 1$-gram
model shortened by one context symbol is used as the more general distribution.
The root node $\perp$ of the tree, therefore, represents the zero-gram model which as-
signs a probability of $\frac{1}{|V|}$ to every event where V denotes the lexicon used. As the
recursive computation procedure for n-gram scores terminates here, no zero probability is stored in the root node. The successors of the tree root, i.e., the tree nodes
on the first level, store the parameters of the uni-gram model and at the same time

---

[8]If the more general distributions are not combined with the special model by interpolation but via
backing-off, the normalization factor K_y must be taken into account (cf. Eq. (6.8)).

n-gram hit
The score of an observed event xyz is retrieved, i.e., $c^*(xyz) > 0$.
$$P(z|xy) \leftarrow f^*(z|xy)$$

n-gram miss (simple):
The event xyz was not observed, i.e., $c^*(xyz) = 0$, but there exist other n-grams with history yz, i.e., $,c(yz) > 0$.
$$P(z|xy) \nleftarrow f^*(\cdot|xy) \Rightarrow P(z|xy) \leftarrow \lambda(xy)K_{xy}P(z|y)$$

history miss (simple):
The history xy of an n-gram does not exist in the current model but only its suffix y.
$$P(z|xy) \nleftarrow f^*(\cdot|x\cdot) \Rightarrow P(z|xy) \leftarrow P(z|y)$$

Fig. 10.5 Possible access types for n-gram model parameters for the example of a tri-gram model using backing-off

define the respective histories of the observed bi-grams. Over the tree nodes of the second level, which contain the bi-gram parameters, one finally reaches nodes that correspond to observed tri-gram events. These will always be leaf nodes. However, depending on the respective sample set, also bi-gram or uni-gram nodes can result that have no successors in the tree.

In a tree-like representation of an n-gram model which is based on the recursive computation scheme for the model parameters, three principally different access types can be distinguished which are summarized in Fig. 10.5. In the style of the terminology used in conjunction with cache memories, we will speak about an *n-gram hit* if the score of an observed event can be retrieved by a direct access to the respective tree node. For unseen events, however, one obtains an *n-gram miss*. This can occur once or multiple times until a corresponding more general event is found. For such an access to succeed, always the complete history of the event considered needs to be represented. If this is not the case, we will call this a *history miss*. In this case the longest suffix of the current history needs to be determined for which model parameters still exist. Consequently, a shortening of the n-gram context by at least one, but eventually more symbols is performed.

The representation of an n-gram model by means of a prefix tree presented above allows an efficient processing of n-gram hits. However, already for an n-gram miss a second pass through the tree from the root is necessary in order to determine the score of the respective $n - 1$-grams. If this does not exist either, the procedure might need to be repeated multiple times. A similar problem arises for history misses. First, an access with the complete history must be attempted in order to find out that this does not exist in the current model. Afterwards, the context can be shortened by one symbol and another access can be tried. This procedure needs to be repeated until an existing suffix of the original history is found.

Fig. 10.6 Combined
suffix–prefix tree for storing
the parameters of an n-gram
model for the example of a
tri-gram model

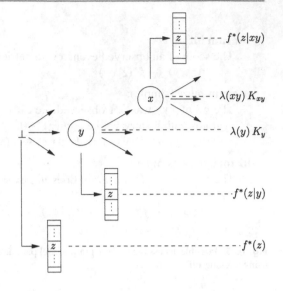

For both n-gram misses as well as history misses unnecessary search effort results from the prefix representation which also increases considerably for n-gram models of higher order. Therefore, it is quite evident to reorganize the tree representation such that the above-mentioned access types can be processed efficiently. Within n-gram contexts, not the prefix but the respective last symbols, which lie closest to the predicted word, have the most significance. Therefore, it is quite obvious to store the n-gram histories in a suffix tree. In addition, the nodes for predicted words need to be accessible from the respective history nodes in the same way as in the simple prefix tree. Consequently, we will call this representation scheme of n-gram parameters a combined suffix–prefix tree.

As shown exemplarily for a tri-gram model in Fig. 10.6, a path from the tree root encodes the history of an n-gram in reverse, i.e., starting from the direct predecessor of the word to be predicted. Thus the longest existing suffix of a given n-gram history is found automatically by traversing the tree from the root. A history miss, therefore, causes no additional search effort at all. The scores of the words z, which were observed in a certain context, are stored compactly as a table per tree node. At this point the passing through the symbol sequence of an n-gram is quasi reversed again. Therefore, these scores cannot be stored in the tree nodes themselves. These only serve the purpose of representing n-gram contexts in a suffix encoding. An n-gram hit can be processed in the combined suffix–prefix representation as efficiently as in the simple prefix tree. As the n-gram contexts become more special when proceeding along a path from the root, one obtains the reversed sequence of the respective more general n-gram histories. In case of an n-gram miss, therefore, the necessary parameters of the more general distributions can be found by simply backtracking the path previously passed through from the root.

Model Adaptation

11

Both HMMs and n-gram models are usually created by estimating their parameters on some sample set. Afterwards, the trained models can be applied for the segmentation of *new* data. This is by definition not part of the training samples and can never be in practical applications. Thus, the characteristic properties of this test data can be predicted to a limited extent only on the basis of the training material. Therefore, in general differences between training and testing material will occur that can not be captured by the statistical models created. Ultimately, this mismatch between training and testing conditions will adversely affect the quality of the results achieved.

Such changes in the characteristics of the input data can be illustrated with examples from automatic speech recognition. Already rather simple deviations in the conditions of the signal recording often lead to significantly increased error rates. This can be caused by the use of a different microphone or be due to the fact that the training data was gathered in a quiet office environment, but the recognition system is used out-doors or in a vehicle. Also unexpected interfering noises caused by wind, cars driving by, or conversations of persons that can be heard in the background on a party lead to a reduced system performance. But also changes in the characteristics of the user of the system cause severe problems. Even so-called speaker-independent recognition systems degrade in performance if they are confronted with an unknown dialect or if children use a speech recognition system that was trained for the speech of adult persons.

All these changes concern the statistical properties of the data to be processed. In contrast, we do not want to consider differences on the semantic-pragmatic level, for example, if somebody tries to order pizza from a flight information system, or a handwriting recognition system is fed with seismic data.

11.1 Basic Principles

The common goal of all methods presented in the following sections is to compensate differences between the training and testing conditions of a recognition system based on Markov models which concern the statistical properties of the data.

G.A. Fink, *Markov Models for Pattern Recognition*,
Advances in Computer Vision and Pattern Recognition,
DOI 10.1007/978-1-4471-6308-4_11, © Springer-Verlag London 2014

A seemingly obvious solution of the problem might be to train specialized models for every single purpose. However, this approach fails for two important reasons. On the one hand, testing material is by its very nature unknown, as already pointed out above, and only in a laboratory environment conditions can be set up which ignore this fact. On the other hand, for the training of statistical models large amounts of data are required. It should, therefore, not be hoped that for every special purpose a complete representative training set can be collected anew.

To a quite limited extent, however, specialized material will always be available. At the least the actual test data itself can be considered as an example for the current properties of the input data to be expected. Often it is even possible to collect a few up to date samples before the actual application of the recognition system. This so-called adaptation set can then be used for adjusting the given system parameters to the respective task. In standard dictation systems, for example, the user is required to read some given texts as adaptation material before the system is ready to use.

In contrast to the training of a model, its adaptation consists in the transformation of a given general parametrization into a special parameter set by means of an extremely limited adaptation set. The adapted special parameter set is assumed to be better suited for the processing of the data actually observed during the current application of the model. Therefore, by their very nature adaptation techniques are methods for parameter estimation, too. They are different from classical estimation methods, however, because they need to cope with some orders of magnitude fewer training samples.

The adaptation of the models can be performed prior to their actual application if adaptation data is available in addition to training and testing material. This adaptation in the manner of batch processing is also called *batch adaptation*. For simplification and for improving the results, the correct annotation of the adaptation set can be given in this approach and one obtains a *supervised* adaptation method. Often, however, this is not possible due to the effort required. Then the annotation of the adaptation data needs to be determined automatically on the basis of the existing general model. The procedure is then called *unsupervised* adaptation. An unsupervised method also is the only possibility if the adaptation cannot be performed on separate sample data but only directly during the evaluation of the models on the test data itself. Such so-called *online* adaptation methods are undoubtedly the most flexible methods for model adaptation as they do not require any changes in the natural use of the respective system. Furthermore, the parameters can be *continuously* adapted to changes in the characteristics of the data.

11.2   Adaptation of Hidden Markov Models

The adaptation of a general HMM to special changed characteristics of the data to be processed can principally be performed by means of the training methods known from Sect. 5.7 (cf. e.g. [59]). However, when following this approach a quite large adaptation set needs to be available in order to be able to robustly estimate the specialized HMM parameters. In the case of speaker adaptation, i.e., the adaptation of an existing speech recognition system to a new user, at least a few 100 utterances of the respective person would be required as adaptation material.

However, parameter estimates which are, e.g., obtained by applying the Baum–Welch algorithm are extremely unreliable if only quite limited example data is available for the adaptation of a given model. Therefore, these parameters are not directly used as specialized models but are interpolated with the parameters of the general model in a suitable way. The interpolation weights are usually dependent on the amount of sample data which is available for estimating certain model parameters. Thus it can be achieved that those parameters, for which many adaptation examples are available, will contribute to the special model almost without modification. In contrast, for rarely observed events the known parameters of the general model will prevail.

Formally, this corresponds to a parameter estimation technique following the principle of *maximum a posteriori estimation* (MAP, cf. Sect. 3.6.2). In contrast to the frequently applied maximum likelihood estimation (ML, cf. Sect. 3.6.1), which is also the basis of the Baum–Welch algorithm, here the posterior probability of the model parameters θ is maximized for given data ω (cf. e.g. [123, pp. 445–446]):

$$\hat{\theta} = \underset{\theta}{\operatorname{argmax}}\, P(\theta|\omega) = \underset{\theta}{\operatorname{argmax}}\, P(\theta)\, p(\omega|\theta)$$

A model adaptation on the basis of the MAP principle offers the advantage that the estimates computed converge to the ones of an ML estimation with increasing size of the adaptation set. Thus the MAP estimation becomes equivalent to the result of a standard training procedure if truly large amounts of adaptation material are available.

However, in practice there are two limitations of MAP adaptation. First, for the application of the MAP principle it is necessary to define estimates for the prior probability $P(\theta)$ of the parameters themselves. This might not be easy for complex model structures with huge numbers of free parameters. Therefore, frequently a simplified version of MAP estimation is used that simply computes new parameters as weighted averages of the current parameters and preliminary estimates obtained on the adaptation data (see Eq. (3.14)). The necessary weights are usually chosen empirically. Interestingly, however, the underlying principle—i.e. the computation of appropriately weighted parameter averages—is valid for the estimation of both mixture densities and HMMs according to the MAP principle [109]. Nevertheless, the computation of optimal weighting coefficients remains a non-trivial problem.

The second limitation of MAP adaptation is its quite slow convergence rate. Therefore, it should not be expected that a fast specialization of a model is possible on only few example data as then the original model parameters still dominate the MAP estimates. Furthermore, for partial models, states, or probability densities for which no adaptation samples are available, improved parameters cannot be derived at all by the MAP method.[1]

---

[1] This effect can be partially avoided in practice by a suitable tying of parameters (cf. Sect. 9.2, p. 169).

A radically different way for the specialization of models to certain application areas is followed by methods that were proposed for improving the modeling of variations in speaking rate by automatic speech recognition systems [194, 282, 321]. There different specialized models, e.g., for slow, medium, and fast speech, are created in advance by classifying the available training material accordingly and splitting it up into separate sample sets. The adaptation to the actual task is then performed in a relatively simple way by choosing the model which matches the data best. In the simplest case the speaking rate of the test data is determined by a classifier, and then the respective model is used for the segmentation [194]. Better results are obtained by a method which, however, is considerably more demanding. There all available models are used in parallel to generate a segmentation of the test data. Afterwards one decides for the result—and consequently also for the respective model—that achieved the best score [321].

Though an adaptation of the HMMs is performed by this method, it can principally only capture variations which were anticipated in advance in the design process and which are covered by sample data from the training set. It is, however, not possible to react upon an unknown variation of the test data using this method.

11.2.1 Maximum-Likelihood Linear-Regression

The most successful method for the fast adaptation of HMM parameters on very limited data is the so-called *maximum likelihood linear regression* (MLLR) [171, 172]. This technique meanwhile belongs to the set of standard methods for applying HMMs to pattern recognition problems (cf. [123, pp. 447ff]).

In contrast to classical training methods which attempt to compute new estimates for *all* model parameters independently on the sample data, MLLR creates a specialized model by means of a transformation. As opposed to the adapted HMM itself, this has only quite few free parameters which can be estimated robustly also on a small adaptation set. As the transformation modifies all model parameters jointly, also such parameters can be adapted for which no adaptation samples were observed.

In order to simplify the method, MLLR assumes that the most important parameters of an HMM are the mean vectors of the probability densities used. In contrast to transition probabilities, mixture weights, and also covariance matrices, changes in the statistical properties of the data affect these the most. By means of an affine transformation, the mean vectors of the general model are adapted to a modified data distribution.[2] Every mean vector μ is transformed into an adapted mean vector μ' by the following formula:

$$\mu' = A\mu + b$$

---

[2] By means of suitable extensions of the MLLR method, the parameters of covariance matrices can be adapted, too [107]. However, the rather moderate improvements observed in practice do usually not justify the considerably increased additional effort.

Here A denotes the rotational part of the transformation and the vector b the associated translation in the feature space. When forming an extended mean vector $\tilde{\mu} = [1, \mu^T]^T$ and a combined transformation matrix $W = [b, A]$, the formula can be compactly written with a single matrix multiplication only:

$$\tilde{\mu}' = W\tilde{\mu}$$

The optimization criterion of the method is the production probability of the data, analogously to the Baum–Welch algorithm. Therefore, the transformation of the model parameters needs to be determined such that the probability for generating the adaptation data is maximized by the specialized model.

As far as the amount of available sample data permits, also multiple independent transforms on different groups of probability densities can be applied to improve the accuracy of the MLLR method. These groups of densities, for which a separate parameter transformation is estimated, are called *regression classes*.[3] As all mean vectors of densities from the same regression class are adapted in an identical way, such distributions should be grouped which describe similar parts of the model. An obvious choice is, for example, to group all densities of a codebook jointly used by multiple states into a regression class.

For computing estimates of the MLLR transformation of one or more regression classes, a mapping between feature vectors x_t from the adaptation set and codebook classes is required. In general, this is performed probabilistically in the same way as when estimating the distribution parameters of continuous HMMs by means of the Baum–Welch algorithm (cf. Sect. 5.7.4). The quantity $\xi_t(j, k)$ represents the probability for using the kth mixture component of state j for generating the data at time t. It can be computed on the basis of the forward and backward probabilities (cf. Eq. (5.20)). Through a formal derivation, which essentially corresponds to the one of the Baum–Welch algorithm, one obtains the following constraint equation for determining the MLLR transformation:

$$\sum_{t=1}^{T} \sum_{g_{jk} \in R} \xi_t(j, k) C_{jk}^{-1} x_t \tilde{\mu}_{jk}^T = \sum_{t=1}^{T} \sum_{g_{jk} \in R} \xi_t(j, k) C_{jk}^{-1} W_R \tilde{\mu}_{jk} \tilde{\mu}_{jk}^T \qquad (11.1)$$

Here R represents the respective regression class which consists of a set of baseline densities g_{jk} of the mixture densities used within the overall model. The associated transformation matrix is denoted by W_R. Additionally the feature vectors x_t as well as the inverse covariance matrices C_{jk}^{-1} and the extended mean vectors $\tilde{\mu}_{jk}$ of the densities enter into the calculation.

However, for the constraint equation in the general form given above no closed form solution exists. In practical applications of HMMs the covariance matrices of normal distributions are frequently described by diagonal covariances only. In this

---

[3]If all mean vectors are adapted by a single affine transformation only, a single regression class comprising all densities is used.

constrained case the transformation matrices W_R can be computed in a row-wise procedure (cf. [172], [123, p. 449]).

A considerable simplification of the MLLR method for practical applications results if the mapping of codebook classes to adaptation samples is uniquely determined. In the same way as in Viterbi training or the segmental k-means algorithm, the Viterbi criterion is used to establish a unique association between model states and feature vectors. In case of a supervised adaptation, for this the correct annotation of the sample data is given, e.g., the correct orthographic transcription of an utterance when considering the task of automatic speech recognition. In contrast, if the MLLR method is applied in an unsupervised manner, the segmentation can also be generated without the respective restrictions by means of the existing model alone.

On the basis of the optimal state sequence, the respective optimal codebook class can then be determined easily as the mixture component m_t of the output distribution of the optimal state s_t which has maximal posterior probability:

$$m_t = \underset{k}{\operatorname{argmax}}\, c_{s_t k}\, g_{s_t k}(x_t) = \underset{k}{\operatorname{argmax}}\, c_{s_t k}\, \mathcal{N}(x_t | \mu_{s_t k}, C_{s_t k})$$

Furthermore, one assumes that the covariance matrices of the individual densities can be neglected or can be assumed to be identity matrices, respectively. One then obtains an estimation procedure which determines the parameter transformation such that the mean squared error between the feature vectors x_t and the associated mean vectors $\mu_{s_t m_t}$ is minimized ([172, Sect. 4.1: Least Squares Regression], [96]). When using a single regression class only, the following simple formula for computing the transformation matrix results:

$$W = \left\{ \sum_{t=1}^{T} x_t \tilde{\mu}_{s_t m_t}^{T} \right\} \left\{ \sum_{t=1}^{T} \tilde{\mu}_{s_t m_t} \tilde{\mu}_{s_t m_t}^{T} \right\}^{-1} \tag{11.2}$$

If multiple regression classes are used, the computation of the individual transformation matrices follows the same scheme. Then only those adaptation vectors x_t are taken into account for which the associated codebook class $g_{s_t m_t}$ belongs to the respective regression class.

Doubtless, the MLLR method offers the fastest possibility for the adaptation of an existing HMM to changed task conditions. For example, in automatic speech recognition, where 39 is a typical dimension of the feature vectors used, less than 1600 parameters need to be estimated for a global transformation matrix W when using a single regression class only. In practice this can be achieved in satisfactory quality with less than a minute of speech material.

Of course, the quality of the adaptation method can principally be arbitrarily increased by the use of many different regression classes. However, then also the demand for adaptation data increases similarly, and in the end the method does not offer any advantages as opposed to a traditional training procedure. In order to achieve an optimal compromise between accuracy of the adaptation and robustness in the estimation of the transformations' parameters, methods were proposed which try to optimally define the number of regression classes depending on the size of the adaptation set [27, 172] or which, starting from a single regression class only, increase their number step by step as soon as sufficient data becomes available [171].

An extension of the MLLR technique, where multiple independent transformations are combined, was proposed by Digalakis and colleagues [27, 28, 57, 58]. For the purpose of speaker adaptation, transforms for typical speaker groups are first estimated on the training material. The number of regression classes used is optimized depending on the available adaptation data. For the adaptation of a general HMM to a specific test speaker, then an optimal linear combination is computed from all available transformations. The estimation of the combination weights requires considerably less data than the computation of an MLLR adaptation rule. Therefore, the method is suited very well for the fast adaptation of large models to changed task conditions.

11.3 Adaptation of *n*-Gram Models

For *n*-gram models it is even more evident than for HMMs that the estimation of a completely new specialized model on a limited adaptation set cannot be achieved. In fact, even on large training sets it is absolutely necessary to determine useful estimates for probabilities of unseen events by smoothing the empirical distributions (cf. Sect. 6.5).

11.3.1 Cache Models

So-called *cache n-gram models* ([162], cf. also [48, 133]) are based on the idea that in texts such words or word combinations re-occur with high probability that were already used before. For the modeling of this effect only special uni-gram statistics are gathered as it is virtually impossible to update statistics for bi-grams or *n*-grams of higher order with only a few adaptation samples. In order to be able to better predict the occurrence of a word w_t at the position t in a text, one calculates the frequency $c(w_t|w_{t-T}, \ldots, w_{t-1})$ of its occurrence in a certain section of past text material of length T, i.e., in the so-called *cache*. The uni-gram probability based on the cache data is then obtained as follows:[4]

$$P_{\text{cache}}(w_t) = \frac{c(w_t|w_{t-T}, \ldots, w_{t-1})}{T}$$

The simple cache uni-gram model estimated such is subsequently interpolated with a standard *n*-gram model $P(z|y)$:

$$P_{\text{cache}}(z|y) = \lambda P(z|y) + (1 - \lambda) P_{\text{cache}}(z)$$

---

[4]Here $c(z|w_1, \ldots, w_n)$ denotes the number of occurrences of word z in the string of words given by $w_1, \ldots, w_n$.

However, the required interpolation weight λ needs to be determined experimentally or be specified heuristically.

In the work of Kuhn & De Mori [162], who coined the term cache n-gram model, a category-based tri-gram model is used. On the basis of the cache memory, merely the probabilities $P(w_i|C_j)$ for mapping between categories and word symbols are adapted so that a good robustness of the model is achieved.

11.3.2 Dialog-Step Dependent Models

A completely different approach for the adaptation of the language modeling is pursued by the so-called *dialog-step dependent language models* (cf. e.g. [68, 245, 306, 307]). In combination with a system for carrying out a natural language dialog, it is possible to use the prediction of the dialog system for the selection of a language model which is adapted to the class of utterances to be expected. In fact, no real adaptation of the model parameters on the basis of example data is performed but a selection based on the internal state of the system.

By splitting up the training material into separate dialog-steps, however, the data for the estimation of the individual n-gram models is considerably reduced [245]. Especially for rare types of dialog-steps possibly not enough material might be available for robustly estimating a specialized n-gram model. In such cases either a suitable grouping of the available dialog states needs to be performed [307], or the robustness of the dialog-step dependent models needs to be improved by interpolation with a general language model [306].

11.3.3 Topic-Based Language Models

A similar basic idea as the dialog-step dependent modeling is followed by the so-called *topic-based language models* (cf. e.g. [19, 48, 133]). In this modeling it is assumed that within large text material certain topics can be identified and that the associated text sections exhibit specific statistical properties. In order to better describe the overall material it is, therefore, quite obvious to use specialized partial models for the individual topics.

In contrast to dialog-step dependent language models, the mapping of a certain text section to a topic and thus to a specialized n-gram model cannot be determined uniquely. Therefore, topic-based n-gram models are mostly used in the form of so-called *topic mixtures*. All partial models $P(z|y, T_i)$ created for a special topic T_i are subsumed into an overall model by a linear combination. The most frequently used model is a combination on the level of individual conditional probabilities for predicting the respective following word:

$$P_{\text{topic}}(z|y) = \sum_i \lambda_i\, P(z|y, T_i) \quad \text{with} \quad \sum_i \lambda_i = 1$$

In contrast to this, in [133] the overall probability of a test text $w_1, w_2, \ldots, w_T$ is defined as a weighted sum of the probability contributions that every individual topic-dependent n-gram model produces for the total word sequence. When using bi-gram models, the following computation rule results:

$$P_{\text{topic}'}(w_1, w_2, \ldots, w_T) = \sum_i \lambda_i \prod_{t=1}^{T} P(w_t | w_{t-1}) \quad \text{with} \quad \sum_i \lambda_i = 1$$

As opposed to the purely local interpolation of the models, this definition can exclusively be used for the re-scoring of segmentation hypotheses which are completely available in a multi-pass recognition system. A time-synchronous combination with the partial path probabilities of an HMM is not possible for such a model.

In the same way as dialog-step dependent n-gram models, the individual topic models are trained in advance on text material which is representative for the respective topic. The adaptation of the overall model to a particular task is then achieved by the adaptation of the interpolation weights λ_i. This can either be performed by an unsupervised estimation procedure as, e.g., the EM algorithm [48], or on the basis of methods for topic identification as they are known from the field of information retrieval [19, 189].

Integrated Search Methods

The probably most challenging applications of Markov model technology are recognition tasks with very large inventories of segmentation units. Typical examples are dictation systems with lexica of some 10,000 or 100,000 words or systems for handwriting recognition with almost unlimited vocabulary. The modeling of the segmentation units—i.e. the spoken or written words—by means of HMMs has virtually become a standard method as in less complex systems, too. However, for such demanding recognition tasks additional restrictions of the possible or plausible sequence of segments are indispensable in order to keep the search effort manageable. The description of such restrictions by n-gram models offers the important advantage over other methods that two compatible formalisms are used and thus a combined application is possible more easily and with greater success.

Formally, this procedure can be derived from a modeling assumption which is mainly used in the field of automatic speech recognition and presumably dates back to work of Jelinek and colleagues [137, 139]. This integrated probabilistic model of signal generation and decoding embeds the segmentation problem into the vocabulary of concepts known from information theory. Figure 12.1 schematically shows the so-called *channel model* as it was formulated for the problem of speech generation and recognition.

In this model it is assumed that first a hypothetical information source generates a sequence of symbolic units $w = w_1, w_2, \ldots, w_N$ with a certain probability $P(w)$. Thus, for example, a human speaker or writer would formulate a word sequence in his brain with the goal to later pronounce it or write it down. The actual realization is then performed in a second step where the symbolic information is transformed or encoded into a signal representation. The thought of word sequence is thus pronounced as an acoustic signal or realized as writing on a sheet of paper. The signal produced is now transmitted over a potentially noisy channel, recorded by a sensor, and transformed into a parametric representation as a sequence of feature vectors $X = x_1, x_2, \ldots, x_T$. For reasons of simplicity the last two steps are subsumed into one for the further considerations. Consequently, an encoding of the symbol sequence w into a feature vector sequence X is performed with a certain probability $P(X|w)$.

G.A. Fink, *Markov Models for Pattern Recognition*,
Advances in Computer Vision and Pattern Recognition,
DOI 10.1007/978-1-4471-6308-4_12, © Springer-Verlag London 2014

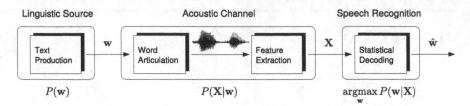

Fig. 12.1 Information-theoretic channel model of speech generation and recognition

The process of decoding or recognition now tries to reconstruct the original "ideal" word sequence on the basis of these features. Due to the probabilistic nature of the generation, which also captures potential errors of the transmission channel, this is not uniquely possible. Therefore, one decides for the solution $\hat{w}$ which maximizes the posterior probability $P(w|X)$ of the word sequence given the observed data X. Thus the following decoding rule results:

$$\hat{w} = \operatorname*{argmax}_{w} P(w|X)$$

Unfortunately, parametric models for the direct description of the probability $P(w|X)$ for inferring the word sequence given the data are generally not known. Therefore, the expression is rewritten using Bayes' rule as follows in order to reduce the problem to probabilistic quantities that can actually be modeled:

$$\hat{w} = \operatorname*{argmax}_{w} P(w|X) = \operatorname*{argmax}_{w} \frac{P(w)P(X|w)}{P(X)}$$

A further simplification results from the fact that the occurrence probability $P(X)$ of the data itself is constant with respect to the maximization and, therefore, can be neglected when determining the optimal word sequence $\hat{w}$:

$$\hat{w} = \operatorname*{argmax}_{w} P(w)\, P(X|w) \tag{12.1}$$

Both probability expressions involved can now be associated with potential modeling parts of a statistical recognition system.

The probability $P(w)$ for generating a symbol sequence w can easily be represented by a Markov chain, i.e., by a statistical n-gram model. The quantity $P(X|w)$, in contrast, is interpreted as the probability to generate a certain observation sequence X with a given model, i.e., the one corresponding to the word sequence w. This part can thus be described by means of a hidden Markov model. Furthermore it can be seen from Eq. (12.1) that the scores of both parts of the model can principally be combined by simple multiplication.

At this point the considerations are discontinued in most presentations found in the literature. Unfortunately, the integrated use of HMMs and n-gram models is not quite so easily achieved in practice. There are two main reasons for this. First, the computation of the combined score has to be complemented by additional means in order to produce useful results in practice. Second, the combined use of an HMM and an n-gram model has to be taken into account in the model decoding process.

Let us first consider the computation of the combined score. It can be easily verified that the dynamic ranges of the two score components usually differ largely. Therefore, without a suitable compensation the HMM score $P(X|w)$ virtually always dominates the score $P(w)$ of the language model.[1] Therefore, the two quantities are combined in a weighted fashion using a constant α according to (cf. e.g. [123, p. 610]):[2]

$$P(w)^\alpha \, P(X|w) \qquad\qquad (12.2)$$

In negative-logarithmic representation (cf. Sect. 7.1) this corresponds to a weighted sum of the scores where the constant α, which is referred to as the *linguistic matching factor*, serves the purpose of adjusting the usually significantly lower costs of the language model to the magnitude of the HMM score. Unfortunately, the choice of α is task specific and suitable values need to be determined in experimental evaluations.[3]

In addition to the adjustment of the relative dynamic ranges by the linguistic matching factor α, sometimes also a so-called *word penalty* score is incorporated per hypothesized word:[4]

$$P(w)^\alpha \, \beta^{|w|} P(X|w)$$

Here β denotes the word penalty which is raised to the power of $|w|$, i.e., the length of the word sequence considered. The parameter β has to be chosen heuristically and can be used to adjust the number of segmentation units that are hypothesized. With small values of β, solutions consisting of a large number of small segmentation hypotheses will hardly be penalized. In contrast, with larger values of β solutions with fewer segmentation units will be favored.

---

[1]This is mainly due to the fact that probabilities on largely differing time-scales enter into the calculations for $P(w)$ and $P(X|w)$, respectively. For determining the HMM score, state transition and output probabilities accumulate per time step, i.e., with the "clock pulse" of the signal. The score of the word sequence, in contrast, is generated by multiplying one conditional probability per word and, therefore, comprises one to two orders of magnitude fewer probability components.

[2]Frequently, the reason for a weighted combination of n-gram and HMM scores being necessary is said to be that the models were generated on different data and, therefore, would not be completely compatible. However, this is at most of marginal importance as, e.g., experiments within the German Verbmobil project showed clearly. For the extensive evaluation in the year 1996 the training data for HMMs and language model was identical. A weighting of the scores was still necessary, though.

[3]In [331] an evaluation of the meta-parameters for combining HMMs and n-gram models is reported for a writer-independent handwriting recognition task.

[4]Without the use of a real n-gram language model the term $\beta^{|w|}$ has the same effect as a simple zero-gram model.

Let us now consider how the score computation interacts with the integrated decoding process. Equation (12.1) specifies that the total score of a word sequence w can be computed by multiplying the scores of the two model components. This computation scheme can only be applied to segmentation hypotheses that are completely available. However, decoding an HMM by applying the Viterbi or the beam-search algorithm produces a single optimal solution only. Evaluating the language model for this result would provide no useful additional information. Therefore, alternative solutions of HMM decoding need to be considered which can be obtained from extensions of the basic Viterbi principle that allow the approximate generation of the top n decoding results (see Sect. 10.3.2). Instead of evaluating the combined score for certain final segmentation results, also partial path scores $\delta_t(i)$ can to be combined with parts of the n-gram score during the Viterbi search. The basis for this is the factorization of $P(w)$ into individual conditional probabilities $P(z|y)$ for the prediction of a word z in the context of y (cf. Sects. 6.1 and 6.3).

Despite the great importance of integrated search methods for the application of Markov models to real-world problems, their presentation is frequently neglected in the literature. For current systems for speech or handwriting recognition, it is often difficult to find out from the respective publications which algorithmic solutions were chosen for the problem of combining HMMs and n-gram models. The primary reason for this is probably that the descriptions are mostly spread across many quite short conference publications and that the focus of those is more on details of the solution than on integrated approaches. Unfortunately, even in monographs on the topic hardly any satisfactory treatments of the problem can be found.[5]

Therefore, we want to present the most important methods for the integration of HMMs and n-gram models in the following. At the beginning the probably oldest and also simplest technique is presented where a model network is created on the basis of partial models in which the n-gram scores serve as transition probabilities. In multi-pass search methods, long-span n-gram restrictions are applied only in a second search process in order to reduce the total search effort. Integrated time-synchronous decoding procedures are usually based on the efficient representation of the recognition lexicon as a prefix tree. In such configurations it is necessary to create copies of the resulting search space in order to be able to integrate the n-gram score directly into the search. The actual methods differ depending on whether the replicated search trees are identified by the n-gram history or by the respective starting time in the signal. The chapter concludes with the presentation of a flexible technique for the integrated time-synchronous search in combined HMM/n-gram models which is also capable of handling long-span context restrictions efficiently.

In summary, the integration of HMMs and n-gram language models requires meta-parameters—at least the linguistic matching factor α—and a substantial enhancement of the usual decoding algorithms for HMMs. An optimal decoding of the combined model is no longer possible as the overall search space would not be manageable any more even for moderately sized problems. Consequently, any

---

[5]A notable exception is the book by Huang and colleagues where a good overview over possible techniques is given [123, Chap. 13, pp. 645–662].

Fig. 12.2 HMM network for
a trivial lexicon $\{a, b, c\}$ and
the use of a bi-gram language
model. For clarity only two
loop edges are shown
explicitly

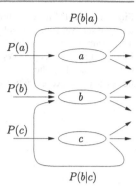

integrated search method will be sub-optimal. Therefore, an important question is
how to evaluate the success of such a model integration or, to put it in more technical terms, how to predict the performance improvement that can be expected from
using a language model in addition to an HMM. Unfortunately, there is no formal
procedure for doing so. However, the relative performances of recognition systems
applying the same underlying HMMs but different language models can be compared on a given benchmark. According to a "rule-of-thumb", the segmentation error rates achieved, i.e., on word or character level, should be roughly proportional to
the square root of the perplexities of the respective language models (cf. [281]). Any
major deviation from this approximate relation strongly suggests a problem with the
correct integration of HMM decoding and language-model evaluation.

12.1   HMM Networks

The technically most simple and probably also the most obvious possibility for combining n-gram models and HMMs offer the so-called *HMM networks*. They were
originally proposed in the field of speech recognition and, therefore, are also referred to as *word networks* (cf. [136, pp. 81–82], [252, pp. 453–454]).

A comparable method was first used in the framework of the HARPY system, yet
without an integrated n-gram model [185]. All utterances accepted by the system
were encoded within a model graph as sequences of the respective word HMMs.

Including an n-gram model into such a structure can principally be achieved at
the edges between consecutive words in the form of transition probabilities. When
using a bi-gram model a simple "looped" lexicon model is sufficient for this procedure. An example of such an HMM network is shown in Fig. 12.2. At the edges
between the partial models a and b the respective bi-gram score $P(b|a)$ can be
combined with the path score of the underlying HMM. The uni-gram scores of the
language model are used as start probabilities of the model as no predecessor words
are available at the beginning of the search process.

However, if n-gram restrictions with larger context lengths as, e.g., tri-gram models are used, this is no longer possible in the framework of this model structure. Due
to its inherent limitations, an HMM is only capable of considering *exactly one* con-

Fig. 12.3 HMM network for
a trivial lexicon $\{a, b, c\}$ and
a tri-gram language model.
Per word model y copies $[x]y$
exist for encoding the
necessary context restrictions

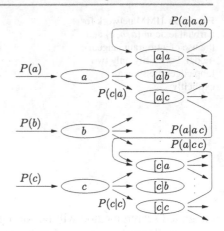

text during the search in the form of the current predecessor state. In the model
structure from Fig. 12.2 this encodes only the current predecessor word.

In order to be able to represent a longer sequence of context words uniquely,
therefore, suitable copies of the partial models need to be created which are specialized to certain long-span context restrictions. Figure 12.3 schematically shows
a simple example of an HMM network that allows the incorporation of a tri-gram
model. In order to be able to represent all contexts relevant for tri-gram decoding,
for every word from the lexicon a copy of the respective partial model exists per potential predecessor word. As in the case of the bi-gram model, the search starts with
the uni-gram score. After passing through the first word model bi-gram scores can
be incorporated and the respective context dependent copies of the partial models
are reached. These now represent the two-symbol tri-gram context uniquely. Therefore, from here on tri-gram scores can be used as transition probabilities provided
that the transition is made to the right context-encoding copy of the successor word.

The comparison with the simpler HMM network from Fig. 12.2, which was sufficient for the integrated decoding of a bi-gram model, shows that a considerably
higher effort is necessary. In general the required number of copies of the word
models involved grows exponentially with the length of the n-gram context. Therefore, in practice HMM networks are almost exclusively used in combination with
bi-gram models.

12.2 Multi-pass Search

The primary goal of multi-pass techniques is to avoid the exponentially increasing
effort required by HMM networks for higher order n-gram models while still being able to exploit their restrictions. The basic idea behind *multi-pass search* is the
application of modeling parts with increasing complexity in multiple subsequent
steps. Therefore, one assumes that the additional restrictions of an $n + k$-gram—
as opposed to the ones of the n-gram model being also available—mainly lead to
a different sorting of the solutions found but not to completely new ones. If this

assumption is fulfilled, the integrated search can use a language model of lower complexity—usually a bi-gram model—for the generation of a set of alternative solutions. These are subsequently re-scored with a more demanding model (cf. e.g. [21, 108, 116]). The computational costs caused by decoding an n-gram model of higher order is thus limited to "relevant" search areas which were already hypothesized in the first phase of decoding.

Consequently, an important prerequisite for the application of multi-pass search strategies is the ability to generate alternative solutions in the decoding steps involved. This is usually achieved by extensions of the Viterbi algorithm that are able to approximately generate the top n best-scoring solutions. In the literature these methods are referred to as techniques for n-best search (see Sect. 10.3.2).

The most straight-forward use of multi-pass decoding it to run a time-synchronous Viterbi beam search for the first pass. This decoding pass could already include a bi-gram language model. From this first pass, recognition results are generated in the form of n-best lists as shown for a simple example from the field of handwriting recognition in Fig. 12.4. These n-best solutions define the search space for all subsequent search processes. In the second pass now a more complex n-gram model, for example, a tri-gram can be used to re-score the solutions hypothesized earlier. However, the application of more complex models in subsequent decoding phases is not limited to language models with increased complexity. It is also possible to use more complex HMMs, i.e., models with larger number of Gaussians per mixture or with increased context-dependency which would be too complex to decode in a one-pass time-synchronous search procedure (see also Sect. 13.2.4).

The main disadvantage of such a multi-pass strategy is that the data to be segmented needs to be completely available before a substantial part of the computations—i.e. the re-scoring steps—can be carried out. For batch processing applications as, e.g., the transcription of broadcast news or the search for interesting samples in large genetic databases, this restriction can be neglected. This is different for interactive applications as, e.g., in multi-modal man-machine communication. For example, in the field of automatic speech recognition demanding computations cannot be started before the end of the spoken utterance when using a multi-pass analysis procedure. Therefore, a fast reaction on user input is hardly possible with such a method.

12.3 Search Space Copies

As already pointed out in Sect. 10.5.1, a substantial increase in the efficiency of HMM search within large lexica can result from a tree-like representation of the models. However, the considerable compression of the HMM state space achieved in this way also has a serious drawback. When a leaf node of the tree is reached, which encodes the end of a word, the identity of the successor word is not known. Therefore, in an integrated model the n-gram score cannot simply be combined with the HMM score in the form of a transition probability. Rather, the information about the word context needs to be saved until the prefix tree has been passed through anew and another leaf node is reached.

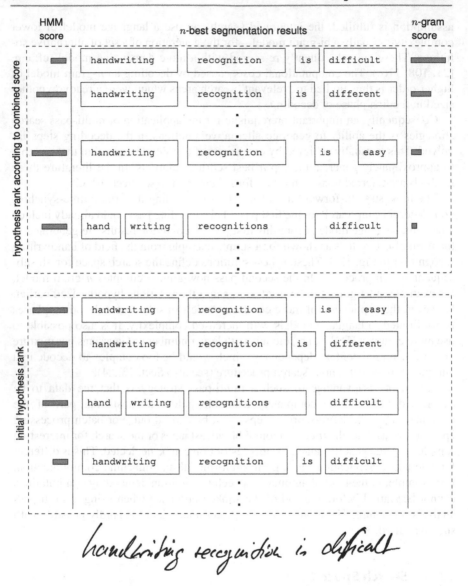

Fig. 12.4 Example of multi-pass decoding on a sample of handwritten script (at the *bottom*). In the *middle*, the (hypothetical) *n*-best recognition results obtained in the first decoding pass are shown. At the *top*, the results are shown that are obtained after re-scoring these hypotheses by taking into account additional language-model scores

12.3.1 Context-Based Search Space Copies

In order to achieve the correct combination of an *n*-gram language model with an HMM organized as a prefix tree, a method was proposed where dynamic copies of the search space are generated depending on the respective context to be encoded

Fig. 12.5 Example of the overall search space when using context-based search-tree copies and a tri-gram model with trivial lexicon $L = \{a, b, c\}$

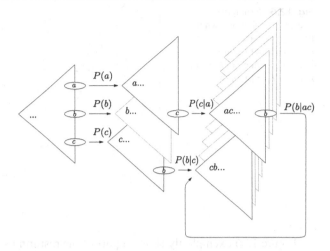

[207]. The algorithm which originally was developed for bi-gram models only was later extended to also handle tri-gram language models [228].

Essentially the method corresponds to the use of a compressed network of word nodes. The resulting model graph is dynamically created as required which, however, is principally also possible for HMM networks. Figure 12.5 exemplarily shows the resulting overall search space when using a tri-gram model with a trivial lexicon. The comparison with Fig. 12.3 makes it clear that the language-model score is integrated in a principally similar way as in an HMM network. However, not before the end of the model actually predicted, the score can be evaluated. It is thus taken into account in the search process with a delay of one word.

In the same way as the method of HMM networks, the resulting search procedure can be realized as a direct extension of the beam-search algorithm. In contrast to multi-pass search strategies, it thus can be applied in a strictly time-synchronous way.

However, also the use of search space copies becomes extremely demanding for n-gram models of higher order. The exponential growth of the search space cannot be counteracted arbitrarily even by a tree-like model organization or by applying pruning strategies. This can also be inferred from the fact that the use of such methods is only documented in the literature up to the complexity of tri-gram models (cf. e.g. [7, 208, 228]). Still, this method probably is the most efficient technique for the combined decoding of HMMs and bi-gram models.

12.3.2 Time-Based Search Space Copies

A variant of the method presented in the previous section was proposed in [228] and independently of that also in [89]. There the search space copies are not generated depending on the language-model context but on the starting time of the respective hypothesis.

Fig. 12.6 Example of the
overall search space when
using time-based search-tree
copies and a bi-gram
language model with trivial
lexicon $L = \{a, b, c\}$

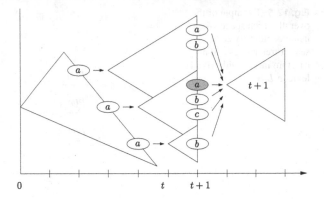

Figure 12.6 exemplarily shows a part of the resulting search space organization. In contrast to the context-based creation of tree copies, in this method different search trees are reached from hypotheses of the same word which end at different times. On the other hand *all* hypotheses with the same end time t are continued in only *a single* search tree with starting time $t + 1$ even though they were possibly created in different search trees. Only the score δ_t^* of the optimal hypothesis ending at time t is taken into account for continuing the decoding process. It serves as the starting score for the newly created search-tree copy. As the locally optimal score is used for starting tree copies, the computation of the correct combined score requires additional effort.

When using time-based search-tree copies, the word context of a search tree is not uniquely defined. Therefore, all potential hypotheses ending in the predecessor tree have to be considered for the evaluation of the language-model score in a word end node in order to be able to correctly integrate n-gram models into the search. As for the partial path of the current solution the optimal score δ_t^* was used up to time t, this score must be replaced by the path score $\delta_t(\dots z)$ of the respective predecessor node for computing the optimal combined score.

In the form described above this method will correctly integrate bi-gram models into a combined search procedure. Already for tri-gram language models, however, an additional context symbol needs to be taken into account which makes the formal presentation of the method considerably more complex [226].

12.3.3 Language-Model Look-Ahead

Within an integrated search process the primary task of a statistical language model is to provide additional knowledge that allows to restrict the search to relevant areas as tightly as possible. Therefore, it is a disadvantage that n-gram scores are evaluated only with rather large temporal difference at the transitions between partial models or words, respectively.

Fig. 12.7 Schematic representation of the computation of the language-model look-ahead in a hypothetical model tree

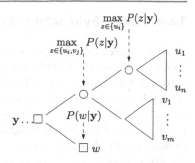

Therefore, the goal of the so-called *language-model look-ahead* is to be able to incorporate language-model restrictions already within a search space organized as a prefix tree [77, 290]. However, this can be achieved only approximately as the identity of the respective successor model is only known when a leaf node is reached (cf. also [223, 225, 227]).

For that purpose all leaf nodes are determined for every model state in the prefix tree that can be reached from there. As soon as the search procedure reaches any of the leaf nodes, the current solution can be extended by one hypothesis and the respective language-model score can be incorporated. Therefore, the current path score is at least augmented by the respective optimum of these n-gram scores. Thus in every model state the n-gram score which is maximum for all reachable word ends can be combined with the path score.

Figure 12.7 schematically shows a search tree which was generated as a copy of an HMM prefix tree within a larger search space. For reasons of simplicity, we assume that the tree copies were created depending on the language-model context. In the example considered let this context be given by y.

With language-model look-ahead the optimal achievable n-gram score is determined for every model state depending on the current n-gram context. If only a single leaf node w can be reached from a state this is exactly given by $P(w|y)$. However, if multiple paths to a set of leaf nodes $v_1, v_2, \ldots, v_n$ exist, the optimal expected language-model score is obtained as the maximum of the respective n-gram probabilities:

$$\max_{z \in \{v_1, v_2, \ldots, v_n\}} P(z|y)$$

Therefore, the preliminary n-gram score defined in this way can be combined with the HMM score already *before* a leaf node is reached. Consequently, a focusing of the search can be achieved in combination with pruning techniques as language-model restrictions are taken into account as early as possible. In general, the set of reachable word end nodes is reduced by every state transition. Therefore, the preliminary language-model score computed for the respective predecessor state needs to be replaced by its actual value after each state transition.

12.4   Time-Synchronous Parallel Model Decoding

In all integrated search algorithms on the basis of search space copies we assumed so far that the scores contributed by the HMMs and the n-gram model, respectively, were combined according to Eq. (12.2) and that all decisions of the search method were taken on the basis of this combined score only. However, in practice it is often desirable to be able to parametrize score-based search space restrictions that follow the principle of beam search separately for HMM states and sequences of segment hypotheses. Furthermore, the use of a combined score in all areas of the search has the consequence that the order of the n-gram models used directly influences the complexity of the search on the level of HMM states.

Therefore, an integrated search technique was developed in [88] which allows a separation of the state-based search process from the level of hypotheses. It originated as a further development of the method presented in Sect. 12.3.2 which works on the basis of time-based search-tree copies. The essential difference from the latter method is that partial path scores within all copies of the HMM search space are computed *without* the influence of the language model. The combined score is only evaluated during the search in the space of segmentation hypotheses. There principally n-gram models of arbitrary order can be used. The complexity of the respective language model does not effect the HMM search, which is realized as a beam-search method extended to the processing of time-based tree copies.

One obtains a time-synchronous search method which consists of two coupled search processes running in parallel. In the first process, HMMs are decoded in order to generate segmentation hypotheses that are passed on to the language-model-based search at every time step. In the second search process, these individual hypotheses are combined into sequences of hypotheses and are evaluated by incorporating the n-gram model.

12.4.1 Generation of Segment Hypotheses

The goal of the hypothesis generation is the creation of a dense lattice of segment hypotheses *without* the influence of the language-model context. Starting at times $t_s = 1, \ldots, T$ all promising segment hypotheses $\hat{w}_i(t_s, t_e)$ are computed. For that purpose a search with all HMMs of the recognition lexicon needs to be carried out from all starting times t_s to be considered. Thus one obtains a copy of the HMM search space for every t_s. The search within these search space copies is, however, not performed in isolation but strictly time-synchronously. The results of the hypothesis generation can thus be collected for every end time t_e and can be passed on to the integrated language-model search, as exemplarily illustrated in Fig. 12.8.

The path hypotheses within all search-tree copies are subject to a joint beam pruning in order to eliminate less promising search paths (see Sect. 10.2). For increased efficiency the models of the recognition lexicon are organized as a prefix tree (see Sect. 10.5.1). This means no limitation for the proposed search method as the language-model scores are handled completely separately from the HMM-based search. Therefore, it is absolutely sufficient that the identities of hypotheses

Fig. 12.8 Exemplary
representation of hypotheses
created by the HMM-based
search with a trivial
recognition lexicon
$L = \{a, b, c\}$ at a given end
time t_1. The hypothesis
$c(t_1 + 1, t_2)$ also shown
represents a solution which
later needs to be integrated
into the overall search space

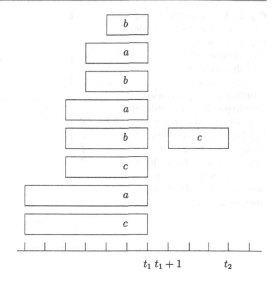

are determined not before a leaf node of the prefix tree is reached. The initial score
for starting a new search-tree copy at time t_s results as the HMM-based path score
of the hypothesis chain that is optimal according to the integrated search and ends
at time $t_s - 1$. Thus it is ensured that the scores of all paths followed in different
search-tree copies always stay comparable and can be used for the mutual pruning
of the search space.

12.4.2 Language-Model-Based Search

The basis of the language-model search is the generation of a search graph on the
level of hypotheses. It is created from the individual hypotheses which are generated
time-synchronously by the HMM-based search. This HMM decoding produces sets
of hypotheses $\hat{w}_i(t_s, t_e)$ for every potential end time t_e. In order to compute the combined score for the newly created hypotheses $\hat{w}_i(t_s, t_e)$ all possible concatenations
with predecessor hypotheses $\hat{w}_j(\dots, t_s - 1)$ are created which are already found in
the search space.

The goal of the method is to determine that path within this huge search space that
is optimal with respect to the combined HMM and n-gram score. For this purpose all
path hypotheses are evaluated which were newly created on the basis of $\hat{w}_i(t_s, t_e)$.
Here the evaluation of a language-model score is possible with arbitrary context
length as the complete context of the preceding hypothesis sequence is known.

In order to effectively avoid an explosion of the search space, a pruning strategy
is necessary that can be applied in a strictly time-synchronous manner. Therefore,
all search paths scored by the language model that were extended up to the current
end time t_e by new hypotheses $\hat{w}_i(\dots, t_e)$ are subject to a beam pruning. Only paths
within a constant score window are considered by the future search depending on the

Fig. 12.9 Representation of the configuration known from Fig. 12.8 after the incorporation of the hypothesis $c(t_1 + 1, t_2)$ into the search space. The resulting search paths with final hypothesis c are ordered from top to bottom according to a fictitious score. With *dashed lines* those path extensions are drawn, which encode a language-model context that is redundant for the future search

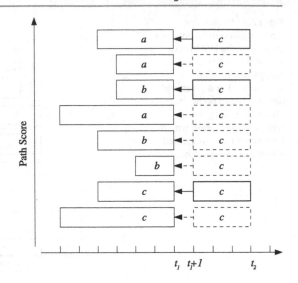

best path score determined for the current set of hypotheses. All remaining solutions are discarded from the search space.

In order to ensure that all relevant n-gram contexts are also available for further path expansions, it is sufficient to save only those of the "surviving" path hypotheses that differ in the respective $n - 1$ final hypotheses. Figure 12.9 shows this exemplarily for the configuration of segmentation hypotheses known from Fig. 12.8.

Therefore, in the case of a bi-gram model, only a single path with end hypothesis $\hat{w}_i(\ldots, t_e)$ is generated at time t_e for the ith entry of the recognition lexicon. For higher order n-grams, however, path hypotheses need to be discriminated according to longer suffixes. In order to be able to manage this efficiently and without the need for a costly backtracking of the respective paths, a hash key is computed for the $n - 2$ predecessor nodes of a path end which, together with the identity of the last hypothesis, compactly encodes the n-gram history. As this encoding is not necessarily unique, not all different n-gram contexts can be discriminated. Informal experiments have shown, however, that this substantial simplification does not lead to measurable losses in quality of the results.

In contrast to comparable approaches the important advantage of this integrated time-synchronous search method lies in the fact that the scoring of the language-model context is *not* transferred into the HMM-based search as, e.g., in [208]. Therefore, the complexity of the n-gram models used does not put additional burden on the already quite considerable cost of the search within the HMM state space.

In addition to a good organizational separability of the internal processes, the strict separation of HMM-based and language-model-based search also leads to a better localization of measures for increasing efficiency. For example, the beam width used for the search within the HMM state space is completely independent of the relative weighting of the two score components as well as of the method for search space pruning used on the level of hypotheses.

Part III
Systems

Introductory Remarks

In the previous chapters, both the theoretical foundations of Markov-model technology were presented and the most important methods were explained that allow their successful application in practice. However, all these methods have configuration parameters which can only be optimized for a certain application scenario. Furthermore, not every combination of individual techniques automatically leads to an improved performance of the overall system.

Therefore, in the following chapters we want to present successful systems for speech and handwriting recognition as well as for the analysis of biological sequences. They will serve as examples for demonstrating which methods from the wealth of available techniques are applied, how they are parametrized in the respective application, and how their combination leads to a powerful overall system. These system presentations partially take us beyond the topic of this book as for a certain task also application specific methods are of great importance in addition to Markov-model-based techniques. However, for application specific methods we will limit ourselves to the explanation of the principal procedures and refer the interested reader to the respective technical literature. The Markov-model techniques used, however, were mostly presented in the scope of the theory and practice parts of this book. Therefore, for those we will always make references to the respective sections in which they are explained further. Additionally, the configuration parameters used are given and their combination with other methods is explained.

In the literature, the efficiency of certain pattern analysis methods is proved by presenting evaluation results. This procedure has an especially long tradition in the field of automatic speech recognition (cf. [105, 325]) where several standardized test scenarios were defined. Nevertheless, also in this area it is extremely difficult to compare systems by the evaluation results documented. Frequently the evaluation configurations considered are slightly different and the results often are hard to interpret for someone less familiar with the respective application. Furthermore, performance measurements once published are quickly outdated. Therefore, in the following we do not want to attempt to compare the systems presented by evaluation results. The interested reader can find those easily in the referenced literature.

Chapters 13, 14 and 15 are devoted to complete systems for one of the three main application areas of Markov models, respectively: Automatic speech recognition, handwriting recognition, and the analysis of biological sequences. As the author's experience in using Markov models is based on extensive research and development of his own, also systems will be presented which are based on ESMERALDA [81, 85]—an open-source software tool for the development of pattern analysis systems based on Markov models. It allows the flexible configuration of the models and offers concrete implementations for most of the methods relevant in practice that were presented in the second part of this book.

Speech Recognition

13

Today, a number of commercial speech recognition systems are available on the market and, just recently, speech enabled assistive services were introduced for smart phones. Nevertheless, the problem of automatic speech recognition should by no means be considered to be solved even if the media and also some researchers sometimes convey that impression. As soon as distant speech sources have to be considered, as, for example, a presenter giving a talk in front of an audience, current speech recognizers will only perform quite poorly. In contrast, impressive performance is possible on speech recorded in more controlled acoustic environments.

In order to build a competitive speech recognition system, the integration of a multitude of techniques is required. Therefore, only a few systems exist today which can sustain their position at the top of the international research community. The probably best documented research systems are the ones developed by Hermann Ney and colleagues at the former Philips research lab in Aachen, Germany, and later at RWTH Aachen University, Aachen, Germany. In the following presentations we want to put the emphasis on the works at RWTH Aachen University. However, many aspects of the systems within the research tradition are identical with those developed by Philips. Afterwards we want to present the speech recognizer of BBN which, in contrast to most systems developed by private companies, is documented by several scientific publications. The chapter concludes with the description of a speech recognition system of our own developed on the basis of ESMERALDA.

13.1 Recognition System of RWTH Aachen University

The recognition system of RWTH Aachen University, which we will be shortly referring to as the *Aachen recognizer* in the following, is a speech recognition system for large vocabularies. In contrast to most other large-vocabulary speech recogniz-

G.A. Fink, *Markov Models for Pattern Recognition*,
Advances in Computer Vision and Pattern Recognition,
DOI 10.1007/978-1-4471-6308-4_13, © Springer-Verlag London 2014

ers, the core system uses a time-synchronous decoding method.[1] The models and algorithms are not applied for the analysis of the complete speech signal in multiple successive phases but are evaluated progressively in only one pass through the data on the utterance to be analyzed. In the following the most important features of the core system are presented which are described in [146, 285] and [18].

Development of the Aachen recognizer is still ongoing. In recent years several refinements were introduced and the recognizer was adapted to a wide variety of languages including Mandarin and Arabic. In 2009 the RWTH Aachen University speech recognition toolkit was made publicly available to the research community [262].

13.1.1 Feature Extraction

The Aachen recognizer uses mel-frequency cepstral coefficients (MFCC) as features as virtually all modern speech recognition systems do. During the frequency analysis of short sections of the signal—so-called frames—which are extracted from the speech signal every 10 ms with a length of 25 ms, the frequency axis is warped approximately logarithmically according to the melody scale following the processing within the human auditory system (cf. [332, p. 112] or [123, p. 34]). Afterwards, the coarse structure of the power spectrum is represented numerically by means of a cosine transform (cf. e.g. [123, pp. 306–315]).

The system uses 15 cepstral coefficients as well as their temporal derivatives which are computed by a regression analysis over a few neighboring frames. Additionally, the signal energy and its first and second temporal derivative are used as features.

The initial feature representation is subject to a linear discriminant analysis in order to optimize the separability of the pattern classes (see Sect. 9.1.6). For this purpose, three successive feature vectors are stacked to form a 99-dimensional vector and subsequently are mapped onto a 35-dimensional sub-space. The pattern classes used are defined by associating HMM states with feature vectors.

The Aachen recognizer also uses a so-called vocal tract length normalization (VTLN) as a further improvement of the feature representation. This method applies a scaling of the frequency axis with the goal of eliminating spectral effects which are caused by the different lengths of the vocal tract—namely the oral and nasal cavities and the pharynx—of different persons (cf. [302]).

13.1.2 Acoustic Modeling

The modeling of acoustic events in the Aachen recognizer is performed on the basis of continuous HMMs (see Sect. 5.2). Triphones are used as sub-word units. Each of these models is realized as a Bakis model with three states (see Sect. 8.1). In

---

[1]Recent extensions to the system also introduced multi-pass decoding in order to be able to exploit the capabilities of speaker adaptation techniques and especially expensive modeling aspects (cf. e.g. [182]).

order to ensure the trainability of the model parameters, model states for which sufficiently many training samples are available are automatically grouped into clusters
by means of decision trees (see Sect. 9.2.2). Additionally, in all mixture densities
used for the modeling of output distributions, only a single shared diagonal covariance is estimated for the underlying normal distributions (see Sect. 9.2.3).

The recognition lexicon is compactly represented as a phonetic prefix tree in
order to be able to efficiently process also large vocabularies of up to 65 000 words
(see Sect. 10.5). A model for speech pauses as well as different models for human
and non-human noises are also part of the lexicon.

13.1.3 Language Modeling

Refined techniques for language modeling and for its integrated use in the search
substantially contribute to the success of the Aachen recognizer. In most configurations, tri-gram models with so-called non-linear interpolation are used. In the
terminology of this book, this corresponds to the application of linear discounting
for gathering probability mass and the subsequent interpolation with the respective
more general distribution (see Sects. 6.5.2 and 6.5.4).

13.1.4 Search

In order to be able to correctly combine an n-gram language model with a tree lexicon, the Aachen recognizer uses an extension of the time-synchronous beam search.
Depending on the respective word context, copies of the lexicon tree are generated
(see Sect. 12.3). When using tri-gram models, HMM states need to be distinguished
according to two predecessor words. Not before a word end node is reached, the respective n-gram score can be determined and taken into account by the search. For
improving this combination of HMMs and n-gram models in the Aachen recognizer,
additionally a so-called language-model look-ahead is used. With this technique the
maximal n-gram scores to be expected are already combined with the path scores
within the acoustic model tree. This makes an early incorporation of the language
model restrictions possible and thus achieves an improved efficiency of the search
method (see Sect. 12.3.3).

13.2   BBN Speech Recognizer BYBLOS

In contrast to the Aachen recognizer, the BYBLOS system developed by BBN—
now Ratheon BBN Technologies—uses a multi-pass search strategy. The modeling
parts used are evaluated in subsequent processing steps which always use more exact
and expensive models and thus more and more constrain the potential final solution.
The details of the system presented in the following are taken from [20, 49, 211]
and [195]. Though no more recent systems-level publications exist for BYBLOS,

the framework is still maintained and developed further by BBN. It is also quite successfully applied to problems of machine-printed or handwritten script recognition (see Sect. 14.1).

13.2.1 Feature Extraction

Similarly to the Aachen recognizer, the feature extraction of BYBLOS computes 14 mel-cepstral coefficients every 10 ms for speech frames with a length of 25 ms. Together with an energy feature and the first and second temporal derivatives of these parameters, a 45-dimensional feature vector is obtained. This feature vector is then projected onto a 39-dimensional sub-space using heteroscedastic linear discriminant analysis with pattern classes defined by the clusters of the tied-mixture codebooks. In contrast to ordinary LDA (see Sect. 9.1.6), this more elaborate method does not assume that all pattern classes involved have the same covariance matrix.

The modeling quality is further improved by applying a gender-dependent vocal tract length normalization (VTLN). Furthermore, the cepstral coefficients are normalized to zero-mean[2] and unit variance on a per-utterance basis. The energy feature, in contrast, is normalized to the respective energy maximum.

13.2.2 Acoustic Modeling

BYBLOS uses HMMs of different complexities for the subsequent decoding phases. The basis forms a so-called phonetically tied-mixture HMM in which all triphone models with the same central phone use a shared codebook of 512 densities (see Sect. 9.2.3). Furthermore, quinphone models are estimated for phones in the context of *two* left and right neighbors, respectively. In order to ensure the trainability of these extremely specialized models, state clusters are formed automatically. For all states of one of these clusters the mixture densities are then defined on the basis of 80 normal distributions. The tri- and quinphones required are described by Bakis models with five states. BBN achieves a further specialization of the modeling by using gender-dependent HMMs. This means that both for triphones as well as for the considerably more complex quinphone models two complete inventories for male and female speakers are estimated.

13.2.3 Language Modeling

As most current speech recognition systems, BYBLOS also uses a tri-gram model for the restriction of the search space on the level of words. The robustness of the model is improved by defining a suitable category system in order to be able to successfully combine models that were estimated for different domains.

---

[2]This corresponds to a quite simple variant of cepstral mean normalization as it is also used in the ESMERALDA system. Further explanations can, therefore, be found in Sect. 13.3.

13.2.4 Search

BYBLOS uses multiple subsequent decoding phases in order to make an efficient evaluation of the complex HMMs and n-gram models possible (see Sect. 12.2). First, an initial restriction of the search space is determined on the basis of the tri-phone models and by using the so-called fast-match method.[3] This technique only uses a bi-gram language model and a compressed phonetic prefix tree during decoding. Subsequently, the quinphone models are adapted on the basis of the current solution by applying MLLR (see Sect. 11.2.1). Then a refinement of the space of possible solutions is computed by means of the adapted models. Afterwards, another adaptation step is carried out which also takes into account sub-word units that extend across word boundaries. The acoustic model already adapted twice is now used together with the tri-gram language model for computing a first intermediate result. This then serves as the basis for another complete pass through the decoding phases outlined above.

13.3 ESMERALDA

ESMERALDA[4] is an integrated development environment for pattern recognition systems based on Markov models. It implements[5] most methods for the estimation and application of HMMs and n-gram models presented in this book (cf. [81, 85]). The core of the ESMERALDA architecture, which is shown in Fig. 13.1, is defined by an incremental recognition system. In different parametrizations and in a variety of scenarios it was applied for tasks of automatic speech recognition [14, 30, 82, 88, 89, 151, 152, 164, 235, 240, 269, 287, 297, 298, 304, 305, 320, 321], for the analysis of prosodic structures [33, 34], for music segmentation [242], for automatic gesture recognition [253], for automatic handwriting recognition [83, 84, 87, 90–92, 243, 258, 259, 313–315, 317] (see also Sect. 14.3), and for the analysis of biological sequences [236–239] (see also Sect. 15.3).

In the following we want to present the important properties of the speech recognition systems developed on the basis of ESMERALDA. For reasons of simplicity we will always be talking about *the* ESMERALDA recognizer, even though there exist many different system configurations and also other application areas for the techniques used.

Similarly to the Aachen recognizer, the ESMERALDA recognizer works strictly time synchronously and also was conceptually influenced in its development by the research at Philips. In contrast to related systems, it offers the possibilities to use a purely declarative grammar as a language model and to incrementally generate

---

[3]The respective efficient decoding method was patented by BBN (cf. [212]).

[4]**E**nvironment for **S**tatistical **M**odel **E**stimation and **R**ecognition on **A**rbitrary **L**inear **D**ata **A**rrays.

[5]ESMERALDA is free software and is distributed under the terms of the GNU Lesser General Public License (LPGL) [86].

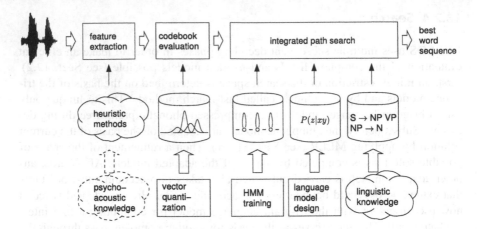

Fig. 13.1 Architecture of the ESMERALDA system: Components of the incremental recognition system are shown (feature extraction, codebook evaluation, path search) as well as the knowledge sources used (HMMs, n-gram model, grammar) and the methods provided for the design of the respective models

recognition hypotheses already during the processing of spoken utterances that are not yet completely available. The basic system features put together in the following are documented in [81, 88, 89, 298] and [235].

13.3.1 Feature Extraction

The ESMERALDA recognizer, similarly to the systems presented in the previous sections, computes mel-cepstral coefficients every 10 ms on frames with a length of 16 ms. In order to eliminate adverse effects which are caused by changes in the signal recording conditions, as, e.g., by the use of a different microphone, a dynamic cepstral mean subtraction is applied (cf. e.g. [255, 309] or [123, pp. 522–525]).

For that purpose a moving cepstral average, which is computed on energetic parts of the utterance, is subtracted from the current cepstrum. Thus changed properties of the recording channel can be compensated well. To a quite limited extent also a form of speaker adaptation is achieved. In addition to the cepstrum, an energy feature is computed. For this purpose a histogram of the signal energies in a certain temporal context is estimated and the energy coefficients are mapped to a an interval between 0.0 and 1.0 with respect to the current local minimum or maximum of the signal energy, respectively. In the same way as the cepstral mean subtraction, this normalization operation can be applied in a strictly causal manner, i.e., without any knowledge about "future" parts of the signal.

The 39-dimensional feature vector is formed from 12 cepstral coefficients, the normalized signal energy, as well as the first and second order temporal derivatives of these parameters. The smoothed temporal derivatives are computed by means of regression polynomials on a window of five neighboring frames.

13.3.2 Acoustic Modeling

The acoustic modeling in the ESMERALDA recognizer is performed by means of semi-continuous HMMs (see Sect. 5.2) with codebook sizes of some 100 up to a few 1000 densities with diagonal covariance matrices.[6]

For all speech recognition applications, triphones with linear model topology are used as sub-word units. The number of states of the individual models varies and is determined by the shortest segment length found for a corresponding speech unit in the sample set.[7] In order to ensure the trainability of the triphone models, state clusters are created automatically which are supported by a certain minimal number of feature vectors in the training set.[8] Only those states are clustered, which occur in triphones for the same baseline phone and at the same model-internal position. The distance between state clusters is determined by the increase in entropy caused by merging the output distributions (see Sect. 9.2.2).

The recognition lexicon is organized as a phonetic prefix tree. In addition to the mandatory silence model, it also contains models for human and non-human noises as well as for hesitations.

13.3.3 Statistical and Declarative Language Modeling

The ESMERALDA recognizer uses statistical bi-gram models during the search by default. However, also the time-synchronous application of higher-order n-gram models is possible. As the most important reduction in perplexity for word-based language models usually is achieved when moving from bi- to tri-gram models, the dramatically increased computational cost for even more complex models can hardly be justified in practice.[9] Even though ESMERALDA provides all techniques for the robust estimation of word-based n-gram models presented in Chap. 6, in practice absolute discounting in combination with back-off smoothing is used (see Sects. 6.5.2 and 6.5.5).

As an important extension compared to other recognition systems, the ESMERALDA recognizer offers the possibility to use a declarative grammar in much the same way as a statistical language model in order to guide the recognition process.

---

[6]ESMERALDA also supports the use of full covariance matrices. However, the large amount of training samples required to estimate such models and the higher costs in decoding cause the simpler diagonal models to become the more favorable alternative. The reduced capabilities for describing correlations between feature vector components are usually outweighed by the additional precision in modeling achieved when using larger numbers of densities.

[7]Most models usually receive 3 states with some 2-state models representing especially short acoustic units.

[8]Good results are achieved for a threshold of 75 samples. More compact and possibly also more robust models are obtained by requiring a few 100 feature vectors to support a state cluster.

[9]However, when using higher-order n-gram models substantial improvements in the accuracy of the results could be achieved in lexicon-free recognition experiments using language models based on phonetic units only [88].

In this way, expert knowledge about utterances from a certain domain can be exploited without the need to gather large amounts of text material for the training of an n-gram model. An LR(1) parser (cf. e.g. [3, pp. 215–247]) derives pseudo-scores for word sequences from the applications of rules defined by the grammar. Thus the restrictions of the grammar are not enforced. Consequently, ungrammatical utterances can be recognized, too, and the use of a grammar is also possible for domains where no full coverage can be achieved. The application of a grammar can always be combined with a statistical language model which is available additionally.

In integrated systems for automatic speech *understanding* it is further possible to output the grammatical structures determined during the recognition process directly as structured recognition hypotheses. Thus the interface between speech recognition and understanding is raised from the level of simple word hypotheses to the one of domain-specific constituents (cf. [30, 234]).

13.3.4 Incremental Search

The ESMERALDA recognizer uses the strictly time-synchronous method for searching combined HMM and n-gram models that was described in detail in Sect. 12.4. There search space copies of the acoustic model tree are created depending on the respective starting time. The search on word hypothesis level is strictly separated from that, which principally makes it possible to take into account arbitrarily long n-gram contexts.

In order to be able to generate results in interactive applications already while the current utterance is still being processed, the ESMERALDA recognizer uses a method for the incremental generation of recognition hypotheses [89]. It assumes that hypotheses for a certain part of the signal become more and more stable the farther the time-synchronous decoding has proceeded beyond this point. Therefore, every 50 ms the currently optimal solution is tracked back a certain time interval into "history" and the prefix of the hypothesis sequence lying *before* that is output as a partial recognition hypothesis. As the actual optimal solution cannot be known before the end of the utterance is reached, such a method necessarily will produce sub-optimal results. With a time delay of two seconds the incremental generation achieves results which are almost identical with those obtained by a method applying the complete optimization. With 750 ms delay one obtains an acceptable reaction time to spoken language input and only a rather low increase in the error rate by approximately 5 % relative.

Handwriting Recognition

In contrast to the field of automatic speech recognition where Markov model-based methods currently represent the state-of-the-art, HMMs and n-gram models are still a rather new approach for the recognition of machine-printed or handwritten texts. This might be due to the fact that data obtained from writing or print can, in general, be segmented into manageable segments, as, e.g., words or characters, much more easily than spoken language. Therefore, especially in the field of OCR, but also for the processing of forms or for the reading of address fields, a number of well established methods exists that rely on the classic distinction between segmentation and classification. Segmentation-free methods on the basis of Markov models, however, are mainly applied by researchers who previously gathered experience with this technology in the field of automatic speech recognition.

In the following we will present typical state-of-the-art systems for offline handwriting recognition. In addition to explanations of how Markov-model technology is applied for the recognition of handwritten script, these presentations will also include brief descriptions of the specialized methods for preprocessing and feature extraction used. More details and more system descriptions including numerous references can be found in our book focusing exclusively on the use of Markov models for handwriting recognition [241].

The first system presented in this chapter is BBN's offline HWR system which explicitly uses the BYBLOS engine originally developed for the purpose of automatic speech recognition. The system can be seen as a typical example for the architecture of an HMM-based system for the recognition of machine-printed or handwritten script. Afterwards, we will present the offline HWR system of RWTH Aachen University, Aachen, Germany. Similarly to the BBN system, its roots lie in the extensive research on automatic speech recognition performed at the Philips Research Labs, Aachen, and later at RWTH Aachen University (see Sect. 13.1). The chapter concludes with a presentation of our own systems for offline handwriting recognition which, just like the speech recognition system presented in Sect. 13.3, were developed using the ESMERALDA tool-kit. We will describe a baseline system following a classical architecture. In addition, we will present a recently pro-

G.A. Fink, *Markov Models for Pattern Recognition*,
Advances in Computer Vision and Pattern Recognition,
DOI 10.1007/978-1-4471-6308-4_14, © Springer-Verlag London 2014

posed extension of the HMM framework that offers the opportunity to estimate feature representations automatically from example data.

14.1 Recognition System by BBN

Ratheon BBN Technologies, Cambridge, USA, undoubtedly is one of the pioneers of transferring Markov-model technology from the domain of automatic speech recognition to the recognition of machine-printed and handwritten script. Already in 1996 BBN proposed a language-independent OCR system based on hidden Markov models [280]. This and all later OCR and HWR systems developed by BBN are based on the BYBLOS engine (cf. e.g. [49]) and are able to handle very large vocabularies. As BYBLOS originally was developed for the purpose of automatic speech recognition (see Sect. 13.2), some modifications for applying the framework to machine-printed or handwritten script recognition are required which are described in [16]. The following description of the system's characteristics is mainly based on [203, 204] and [264].

14.1.1 Preprocessing

The basis of offline handwriting recognition is the optical capturing of a complete document page with a resolution of 600 dpi.[1] The digitized page image obtained is then first de-skewed, i.e., a global rotation of the text caused by imperfect scanning is compensated. Afterwards, the document image is segmented into text lines by either applying a method based on connected components or on HMMs [186]. Both procedures assume that text lines are oriented more or less horizontally and do not exhibit severe baseline drift.

14.1.2 Feature Extraction

In order to compute a serialized feature representation from the extracted text-line images, BBN's handwriting recognition system applies the so-called sliding-window approach (see also Sect. 2.2). Every text line is subdivided into a sequence of small vertical stripes—usually referred to as frames—which overlap each other by two thirds. The width of the frames is 1/15 of the line height which has been normalized in order to compensate for different script sizes.

This sliding-window technique was first applied to the problem of offline handwriting recognition by researchers at the Daimler-Benz Research Center, Ulm, Germany [38]. Later, the method was pioneered by BBN especially in the context of offline recognition of machine-printed text [280]. It is fundamental for transforming images of machine-printed or handwritten script into a chronological sequence

---

[1] Abbreviation for *dots per inch*.

of feature vectors that can later be fed into an HMM-based analysis system. Today the sliding-window approach can be found in the majority of HMM-based offline recognizers.

After the individual analysis windows have been generated by the sliding-window approach, an intermediate feature representation is computed for each of them. It mainly consists of so-called percentile features which are obtained from equidistantly sampling a cumulative vertical gray-level histogram of the frame-image analyzed. The percentile features are complemented by angular, correlation, and energy features resulting in a 33 to 81-dimensional intermediate feature representation, depending on the system version considered. This intermediate feature representation is then subject to an LDA transform (see Sect. 9.1.6) which reduces the dimensionality of the final feature vector to 15.

14.1.3 Script Modeling

In the BBN recognizer, the statistical modeling of script appearance is performed on the basis of character models. Usually, these are context independent. However, for the recognition of Arabic script BBN could show improvements in recognition accuracy when using context-dependent character models that account for the contextual variations in the character shapes of Arabic writing [246, 264] (see also Sect. 8.2.2).

Both context-independent and context-dependent character models use the Bakis topology with a fixed number of 14 states per model (see Sect. 8.1).

The output probability densities of the particular model states are defined on the basis of shared sets of component densities realizing different degrees of mixture tying (see Sect. 5.2). With a single global set of Gaussians, tied-mixture or semi-continuous HMMs are realized. More degrees of freedom and a greater model complexity result from sharing component densities among character models only. The most advanced mixture-tying scheme proposed by BBN is realized by so-called position-dependent tied-mixture HMMs. With the use of context-dependent character units, these models share sets of mixture components among all states at the same logical position within a model set representing the same base character.

The training of the models is achieved by means of the Baum–Welch algorithm (see Sect. 5.7.4). Similarly to automatic speech recognition, only the orthographic transcription of every text line—i.e. the actual character or word sequence—is given during training. At the beginning of the training all HMM parameters are initialized uniformly. Unfortunately, it is not documented in the literature how initial parameters are derived for the mixture codebooks used. However, it may be assumed that initial codebooks are generated in an unsupervised manner by means of a method for vector quantizer design (see Sect. 4.3).

14.1.4 Language Modeling and Search

n-Gram language models are an integral component of BBN's handwriting recognition system. The integrated decoding of the HMMs used for modeling the script appearance and the word or character-based language models is achieved by a multi-pass search algorithm (see Sects. 12.2 and 13.2.4). First, a forward decoding pass is carried out using the fast-match beam-search algorithm and an approximate bi-gram model. In a subsequent backward decoding pass, a tri-gram model is used for generating n-best results. These recognition hypotheses are afterwards rescored based on detailed match scores and the language-model scores.

In order to account for mismatches in the characteristics of the data between training and testing conditions, the BBN handwriting recognizer applies unsupervised adaptation. Therefore, based on the first-best recognition result generated using the un-adapted models, an MLLR transformation is estimated distinguishing 10 regression classes (see Sect. 11.2.1). The estimated transform parameters are then applied to obtain an adapted HMM. Using this adapted writing model a second pass through the multi-pass decoding method outline above is carried out in order to obtain the final transcription hypothesis.

14.2 Recognition System of RWTH Aachen University

Similarly to the BBN recognizer, the RWTH Aachen handwriting recognition system was derived from the group's speech recognition framework (see Sect. 13.1). The first publication applying these Markov-model-based techniques to problems of document image analysis was concerned with white-space modeling for Arabic script recognition [61]. Also in later works the group put a strong focus on the recognition of Arabic handwriting (cf. e.g. [63]) though impressive recognition performance was also reported for the recognition of Roman script (cf. [159]). The following description of the system's characteristics is mainly based on [159].

14.2.1 Preprocessing

In the most recent version, the RWTH Aachen recognizer does not include methods for page segmentation or text-line extraction [159]. Rather, it is assumed that handwritten script to be transcribed is given as previously extracted text-line images.

These text-line images are then subject to normalization operations. First, the contrast of the line images is normalized such that a pre-set proportion of the lightest or darkest image pixels are set to white or black, respectively, while linearly normalizing the in-between intensity range. Afterwards, the slant angle of the handwritten text lines is compensated by applying a shear transform. The slant angle is estimated by applying different slant-angle estimation methods and computing the median of the resulting angles.

14.2.2 Feature Extraction

As most HMM-based recognizers for handwritten or machine-printed script, the
RWTH Aachen system uses the sliding-window approach for feature extraction. The
analysis windows extracted are 30 pixels wide[2] and are shifted along the text-line
with an offset of 3 pixels, which means that successive frames overlap by 90 %. In
order to smooth the borders of the extracted analysis windows, a horizontal cosine
window is applied.

Afterwards, the individual frame images are normalized with respect to their center of gravity and their scale based on the first- and second-order image moments.
These moments are not computed on the gray-scale images directly but are obtained
after computing a gradient-magnitude image using the Sobel operator. Thus the normalization operation might be less susceptible to variations in the width of the pen
strokes. Finally, all frame images are normalized to a pre-defined size of 8×32
pixels.

Based on the normalized frame images the feature representation is computed
by applying a PCA transform to the gray-scale images. Thereby, the dimensionality
is reduced to 20. Finally, the 4 original normalized moments are added to the feature vector as the normalizations performed so far remove all information about the
actual size of the original script components contained within the frame images.

14.2.3 Script Modeling

The script appearance model used by the RTWH Aachen recognizer is based in
HMMs for context-independent character models. All character HMMs use the
Bakis topology. Interestingly, no individual state transition probabilities are used
but rather these are shared across all models. Furthermore, the shared exit, loop, and
skip probabilities are not trained from data but pre-set heuristically.

The number of states for individual character HMMs, i.e., the length of the models, may vary and is estimated on the basis of alignment information obtained during
training. Within each model the respective HMM states are grouped into pairs that
share the same output probability density functions.

These output probability densities are described by Gaussian mixtures using a
set of 64 component densities and a single, global diagonal covariance matrix that
is shared between all mixtures. This effectively means that no real covariance modeling is performed but rather a single scaling parameter is estimated for every component of the 24-dimensional feature vectors.

The script appearance model is estimated by applying the approximate Viterbi
training procedure described in detail in Sect. 5.7.5. Similarly to the BBN recognizer, the RWTH Aachen system performs unsupervised writer adaptation in order
to compensate for mismatches between training and testing conditions. MLLR adaptation transforms using a single regression class (see Sect. 11.2.1) are estimated per
writer during training and per text paragraph during recognition.

---

[2]According to [159] no size or height normalization of the line images is performed.

14.2.4 Language Modeling and Search

As a consequence of the adaptation procedure applied, the decoding within the RWTH Aachen recognizer has to be performed in a two-pass process. In the first pass, the pre-trained appearance model is used in decoding. After applying the MLLR-based adaptation, a second decoding pass is carried out using the adapted models.

In order to be able to handle out-of-vocabulary words during decoding, i.e., words in the test material that are not part of the recognition lexicon, the RTWH Aachen system uses a hybrid combination of word-level and character-level language models [13]. The word-level tri-gram model is obtained by applying discounting and Kneser–Ney smoothing to the raw n-gram statistics (see Sect. 6.5.6). The character-level 10-gram language model being used is estimated from character sequences that were extracted from out-of-vocabulary words observed during training.

14.3   ESMERALDA Offline Recognition System

Development of the ESMERALDA offline HWR system dates back to [93] and the first research efforts aiming at automatic video-based whiteboard reading (cf. [91, 316]). Since then it has been successfully applied to a number of recognition tasks (cf. [84, 87, 90, 243, 317]) and serves as a baseline system for new developments (cf. [83, 117, 258, 259]). Just as the systems described in the previous sections, it can be considered as a classical descendant of a speech recognition framework following quite closely the general architecture of HMM-based systems for the recognition of machine-printed or handwritten script. The system is different from other state-of-the-art HWR recognizers as it was mainly developed for camera-based recognition tasks that require robust modeling techniques (cf. [243, 317]).

The following description of the ESMERALDA offline HWR systems is mainly based on [317] and [243]. Recent developments towards HWR systems based on an extension of the HMM framework offering the capability to learn feature representations automatically from data will be described in the next section.

14.3.1 Preprocessing

In offline handwriting recognition, the preprocessing of the document images captured is of fundamental importance. Similarly to the system by BBN, the ESMERALDA offline HWR system includes a relatively straight-forward page-segmentation module. After a skew normalization of the document page, a segmentation of the individual text lines is performed by evaluating the horizontal projection histogram. The text lines extracted such are then normalized in subsequent processing steps. First, a local estimation of the baseline is computed by a three-step procedure. Initially, the position of the core area of the writing, i.e., the area between upper and lower baseline, is derived from the horizontal projection histogram.

Then the local contour minima of the writing are extracted and approximated by a straight line using linear regression. In the final step, this baseline estimate is refined by removing outliers from the set of contour minima. Based on this estimate, the baseline and also line internal offsets between word-images are normalized. Afterwards, the slant angle of the writing is estimated by computing the median of a gradient histogram extracted from the text line in question. The estimated slant is then compensated by a shear transform of the text-line image. The next normalization operation is extremely important for tasks where the apparent size of the script to be transcribed may vary widely. In order to compensate such variation, a robust size normalization is applied. It is based on an estimate of the average character width which is computed as the average distance between local contour minima [188]. Based on the character-width estimate the line image is re-scaled such that the average distance between local contour minima matches a pre-defined constant.[3] Finally a local binarization of the text-line image is performed by applying a modified version of the Niblack method [330]. As the ESMERALDA offline recognizer was primarily intended for the recognition of texts in video data, this ensures that intensity variations of both writing and background do not adversely affect the subsequent feature extraction process.

14.3.2 Feature Extraction

Similarly to all major HMM-based handwriting recognition systems, the ESMER-ALDA offline recognizer uses the sliding-window technique to convert text-line images into sequences of feature vectors. Pre-segmented and normalized text-line images are subdivided into small stripes or analysis windows which are 8 pixels wide and overlap each other by 75 %. The height of these analysis windows varies depending on the results of the size normalization performed before. For each of these windows nine geometrical features inspired by [191] are computed from the associated stripe of the binarized text image. The first group of features describes the coarse shape of the writing within the local analysis window. The average distance of the lower baseline to both the upper and the lower contour of the writing is computed, and the distance of the center of gravity of the text pixels to the baseline. These features are then normalized by the core size, i.e., the distance between upper and lower baseline in order to increase the robustness against variations in the size of the writing. Furthermore, three local directional features are calculated describing the orientation of the lower and upper contour as well as the gradient of the mean of the column-wise pixel distributions. Finally, the average number of black-to-white transitions per column, the average number of text pixels per column, and the average number of text pixels between upper and lower contour are calculated.

---

[3]This size normalization operation is script dependent. For Roman script the implicit assumption that average character width is correlated with the average distances between contour minima is justified quite well. In contrast, for Arabic script this size normalization technique does not produce useful results.

Subsequently, dynamic features are added to the basic feature vector computed so far in order to be able to consider a wider temporal context in the feature representation. Therefore, discrete approximations of the temporal derivatives of the 9 baseline features are computed over a context of five analysis windows by linear regression (cf. [60]). Taken together, the baseline features and the dynamic features form a 18-dimensional feature vector.

14.3.3 Handwriting Model

The statistical modeling of handwriting is performed on the basis of semi-continuous HMMs (see Sect. 5.2) with a shared codebook of approximately 2,000 Gaussians with individual diagonal covariances. For Roman script, a total of 75 context-independent HMMs is created for modeling 52 letters, ten digits, 12 punctuation symbols, and white space. The number of model states is automatically determined depending on the length of the respective unit in the training material. All these models use the Bakis topology in order to be able to capture a wider variability in the length of the character patterns described (see Sect. 8.1).

14.3.4 Language Modeling and Search

In order to make handwriting recognition with "unlimited" lexicon possible on the basis of character models only, sequencing restrictions between HMMs for individual symbols are represented by means of character n-gram models of increasing complexity.[4] For all models estimated the raw n-gram probabilities are smoothed by applying absolute discounting and backing off (see Sect. 6.5). The integrated decoding of HMMs for describing the handwriting and n-gram language models defining the sequencing restrictions is achieved in the ESMERALDA offline recognizer by applying the time-synchronous search method described in detail in Sect. 12.4.

14.4 Bag-of-Features Hidden Markov Models

In the previous sections we saw that in successful HWR systems a number of preprocessing steps is applied. The preprocessing methods being used are chosen heuristically and their parameters are fine-tuned on some set of development data. After preprocessing the sliding-window approach is applied and features are extracted from the analysis windows obtained. Again, the feature extraction methods being used are chosen heuristically and their parameters can only be tuned on development data.

---

[4]In [317] lexicon free experiments are reported for bi-gram up to 5-gram models.

Only after preprocessing and feature extraction is complete, machine learning methods are applied, i.e., HMMs and n-gram models for which parameters can be learned from example data. Consequently, the heuristics involved in choosing suitable preprocessing and feature extraction methods severely affect the overall performance of any HWR system.

Therefore, one long-term goal of the author's research group is to develop methods for feature extraction—and ideally preprocessing—in HWR that also apply machine learning techniques such that learning from example data becomes possible and expert knowledge is only applied on a more abstract, structural level. In our first efforts towards this goal we applied analytical feature extraction methods as, for example, PCA in order to obtain feature representations for HWR that are automatically derived from sample data [83] (see also Sect. 9.1). In [117] a method based on auto-encoder neuronal networks was used in order to automatically obtain non-linear feature representations from sample data.

Recently, we developed a method for learning feature representations for HWR that is based on the *Bag-of-Features* (BoF) paradigm which has been successfully applied to tasks of object recognition and scene categorization in the field of computer vision before (cf. [221]). BoF representations are actually a generalization of so-called *Bag-of-Words* (BoW) models that were developed for the task of text categorization and retrieval (cf. e.g. [265]).

In the BoW framework a text is characterized by the frequency of occurrence of content words contained therein. In order to do so, first all words that most likely do not contribute useful information for characterizing the textual content are discarded as, for example, determiners, prepositions, and other function words. The remaining words are mapped to their stems, for example, `script` and `scripts` are represented as `script` and `write`, `writes`, `writing`, and `written` are mapped to `write`. Finally, the frequencies of occurrence of all word stems are collected in a histogram. This representation is referred to as a *bag* of words as all information about the position of words within the text encoded in such a way is lost.

The BoW representation now serves as a compact model of the respective text. It can be used to measure similarity between texts and to retrieve texts from a database that are similar to a given query BoW representation.

In the same way as BoW representations are statistical representations of texts, BoF models are statistical representations of images. The challenge is to find a suitable equivalent for words in the visual domain. So-called *visual words* are derived from image data by clustering certain local image descriptors. An element of the codebooks computed thus is referred to as a visual word. Here the clustering or quantization process corresponds to the stemming operation known from the BoW approach. Local image descriptors may be simple image patches of fixed size that are extracted from the image to be analyzed in a dense grid (cf. [78]). The most widely used descriptor type in the context of BoF models is, however, the well known SIFT descriptor ([183], cf. [221, 284]).

A fundamental characteristic of the BoF approach is that all spatial information not implicitly encoded by the image descriptors is lost in the feature statistics computed. Therefore, BoF models are able to cover a significant variation in the spatial configuration of the image features considered. However, completely ignoring spatial relations can also be regarded as a limitation of the approach. Therefore, recently several approaches where proposed that aim at reducing this limitation by reintroducing spatial information into an augmented BoF model. The probably most well known of these approaches is the so-called *spatial pyramid* model proposed in [167]. In this model BoF representations are extracted in a hierarchical fashion and combined into an overall model. This approach achieves superior performance compared to plain BoF models but also increases the dimensionality of the model considerably. A more compact modeling with comparable performance can be obtained by introducing explicit spatial information into the descriptors themselves obtaining so-called *spatial visual vocabularies* [113].

On the one hand side, BoF models are powerful statistical representations of visual appearance. On the other hand side, in HWR the description of visual appearance of handwritten script is considered as a statistical sequence modeling problem that is mainly approached by Markov-model technology. Therefore, we recently proposed a combination of the two fundamental methods resulting in so-called *Bag-of-Features hidden Markov models* (BoF-HMMs) [259].

In BoF-HMMs the BoF representations take over the task of modeling the local appearance of handwriting as seen by the sliding-window approach. Consequently, BoF models are computed in a sequential manner for images of handwritten script. The BoF representations obtained can then either be considered as feature representations or can directly be used as the basis of the modeling of output probability distributions. In the first case, the application of a suitable method for dimensionality reduction is advisable (see Sect. 9.1) as BoF models usually are extremely high-dimensional. The resulting low-dimensional feature representations can then serve as the basis for continuous or tied-mixture HMMs [259]. Alternatively, the discrete probability distributions defined by BoF models can directly be combined with state-specific mixture weights in order to compute approximations of output probabilities [259].

We applied BoF-HMMs first to the task of handwriting recognition, more specifically the recognition of Arabic script achieving highly competitive results [259]. However, the greatest success of the method was achieved in the domain of segmentation-free handwritten word spotting [258]. In previous work on that topic, Rusiñol and colleagues proposed to use an adapted spatial-pyramid modeling for query-by-example word spotting in a segmentation-free framework [261]. The BoF-HMM approach can be seen as a generalization of that method offering both a more detailed modeling of script appearance and more flexibility in the sequence representation due to the incorporation of HMMs [258].

Consequently, our method achieved the best performance reported so far on a widely recognized word-spotting benchmark defined by Rusiñol and colleagues [261] on the basis of the George-Washington dataset [95] outperforming other approaches with a mean average precision of more than 67 % [257]. The impressive performance of BoF-HMMs on word-spotting tasks is only possible because the method works well for query words of any length, i.e., also for extremely short queries that usually are the most problematic ones to spot.

Dense grid of image features

Quantized visual words

Query modeling

Patch-based decoding

Visualization of match scores

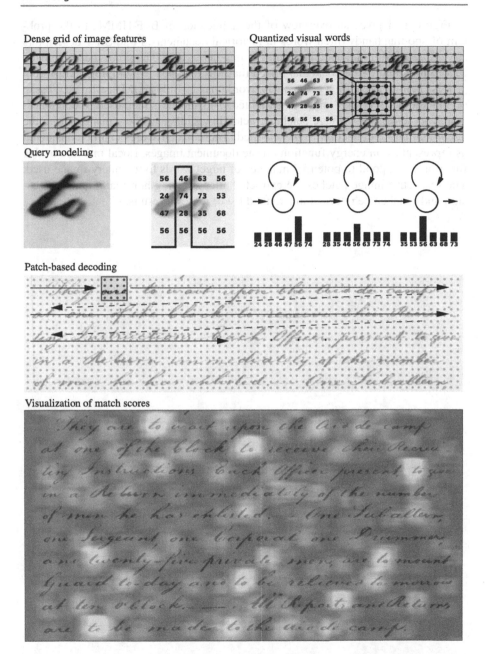

Fig. 14.1 Overview of the application of BoF-HMMs to the task of word spotting: Dense grid of image descriptors and quantized visual words (*top row*), query image, sliding BoF representation, and query model (*second row*), patch-based decoding (*third row*), and visualization of match scores obtained (example based on the document image known from Fig. 2.3, used with permission; visualization courtesy of Leonard Rothacker)

Figure 14.1 gives an overview of the application of BoF-HMMs to the problem of spotting handwritten words in historical documents. First, SIFT descriptors are extracted from the document images in a dense grid. These are then quantized according to the visual vocabulary used that was obtained by applying a clustering process before. Then, for a given query-word image a BoF-HMM is estimated based on the sliding-BoF representation extracted. This model is then used to compute a match score for every image patch extracted in a sliding-window manner from the document image collection to be searched. These match scores can be considered as representing an energy function on the document images. Local maxima of this function correspond to potential matches of target words to the query image used. The respective image patches are extracted after applying non-maximum suppression and can then be returned in a ranked list of retrieval results.

Analysis of Biological Sequences

15

When considering applications of HMMs in the field of bioinformatics, an interesting observation can be made. Researchers in this area frequently try to influence as many details of the models as possible by introducing expert knowledge, i.e., they specify model parameters manually in a heuristic way. This procedure is rather counterintuitive in the context of a statistical modeling framework as one of the main advantages of HMMs, namely the possibility to estimate their parameters automatically from sample data, is not exploited. To some extent this situation might be explained by a lack of sufficiently large sets of annotated sample data that still exists despite the considerable advances that have been made in the sequencing of the human genome and the genomes of other species.

Here parallels can be drawn to the times when statistical speech recognition was in its infancy. Then also substantial influence was exerted on the model structure. With the availability of ever larger sample sets that were annotated or could be annotated semi-automatically such techniques, however, were applied to a ever lesser extent and were replaced by methods which allowed to estimate the necessary configurations from example data automatically. Usually, also the former expensive model structures, which needed to be optimized manually, gave way to drastically simplified structures with considerably increased degrees of freedom.

Furthermore, in the field of biological sequence analysis there still seem to exist strong reservations against the application of techniques of statistical pattern recognition such as HMMs. These reservations are most probably due to the fact that research in the field of biological sequence analysis have the strong desire to be able to explain every detail of a model from a biological viewpoint. Therefore, in several publications on HMM-based biological sequence analysis, as, for example, in [70], sections can be found in which it is explicitly pointed out that HMMs principally achieve the same results as more traditional methods for score-based sequence comparison. Usually only the underlying mathematical theory is given as their main advantage and less frequently the automatic trainability of the model parameters required.

In the following we will first briefly present the two most important software tools that were developed for the analysis of biological sequences by means of hidden

G.A. Fink, *Markov Models for Pattern Recognition*,
Advances in Computer Vision and Pattern Recognition,
DOI 10.1007/978-1-4471-6308-4_15, © Springer-Verlag London 2014

Markov models. In these systems Markov chain models play just as little a role as the detection of genes within a complete genome. In the final section of the chapter we will present a system for the classification of proteins which was developed on the basis of ESMERALDA and which follows a radically different approach in many respects.

15.1 HMMER

The *HMMER* system (pronounced[1] *hammer*) was developed by Eddy and colleagues, first at Washington University, Saint Louis, and meanwhile at the Janelia Farm Research Campus of the Howard Hughes Medical Institute, Chevy Chase, [94, 122]. The underlying techniques are described in detail in the monograph by Durbin and colleagues [67].

15.1.1 Model Structure

HMMER exclusively uses profile HMMs as the overall model structure (see Sect. 8.4). Already in version 2.2 (current version is 3.1) their architecture was extended such that in addition to the detection of similar sequences also the search for similar partial sequences was possible which are embedded in longer sequences of amino acids. The model structure denoted as "Plan 7" results from the one shown in Fig. 8.6 by reducing the potential state transitions within a group of match, insert, and delete states from 9 to 7.[2] With this simplification no transitions from delete to insert states and vice versa are possible any more.

15.1.2 Parameter Estimation

The estimation of model parameters in HMMER is exclusively performed on the basis of pre-existing multiple alignments that have been created by experts. The empirical distributions of the amino acids can directly be given as the mapping between the columns of the alignment and model states is fixed and is not modified. In order to improve the robustness of the estimates, prior probabilities of the parameter values are incorporated following the principle of MAP estimation (see Sect. 3.6.2). The output probability densities are modeled as mixtures of Dirichlet distributions (cf. [67, pp. 116–117]). However, the model created such is not further optimized by means of the Baum–Welch algorithm or a similar method for HMM training.

---

[1]The original HMMER 2.1.1 documentation, which today is only partially available via archive.org, says that '*It's "hammer": as in, a more precise tool than a BLAST. :)*'.

[2]The name "Plan 7" for the structure improved with respect to the older "Plan 9" model architecture was an allusion to the title of a science fiction movie—sometimes referred to as the worst movie ever made. Unfortunately, this humorous remark can no longer be found in the HMMER documentation.

When searching for matching sequences, the decision about the similarity to the sequence family considered is based on the log-odds score between the score of the target model and the one of an appropriately chosen background model (see Sect. 7.4). Therefore, HMMER offers the possibility to automatically adjust the parameters of the background distribution and the necessary thresholds in a calibration step.

15.1.3 Interoperability

An essential aspect of HMMER is the interoperability with other systems. Ready-made profile HMMs, which are available in a certain data format as, e.g., the one defined in the PFAM database [250], can be used directly for sequence analysis by the software tools. Furthermore, for arbitrary models HMMER is capable of applying the search algorithms provided to different sequence databases available on the Internet, as e.g. the protein database SWISS-PROT [12].

15.2 SAM

The *Sequence Alignment and Modeling System* (SAM) resulted from works of Hughey and colleagues at the University of California, Santa Cruz, CA [128]. From the principal algorithmic capabilities it is very similar to HMMER. Profile HMMs[3] are used as the overall model structure though without the modifications of the "Plan 7" architecture. The parameter estimation is performed on pre-existing multiple alignments by default. A calibration of models is provided in order to enable a purely score-based decision about the similarity of sequences. In the same way as HMMER, SAM offers the possibility to import ready-made models from external data formats and to directly apply models for the search on sequence databases.

The important difference between HMMER and SAM lies in the fact that the latter system offers different iteratively optimizing training methods for profile HMMs. By default the Baum–Welch algorithm is used (see Sect. 5.7.4), which in the SAM documentation, however, is only referred to as EM algorithm. In order to modify the convergence properties and to avoid finding local maxima only during the optimization procedure, the parameter estimation can be overlaid by a noise process following the principle of simulated annealing. The parameter estimates are randomly modified according to a statistical model while the degree of the modification decreases with increasing number of training iterations. SAM also offers the application of the Viterbi training (see Sect. 5.7.5) for a substantially accelerated but also qualitatively less satisfactory parameter training. Furthermore, in SAM there exist various heuristic methods for optimizing the structure of the model to be estimated during the training process depending on the current model parameters. However,

---

[3]The profile HMM structure with match, insert, and delete states is incorrectly referred to as a "linear HMM" in the SAM documentation.

all these methods are highly specific to the problem of modeling protein sequences by profile HMMs.

In contrast to HMMER, SAM furthermore offers the possibility to generate multiple alignments from initially un-aligned sequences in a purely data-driven manner. For HMMER multiple alignments need to be pre-specified and can only be augmented by additional members of the respective sequence family, which were found during the similarity search in certain databases.

Despite these distinguishing features, one may say that from the purely discrete view on sequence data both systems implement all relevant aspects of research on the topic of profile HMMs. In contrast to the fields of speech and handwriting recognition, both HMMER as well as SAM are available on the Internet as software tools for several system architectures and with detailed documentation.

15.3   ESMERALDA

Though it might seem obvious that sequence data, which can be described by a series of symbols taken from a small finite alphabet, is modeled using discrete HMMs, alternative data representations can lead to considerably improved modeling capabilities. The ESMERALDA-based system for modeling families of remotely homologous proteins, which was developed by Thomas Plötz and the author at Bielefeld University, Germany, follows such a radically different approach. As the first system of its kind it used a biologically motivated *continuous* multi-channel representation of protein sequence data in conjunction with semi-continuous HMMs for describing families of remotely homologous sequences [236–239].

15.3.1   Feature Extraction

The function of the residues within a protein sequence—i.e. the individual amino acids—can be abstractly characterized on a symbolic level, but it is actually realized by their bio-chemical properties. Therefore, the symbolic sequence representation of proteins is first mapped onto a suitable continuous representation of relevant bio-chemical properties of amino acids. As it is not clear which single property might be the most relevant, multiple properties complementing each other—here 35—are considered which are defined by so-called amino acid indices. Therefore, protein sequences are now represented as multi-channel real-valued signals where each channel encodes one bio-chemical property of amino acids.

This signal representation is then analyzed locally by sliding along a small analysis window with a length of 16 residues and an overlap of 15. Thus for every position in the original symbolic sequence representation a local analysis is performed. For this purpose first a channel-wise discrete wavelet transform is applied using two-stage multi-scale analysis. Secondly, after a first reduction of the dimension per channel to 11, the collection of coefficients obtained such is subject to a principal component analysis (see Sect. 9.1.5) obtaining a 99-dimensional feature vector (cf. [236, 238]).

15.3.2 Statistical Models of Proteins

The statistical models of proteins are based on semi-continuous HMMs (see Sect. 5.2). When structured equivalently to profile HMMs, the difference from the classical modeling of proteins is completely concentrated in the modified data representation. However, as continuous models based on mixture densities in conjunction with a feature representation encoding local context information are much more powerful than discrete models, the tight structural restrictions of profile HMMs, which encode the prior expert knowledge, no longer are of fundamental importance. Rather, the actual structures can be inferred from training data within the framework of a greatly simplified model topology. Therefore, so-called bounded left-right models were introduced [239]. These are principally equivalent to ordinary left-to-right models with the notable distinction that the distance for skipping states forward in the model is limited to a maximum number of states. As arbitrarily long forward skips are hardly necessary to represent sequential data, this measure ensures that the number of transition probabilities reduced thus can actually be trained on the sample data available.

As the problem of data sparseness is especially extreme in the field of bioinformatics, it is of fundamental importance to define robust procedures for parameter training. Usually this is achieved by incorporating certain prior knowledge into the estimation process or by heuristic methods for model regularization, i.e. suitable modifications of the parameter estimates. In the ESMERALDA-based protein modeling framework, a training procedure was defined which combines several estimation steps producing more and more specialized models. As semi-continuous HMMs are used, annotated data is not required for the initial estimation of the shared set of codebook densities. Therefore, this can be achieved on large databases of general protein sequences. The remaining model parameters, namely transition probabilities and mixture density weights, can then be estimated on family-specific data. As this data usually is too limited to achieve a robust re-estimation of the codebook densities, too, these are merely adapted to the special data by means of maximum likelihood linear regression (see Sect. 11.2.1).

15.2.2 Statistical Models of Proteins

References

1. Adda, G., Adda-Decker, M., Gauvain, J.-L., Lamel, L.: Text normalization and speech recognition in French. In: Proc. European Conf. on Speech Communication and Technology, vol. 5, pp. 2711–2714 (1997)
2. Adda-Decker, M.: Towards multilingual interoperability in automatic speech recognition. Speech Communication 35(1–2), 5–20 (2001)
3. Aho, A.V., Sethi, R., Ullman, J.D.: Compilers: Principles, Techniques, and Tools. Addison-Wesley, Reading (1986)
4. Andreao, R.V., Dorizzi, B., Boudy, J.: ECG signal analysis through hidden Markov models. IEEE Trans. on Biomedical Engineering 53(8), 1541–1549 (2006)
5. Ariso, E., Kurimo, M., Saraçlar, M., Hirsimäki, T., Pylkkönen, J., Alumäe, T., Sak, H.: Statistical language modeling for automatic speech recognition of agglutinative languages. In: Mihelic, F., Zibert, J. (eds.) Speech Recognition, Technologies and Applications, pp. 193–204. I-Tech, Vienna (2008)
6. Asadi, A., Schwartz, R., Makhoul, J.: Automatic detection of new words in a large vocabulary continuous speech recognition system. In: Proc. Int. Conf. on Acoustics, Speech, and Signal Processing, Albuquerque, pp. 125–128 (1990)
7. Aubert, X., Dugast, C., Ney, H., Steinbiss, V.: Large vocabulary continuous speech recognition of Wall Street Journal data. In: Proc. Int. Conf. on Acoustics, Speech, and Signal Processing, Adelaide, vol. II, pp. 129–132 (1994)
8. Aubert, X., Haeb-Umbach, R., Ney, H.: Continuous mixture densities and linear discriminant analysis for improved context-dependent acoustic models. In: Proc. Int. Conf. on Acoustics, Speech, and Signal Processing, Minneapolis, vol. II, pp. 648–651 (1993)
9. Avendaño, C., Deng, L., Hermansky, H., Gold, B.: The analysis and representation of speech. In: Greenberg, S., Ainsworth, W.A., Popper, A.N., Fay, R.R. (eds.) Speech Processing in the Auditory System. Springer Handbook of Auditory Research, vol. 18, pp. 63–100. Springer, Berlin (2004)
10. Bahl, L.R., Brown, P.F., de Souza, P.V., Mercer, R.L.: Estimating hidden Markov model parameters so as to maximize speech recognition accuracy. IEEE Trans. on Speech and Audio Processing 1(1), 77–83 (1993)
11. Bahl, L.R., Jelinek, F.: Decoding for channels with insertions, deletions, and substitutions with applications to speech recognition. IEEE Trans. on Information Theory 21(4), 404–411 (1975)
12. Bairoch, A., Apweiler, R.: The SWISS-PROT protein sequence database and its supplement TrEMBL in 2000. Nucleic Acids Research 28(1), 45–48 (2000)
13. Basha Shaik, M.A., Rybach, D., Hahn, S., Schlüter, R., Ney, H.: Hierarchical hybrid language models for open vocabulary continuous speech recognition using wfst. In: Proc. Workshop on Statistical and Perceptual Audition, Portland, OR, USA, pp. 46–51 (2012)

14. Bauckhage, C., Fink, G.A., Fritsch, J., Kummert, F., Lömker, F., Sagerer, G., Wachsmuth, S.: An integrated system for cooperative man-machine interaction. In: IEEE International Symposium on Computational Intelligence in Robotics and Automation, Banff, Canada, pp. 328–333 (2001)

15. Baum, L.E., Petrie, T., Soules, G., Weiss, N.: A maximization technique occurring in the statistical analysis of probabilistic functions of Markov chains. The Annals of Mathematical Statistics **41**, 164–171 (1970)

16. Bazzi, I., Schwartz, R., Makhoul, J.: An omnifont open-vocabulary OCR system for English and Arabic. IEEE Trans. on Pattern Analysis and Machine Intelligence **21**(6), 495–504 (1999)

17. Bell, T.C., Cleary, J.G., Witten, I.H.W.: Text Compression. Prentice Hall, Englewood Cliffs (1990)

18. Beyerlein, P., Aubert, X.L., Haeb-Umbach, R., Harris, M., Klakow, D., Wendemuth, A., Molau, S., Pitz, M., Sixtus, A.: The Philips/RWTH system for transcription of broadcast news. In: Proc. European Conf. on Speech Communication and Technology, Budapest, vol. 2, pp. 647–650 (1999)

19. Bigi, B., De Mori, R., El-Béze, M., Spriet, T.: Combined models for topic spotting and topic-dependent language modeling. In: Furui, S., Huang, B.H., Chu, W. (eds.) Proc. Workshop on Automatic Speech Recognition and Understanding, pp. 535–542 (1997)

20. Billa, J., Colhurst, T., El-Jaroudi, A., Iyer, R., Ma, K., Matsoukas, S., Quillen, C., Richardson, F., Siu, M., Zvaliagkos, G., Gish, H.: Recent experiments in large vocabulary conversational speech recognition. In: Proc. Int. Conf. on Acoustics, Speech, and Signal Processing, Phoenix, AZ (1999)

21. Billa, J., Ma, K., McDonough, J.W., Zavaliagkos, G., Miller, D.R., Ross, K.N., El-Jaroudi, A.: Multilingual speech recognition: the 1996 Byblos Callhome system. In: Proc. European Conf. on Speech Communication and Technology, Rhodes, Greece, vol. 1, pp. 363–366 (1997)

22. Bilmes, J.: A gentle tutorial of the EM algorithm and its application to parameter estimation for Gaussian mixture and hidden Markov models. Technical report TR-97-021, International Computer Science Institute, Berkeley (1997)

23. Bishop, C.M.: Pattern Recognition and Machine Learning. Springer, New York (2006)

24. Bocchieri, E.: Vector quantization for efficient computation of continuous density likelihoods. In: Proc. Int. Conf. on Acoustics, Speech, and Signal Processing, Minneapolis, vol. 2, pp. 692–695 (1993)

25. Bock, H.-H.: Origins and extensions of the k-means algorithm in cluster analysis. J. Électron. Hist. Probab. Stat. **4**(2) (2008)

26. Bogert, B.P., Healy, M.J.R., Tukey, J.W.: The frequency analysis of time series for echoes: cepstrum, pseudo-autocovariance, cross-cepstrum and saphe cracking. In: Rosenblatt, M. (ed.) Proceedings of the Symposium on Time Series Analysis (1962, Providence, Rhode Island), pp. 209–243. Wiley, New York (1963)

27. Boulis, C., Diakoloukas, V.D., Digalakis, V.V.: Maximum likelihood stochastic transformation adaptation for medium and small data sets. Computer Speech & Language **15**, 257–285 (2001)

28. Boulis, C., Digalakis, V.V.: Fast speaker adaptation of large vocabulary continuous density HMM speech recognizer using a basis transform approach. In: Proc. Int. Conf. on Acoustics, Speech, and Signal Processing, Istanbul, pp. 3630–3633 (2000)

29. Brand, M., Oliver, N., Pentland, A.: Coupled hidden Markov models for complex action recognition. In: Proc. Int. Conf. on Computer Vision and Pattern Recognition, San Juan, Puerto Rico, pp. 994–999 (1997)

30. Brandt-Pook, H., Fink, G.A., Wachsmuth, S., Sagerer, G.: Integrated recognition and interpretation of speech for a construction task domain. In: Bullinger, H.-J., Ziegler, J. (eds.) Proceedings 8th International Conference on Human-Computer Interaction, München, vol. 1, pp. 550–554 (1999)

31. Bregler, C.: Learning and recognizing human dynamics in video sequences. In: Proc. Int. Conf. on Computer Vision and Pattern Recognition, San Juan, Puerto Rico, pp. 568–571 (1997)

32. Breiman, L., Friedman, J.H., Olshen, R.A., Stone, C.J.: Classification and Regression Trees. The Wadsworth Statistics/Probability Series. Wadsworth Publishing Company, Belmont (1984)

33. Brindöpke, C., Fink, G.A., Kummert, F.: A comparative study of HMM-based approaches for the automatic recognition of perceptively relevant aspects of spontaneous German speech melody. In: Proc. European Conf. on Speech Communication and Technology, Budapest, vol. 2, pp. 699–702 (1999)

34. Brindöpke, C., Fink, G.A., Kummert, F., Sagerer, G.: An HMM-based recognition system for perceptive relevant pitch movements of spontaneous German speech. In: Proc. Int. Conf. on Spoken Language Processing, Sydney, vol. 7, pp. 2895–2898 (1998)

35. Brown, P.F., Pietra, V.J.D., deSouza, P.V., Lai, J.C., Mercer, R.L.: Class-based n-gram models of natural language. Comput. Linguist. 18(4), 467–479 (1992)

36. Bunke, H., Wang, P.S.P. (eds.): Handbook of Character Recognition and Document Image Analysis. World Scientific, Singapore (1997)

37. Burshtein, D.: Robust parametric modelling of durations in hidden Markov models. IEEE Trans. Acoust. Speech Signal Process. 3(4), 240–242 (1996)

38. Caesar, T., Gloger, J.M., Mandler, E.: Preprocessing and feature extraction for a handwriting recognition system. In: Proc. Int. Conf. on Document Analysis and Recognition, Tsukuba Science City, Japan, pp. 408–411 (1993)

39. Calinon, S., Billard, A.: Recognition and reproduction of gestures using a probabilistic framework combining PCA, ICA and HMM. In: Proc. Int. Conf. on Machine Learning, Bonn, Germany, pp. 105–112 (2005)

40. Çarkı, K., Geutner, P., Schultz, T.: Turkish LVCSR: towards better speech recognition for agglutinative languages. In: Proc. Int. Conf. on Acoustics, Speech, and Signal Processing, Istanbul (2000)

41. Chen, C., Liang, J., Zhao, H., Hu, H.: Gait recognition using hidden Markov model. In: Jiao, L., Wang, L., Gao, X.-b., Liu, J., Wu, F. (eds.) Advances in Natural Computation. Lecture Notes in Computer Science, vol. 4221, pp. 399–407. Springer, Berlin (2006)

42. Chen, S.F., Goodman, J.: An empirical study of smoothing techniques for language modeling. Technical report TR-10-98, Center for Research in Computing Technology, Harvard University, Cambridge, MA (1998)

43. Chen, S.F., Goodman, J.: An empirical study of smoothing techniques for language modeling. Comput. Speech Lang. 13, 359–394 (1999)

44. Chow, Y.-L.: Maximum Mutual Information estimation of HMM parameters for continuous speech recognition using the N-best algorithm. In: Proc. Int. Conf. on Acoustics, Speech, and Signal Processing, pp. 701–704 (1990)

45. Chow, Y.-L., Schwartz, R.: The N-best algorithm. In: Speech and Natural Language Workshop, pp. 199–202. Morgan Kaufmann, San Mateo (1989)

46. Chung, K.L., AitSahlia, F.: Elementary Probability Theory, 4th edn. Springer, Berlin (2003)

47. Clark, J., Yallop, C.: An Introduction to Phonetics and Phonology. Blackwell, Oxford (1990)

48. Clarkson, P.R., Robinson, A.J.: Language model adaptation using mixtures and an exponentially decaying cache. In: Proc. Int. Conf. on Acoustics, Speech, and Signal Processing, München, vol. 2, pp. 799–802 (1997)

49. Colthurst, T., Kimball, O., Richardson, F., Shu, H., Wooters, C., Iyer, R., Gish, H.: The 2000 BBN Byblos LVCSR system. In: 2000 Speech Transcription Workshop, Maryland (2000)

50. D'Amato, D.P., Kuebert, E.J., Lawson, A.: Results from a performance evaluation of handwritten address recognition systems for the United States postal service. In: Proc. 7th Int. Workshop on Frontiers in Handwriting Recognition, Amsterdam, pp. 249–260 (2000)

51. Daniels, P.T., Bright, W. (eds.): The World's Writing Systems. Oxford University Press, New York (1996)

52. Davenport, J., Nguyen, L., Matsoukas, S., Schwartz, R., Makhoul, J.: The 1998 BBN BYBLOS 10x real time system. In: Proc. DARPA Broadcast News Workshop, Herndon, VA (1999)

53. Dempster, A.P., Laird, N.M., Rubin, D.B.: Maximum likelihood from incomplete data via the EM algorithm. J. R. Stat. Soc. B **39**(1), 1–22 (1977)

54. Deng, L.: The semi-relaxed algorithm for estimating parameters of Hidden Markov Models. Comput. Speech Lang. **5**(3), 231–236 (1991)

55. Dengel, A., Hoch, R., Hönes, F., Jäger, T., Malburg, M., Weigel, A.: Techniques for improving OCR results. In: Bunke, H., Wang, P.S.P. (eds.) Handbook of Character Recognition and Document Image Analysis, pp. 227–258. World Scientific, Singapore (1997)

56. Devijver, P.A., Kittler, J.: Pattern Recognition. A Statistical Approach. Prentice Hall, London (1982)

57. Diakoloukas, V.D., Digalakis, V.V.: Adaptation of Hidden Markov Models using multiple stochastic transformations. In: Proc. European Conf. on Speech Communication and Technology, pp. 2063–2066 (1997)

58. Diakoloukas, V.D., Digalakis, V.V.: Maximum-likelihood stochastic-transformation adaptation of Hidden Markov-Models. IEEE Trans. Audio Speech Lang. Process. **7**(2), 177–187 (1999)

59. Digalakis, V.V.: Online adaptation of hidden Markov models using incremental estimation algorithms. IEEE Trans. Audio Speech Lang. Process. **7**(3), 253–261 (1999)

60. Dolfing, J.G.A., Haeb-Umbach, R.: Signal representations for Hidden Markov Model based on-line handwriting recognition. In: Proc. Int. Conf. on Acoustics, Speech, and Signal Processing, München, vol. IV, pp. 3385–3388 (1997)

61. Dreuw, P., Jonas, S., Ney, H.: White-space models for offline Arabic handwriting recognition. In: Proc. Int. Conf. on Pattern Recognition, Tampa, FL, USA, pp. 1–4 (2008)

62. Dreuw, P., Rybach, D., Deselaers, T., Zahedi, M.t., Ney, H.: Speech recognition techniques for a sign language recognition system. In: Interspeech, Antwerp, Belgium, pp. 2513–2516 (2007)

63. Dreuw, P., Rybach, D., Heigold, G., Ney, H.: Rwth ocr: a large vocabulary optical character recognition system for Arabic scripts. In: Märgner, V., El Abed, H. (eds.) Guide to OCR for Arabic Scripts, pp. 215–254. Springer, London, UK (2012). Chap. Part II: Recognition

64. Duda, R.O., Hart, P.E.: Pattern Classification and Scene Analysis. Wiley, New York (1973)

65. Duda, R.O., Hart, P.E., Stork, D.G.: Pattern Classification, 2nd edn. Wiley, New York (2001)

66. Dugast, C., Beyerlein, P., Haeb-Umbach, R.: Application of clustering techniques to mixture density modelling for continuous-speech recognition. In: Proc. Int. Conf. on Acoustics, Speech, and Signal Processing, Detroit, MI, vol. 1, pp. 524–527 (1995)

67. Durbin, R., Eddy, S.R., Krogh, A., Mitchison, G.: Biological Sequence Analysis: Probabilistic Models of Proteins and Nucleic Acids. Cambridge University Press, Cambridge (1998)

68. Eckert, W., Gallwitz, F., Niemann, H.: Combining stochastic and linguistic language models for recognition of spontaneous speech. In: Proc. Int. Conf. on Acoustics, Speech, and Signal Processing, Atlanta, vol. 1, pp. 423–426 (1996)

69. Eddy, S.R.: Multiple alignment using Hidden Markov Models. In: Proc. Int. Conf. on Intelligent Systems for Molecular Biology, pp. 114–120 (1995)

70. Eddy, S.R.: Profile Hidden Markov Models. Bioinformatics **14**(9), 755–763 (1998)

71. Efron, B., Gong, G.: A leisury look at the bootstrap, the jackknife, and cross-validation. Am. Stat. **37**(1), 36–48 (1983)

72. Eickeler, S., Kosmala, A., Rigoll, G.: Hidden Markov Model based continuous online gesture recognition. In: Proc. Int. Conf. on Pattern Recognition, vol. 2, pp. 1206–1208 (1998)

73. Eickeler, S., Müller, S., Rigoll, G.: High performance face recognition using pseudo 2D-Hidden Markov Models. In: Proc. European Control Conference, Karlsruhe (1999)

74. Elmezain, M., Al-Hamadi, A., Appenrodt, J., Michaelis, B.: A hidden Markov model-based
     continuous gesture recognition system for hand motion trajectory. In: Proc. Int. Conf. on
     Pattern Recognition, Tampa, FL, USA (2008)
75. Elms, A.J., Procter, S., Illingworth, J.: The advantage of using an HMM-based approach
     for faxed word recognition. Int. J. Doc. Anal. Recognit. **1**(1), 18–36 (1998)
76. Ewens, W.J., Grant, G.R.: Statistical Methods in Bioinformatics: An Introduction, 2nd edn.
     Statistics for Biology and Health. Springer, Berlin (2001)
77. Federico, M., Cettelo, M., Brugnara, F., Antoniol, G.: Language modelling for efficient
     beam-search. Comput. Speech Lang. **9**, 353–379 (1995)
78. Fei-Fei, L., Perona, P.: A Bayesian hierarchical model for learning natural scene categories.
     In: Proc. IEEE Comp. Soc. Conf. on Computer Vision and Pattern Recognition, vol. 2, pp.
     524–531 (2005)
79. Ferguson, J.D.: Hidden Markov analysis: an introduction. In: Ferguson, J.D. (ed.) Sympo-
     sium on the Application of Hidden Markov Models to Text and Speech, pp. 8–15. Institute
     for Defense Analyses, Communications Research Division, Princeton (1980)
80. Ferguson, T.S.: Bayesian density estimation by mixtures of normal distributions. In:
     Rizvi, M., Rustagi, J., Siegmund, D. (eds.) Recent Advances in Statistics, pp. 287–302.
     Academic Press, New York (1983)
81. Fink, G.A.: Developing HMM-based recognizers with ESMERALDA. In: Matoušek, V.,
     Mautner, P., Ocelíková, J., Sojka, P. (eds.) Text, Speech and Dialogue. Lecture Notes in
     Artificial Intelligence, vol. 1692, pp. 229–234. Springer, Berlin (1999)
82. Fink, G.A., Plötz, T.: Integrating speaker identification and learning with adaptive speech
     recognition. In: 2004: A Speaker Odyssey – The Speaker and Language Recognition Work-
     shop, Toledo, pp. 185–192 (2004)
83. Fink, G.A., Plötz, T.: On appearance-based feature extraction methods for writer-
     independent handwritten text recognition. In: Proc. Int. Conf. on Document Analysis and
     Recognition, Seoul, Korea, vol. 2, pp. 1070–1074 (2005)
84. Fink, G.A., Plötz, T.: Unsupervised estimation of writing style models for improved un-
     constrained off-line handwriting recognition. In: Proc. Int. Workshop on Frontiers in Hand-
     writing Recognition, La Baule, France, pp. 429–434 (2006)
85. Fink, G.A., Plötz, T.: ESMERALDA: a development environment for HMM-based pattern
     recognition systems. In: 7th Open German/Russian Workshop on Pattern Recognition and
     Image Understanding, Ettlingen, Germany (2007)
86. Fink, G.A., Plötz, T.: ESMERALDA: a development environment for HMM-based pattern
     recognition systems (2007). http://sourceforge.net/projects/esmeralda
87. Fink, G.A., Plötz, T.: On the use of context-dependent modelling units for HMM-based of-
     fline handwriting recognition. In: Proc. Int. Conf. on Document Analysis and Recognition,
     Curitiba, Brazil, vol. 2, pp. 729–733 (2007)
88. Fink, G.A., Sagerer, G.: Zeitsynchrone Suche mit n-Gramm-Modellen höherer Ord-
     nung (Time-synchonous search with higher-order n-gram models). In: Konvens
     2000/Sprachkommunikation. ITG-Fachbericht, vol. 161, pp. 145–150. VDE Verlag, Berlin
     (2000) (in German)
89. Fink, G.A., Schillo, C., Kummert, F., Sagerer, G.: Incremental speech recognition for mul-
     timodal interfaces. In: Proc. Annual Conference of the IEEE Industrial Electronics Society,
     Aachen, vol. 4, pp. 2012–2017 (1998)
90. Fink, G.A., Vajda, S., Bhattacharya, U., Parui, S.K., Chaudhuri, B.B.: Online Bangla word
     recognition using sub-stroke level features and hidden Markov models. In: Proc. Int. Conf.
     on Frontiers in Handwriting Recognition, Kolkata, India, pp. 393–398 (2010)
91. Fink, G.A., Wienecke, M.: Experiments in video-based whiteboard reading. In: First Int.
     Workshop on Camera-Based Document Analysis and Recognition, Seoul, Korea, pp. 95–
     100 (2005)
92. Fink, G.A., Wienecke, M., Sagerer, G.: Video-based on-line handwriting recognition. In:
     Proc. Int. Conf. on Document Analysis and Recognition, pp. 226–230 (2001)

93. Fink, G.A., Wienecke, M., Sagerer, G.: Video-based on-line handwriting recognition. In: Proc. Int. Conf. on Document Analysis and Recognition, pp. 226–230. IEEE, Seattle (2001)

94. Finn, R.D., Clements, J., Eddy, S.R.: HMMER web server: interactive sequence similarity searching. Nucleic Acids Res. **39**(suppl 2), 29–37 (2011)

95. Fischer, A., Keller, A., Frinken, V., Bunke, H.: Lexicon-free handwritten word spotting using character hmms. Pattern Recognit. Lett. **33**(7), 934–942 (2012)

96. Fischer, A., Stahl, V.: Database and online adaptation for improved speech recognition in car environments. In: Proc. Int. Conf. on Acoustics, Speech, and Signal Processing, Phoenix, AZ (1999)

97. Flach, G., Hoffmann, R., Rudolpy, T.: Eine aktuelle Evaluation kommerzieller Diktiersysteme (An up to date evaluation of commercial dictation systems). In: Konvens 2000/Sprachkommunikation. ITG-Fachbericht, vol. 161, pp. 51–55. VDE Verlag, Berlin (2000) (in German)

98. Forney, G.D.: The Viterbi algorithm. Proc. IEEE **61**(3), 268–278 (1973)

99. Fritsch, J., Finke, M., Waibel, A.: Context-dependent hybrid HME/HMM speech recognition using polyphone clustering decision trees. In: Proc. Int. Conf. on Acoustics, Speech, and Signal Processing, München, vol. 3, pp. 1759–1762 (1997)

100. Fritsch, J., Rogina, I.: The bucket box intersection (BBI) algorithm for fast approximative evaluation of diagonal mixture Gaussians. In: Proc. Int. Conf. on Acoustics, Speech, and Signal Processing, Atlanta, vol. 1, pp. 837–840 (1996)

101. Fukunaga, K.: Introduction to Statistical Pattern Recognition. Academic Press, New York (1972)

102. Fukunaga, K.: Introduction to Statistical Pattern Recognition, 2nd edn. Academic Press, New York (1990)

103. Furui, S.: Digital Speech Processing, Synthesis, and Recognition. Signal Processing and Communications Series. Marcel Dekker, New York (2000)

104. Gader, P.D., Mystkowski, M., Zhao, Y.: Landmine detection with ground penetrating radar using hidden Markov models. IEEE Trans. Geosci. Remote Sens. **39**(6), 1231–1244 (2001)

105. Gaizauskas, R.: Evaluation in language and speech technology. Comput. Speech Lang. **12**, 249–262 (1998)

106. Gales, M.J.F.: Semi-tied covariance matrices for hidden Markov models. IEEE Trans. Audio Speech Lang. Process. **7**(3), 272–281 (1999)

107. Gales, M.J.F., Woodland, P.C.: Variance compensation within the MLLR framework. Technical report, Cambridge University Engineering Department (1996)

108. Gauvain, J.L., Lamel, L.F., Adda, G., Adda-Decker, M.: The LIMSI continuous speech dictation system: evaluation on the ARPA Wall Street Journal task. In: Proc. Int. Conf. on Acoustics, Speech, and Signal Processing, Adelaide, vol. I, pp. 557–560 (1994)

109. Gauvain, J.-L., Lee, C.-H.: Maximum a posteriori estimation for multivariate Gaussian mixture observations of Markov chains. IEEE Trans. Audio Speech Lang. Process. **2**(2), 291–298 (1994)

110. Gersho, A., Gray, R.M.: Vector Quantization and Signal Compression. Communications and Information Theory. Kluwer Academic, Boston (1992)

111. Geutner, P.: Using morphology towards better large-vocabulary speech recognition systems. In: Proc. Int. Conf. on Acoustics, Speech, and Signal Processing, Detroit, vol. 1, pp. 445–448 (1995)

112. Ghosh, D., Dube, T., Shivaprasad, A.P.: Script recognition – a review. IEEE Trans. Pattern Anal. Mach. Intell. **32**(12), 2142–2161 (2010)

113. Grzeszick, R., Rothacker, L., Fink, G.A.: Bag-of-features representations using spatial visual vocabularies for object classification. In: IEEE Intl. Conf. on Image Processing, Melbourne, Australia (2013)

114. Haeb-Umbach, R.: Investigations on inter-speaker variability in the feature space. In: Proc. Int. Conf. on Acoustics, Speech, and Signal Processing, Phoenix, AZ (1999)

115. Haeb-Umbach, R., Ney, H.: Linear discriminant analysis for improved large vocabulary continuous speech recognition. In: Proc. Int. Conf. on Acoustics, Speech, and Signal Processing, San Francisco, vol. 1, pp. 13–16 (1992)

116. Hain, T., Woodland, P.C., Niesler, T.R., Whittaker, E.W.D.: The 1998 HTK system for transcription of conversational telephone speech. In: Proc. Int. Conf. on Acoustics, Speech, and Signal Processing, Phoenix, AZ (1999)

117. Hammerla, N.Y., Plötz, T., Vajda, S., Fink, G.A.: Towards feature learning for HMM-based offline handwriting recognition. In: International Workshop on Frontiers of Arabic Handwriting Recognition, Istanbul, Turkey (2010)

118. Haussler, D., Kulp, D., Reese, M.G., Eckmann, F.H.: A generalized Hidden Markov Model for the recognition of human genes in DNA. In: Proc. Int. Conf. on Intelligent Systems for Molecular Biology, St. Louis, pp. 134–142 (1996)

119. Hayamizu, S., Itou, K., Takaka, K.: Detection of unknown words in large vocabulary speech recognition. In: Proc. European Conf. on Speech Communication and Technology, Berlin, pp. 2113–2116 (1993)

120. Hoey, J., Little, J.J.: Representation and recognition of complex human motion. In: Proc. Int. Conf. on Computer Vision and Pattern Recognition, pp. 752–759 (2000)

121. Hovland, G.E., Sikka, P., McCarragher, B.J.: Skill acquisition from human demonstration using a Hidden Markov Model. In: Proc. IEEE Int. Conf. on Robotics and Automation, Minneapolis, pp. 2706–2711 (1996)

122. Howard Hughes Medical Institute: HMMER: biological sequence analysis using profile hidden Markov models (2013). http://hmmer.janelia.org/

123. Huang, X., Acero, A., Hon, H.-W.: Spoken Language Processing: A Guide to Theory, Algorithm, and System Development. Prentice Hall, Englewood Cliffs (2001)

124. Huang, X., Alleva, F., Hon, H.-W., Hwang, M.-Y., Lee, K.-F., Rosenfeld, R.: The SPHINX-II speech recognition system: An overview. Comput. Speech Lang. **2**, 127–148 (1993)

125. Huang, X.D., Ariki, Y., Jack, M.A.: Hidden Markov Models for Speech Recognition. Information Technology Series, vol. 7. Edinburgh University Press, Edinburgh (1990)

126. Huang, X.D., Jack, M.A.: Semi-continuous Hidden Markov Models for speech signals. Comput. Speech Lang. **3**(3), 239–251 (1989)

127. Hughes, N.P., Tarassenko, L., Roberts, S.J.: Markov models for automated ecg interval analysis. In: Thrun, S., Saul, L., Schölkopf, B. (eds.) Advances in Neural Information Processing Systems, vol. 16. MIT Press, Cambridge (2004)

128. Hughey, R., Karplus, K., Krogh, A.: SAM: Sequence alignment and modeling software system (2005). http://www.cse.ucsc.edu/research/compbio/sam.html

129. Human Genome Project: (2003). http://www.ornl.gov/sci/techresources/Human_Genome/home.shtml

130. IEEE Computer Society. Technical Committee on Microprocessors and Microcomputers, IEEE Standards Board: IEEE Standard for Radix-Independent Floating-Point Arithmetic. ANSI/IEEE Std 854-1987, p. 16. IEEE Computer Society Press, 1109 Spring Street, Suite 300, Silver Spring, MD 20910, USA (1987)

131. International Human Genome Sequencing Consortium: Initial sequencing and analysis of the human genome. Nature **409**, 860–921 (2001)

132. International Human Genome Sequencing Consortium: Fishing the euchromatic sequence of the human genome. Nature **43**, 931–945 (2004)

133. Iyer, R.M., Ostendorf, M.: Modeling long distance dependence in language: topic mixtures versus dynamic cache models. IEEE Trans. Audio Speech Lang. Process. **7**(1), 30–39 (1999)

134. Jelinek, F.: A fast sequential decoding algorithm using a stack. IBM J. Res. Dev. **13**(6), 675–685 (1969)

135. Jelinek, F.: Self-organized language modeling for speech recognition. In: Waibel, A., Lee, K.F. (eds.) Readings in Speech Recognition, pp. 450–506. Morgan Kaufmann, San Mateo (1990)

136. Jelinek, F.: Statistical Methods for Speech Recognition. MIT Press, Cambridge (1997)

137. Jelinek, F., Bahl, L.R., Mercer, R.L.: Design of a linguistic statistical decoder for the recognition of continuous speech. IEEE Trans. Inf. Theory **21**(3), 250–256 (1975)
138. Jelinek, F., Mercer, R.L.: Interpolated estimation of Markov source parameters from sparse data. In: Gelsema, E., Kanal, L. (eds.) Pattern Recognition in Practice, pp. 381–397. North-Holland, Amsterdam (1980)
139. Jelinek, F., Mercer, R.L., Bahl, L.R.: Continuous speech recognition. In: Krishnaiah, P.R., Kanal, L.N. (eds.) Handbook of Statistics, vol. 2, pp. 549–573. North-Holland, Amsterdam (1982)
140. Jennings, A., McKeown, J.J.: Matrix Computation, 2nd edn. Wiley, New York (1992)
141. Joshi, D., Li, J., Wang, J.Z.: A computationally efficient approach to the estimation of two- and three-dimensional hidden Markov models. IEEE Trans. Image Process. **15**(7), 1871–1886 (2006)
142. Juang, B.-H., Rabiner, L.R.: The segmental k-means algorithm for estimating parameters of Hidden Markov Models. IEEE Trans. Acoust. Speech Signal Process. **38**(9), 1639–1641 (1990)
143. Jusek, A., Fink, G.A., Kummert, F., Sagerer, G.: Automatically generated models for unknown words. In: Proc. Australian International Conference on Speech Science and Technology, Adelaide, pp. 301–306 (1996)
144. Kale, A., Sundaresan, A., Rajagopalan, A.N., Cuntoor, N.P., Roy-Chowdhury, A.K., Krüger, V., Chellappa, R.: Identification of humans using gait. IEEE Trans. Image Process. **13**(9), 1163–1173 (2004)
145. Kannan, A., Ostendorf, M., Rohlicek, J.R.: Maximum likelihood clustering of Gaussians for speech recognition. IEEE Trans. Audio Speech Lang. Process. **2**(3), 453–455 (1994)
146. Kanthak, S., Molau, S., Sixtus, A., Schlüter, R., Ney, H.: The RWTH large vocabulary speech recognition system for spontaneous speech. In: Konvens 2000/Sprachkommunikation. ITG-Fachbericht, vol. 161, pp. 249–256. VDE Verlag, Berlin (2000)
147. Kapadia, A.S., Chan, W., Moyé, L.: Mathematical Statistics with Applications. Chapman & Hall/CRC, Boca Raton (2005)
148. Katz, S.M.: Estimation of probabilities from sparse data for the language model component of a speech recognizer. IEEE Trans. Acoust. Speech Signal Process. **35**(3), 400–401 (1987)
149. Kim, D., Song, J., Kim, D.: Simultaneous gesture segmentation and recognition based on forward spotting accumulative HMMs. Pattern Recognit. **40**, 3012–3026 (2007)
150. Kingsbury, N.G., Rayner, P.J.W.: Digital filtering using logarithmic arithmetic. Electron. Lett. **7**(2), 56–58 (1971)
151. Kirchhoff, K., Fink, G.A., Sagerer, G.: Conversational speech recognition using acoustic and articulatory input. In: Proc. Int. Conf. on Acoustics, Speech and Signal Processing, Istanbul (2000)
152. Kirchhoff, K., Fink, G.A., Sagerer, G.: Combining acoustic and articulatory information for robust speech recognition. Speech Commun. **37**(3–4), 303–319 (2002)
153. Kneser, R., Ney, H.: Improved backing-off for M-gram language modeling. In: Proc. Int. Conf. on Acoustics, Speech, and Signal Processing, Adelaide, vol. 1, pp. 181–184 (1995)
154. Kneser, R., Peters, J.: Semantic clustering for adaptive language modeling. In: Proc. Int. Conf. on Acoustics, Speech, and Signal Processing, München, vol. 2, pp. 779–782 (1997)
155. Knight, K.: Mathematical Statistics. Chapman & Hall/CRC, Boca Raton (2000)
156. Knill, K.M., Gales, M.J.F., Young, S.J.: Use of Gaussian selection in large vocabulary continuous speech recognition using HMMs. In: International Conference on Spoken Language Processing, Philadelphia, PA, Oct 1996, vol. 1, pp. 470–473 (1996)
157. Kosmala, A., Rigoll, G.: Tree-based state clustering using self-organizing principles for large vocabulary on-line handwriting recognition. In: Proc. Int. Conf. on Pattern Recognition, Brisbane, vol. 3I, pp. 1313–1316 (1998)
158. Kosmala, A., Rottland, J., Rigoll, G.: Improved on-line handwriting recognition using context dependent hidden Markov models. In: Proc. Int. Conf. on Document Analysis and Recognition, Ulm, Germany, vol. 2, pp. 641–644 (1997)

159. Kozielski, M., Doetsch, P., Ney, H.: Improvements in RWTH's system for off-line handwriting recognition. In: Proc. Int. Conf. on Document Analysis and Recognition, Washington, DC, USA (2013)

160. Krogh, A.: An introduction to Hidden Markov Models for biological sequences. In: Salzberg, S.L., Searls, D.B., Kasif, S. (eds.) Computational Methods in Molecular Biology, pp. 45–63. Elsevier, New York (1998)

161. Krogh, A., Brown, M., Mian, I.S., Sjölander, K., Haussler, D.: Hidden Markov Models in computational biology: applications to protein modeling. J. Mol. Biol. **235**, 1501–1531 (1994)

162. Kuhn, R., De Mori, R.: A cache-based natural language model for speech recognition. IEEE Trans. Pattern Anal. Mach. Intell. **12**(6), 570–583 (1990)

163. Kuhn, R., Lazarides, A., Normandin, Y., Brousseau, J., Nöth, E.: Applications of decision tree methodology in speech recognition and understanding. In: Niemann, H., de Mori, R., Harnrieder, G. (eds.) Proceedings in Artificial Intelligence, vol. 1, pp. 220–232. Infix, Sankt Augustin (1994)

164. Kummert, F., Fink, G.A., Sagerer, G.: A hybrid speech recognizer combining HMMs and polynomial classification. In: Proc. Int. Conf. on Spoken Language Processing, Beijing, China, vol. 3, pp. 814–817 (2000)

165. Lam, L., Suen, C.Y., Guillevic, D., Strathy, N.W., Cheriet, M., Liu, K., Said, J.N.: Automatic processing of information on cheques. In: Proc. Int. Conf. on Systems, Man & Cybernetics, Vancouver, vol. 3, pp. 2353–2358 (1995)

166. Larsen, R.J., Marx, M.L.: An Introduction to Mathematical Statistics and Its Applications, 3rd edn. Prentice-Hall, Upper Saddle River (2001)

167. Lazebnik, S., Schmid, C., Ponce, J.: Beyond bags of features: spatial pyramid matching for recognizing natural scene categories. In: Proc. IEEE Comp. Soc. Conf. on Computer Vision and Pattern Recognition, vol. 2, pp. 2169–2178 (2006)

168. Lee, C.H., Rabiner, L.R., Pieraccini, R., Wilpon, J.G.: Acoustic modeling for large vocabulary speech recognition. Comput. Speech Lang. **4**, 127–165 (1990)

169. Lee, K.-F.: Automatic Speech Recognition: The Development of the SPHINX System. Kluwer Academic, Boston (1989)

170. Lee, K.-F.: Context dependent phonetic hidden Markov models for continuous speech recognition. IEEE Trans. Acoust. Speech Signal Process. **38**(4), 599–609 (1990)

171. Leggetter, C.J., Woodland, P.C.: Flexible speaker adaptation using maximum likelihood linear regression. In: Workshop on Spoken Language Systems Technology, pp. 110–115 (1995). ARPA

172. Leggetter, C.J., Woodland, P.C.: Maximum likelihood linear regression for speaker adaptation of continuous density Hidden Markov Models. Comput. Speech Lang. **9**, 171–185 (1995)

173. Leite, P.B.C., Feitosa, R.Q., Formaggio, A.R., da Costa, G.A.O.P., Pakzad, K., Sanches, I.D.: Hidden Markov models for crop recognition in remote sensing image sequences. Pattern Recognit. Lett. **32**(1), 19–26 (2011)

174. Levinson, S.E.: Continuously variable duration Hidden Markov Models for automatic speech recognition. Comput. Speech Lang. **1**(1), 29–45 (1986)

175. Li, J., Gray, R.M., Olshen, R.A.: Multiresolution image classification by hierarchical modeling with two-dimensional hidden Markov models. IEEE Trans. Inf. Theory **46**(5), 1826–1841 (2000)

176. Li, J., Najmi, A., Gray, R.M.: Image classification by a two-dimensional Hidden Markov Model. IEEE Trans. Signal Process. **48**(2), 517–533 (2000)

177. Lien, J.J., Kanade, T., Zlochower, A.J., Cohn, J.F., Li, C.-C.: Automatically recognizing facial expressions in the spatio-temporal domain. In: Proc. Workshop on Perceptual User Interfaces, Banff, Alberta, Canada, pp. 94–97 (1997)

178. Linde, Y., Buzo, A., Gray, R.M.: An algorithm for vector quantizer design. IEEE Trans. Commun. **28**(1), 84–95 (1980)

179. Liu, Z., Sarkar, S.: Improved gait recognition by gait dynamics normalization. IEEE Trans. Pattern Anal. Mach. Intell. **28**(6), 863–876 (2006)

180. Lloyd, S.P.: Least squares quantization in PCM. IEEE Trans. Inf. Theory **28**(2), 129–137 (1982)

181. Lombard, E.: Le signe de l'élévation de la voix. Annales des maladies de l'oreilles, du larynx, du nez et du pharynx **37**, 101–119 (1911)

182. Lööf, J., Bisani, M., Gollan, C., Heigold, G., Hoffmeister, B., Plahl, C., Schlüter, R., Ney, H.: The 2006 RWTH parliamentary speeches transcription system. In: TC-STAR Workshop on Speech-to-Speech Translation, Barcelona, Spain, pp. 133–138 (2006)

183. Lowe, D.: Distinctive image features from scale-invariant keypoints. Int. J. Comput. Vis. **60**(2), 91–110 (2004)

184. Lowerre, B., Reddy, R.: The Harpy speech understanding system. In: Lea, W.A. (ed.) Trends in Speech Recognition, pp. 340–360. Prentice-Hall, Englewood Cliffs (1980)

185. Lowerre, B.T.: The HARPY speech recognition system. PhD thesis, Carnegie-Mellon University, Department of Computer Science, Pittsburgh (1976)

186. Lu, Z., Schwartz, R., Raphael, C.: Script-independent, HMM-based text line finding for OCR. In: Proc. Int. Conf. on Pattern Recognition, Barcelona, vol. 4, pp. 551–554 (2000)

187. MacQueen, J.: Some methods for classification and analysis of multivariate observations. In: Cam, L.M.L., Neyman, J. (eds.) Proc. Fifth Berkeley Symposium on Mathematical Statistics and Probability, vol. 1, pp. 281–296 (1967)

188. Madhvanath, S., Kim, G., Govindaraju, V.: Chaincode contour processing for handwritten word recognition. IEEE Trans. Pattern Anal. Mach. Intell. **21**(9), 928–932 (1999)

189. Mahajan, M., Beeferman, D., Huang, X.D.: Improved topic-dependent language modeling using information retrieval techniques. In: Proc. Int. Conf. on Acoustics, Speech, and Signal Processing, Phoenix, AZ, vol. 1, pp. 15–19 (1999)

190. Markov, A.A.: Примѣръ статистическаго изслѣдованія надъ текстомъ "Евгенія Онѣгина" иллюстрирующій связь испытаній в цѣпь (Example of statistical investigations of the text of "Eugen Onegin", wich demonstrates the connection of events in a chain). In: Извѣстія Императорской Академій Наукъ (Bulletin de l'Académie Impériale des Sciences de St.-Pétersbourg), Sankt-Petersburg, pp. 153–162 (1913) (in Russian)

191. Marti, U.-V., Bunke, H.: Handwritten sentence recognition. In: Proc. Int. Conf. on Pattern Recognition, Barcelona, vol. 3, pp. 467–470 (2000)

192. Marti, U.-V., Bunke, H.: The IAM-database: an English sentence database for offline handwriting recognition. Int. J. Doc. Anal. Recognit. **5**(1), 39–46 (2002)

193. Martin, S., Hamacher, C., Liermann, J., Wessel, F., Ney, H.: Assessment of smoothing methods and complex stochastic language modeling. In: Proc. European Conf. on Speech Communication and Technology, Budapest, pp. 1939–1942 (1999)

194. Martínez, F., Tapias, D., Álvarez, J.: Towards speech rate independence in large vocabulary continuous speech recognition. In: Proc. Int. Conf. on Acoustics, Speech, and Signal Processing, pp. 725–728 (1998)

195. Matsoukas, S., Colthurst, T., Kimball, O., Solomonoff, A., Richardson, F., Quillen, C., Gish, H., Dognin, P.: The 2001 BYBLOS English large vocabulary conversational speech recognition system. In: Proc. Int. Conf. on Acoustics, Speech, and Signal Processing, vol. 1, pp. 721–724 (2002)

196. Mercer, R.L.: Language modeling for speech recognition. In: IEEE Workshop on Speech Recognition, Arden House, Harriman, NY (1988)

197. Merhav, N., Ephraim, Y.: Hidden Markov Modeling using a dominant state sequence with application to speech recognition. Comput. Speech Lang. **5**(4), 327–339 (1991)

198. Merhav, N., Lee, C.-H.: On the asymptotic statistical behavior of empirical cepstral coefficients. IEEE Trans. Signal Process. **41**(5), 1990–1993 (1993)

199. Morgan, N., Bourlard, H.: Continuous speech recognition. IEEE Signal Process. Mag. **12**(3), 24–42 (1995)

200. Mori, S., Nishida, H.: Optical Character Recognition. Wiley, New York (1998)

201. Munich, M.E., Perona, P.: Visual input for pen-based computers. IEEE Trans. Pattern Anal. Mach. Intell. **24**(3), 313–328 (2002)
202. Nam, Y., Wohn, K.: Recognition of hand gestures with 3D, nonlinear arm movement. Pattern Recognit. Lett. **18**(1), 105–113 (1997)
203. Natarajan, P., Lu, Z., Schwartz, R., Bazzi, I., Makhoul, J.: Multilingual machine printed OCR. Int. J. Pattern Recognit. Artif. Intell. **15**(1), 43–63 (2001)
204. Natarajan, P., Saleem, S., Prasad, R., MacRostie, E., Subramanian, K.: Multi-lingual offline handwriting recognition using hidden Markov models: a script-independent approach. In: Doermann, D.S., Jaeger, S. (eds.) SACH 2006: Arabic and Chinese Handwriting Recognition. Lecture Notes in Computer Science, vol. 4768, pp. 231–250. Springer, Berlin (2008)
205. Ney, H., Essen, U., Kneser, R.: On structuring probabilistic dependencies in stochastic language modelling. Comput. Speech Lang. **8**, 1–38 (1994)
206. Ney, H., Essen, U., Kneser, R.: On the estimation of 'small' probabilities by leaving-one-out. IEEE Trans. Pattern Anal. Mach. Intell. **17**(12), 1202–1212 (1995)
207. Ney, H., Haeb-Umbach, R., Tran, B.H., Oerder, M.: Improvements in beam search for 10000-word continuous speech recognition. In: Proc. Int. Conf. on Acoustics, Speech, and Signal Processing, San Francisco, vol. 1, pp. 9–12 (1992)
208. Ney, H., Ortmanns, S.: Dynamic programming search for continuous speech recognition. IEEE Signal Process. Mag. **16**(5), 64–83 (1999)
209. Ney, H., Steinbiss, V., Haeb-Umbach, R., Tran, B.-H., Essen, U.: An overview of the Philips research system for large vocabulary continuous speech recognition. Int. J. Pattern Recognit. Artif. Intell. **8**(1), 33–70 (1994)
210. Ney, H., Welling, L., Beulen, K., Wessel, F.: The RWTH speech recognition system and spoken document retrieval. In: Proc. Annual Conference of the IEEE Industrial Electronics Society, Aachen, vol. 4, pp. 2022–2027 (1998)
211. Nguyen, L., Matsoukas, S., Billa, J., Schwartz, R., Makhoul, J.: The 1999 BBN BYB-LOS 10xRT broadcast news transcription system. In: 2000 Speech Transcription Workshop, Maryland (2000)
212. Nguyen, L., Schwartz, R.: The BBN single-phonetic-tree fast-match algorithm. In: Proc. Int. Conf. on Spoken Language Processing, Sydney (1998)
213. Nickel, K., Stiefelhagen, R.: Visual recognition of pointing gestures for human-robot interaction. Image Vis. Comput. **25**(12), 1875–1884 (2007)
214. Niemann, H.: Pattern Analysis and Understanding, 2nd edn. Series in Information Sciences, vol. 4. Springer, Berlin (1990)
215. Niesler, T.R., Whittaker, E.W.D., Woodland, P.C.: Comparison of part-of-speech and automatically derived category-based language models for speech recognition. In: Proc. Int. Conf. on Acoustics, Speech, and Signal Processing, Seattle, vol. 1, pp. 177–180 (1998)
216. Niesler, T.R., Woodland, P.C.: Combination of word-based and category-based language models. In: Proc. Int. Conf. on Spoken Language Processing, Philadelphia, vol. 1, pp. 220–223 (1996)
217. Nilsson, N.J.: Artificial Intelligence: A New Synthesis. Morgan Kaufmann, San Francisco (1998)
218. Nock, H.J., Gales, M.J.F., Young, S.J.: A comparative study of methods for phonetic decision-tree state clustering. In: Proc. European Conf. on Speech Communication and Technology (1997)
219. Nwe, T.L., Foo, S.W., Silva, L.C.D.: Speech emotion recognition using hidden Markov models. Speech Commun. **41**(4), 603–623 (2003)
220. Obermaier, B., Guger, C., Neuper, C., Pfurtscheller, G.: Hidden Markov models for online classification of single trial EEG data. Pattern Recognit. Lett. **22**(12), 1299–1309 (2001)
221. O'Hara, S., Draper, B.A.: Introduction to the bag of features paradigm for image classification and retrieval. Comput. Res. Repository (2011). arXiv:1101.3354v1
222. Ohler, U., Harbeck, S., Niemann, H., Nöth, E., Reese, M.G.: Interpolated Markov chains for eukaryotic promoter recognition. Bioinformatics **15**(5), 362–369 (1999)

223. Ortmanns, S., Eiden, A., Ney, H., Coenen, N.: Look-ahead techniques for fast beam search. In: Proc. Int. Conf. on Acoustics, Speech, and Signal Processing, München, vol. 3, pp. 1783–1786 (1997)

224. Ortmanns, S., Firzlaff, T., Ney, H.: Fast likelihood computation methods for continuous mixture densities in large vocabulary speech recognition. In: Proc. European Conf. on Speech Communication and Technology, Rhodes, vol. 1, pp. 139–142 (1997)

225. Ortmanns, S., Ney, H.: Look-ahead techniques for fast beam search. Comput. Speech Lang. **14**, 15–32 (2000)

226. Ortmanns, S., Ney, H.: The time-conditioned approach in dynamic programming search for LVCSR. IEEE Trans. Audio Speech Lang. Process. **8**(6), 676–687 (2000)

227. Ortmanns, S., Ney, H., Eiden, A.: Language-model look-ahead for large vocabulary speech recognition. In: Proc. Int. Conf. on Spoken Language Processing, Philadelphia, pp. 2095–2098 (1996)

228. Ortmanns, S., Ney, H., Seide, F., Lindam, I.: A comparison of time conditioned and word conditioned search techniques for large vocabulary speech recognition. In: Proc. Int. Conf. on Spoken Language Processing, Philadelphia, pp. 2091–2094 (1996)

229. O'Shaughnessy, D.: Speech Communications: Human and Machine, 2nd edn. Addison-Wesley, Reading (2000)

230. Paul, D.B.: The Lincoln robust continuous speech recognizer. In: Proc. Int. Conf. on Acoustics, Speech, and Signal Processing, Glasgow, pp. 449–452 (1989)

231. Paul, D.: An investigation of Gaussian shortlists. In: Furui, S., Huang, B.H., Chu, W. (eds.) Proc. Workshop on Automatic Speech Recognition and Understanding. IEEE Signal Processing Society, Piscataway (1997)

232. Paul, D.B.: An efficient A* stack decoder algorithm for continuous speech recognition with a stochastic language model. In: Proc. Int. Conf. on Acoustics, Speech, and Signal Processing, San Francisco, pp. 25–28 (1992)

233. Pestman, W.R.: Mathematical Statistics. de Gruyter, Berlin (1998)

234. Pfeiffer, M.: Architektur eines multimodalen Forschungssystems zur iterativen inhaltsbasierten Bildsuche (Architecture of a multimodal research system for iterative interactive image retrieval). PhD thesis, Bielefeld University, Faculty of Technology, Bielefeld, Germany (2006) (in German)

235. Plötz, T., Fink, G.A.: Robust time-synchronous environmental adaptation for continuous speech recognition systems. In: Proc. Int. Conf. on Spoken Language Processing, Denver, vol. 2, pp. 1409–1412 (2002)

236. Plötz, T., Fink, G.A.: Feature extraction for improved profile HMM based biological sequence analysis. In: Proc. Int. Conf. on Pattern Recognition, pp. 315–318 (2004)

237. Plötz, T., Fink, G.A.: A new approach for HMM based protein sequence modeling and its application to remote homology classification. In: Proc. Workshop Statistical Signal Processing, Bordeaux, France (2005)

238. Plötz, T., Fink, G.A.: Robust remote homology detection by feature based Profile Hidden Markov Models. Stat. Appl. Genet. Mol. Biol. **4**(1) (2005)

239. Plötz, T., Fink, G.A.: Pattern recognition methods for advanced stochastic protein sequence analysis using HMMs. Pattern Recognit. **39**, 2267–2280 (2006). Special Issue on Bioinformatics

240. Plötz, T., Fink, G.A.: An efficient method for making un-supervised adaptation of HMM-based speech recognition systems robust against out-of-domain data. In: Proc. 4th Int. Workshop on Natural Language Processing and Cognitive Science, Funchal, Portugal, June 2007

241. Plötz, T., Fink, G.A.: Markov Models for Handwriting Recognition. Springer Briefs in Computer Science. Springer, Berlin (2011)

242. Plötz, T., Fink, G.A.., Husemann, P., Kanies, S., Lienemann, K., Marschall, T., Martin, M., Schillingmann, L., Steinrücken, M., Sudek, H.: Automatic detection of song changes in music mixes using stochastic models. In: Proc. Int. Conf. on Pattern Recognition, pp. 665–668 (2006)

243. Plötz, T., Thurau, C., Fink, G.A.: Camera-based whiteboard reading: new approaches to a challenging task. In: Proc. Int. Conf. on Frontiers in Handwriting Recognition, Montreal, Canada, pp. 385–390 (2008)
244. Ponte, J.M., Croft, W.B.: A language modeling approach to information retrieval. In: Research and Development in Information Retrieval, pp. 275–281 (1998)
245. Popovici, C., Baggia, P.: Specialized language models using dialogue predictions. In: Proc. Int. Conf. on Acoustics, Speech, and Signal Processing, München, vol. 2, pp. 779–782 (1997)
246. Prasad, R., Saleem, S., Kamali, M., Meermeier, R., Natarajan, P.: Improvements in hidden Markov model based Arabic OCR. In: Proc. Int. Conf. on Pattern Recognition, pp. 1–4 (2008)
247. Pratt, J.W., Raiffa, H., Schlaifer, R.: Introduction to Statistical Decision Theory, 2nd edn. MIT Press, Cambridge (1996)
248. Press, W.H., Flannery, B.P., Teukolsky, S.A., Vetterling, W.T.: Numerical Recipies in C: the Art of Scientific Computing. Cambridge University Press, Cambridge (1988)
249. Pruteanu-Malinici, I., Carin, L.: Infinite hidden Markov models and ISA features for unusual-event detection in video. In: IEEE Int. Conf. on Image Processing, vol. 5, pp. 137–140 (2007)
250. Punta, M., Coggill, P.C., Eberhardt, R.Y., Mistry, J., Tate, J., Boursnell, C., Pang, N., Forslund, K.f., Ceric, G., Clements, J., Heger, A., Holm, L., Sonnhammer, E.L.L., Eddy, S.R., Bateman, A., Finn, R.D.: The Pfam protein families database. Nucleic Acids Res. **40**(D1), 290–301 (2012). http://nar.oxfordjournals.org/content/40/D1/D290.full.pdf+html
251. Rabiner, L.R.: A tutorial on Hidden Markov Models and selected applications in speech recognition. Proc. IEEE **77**(2), 257–286 (1989)
252. Rabiner, L.R., Juang, B.-H.: Fundamentals of Speech Recognition. Prentice-Hall, Englewood Cliffs (1993)
253. Richarz, J., Fink, G.A.: Visual recognition of 3d emblematic gestures in an hmm framework. J. Ambient Intell. Smart Environ. **3**(3), 193–211 (2011). Thematic Issue on Computer Vision for Ambient Intelligence
254. Rigoll, G.: Maximum Mutual Information Neural Networks for hybrid connectionist-HMM speech recognition systems. IEEE Trans. Audio Speech Lang. Process. **2**(1), 175–184 (1994)
255. Rosenberg, A.E., Lee, C.-H., Soong, F.K.: Cepstral channel normalization techniques for HMM-based speaker verification. In: Proc. Int. Conf. on Spoken Language Processing, Yokohama, Japan, vol. 4, pp. 1835–1838 (1994)
256. Rosenfeld, R.: Two decades of statistical language modeling: where do we go from here? Proc. IEEE **88**(8), 1270–1278 (2000)
257. Rothacker, L., Fink, G.A., Banerjee, P., Bhattacharya, U., Chaudhuri, B.B.: Bag-of-features hmms for segmentation-free bangla word spotting. In: International Workshop on Multilingual OCR (MOCR), Washington DC, USA (2013)
258. Rothacker, L., Rusinol, M., Fink, G.A.: Bag-of-features HMMs for segmentation-free word spotting in handwritten documents. In: Proc. Int. Conf. on Document Analysis and Recognition, Washington DC, USA (2013)
259. Rothacker, L., Vajda, S., Fink, G.A.: Bag-of-features representations for offline handwriting recognition applied to Arabic script. In: Proc. Int. Conf. on Frontiers in Handwriting Recognition, Bari, Italy (2012)
260. Rottland, J., Rigoll, G.: Tied posteriors: an approach for effective introduction of context dependency in hybrid NN/HMM LVCSR. In: Proc. Int. Conf. on Acoustics, Speech, and Signal Processing, Istanbul (2000)
261. Rusiñol, M., Aldavert, D., Toledo, R., Llados, J.: Browsing heterogeneous document collections by a segmentation-free word spotting method. In: Proc. Int. Conf. on Document Analysis and Recognition, Bejing, China, pp. 63–67 (2011)

262. Rybach, D., Gollan, C., Heigold, G., Hoffmeister, B., Lööf, J., Schlüter, R., Ney, H.:
      The RWTH Aachen University open source speech recognition system. In: Interspeech,
      Brighton, UK, pp. 2111–2114 (2009)
263. Sabin, M., Gray, R.: Global convergence and empirical consistency of the generalized
      Lloyd algorithm. IEEE Trans. Inf. Theory **32**(2), 148–155 (1986)
264. Saleem, S., Cao, H., Subramanian, K., Kamali, M., Prasad, R., Natarajan, P.: Improvements
      in bbn's hmm-based offline Arabic handwriting recognition system. In: Proc. Int. Conf. on
      Document Analysis and Recognition, pp. 773–777 (2009)
265. Salton, G., McGill, J.M.: Introduction to Modern Information Retrieval. McGraw-Hill,
      New York (1983)
266. Salzberg, S.L., Delcher, A.L., Kasif, S., White, O.: Microbial gene identification using
      interpolated Markov models. Nucleic Acids Res. **26**(2), 544–548 (1998)
267. Samaria, F., Young, S.: HMM-based architecture for face identification. Image Vis. Com-
      put. **12**, 537–543 (1994)
268. Samuelsson, C., Reichl, W.: A class-based language model for large-vocabulary speech
      recognition extracted from part-of-speech statistics. In: Proc. Int. Conf. on Acoustics,
      Speech, and Signal Processing, Phoenix, Arizona (1999)
269. Schillo, C., Fink, G.A., Kummert, F.: Grapheme based speech recognition for large vocab-
      ularies. In: Proc. Int. Conf. on Spoken Language Processing, Beijing, China, vol. 4, pp.
      584–587 (2000)
270. Schmid, G., Schukat-Talamazzini, E.G., Niemann, H.: Analyse mehrkanaliger Meßreihen
      im Fahrzeugbau mit Hidden Markovmodellen (Analysis of multi-channel measurement
      data in car manufacturing by hidden Markov models). In: Pöppl, S. (ed.) Mustererken-
      nung 1993, 15. DAGM Symposium. Informatik aktuell, pp. 391–398. Springer (1993) (in
      German)
271. Schukat-Talamazzini, E.G., Bielecki, M., Niemann, H., Kuhn, T., Rieck, S.: A non-metrical
      space search algorithm for fast Gaussian vector quantization. In: Proc. Int. Conf. on Acous-
      tics, Speech, and Signal Processing, Minneapolis, pp. 688–691 (1993)
272. Schukat-Talamazzini, E.G., Kuhn, T., Niemann, H.: Das POLYPHON – eine neue Wortun-
      tereinheit zur automatischen Spracherkennung (The polyphone—A new sub-word unit for
      automatic speech recognition). In: Fortschritte der Akustik, Frankfurt, pp. 948–951 (1993)
      (in German)
273. Schukat-Talamazzini, E.G., Niemann, H., Eckert, W., Kuhn, T., Rieck, S.: Automatic
      speech recognition without phonemes. In: Proc. European Conf. on Speech Communi-
      cation and Technology, Berlin, pp. 129–132 (1993)
274. Schultz, T., Rogina, I.: Acoustic and language modeling of human and nonhuman noises
      for human-to-human spontaneous speech recognition. In: Proc. Int. Conf. on Acoustics,
      Speech, and Signal Processing, Detroit (1995)
275. Schürmann, J.: Pattern Classification. Wiley, New York (1996)
276. Schwartz, R., Austin, S.: A comparison of several approximate algorithms for finding mul-
      tiple (n-best) sentence hypotheses. In: Proc. Int. Conf. on Acoustics, Speech, and Signal
      Processing, Toronto, pp. 701–704 (1991)
277. Schwartz, R., Chow, Y., Kimball, O., Roucos, S., Krasner, M., Makhoul, J.: Context-
      dependent modeling for acoustic-phonetic recognition of continuous speech. In: Proc. Int.
      Conf. on Acoustics, Speech, and Signal Processing, Tampa, Florida, pp. 1205–1208 (1985)
278. Schwartz, R.M., Chow, Y.L., Roucos, S., Krasner, M., Makhoul, J.: Improved hidden
      Markov modelling of phonemes for continuous speech recognition. In: Int. Conf. on
      Acoustics, Speech and Signal Processing, San Diego, pp. 35.6.1–35.6.4 (1984)
279. Schwartz, R., Chow, Y.-L.: The n-best algorithms: an efficient and exact procedure for
      finding the N most likely sentence hypotheses. In: Proc. Int. Conf. on Acoustics, Speech,
      and Signal Processing, vol. 1, pp. 81–84 (1990)
280. Schwartz, R., LaPre, C., Makhoul, J., Raphael, C., Zhao, Y.: Language-independent OCR
      using a continuous speech recognition system. In: Proc. Int. Conf. on Pattern Recognition,
      Vienna, Austria, vol. 3, pp. 99–103 (1996)

281. Schwartz, R., Nguyen, L., Kubala, F., Chou, G., Zavaliagkos, G., Makhoul, J.: On using written language training data for spoken language modeling. In: Proc. Workshop on Human Language Technology, HLT '94, pp. 94–98 (1994)

282. Siegler, M.A., Stern, R.M.: On the effects of speech rate in large vocabulary speech recognition systems. In: Proc. Int. Conf. on Acoustics, Speech, and Signal Processing, Detroit, vol. 1, pp. 612–615 (1995)

283. Siivola, V., Kurimo, M., Lagus, K.: Large vocabulary statistical language modeling for continuous speech recognition in Finnish. In: Proc. European Conf. on Speech Communication and Technology, Aalborg (2001)

284. Sivic, J., Zisserman, A.: Video Google: a text retrieval approach to object matching in videos. In: Proc. Int. Conf. on Computer Vision, vol. 2, pp. 1470–1477 (2003)

285. Sixtus, A., Molau, S., Kanthak, S., Schlüter, R., Ney, H.: Recent improvements of the RWTH large vocabulary speech recognition system on spontaneous speech. In: Proc. Int. Conf. on Acoustics, Speech, and Signal Processing, Istanbul, pp. 1671–1674 (2000)

286. Soong, F.K., Huang, E.-F.: A tree-trellis based fast search for finding the n best sentence hypotheses in continuous speech recognition. In: Speech and Natural Language Workshop, pp. 12–19. Morgan Kaufmann, Hidden Valley (1990)

287. Spiess, T., Wrede, B., Kummert, F., Fink, G.A.: Data-driven pronunciation modeling for ASR using acoustic subword units. In: Proc. European Conf. on Speech Communication and Technology, Geneva, pp. 2549–2552 (2003)

288. Starner, T., Pentland, A.: Visual recognition of American Sign Language using Hidden Markov Models. In: International Workshop on Automatic Face and Gesture Recognition, Zürich, pp. 189–194 (1995)

289. Steinbiss, V., Ney, H., Aubert, X., Besling, S., Dugast, C., Essen, U., Haeb-Umbach, R., Kneser, R., Meier, H.-G., Oerder, M., Tran, B.-H.: The Philips research system for continuous-speech recognition. Philips J. Res. **49**(4), 317–352 (1996)

290. Steinbiss, V., Tran, B.-H., Ney, H.: Improvements in beam search. In: Proc. Int. Conf. on Spoken Language Processing, Yokohama, Japan, vol. 4, pp. 2143–2146 (1994)

291. Sundaresan, A., Chowdhury, A.R., Chellappa, R.: A hidden Markov model based framework for recognition of humans from gait sequences. In: Int. Conf. on Image Processing (2003)

292. Terrell, G.R.: Mathematical Statistics. Springer Texts in Statistics. Springer, Berlin (1999)

293. Tokuda, K., Nankaku, Y., Toda, T., Zen, H., Yamagishi, J., Oura, K.: Speech synthesis based on hidden Markov models. Proc. IEEE **101**(5), 1234–1252 (2013)

294. Tokuno, J., Inami, N., Matsuda, S., Nakai, M., Shimodaira, H., Sagayama, S.: Context-dependent substroke model for HMM-based on-line handwriting recognition. In: Proc. Int. Workshop on Frontiers in Handwriting Recognition, pp. 78–83 (2002)

295. Venter, J.C., et al.: The sequence of the human genome. Science **291**, 1304–1351 (2001)

296. Viterbi, A.J.: Error bounds for convolutional codes and an asymptotically optimum decoding algorithm. IEEE Trans. Inf. Theory **13**(2), 260–269 (1967)

297. Wachsmuth, S., Fink, G.A., Kummert, F., Sagerer, G.: Using speech in visual object recognition. In: Sommer, G., Krüger, N., Perwass, C. (eds.) Mustererkennung 2000, 22. DAGM-Symposium Kiel. Informatik Aktuell, pp. 428–435. Springer, Berlin (2000)

298. Wachsmuth, S., Fink, G.A., Sagerer, G.: Integration of parsing and incremental speech recognition. In: Proceedings of the European Signal Processing Conference, Rhodes, Sep. 1998, vol. 1, pp. 371–375 (1998)

299. Waibel, A., Geutner, P., Tomokiyo, L.M., Schultz, T., Woszczyna, M.: Multilinguality in speech and spoken language systems. Proc. IEEE **88**(8), 1297–1313 (2000)

300. Weitzenberg, J., Posch, S., Rost, M.: Diskrete Hidden Markov Modelle zur Analyse von Meßkurven amperometrischer Biosensoren (Discrete hidden Markov models for the analysis of measurement curves of amperometric biosensors). In: Sommer, G., Krüger, N., Perwass, C. (eds.) Mustererkennug 2000. Proceedings 22. DAGM-Symposium. Informatik Aktuell, pp. 317–324. Springer, Berlin (2000) (in German)

301. Wellekens, C.J.: Mixture density estimators in Viterbi training. In: Proc. Int. Conf. on Acoustics, Speech, and Signal Processing, vol. 1, pp. 361–364 (1992)

302. Welling, L., Kanthak, S., Ney, H.: Improved methods for vocal tract normalisation. In: Proc. Int. Conf. on Acoustics, Speech, and Signal Processing, Phoenix, AZ, pp. 761–764 (1999)

303. Wells, J.: SAMPA – Computer Readable Phonetic Alphabet (2005). http://www.phon.ucl.ac.uk/home/sampa/home.htm

304. Wendt, S., Fink, G.A., Kummert, F.: Forward masking for increased robustness in automatic speech recognition. In: Proc. European Conf. on Speech Communication and Technology, Aalborg, vol. 1, pp. 615–618 (2001)

305. Wendt, S., Fink, G.A., Kummert, F.: Dynamic search-space pruning for time-constrained speech recognition. In: Proc. Int. Conf. on Spoken Language Processing, Denver, vol. 1, pp. 377–380 (2002)

306. Wessel, F., Baader, A.: Robust dialogue-state dependent language modeling using leaving-one-out. In: Proc. Int. Conf. on Acoustics, Speech, and Signal Processing, Phoenix, AZ (1999)

307. Wessel, F., Baader, A., Ney, H.: A comparison of dialogue-state dependent language models. In: Proc. ECSA Workshop on Interactive Dialogue in Multi-Modal Systems, Irsee, Germany, pp. 93–96 (1999)

308. Wessel, F., Ortmanns, S., Ney, H.: Implementation of word based statistical language models. In: Proc. SQEL Workshop on Multi-Lingual Information Retrieval Dialogs, Plzen, pp. 55–59 (1997)

309. Westphal, M.: The use of cepstral means in conversational speech recognition. In: Proc. European Conf. on Speech Communication and Technology, Rhodes, Greece, vol. 3, pp. 1143–1146 (1997)

310. White, D.J.: Markov Decision Processes. Wiley, New York (1993)

311. Whittaker, E.W.D., Woodland, P.C.: Comparison of language modelling techniques for Russian and English. In: Proc. Int. Conf. on Spoken Language Processing, Sydney (1998)

312. Whittaker, E.W.D., Woodland, P.C.: Particle-based language modelling. In: Proc. Int. Conf. on Spoken Language Processing, Beijing (2000)

313. Wienecke, M., Fink, G.A., Sagerer, G.: A handwriting recognition system based on visual input. In: Schiele, B., Sagerer, G. (eds.) Computer Vision Systems. Lecture Notes in Computer Science, pp. 63–72. Springer, Berlin (2001)

314. Wienecke, M., Fink, G.A., Sagerer, G.: Experiments in unconstrained offline handwritten text recognition. In: Proc. 8th Int. Workshop on Frontiers in Handwriting Recognition, Niagara on the Lake, Canada, August 2002

315. Wienecke, M., Fink, G.A., Sagerer, G.: Towards automatic video-based whiteboard reading. In: Proc. Int. Conf. on Document Analysis and Recognition, Edinburgh, vol. 1, pp. 87–91 (2003)

316. Wienecke, M., Fink, G.A., Sagerer, G.: Towards automatic video-based whiteboard reading. In: Proc. Int. Conf. on Document Analysis and Recognition, Edinburgh, Scotland, pp. 87–91 (2003)

317. Wienecke, M., Fink, G.A., Sagerer, G.: Toward automatic video-based whiteboard reading. Int. J. Doc. Anal. Recognit. 7(2–3), 188–200 (2005)

318. Winograd, T.: Language as a Cognitive Process, vol. 1: Syntax. Addison-Wesley, Reading (1983)

319. Witten, I.H., Bell, T.C.: The zero-frequency problem: estimating the probabilities of novel events in adaptive text compression. IEEE Trans. Inf. Theory 37(4), 1085–1094 (1991)

320. Wrede, B., Fink, G.A., Sagerer, G.: Influence of duration on static and dynamic properties of German vowels in spontaneous speech. In: Proc. Int. Conf. on Spoken Language Processing, Beijing, China, vol. 1, pp. 82–85 (2000)

321. Wrede, B., Fink, G.A., Sagerer, G.: An investigation of modelling aspects for rate-dependent speech recognition. In: Proc. European Conf. on Speech Communication and Technology, Aalborg, vol. 4, pp. 2527–2530 (2001)

322. Yakowitz, S.J.: Unsupervised learning and the identification of finite mixtures. IEEE Trans. Inf. Theory **16**(3), 330–338 (1970)

323. Yamamoto, J., Ohya, J., Ishii, K.: Recognizing human action in time-sequential images using Hidden Markov Models. In: Proc. Int. Conf. on Computer Vision and Pattern Recognition, pp. 379–387 (1992)

324. Young, S.J., Woodland, P.C.: State clustering in hidden Markov model-based continuous speech recognition. Comput. Speech Lang. **8**(4), 369–383 (1994)

325. Young, S.J., Chase, L.L.: Speech recognition evaluation: a review of the U.S. CSR and LVCSR programmes. Comput. Speech Lang. **12**, 263–279 (1998)

326. Young, S.J., Russell, N.H., Thornton, J.H.S.: Token passing: a simple conceptual model for connected speech recognition systems. Technical report, Cambridge University Engineering Department (1989)

327. Young, S.R.: Detection of misrecognitions and out-of-vocabulary words in spontaneous speech. In: McKevitt, P. (ed.) AAAI-94 Workshop Program: Integration of Natural Language and Speech Processing, Seattle, Washington, pp. 31–36 (1994)

328. Zavaliagkos, G., McDonough, J., Miller, D., El-Jaroudi, A., Billa, J., Richardson, F., Ma, K., Siu, M., Gish, H.: The BBN Byblos 1997 large vocabulary conversational speech recognition system. In: Proc. Int. Conf. on Acoustics, Speech, and Signal Processing, vol. 2, pp. 905–9082 (1998)

329. Zhang, D., Gatica-Perez, D., Bengio, S., McCowan, I.: Semi-supervised adapted HMMs for unusual event detection. In: Proc. IEEE Comp. Soc. Conf. on Computer Vision and Pattern Recognition, vol. 1, pp. 611–618 (2005)

330. Zhang, Z., Tan, C.L.: Restoration of images scanned from thick bound documents. In: Int. Conf. on Image Processing, Thessaloniki, Greece, October 2001, pp. 1074–1077 (2001)

331. Zimmermann, M., Bunke, H.: Optimizing the integration of a statistical language model in HMM based offline handwritten text recognition. In: Proc. Int. Conf. on Pattern Recognition, Cambridge, UK, vol. 2, pp. 541–544 (2004)

332. Zwicker, E., Fastl, H.: Psychoacoustics: Facts and Models, 2nd edn. Springer Series in Information Sciences, vol. 22. Springer, Berlin (1999)

Index

Printed in the United States
By Bookmasters